Africa's Future, Africa's Challenge

Africa's Future, Africa's Challenge

Early Childhood Care and Development in Sub-Saharan Africa

Editors
Marito Garcia
Alan Pence
Judith L. Evans

 THE WORLD BANK

1818 H Street NW
Washington, DC 20433
Telephone: 202-473-1000
Internet: www.worldbank.org
E-mail: feedback@worldbank.org

1 2 3 4 11 10 09 08

ISBN: 978-0-8213-6886-2
eISBN: 978-0-8213-6887-9
DOI: 10.1596/978-0-8213-6886-2

Cover photographs: *Left:* © Bernard van Leer Foundation/Jim Holmes (2003); Edines Lyakurwa's children near Moshi, Tanzania, photographed during a field visit with *Kiwakkuki*, a women's organization working with rural Tanzanian communities affected by HIV/AIDS.
Right: © Aga Khan Foundation (AKF)/Jean-Luc Ray (1991); two boys in Mombasa, Kenya, photographed sorting beans in a counting and color identification exercise.
Cover design: Naylor Design

Library of Congress Cataloging-in-Publication Data

Africa's future, Africa's challenge: early childhood care and development in sub Saharan Africa / Marito Garcia, Alan Pence & Judith Evans, editors.
   p. cm.
ISBN: 978-0-8213-6886-2
   1. Child care—Africa, Sub-Saharan. 2. Early childhood education—Africa, Sub-Saharan. 3. Child development—Africa, Sub-Saharan. I. Garcia, Marito, 1951– II. Pence, Alan R., 1948– III. Evans, Judith L.

HQ778.7.A35A37 2007
362.70967—dc22

                2007008823

Contents

Boxes

Figures

Tables

Foreword

The launching of the *Education for All Global Monitoring Report 2007* (EFA GMR 2007), in Dakar, Senegal, in November 2006, called on African countries "to expand and improve comprehensively early childhood care and development, especially for the most disadvantaged children." Indeed, children are our future and investing in Africa's young children is an investment in Africa's future. This book contributes a wide perspective on how to address this challenge, with chapters written by African and other scholars and practitioners in the field.

Coverage of early childhood development programs remains very low in Sub-Saharan Africa, especially among children under 3. The *EFA GMR 2007* indicates that Sub-Saharan Africa's gross preprimary enrollment ratio of 12 percent (compared with 48 percent for all other developing regions worldwide) is contributing to low primary completion and poor performance in primary grades. Early learning experiences help young children transition to primary school and make it more likely that they begin and complete primary school. By reducing dropout rates, repetition, and special education placements, early childhood development programs can improve the efficiency of primary education and reduce the costs for governments and households.

Recent trends have increased the need for early childhood development policies and programs. Today, the challenge is to provide good beginnings for the 130 million children under 6 in Sub-Saharan Africa. Urbanization, with attendant changes in household structures, has reduced the role of extended family members as caregivers. The growing number of working mothers with young children has increased the demand for nonparental child care. This demand is further exacerbated by the newest challenge, which is the rising number of orphans—now totaling 12 million—from the HIV/AIDS pandemic. Malnutrition of children under 5 in Africa has increased in the last 10 years: 75 million of these children are chronically malnourished and stunted. Iodine deficiency disorders have been found to reduce the IQs of school children by 13 points; anemia causes many pupils to achieve less than their potential. These factors lead to later enrollment and reduce primary school completion rates.

This book draws from views of authors and watchers of African trends. It presents the case for investment in early childhood development based on new findings from neuroscience. Trends in early childhood development from sociohistorical perspectives—including the new threats to early childhood such as HIV/AIDS, the challenges of caring for children under 3, and the role of African fathers—are presented to provide the context of how households, communities, and the public sector care for Africa's children. Similarly, comparative studies on how various countries are addressing early childhood development policy indicate a variety of approaches including participatory early childhood development planning and community-based approaches that work. This book includes several results of evaluations of the impact of programs designed to promote children's care and development in various countries. As ways forward, this book also describes financing of early childhood programs and the approaches being taken toward capacity building and knowledge dissemination.

The Communiqué from the Third African Early Childhood Development Conference in Accra, Ghana, in June 2005, called upon the African Commission and Secretariats of the subregional bodies of ECOWAS, COMESA, SADC, and the NEPAD to promote and support holistic development and lifesaving interventions for all infants and young children, starting with the most vulnerable. It also called on the heads of states and governments of the African Union and of the regional bodies of ECOWAS, COMESA, and SADC to make the development of infants and young children an urgent priority. This book reiterates that message and offers pathways for investing in Africa's children to develop strong beginnings for a brighter future.

Yaw Ansu
Director, Human Development Department
Africa Region
The World Bank

Acknowledgments

This book is a product of close collaboration among many individuals and organizations. We would like to thank all the participants in the Third African International Conference on Early Childhood Care and Development held in Accra, Ghana, in 2005, whose insights have made their way into several chapters of this book. As evidenced at that Conference and the two preceding it, significant challenges—as well as significant and creative responses to those challenges—face children's care and development in Africa. We acknowledge the dedication shown by all those who promote the well-being of children in Africa.

The Working Group on Early Childhood Development (WGECD) for the Association for the Development of Education in Africa (ADEA), the World Bank, the Early Childhood Development Virtual University (ECDVU) at the University of Victoria (Canada) School of Child and Youth Care, UNICEF, WHO, and UNESCO played key roles in supporting the Ghana Planning Committee in mounting the Third Conference; those organizations, joined by others from governmental, nongovernmental, and the private sector, have worked cooperatively to complete this book. The funding from the Norwegian Education Trust Fund (NETF) and the Education Program Development Trust Fund (EPDF) in the preparation of this book is gratefully acknowledged.

Thanks for the tireless efforts in technical editing and copyediting of this book go to Gillian Virata, Janice Tuten, and Leslie Prpich. Finally, we would like to thank Aziz Gökdemir, Nora Ridolfi, Jonathan Tin, and Richard Crabbe at the World Bank's Office of the Publisher, which produced the book.

Contributors

Madeez Adamu-Issah is an Education Project Officer for UNICEF in Ghana.

Agnes Akosua Aidoo is a member of the Committee on the Rights of the Child, Geneva, Switzerland.

Harold Alderman is the Adviser for Social Protection for the World Bank's Africa Region.

Linda Biersteker is Head of Research at the Early Learning Resource Unit in Cape Town, South Africa.

Joseph Kwasi Ayim Boakye is an early childhood development consultant in Ghana.

Cecilia Cabañero-Verzosa is the unit head for knowledge and capacity building in the World Bank's Development Communication Division.

Francis R. W. Chalamanda is the National Coordinator for ECD at the Ministry of Women and Child Development in Malawi.

Gilberte Chung Kim Chung is Director of the Bureau de l'Education Catholique (BEC), Mauritius.

Cyril Dalais is a consultant and adviser on child protection and child development for the Ministry of Education and Human Resources in Mauritius.

Erika Dunkelberg is a member of the Early Child Development Team for the World Bank's Human Development Network for Children and Youth.

Nawsheen Elaheebocus works in the World Bank's Development Communication Division.

Patrice L. Engle is a professor at the California Polytechnic State University in San Luis Obispo, California, United States.

Stella Etse is a consultant and Coordinator for the Association for the Development of Education in Africa's Working Group on Early Child Development. She is based in Ghana.

Judith L. Evans is Director Emeritus for the Consultative Group on Early Childhood Care and Development and Adjunct Professor, School of Child and Youth Care, Faculty of Human and Social Development, University of Victoria, Canada.

Jodie Fonseca is an education and HIV/AIDS adviser for Save the Children USA.

Marito Garcia is a lead human development economist at the World Bank's Human Development Department, Africa Region.

Elena Glinskaya is a Senior Economist for the World Bank's Economic Policy and Poverty Reduction Department, South Asia Region.

Sarah Gudyanga is a consultant on life skills and early childhood in Zimbabwe.

Abeba Habtom is Head of the ECCE and Special Needs Unit for the Ministry of Education in Eritrea.

Shireen Issa is a consultant for UNICEF.

Adriana Jaramillo is Senior Education Specialist for human development for the World Bank's Middle East and North Africa Region.

Jessica Jitta is director of the Child Health and Development Center at Makerere University in Kampala, Uganda.

Gareth Jones is a statistician for Adeni Consulting in Ottawa, Canada.

Margaret Kabiru is a consultant and Director of the Mwana Mwende ECDE Training Center in Kenya.

Michael M. Lokshin is a Senior Economist for the World Bank's Development Research Group.

Jane E. Lucas is a consultant in child health and development.

Kofi Marfo is Professor of Educational Psychology and Director of the Center for Research on Children's Development and Learning at the University of South Florida in the United States.

Juditha Leketo Matjila is a Communication Officer for UNICEF in Namibia.

Chalizamudzi Elizabeth Matola is an Assistant Project Officer for UNICEF's program on Orphans and Vulnerable Children and Child Protection in Malawi.

Alain Mingat is Director of Research at CNRS, IREDU, and University of Burgundy in France.

Bishara T. Mohamed is technical adviser for Radio Instruction to Strengthen Education in Tanzania/Zanzibar, formerly Director of the Madrasa Resource Center in East Africa.

Carlinda Monteiro is the deputy director of the Christian Children's Fund in Angola.

Robert Morrell is a professor at the School of Education at the University of KwaZulu-Natal in South Africa.

Medha Devi Moti is an education consultant and former Chief Technical Officer of the Ministry of Education in Mauritius.

Fraser Mustard is the founding President and a Fellow at the Canadian Institute for Advanced Research.

Peter Mwaura is lead researcher of the Madrasa Regional Research Program for the Madrasa Resource Center in East Africa.

Samuel Ngaruiya is a Senior Education Officer for ECD at the Ministry of Education in Kenya.

Anne Njenga is a consultant and Training and Research Coordinator for the Mwana Mwende ECDE Centre in Kenya.

A. Bame Nsamenang is an Associate Professor of Psychology and Counseling at the University of Yaounde I in Cameroon.

Jolly P. T. Nyeko is the founder and Chairperson of Action for Children in Uganda.

Chloe O'Gara is Associate Vice President and Director of Education for Save the Children USA.

Alan Pence is the Director of the Early Childhood Development Virtual University and Professor, School of Child and Youth Care, Faculty of Human and Social Development, University of Victoria, Canada.

Larry Prochner is an Associate Professor of Elementary Education at the University of Alberta in Canada.

Linda M. Richter is Executive Director for Child, Youth, Family, and Social Development at the Human Sciences Research Council in South Africa.

Jenieri Sagnia is an Education Project Officer for UNICEF's Basic Services Program in The Gambia.

Edith Sebatane is an Inspector at the Ministry of Education and Training in Lesotho.

Shamani-Jeffrey Shikwambi is a Program Coordinator at Augsburg College in Minneapolis, Minnesota, the United States.

Linda Sussman is a consultant on HIV/AIDS prevention and care.

Elizabeth Swadener is Chair and Professor of Early Childhood Education, and a Professor of Policy Studies at Arizona State University in the United States.

Emily Vargas-Barón is Director of the Institute for Reconstruction and International Security through Education in Washington, DC.

Gillian Virata is a consultant in early childhood development for the World Bank.

Patrick Wachira is an assistant professor in the Department of Teacher Education and Mathematics at Cleveland State University, Cleveland, Ohio, the United States.

Michael Wessells is a senior adviser on child protection for the Christian Children's Fund, and professor of clinical population and family health at Columbia University, New York, the United States.

Katarzyna Wilczynska-Ketende is a consultant in international child health, an honorary research fellow at the Institute of Child Health, and consultant project coordinator for the Interagency Group on Breastfeeding Monitoring (IGBM)/UNICEF UK in London.

John Williamson is a senior technical adviser for USAID's Displaced Children and Orphans Fund.

Mary Eming Young is lead specialist of the World Bank's Early Child Development Team, Human Development Network for Children and Youth.

Abbreviations

ACRWC	African Charter on the Rights and Welfare of the Child
ADEA	Association for the Development of Education in Africa
AIDS	acquired immune deficiency syndrome
ART	antiretroviral therapy
AU	African Union
BFCI	baby friendly community initiative
CBCC	community-based child care center
CBO	community-based organization
CEDAW	Convention on the Elimination of All Forms of Discrimination Against Women
CHH	child-headed household
CHW	community health worker
CRC	Convention on the Rights of the Child (United Nations)
CSO	civil society organization
DICECE	District Centers for Early Childhood Education (Kenya)
ECA	Economic Commission for Africa
ECCD	early childhood care and development
ECD	early childhood development
ECDVU	Early Childhood Development Virtual University
ECERS	Early Childhood Environment Rating Scale
ECI	early childhood intervention
EFA	*Education for All*
ELRU	Early Learning Resource Unit
ESAR	Eastern and Southern Africa Region (UNICEF)
FBO	faith-based organization

FCM	family and community motivator
FTI	Fast-Track Initiative (*Education for All*)
GDP	gross domestic product
GER	gross enrollment ratio
GNCC	Ghana National Commission on Children
GNP	gross national product
HIPC	heavily indebted poor countries
HIV	human immunodeficiency virus
IDA	International Development Association (of the World Bank Group)
IECD	integrated early childhood development
IMCI	Integrated Management of Childhood Illnesses
IQ	intelligence quotient
LAC	Latin America and the Caribbean (World Bank region)
LICUS	low-income countries under stress
MAP	Multicountry HIV/AIDS Program
MDGs	Millennium Development Goals
MGECW	Ministry of Gender Equality and Child Welfare (Namibia)
MINEDAF	Ministers of Education of African Member States
MOEST	Ministry of Education, Science, and Technology (Kenya)
MOWAC	Ministry of Women and Children's Affairs (Ghana)
MRC	Madrasa Resource Center
MRLGH	Ministry of Regional Local Government and Housing (Namibia)
MWRCDFW	Ministry of Women's Rights, Child Development, and Family Welfare (Mauritius)
NACECE	National Center for Early Childhood Education (Kenya)
NECDP	Nutrition and ECD Project (Uganda)
NEPA	National ECD Plan of Action
NEPAD	New Partnership for Africa's Development
NGO	nongovernmental organization
NPA	National Plan of Action (Mauritius)
NPC	National Policy for Children (Mauritius)
OECD	Organisation for Economic Co-operation and Development
ORT	oral rehydration therapy
OVC	orphans and vulnerable children

PLWHA	people living with HIV/AIDS
PMTCT	prevention of mother-to-child transmission
PRSP	Poverty Reduction Strategy Paper
SAP	Structural Adjustment Program
SMC	school management committee
SSA	Sub-Saharan Africa
SWAp	sectorwide approach
UNESCO	United Nations Educational, Scientific and Cultural Organization
UNICEF	United Nations Children's Fund
USAID	U.S. Agency for International Development
VSG	village support group
WGECD	Working Group for ECD (of the ADEA)
WHO	World Heath Organization

All dollar amounts are U.S. dollars unless otherwise indicated.

Introduction

Alan Pence, Judith L. Evans, and Marito Garcia

Much is written about Africa today, and much of it is not hopeful. Daily, the world hears stories of disease, despair, and death. Such a litany of misery is not unfounded—but there are also stories of hope, promise, and potential. They too are a critically important part of the complex story of Sub-Saharan Africa (SSA) in the first years of the 21st century. Just as multiple stories exist, so are multiple perspectives needed to understand, envision, and plan a hopeful future for Africa's children.

This book seeks to achieve a balance, describing challenges that are being faced as well as developments that are underway. It seeks a balance in terms of the voices heard, including not just voices of the North commenting on the South, but voices from the South, and in concert with the North. It seeks to provide the voices of specialists and generalists, of those from international and local organizations, from academia and the field. It seeks a diversity of views and values. Such diversity and complexity are the reality of Sub-Saharan Africa today.

Children in Sub-Saharan Africa

There are 54 African countries and 48 in Sub-Saharan Africa,[1] including the Sahel. The major focus of this book is on SSA from the Sahel south. Approximately 130 million children between birth and age 6 live in SSA. Every year 27 million children are born, and every year 4.7 million children under age 5 die. Rates of birth—and of child deaths—are consistently higher in SSA than in any other part of the world; the under-5 mortality rate of 163 per 1,000 is twice that of the rest of the developing world and 30 times that of industrialized countries (UNICEF 2006). Of the children who are born, 65 percent will experience poverty, 14 million will be orphans affected by HIV/AIDS—directly and within their families—and one-third will experience exclusion because of their gender or ethnicity. These are the kinds of numbers typically reported out of Africa. Typically *not* reported are the increasing percentage of children who enter grade 1 and the increasing number who graduate from primary school—both boys and girls. We seldom hear about the increase in the number of children who have access to a preprimary program, or about the wide variety of alternative programs that are being created to meet multiple needs in a variety of contexts. These, too, are important child stories in Africa.

Children as Social Entities

For much of the 20th century and throughout most of the world, early childhood (from birth through school entry) was largely invisible as a state-policy concern. Children, in the eyes of most states, were an appendage of their parents, or were simply embedded in the larger family structure. The child as an individual social entity was largely formless. Children did not emerge from the shadow of their families until they entered school, typically at age 6 or 7. Until that emergence, children were accessed only through their parents or family.

In the latter decades of the 20th century, children became more visible as individuals in their own right. In November 1989 the *Convention on the Rights of the Child* (CRC; United Nations 1989) was formally adopted by the UN General Assembly. By September 1990, 20 countries had ratified the CRC, bringing it into international law; today it has been ratified by all but one country internationally. It was ratified "more quickly and by more countries than any other human rights instrument" (Annan 2001, 1). A conscious inclusion of the rights of young children became evident in 1990 at the World Conference on *Education for All* (EFA) in Jomtien, Thailand. Through an effective advocacy effort, a significant advance was made in bringing the youngest children onto the education agenda: "Learning begins at birth . . . This calls for early childhood care and initial education" (UNESCO 1990, art. 5). At the EFA follow-up conference in Dakar, Senegal in 2000, the delegates committed themselves to six key goals, the first of which was "expanding and improving early childhood care and education, especially for the most vulnerable and disadvantaged children" (UNESCO 2000). Early childhood care and education was the focus of UNESCO's (2006) EFA Global Monitoring Report, *Strong Foundations*. That report makes the argument that the EFA and Millennium Development Goals (MDGs) cannot be achieved without significant investment in young children's well-being.

Children on the Agenda in Africa

The impact of these conventions and statements was felt in Africa as in the rest of the world. Indeed Mali President Traore cohosted the 1990 CRC Summit held in New York and Senegalese President Diouf was a key figure in promoting the CRC Summit.

In 1993 the Donors to African Education (now the Association for the Development of Education in Africa, ADEA) created a Working Group on Early Childhood Development (WGECD). In 1999 the World Bank took the lead, with support from United Nations Children's Fund (UNICEF) and other international organizations, to organize a continentwide African International Conference on Early Childhood Development. The first conference, held in Kampala, Uganda, was followed by conferences in Asmara, Eritrea (2002), and Accra, Ghana (2005). (See chapter 24 for more details on the conference series.) The 2002 Asmara Conference produced a declaration on early childhood development (*Asmara Declaration on ECD* 2002) supported by those in attendance, while the Accra Conference held a special one-day concurrent session with government representatives from 39 African countries that led to the endorsement by those governments of a multipoint communiqué supporting early childhood development (ECD)[2] in Africa (*Accra Communiqué* 2005). Another indication of the growing strength of ECD in Africa was its selection as a focal theme for the Eighth ADEA Biennial Meeting of the Ministries of Education held in Libreville, Gabon in March 2006 (ADEA 2006). In a relatively short period, ECD has moved from the margins to become a shared and central concern for many countries in Africa. It is critical that the support engendered to date continues.

Why This Volume?

This volume is the direct result of the forces briefly described above and represents one expression of continuing to build infrastructure and momentum for ECD. Early childhood care and development is on the policy and program agendas in many SSA countries. And, while a growing body of research is available about young children and their families from other parts of the world, particularly from the United States and Europe, there is a paucity of such information available within and about Africa.

This volume seeks to address that gap to some extent and reflects the current diversity of early childhood work in Africa. The topics were chosen based on their importance in their own right, but also on what was known about and possible to capture for the broad-ranging overview intended for this volume. The book is not authoritative in the sense of representing a "final word" on any given topic, nor is it exhaustive of all that is important regarding ECD in SSA. It is instead one step to inform readers about the early years of ECD as a discipline and as an interrelated set of activities in Africa. Its greatest achievement would be to stimulate more steps.

Sections and Chapters

The volume is organized in six sections. Section 1, **Contexts**, leads with an overview of the state of young children in Sub-Saharan Africa and compares these with the status in other regions of the world in the opening years of the 21st century (chapter 1). The chapter includes a review of childhood indicators on poverty, demography, nutrition, health, and early education before children enter school. Chapter 2 follows with a description of how ECD has become positioned as a national priority in several African countries and the mechanisms that are being used to bring increased investment in services and implementation of policies supportive of young children and their families. Chapter 3 provides an analysis of the relationship between investment in ECD and the potential for a country to achieve the child-related Millennium Development Goals and the goals established in the *Education for All* Dakar Forum. Chapter 4 describes an area of research, neurological development, that has stimulated heightened international awareness of the importance of the early years as a key contributor to social and economic development. Chapter 5 provides an overview of the current HIV/AIDS pandemic in Africa with a particular focus on the implications for young children.

Section 2, **Sociohistorical Perspectives**, provides three views of the development of ECD in Africa that are seldom considered, either in ECD literature or in studies of international development. Chapter 6 examines the long history of ECD in Africa with roots in early 19th-century colonization activities. ECD's historic mission of transformation is considered alongside postindependence movements to address the care and education needs of children in newly independent African states. Chapter 7 argues that colonization practices remain a key part of the international ECD dynamic in Africa today, ignoring and threatening indigenous approaches to early childhood that have deep and complex histories based on "other" understandings of child and social development. Chapter 8 discusses another neglected area of ECD, fathers' roles in the care and development of young children, considered both from the international literature (primarily Euro-Western) and from recent studies in South Africa.

Section 3, **Policy Development**, provides an update on three case studies that took place in 2000/1 focusing on ECD policy development in Ghana, Mauritius, and Namibia (chapter 9), while chapter 10 describes related work in three Francophone countries: Burkina Faso, Mauritania, and Senegal. Such case studies are an important contribution to the future of ECD in Africa as ECD policy development becomes a central concern for various international organizations (such as United Nations Educational, Scientific, and Cultural Organization [UNESCO]) and for certain African states.

Section 4, **Programming**, touches on a broad range of approaches providing support to young children and their families in SSA. Chapter 11 considers programming for children under 3, first discussing frameworks for understanding and promoting early development, then presenting case information from The Gambia, Kenya, and South Africa. Chapter 12 uses a case description approach to look more closely at the emergence of a preprimary year of education in Kenya, Lesotho, South Africa, and Zimbabwe. Chapter 13 describes an ambitious and multifaceted approach to special needs care that has evolved in Mauritius, and chapter 14 considers approaches to parent support programs that are evolving in Malawi, Nigeria, and Uganda as a result of the changing African family. Chapter 15 provides an extensive description of HIV/AIDS initiatives from various parts of SSA (Ghana, Malawi, Rwanda, Tanzania, and Zambia). Chapter 16 discusses the importance and ways of promoting children's well-being in conflict and postconflict situations, with a focus on Angola. The section concludes with a discussion of the importance of strategic communication initiatives for ECD, with a case study based on project experience in Uganda (chapter 17).

Section 5, **Evaluations and Research**, provides a range of recent approaches to better understand the impact of programs designed to promote children's care and development in SSA. Chapter 18 addresses an experimental approach to assess the impact of growth monitoring and promotion on nutrition and ECD in Uganda, as well as an approach of nonparametric score matching to assess the effects of longer exposure to growth promotion programs on child nutrition in Madagascar. Chapter 19 looks at the impact of ECD on women's participation in the labor force and girls in school based on household survey data in Kenya. Chapter 20 uses a quasi-experimental design to assess the impact of Madrasa-based ECD on primary school participation in Kenya, Tanzania, and Uganda, while chapter 21 uses a qualitative- and critical-theories approach to better understand local care provision practices in Kenya. Chapter 22 describes an evaluation of the Integrated Management of Childhood Illness (IMCI) community-based programs being implemented in 18 African countries. The chapter focuses on evaluations from four countries: Malawi, South Africa, Tanzania, and Uganda.

In Section 6, **Challenges and Ways Forward**, chapter 23 focuses on the cost and financing of alternative approaches to ECD in SSA, then chapter 24 concludes the volume with a description of an interrelated set of ECD leadership-promotion and capacity-building activities that commenced in 1995 and continue to the present. This volume is one of the more recent facets of this multipronged undertaking.

As noted earlier, this book does not speak with one voice. It is polyphonic, as is Sub-Saharan Africa. The influences of tradition, globalization, and local and international communities can all be seen and felt in the complex tapestry of early childhood care and development in Africa. This book need not be read in any particular sequence; undoubtedly, some chapters will be of greater interest to some readers than will others. We invite you to browse, to reflect, and to act.

Notes

1. The numbers of countries vary according to source. Sudan, for example, is not included in the United Nation's list of SSA countries, but is often included in other lists. Numbers also vary depending on whether islands are included.

2. In this publication, the acronym ECD refers to both "early childhood development" and "early childhood care and development." The acronym ECCD is also commonly used in this field.

References

Accra Communiqué. 2005. Retrieved August 16, 2006, from http://www.adeanet. org/downloadcenter/Focus/COMMUNIQUE%20-%20final.doc.

ADEA (Association for the Development of Education in Africa). 2006. Biennial meeting. Retrieved November 12, 2006, from http://www.adeanet.org/biennial-2006/en_index.html.

Annan, K. 2001. *We the Children: Meeting the Promises of the World Summit for Children.* United Nation's Secretary-General's Report. Retrieved November 12, 2006, from http://www.unicef.org/specialsession/about/sgreport-pdf/sgreport_adapted_eng.pdf.

Asmara Declaration on ECD. 2002. Retrieved August 10, 2006, from http://www.ecdgroup.com/asmara_declaration_on_ECD.asp.

UNESCO (United Nations Educational, Scientific, and Cultural Organization). 1990. *World Declaration on Education for All.* Retrieved November 12, 2006, from http://www.unesco.org/.

——. 2000. *World Education Forum.* Retrieved November 12, 2006, from http://unesco.org/.

——. 2006. *Strong Foundations.* EFA Global Monitoring Report 2007. Paris: UNESCO.

UNICEF (United Nations Children's Fund). 2006. *The State of the World's Children 2007.* New York: UNICEF.

United Nations. 1989. *Convention on the Rights of the Child.* Retrieved September 5, 2006, from http://www.unicef.org/crc/.

Contexts

CHAPTER 1

The State of Young Children in Sub-Saharan Africa

Marito Garcia, Gillian Virata, and Erika Dunkelberg

Sub-Saharan Africa (SSA) is home to 130 million children under age 6, many of whom live in dire conditions (see table 1.1). Millions of young children need rapid and intense interventions.

This chapter examines the conditions these children face, as measured by a child welfare index that combines national economic well-being and child-level indicators in health, nutrition, and early learning. This chapter also highlights findings on the status of young children in the region in terms of poverty, health, nutrition, orphanhood, and early education and care. Finally, it estimates the effect of various early childhood indicators on school performance, measured by primary completion rates.

Several important findings emerge:

- Countries that are richer, less stressed, or have better development indicators for the general population do not always provide better environments for their children.
- Sub-Saharan Africa has the highest rates of absolute child poverty in the world. More than half of all children in the region are severely shelter-deprived and 45 percent are water-deprived. The region also suffers from the highest rates of deprivation in education (30 percent) and health (27 percent).

Table 1.1. Selected National Health and Education Indicators in Sub-Saharan Africa

Country	Infant mortality rate (per 1,000 live births) 2005	Under-5 mortality rate (per 1,000) 2005	Stunting[a] (% of children under 5) 2005	Preprimary gross enrollment rate (%) 2004	Primary gross enrollment rate (%) 2004	Primary completion rates (%) 2005	Primary repetition rate (% of total enrollment) MRY 1998–2002
Angola	154	260	45	4	101	—	29
Benin	91	150	31	4	96	65	20
Botswana	82	120	23	—	105	92	3
Burkina Faso	107	191	39	1	58	31	15
Burundi	114	190	57	1	85	36	26
Cameroon	87	149	32	20	117	62	26
Cape Verde	26	35	—	53	121	96	13
Central African Republic	115	193	39	2	56	23	—
Chad	124	208	41	—	77	32	25
Comoros	53	71	44	3	90	58	28
Congo, Dem. Rep. of	129	205	38	1	62	39	16
Congo, Rep.	81	108	26	6	88	57	28
Côte d'Ivoire	118	195	21	3	72	51	18
Djibouti	88	133	23	3	40	35	18
Equatorial Guinea	123	205	39	40	126	45	40
Eritrea	50	78	38	7	64	51	21
Ethiopia	109	164	47	2	93	55	11
Gabon	60	91	21	14	130	66	34
Gambia, The	97	137	19	18	81	68	8
Ghana	68	112	30	42	79	72	6
Guinea	98	150	35	6	81	55	20

Country						
Guinea-Bissau	124	200	30	—	—	28	24
Kenya	79	120	30	53	114	95	6
Lesotho	102	132	38	31	132	67	21
Liberia	157	235	39	56	—	—	3
Madagascar	74	119	48	10	138	58	29
Malawi	79	125	48	—	122	61	16
Mali	120	218	38	2	66	38	20
Mauritania	78	125	35	2	93	45	15
Mauritius	13	15	10	95	122	97	4
Mozambique	100	145	41	—	105	42	23
Namibia	46	62	24	29	99	75	13
Niger	150	256	40	1	47	28	7
Nigeria	100	194	38	5	103	82	3
Rwanda	118	203	45	3	120	39	17
São Tomé and Príncipe	75	118	29	42	126	61	26
Senegal	77	136	16	6	88	52	14
Seychelles	12	13	—	102	114	118	—
Sierra Leone	165	282	34	4	155	56	—
Somalia	133	225	23	—	17	—	—
South Africa	68	55	25	33	104	99	7
Sudan	62	90	43	27	60	56	5
Swaziland	110	160	30	14	107	64	15
Tanzania	76	122	38	29	106	54	3
Togo	78	139	22	2	100	65	24
Uganda	79	136	39	2	118	57	11
Zambia	102	182	50	2	28	78	8
Zimbabwe	81	132	26	43	36	80	—

Sources: World Bank 2007 and UNESCO 2006.

Note: a. Prevalence of malnutrition (height for age). MRY = most recent year. — = not available.

- About 96 of every 1,000 children born in SSA in 2005 did not reach their first birthday. Another 163 of every 1,000 children will not reach their fifth birthday. These figures are twice the world averages.
- Improvements in infant mortality rates that occurred between the 1960s and the 1990s were negated by reversals in trends in many countries in the late 1990s and early 2000s.
- Malaria is the cause of death for about 1 million children under age 5 in SSA each year. This age group has 75 percent of all deaths from this disease in the region. Malaria accounts for 20 percent of all deaths among children under age 5.
- Nutrition indicators in SSA are average for developing countries, but the number of stunted children increased from 28 million in 1990 to 36 million in 2000, and further increased to 40 million in 2005.
- The orphan population in SSA rose to 46.6 million in 2005. For 12.3 million of these children, AIDS took the lives of one or more parents.
- Preschool gross enrollment ratio is extremely low, averaging 12 percent,[1] which is far below the developing world's average of 36 percent. However, the total enrollment rose in absolute numbers between 1999 and 2004.
- Analysis of national data from 47 SSA countries confirms the strong contribution of early childhood factors to success in primary school. Average primary completion rates in these countries are associated with preprimary enrollment and with health and nutrition status early in life.

Indexes Indicate the Conditions of Children

Children's welfare can be assessed using the child welfare index, based on under-5 mortality rates, gross primary and secondary enrollment rates, and per capita GDP (purchasing power parity). Although countries with higher incomes generally also provide better for their children, in many countries higher income does not translate into better conditions for children (see figure 1.1). Liberia, for example, has a lower child welfare index than countries with lower incomes; Malawi, one of the poorest countries in the world, has a much higher child welfare index than many richer countries. Many countries with the lowest child welfare index scores are low-income countries under stress (LICUS), but some LICUS, such as Comoros and The Gambia, have high indexes.

Some countries provide for the general population better than for their children (see figure 1.2). Human development index scores are

Figure 1.1. Higher National Income Does Not Always Translate into Better Conditions for Children

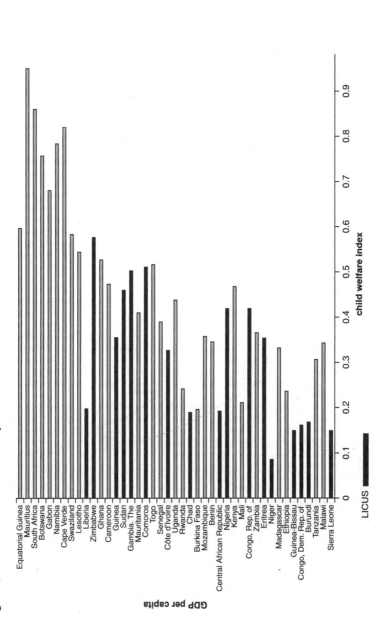

LICUS

Source: Authors computed scores using the child welfare index formula developed by van der Gaag and Dunkelberg (2004) using 2003 SSA data from the World Bank's World Development Indicators database.

Note: Countries are displayed from highest to lowest per capita GDP. LICUS = low-income countries under stress.

Figure 1.2. Countries with Better Human Development Indexes Tend to Have Stronger Child Welfare Indexes

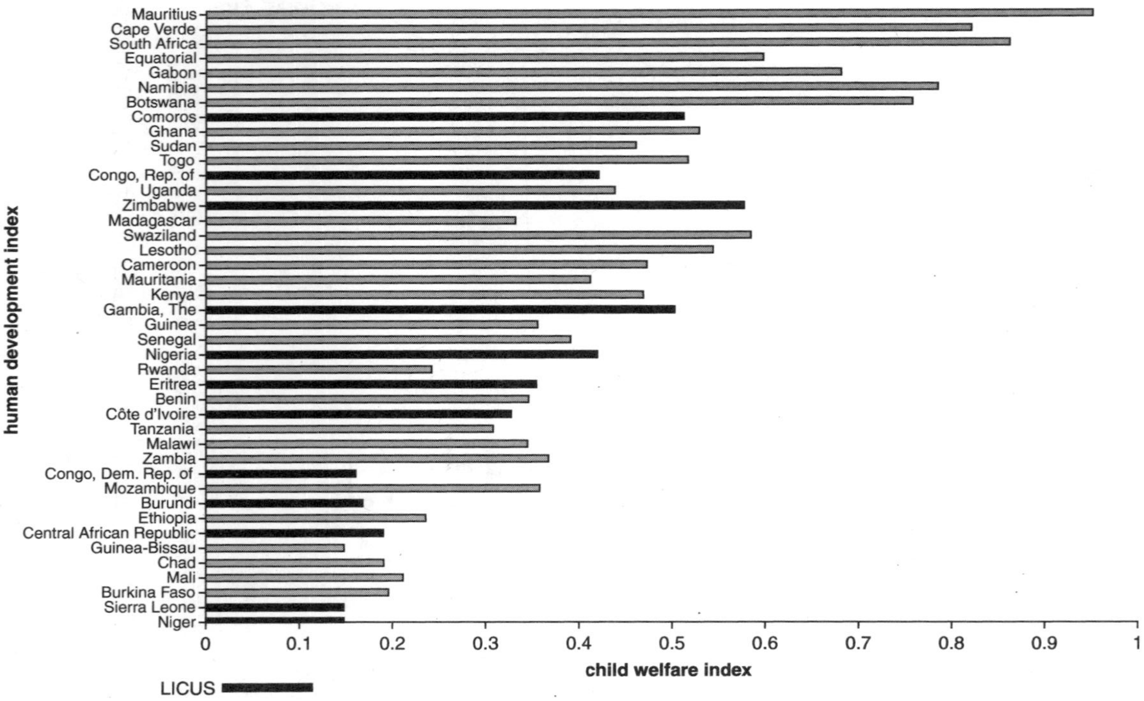

■ LICUS

Source: Authors computed scores using the child welfare index formula developed by van der Gaag and Dunkelberg (2004) using 2003 SSA data from the World Bank's World Development Indicators database.

Note: Countries are displayed from highest to lowest Human Development Index. LICUS = low-income countries under stress.

more closely matched to child welfare index scores than are rankings by per capita GDP.[2]

Children in Sub-Saharan Africa Fare Worse than Children in Most Other Regions

Gordon et al. (2003) present results on child poverty in developing countries in an holistic manner. They define poverty not in terms of income but in terms of "severe deprivation" of food, safe drinking water, sanitation facilities, health, shelter, education, information, and basic social services.

The results in Sub-Saharan Africa are stark. The region has the highest rates of absolute child poverty in the world: 207 million children—65 percent of all children in the region—suffer from two or more types of severe deprivation; more than 80 percent are severely deprived of one or more basic needs. Among rural children, more than 70 percent live in absolute poverty and 90 percent suffer from severe deprivation (see figures 1.3 and 1.4).[3]

Figure 1.3. More Children Suffer from Severe Deprivation in Sub-Saharan Africa than in Any Region except South Asia (2000)

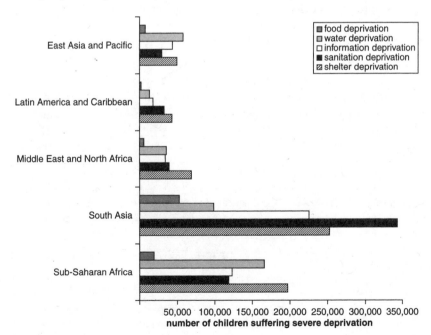

Source: Based on data from Gordon et al. (2003).

Figure 1.4. The Proportion of Children in Sub-Saharan Africa Suffering from Severe Shelter and Water Deprivation Is the Highest in the World (2000)

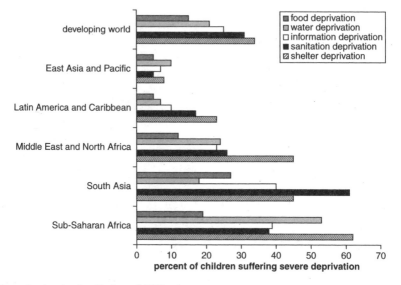

Source: Based on data from Gordon et al. (2003).

Improvements in Child Mortality Have Slowed But Improved in a Number of Countries

Child mortality rates in Sub-Saharan Africa are high; the rates are also far worse, relative to rich countries, than they were a generation ago. In 1980 child mortality rates in SSA were 13 times higher than in rich countries; in 2005 they were 29 times higher (Watkins 2005). None of the larger SSA countries will meet Millennium Development Goal 4, to reduce the under-5 mortality rate by two-thirds between 1990 and 2015. In fact, at current rates, SSA will not reach the target before 2015 (p. 42).

The World Health Organization (2005) confirms these dire findings. Although child mortality is declining globally, improvements in child mortality indicators in Sub-Saharan Africa have been reversed over the past decade. Overall, 35 percent of Africa's children face a greater risk of dying today, compared with 10 years ago.

Not all the news is gloomy, however. Several countries have shown success in reducing child mortality in recent years. Between 2000 and 2004, for example, Malawi reduced under-5 child mortality by 24 percent and Tanzania by 20 percent. Other countries—including Ethiopia, Mozambique, Namibia, Niger, and Rwanda—also showed significant reductions in child mortality during the same period.

The World Health Organization attributes the stubbornly high under-5 mortality rates in the region to "lack of preventive care and treatment, fragile health systems, and socioeconomic stagnation due to conflicts, instability, and HIV/AIDS" (WHO 2005, p. 52). These causes have led to increases in under-5 mortality rate in 14 African countries since 1990. The region as a whole has seen only a slight decrease in its under-5 mortality rate, from 185 deaths for every 1,000 live births in 1990 to 163 in 2005.

An average of 68 of every 1,000 children in the region's middle-income countries die before their fifth birthday (54 of them die before their first birthday), while as many 189 die in LICUS countries (107 of them before their first birthday; World Bank 2005). Children in Mauritius and the Seychelles have the best chance of survival (with an under-5 mortality rate of 15 and 13 per 1,000, respectively), while those in Sierra Leone face the worst odds (an under-5 mortality rate of 282 per 1,000 and infant mortality rate of 165).

Of the world's 2.3 million children under age 14 living with HIV, 2.0 million—more than 86 percent—are in Sub-Saharan Africa (UNAIDS 2006). These children are so vulnerable to HIV because 6.1 percent of parents 15 years and older are HIV-positive, which is about seven times the average world prevalence rate.

Malaria also poses a major threat to children in Africa. Just 14 percent of children under age 5 in the region slept under bed nets, only 4 percent slept under treated bed nets, and just 37 percent of those with fevers received antimalarial drugs between 1999 and 2003 (UNICEF 2006). The prevention and treatment rates are low despite the fact that 200–450 million young children are infected by the disease. Malaria kills 1 million people in Africa every year, more than 75 percent of them are children (Mills and Shillcutt 2004). It accounts for about 20 percent of deaths among children under age 5.

Governments in Sub-Saharan Africa financed just 50 percent of routine Expanded Program on Immunization (EPI) vaccines in 2005; donors and the private sector financed the other half. About 76 percent of 1-year-olds are immunized against tuberculosis and 66–77 percent are immunized against DPT (diptheria, pertussis, and tetanus), polio, and measles, but these figures are still the lowest in the world. Measles vaccination improved to 65 percent in 2005, but it remains lower than in any other region.

Thirty-seven percent of children under the age of 1 in Sub-Saharan Africa are immunized against hepatitis, which is the second-lowest rate in the world after South Asia (where only 1 percent of the population is immunized). Tetanus vaccination in pregnant women is lower in Sub-Saharan Africa (61 percent) than in South Asia (77 percent; UNICEF 2006).

Rising living standards and a decline in the number of deaths from diarrheal disease and vaccine-preventable conditions have reduced child mortality rates since 1970, but this decline is slowing. Malnutrition and acute respiratory infection are declining more slowly than they were, and the number of deaths from malaria has been increasing.

Malnutrition Is High and the Number of Underweight Children Has Risen

Chronic malnutrition measured by stunting (or low height for age) affects 37 percent of all under-5 children in Sub-Saharan Africa, a prevalence rate that has not changed at all since 1990. The number of stunted children has risen from 28 million in 1990 to 36 million in 2000 (ACC/SCN and IFPRI 2000) and the most recent estimate shows an increase to 40 million in 2005 (World Bank 2007). Sub-Saharan Africa is the only region in the world where the incidence of malnutrition is increasing. The countries experiencing very high rates of stunting are Burundi, Ethiopia, Madagascar, Malawi, and Zambia, where more than 45 percent of children are affected. Figure 1.5 shows the stunting prevalence across the continent.

Malnutrition is a major risk factor to other health problems; it is associated with more that 52 percent of all child mortality in Sub-Saharan Africa (WHO 2007). Apart from protein-energy malnutrition, which is reflected in child stunting, other major nutrition problems of young children in SSA include vitamin A deficiency, which compromises the immune systems, causing partial and total blindness and contributing to 22 percent of all childhood deaths in these countries. International agencies such as the United Nations Children's Fund (UNICEF) have increased efforts to fight the problem through vitamin A supplementation; coverage has risen to an estimated 73 percent in the region in 2004, from a low level in the 1990s. Iron deficiency anemia is one of the most widespread health problems among young children, impairing normal mental development of 40–60 percent of infants in SSA. More than two-thirds of children under 6 years in SSA are anemic, with Benin, Burkina Faso, Burundi, Mozambique, and Sierra Leone hit hardest with more than 80 percent prevalence (UNICEF 2006).

It is estimated that malnutrition robs at least 2–3 percent of GDP growth in Sub-Saharan Africa due to losses from increased health care costs in addition to losses from poor cognitive function and the deficits it causes on schooling and learning ability. Micronutrient deficiency

Figure 1.5. Prevalence of Stunting among Children under 5 in Sub-Saharan Africa (2005)

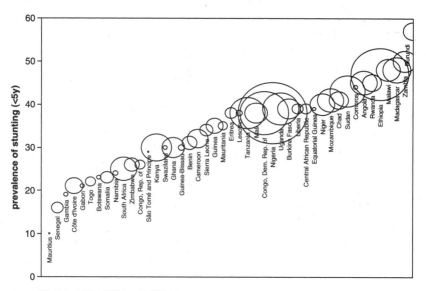

Sources: World Bank 2006, DHS data, UNICEF 2004.
Note: The bubble size indicates the relative number of children affected.

inflicts anemia, which perpetuates poverty due to direct losses from productivity from poor physical status. Micronutrient deficiency also causes cretinism and blindness in children. Even subclinical micronutrient deficiency that does not have overt symptoms impairs intellectual development, compromises the immune systems, causes birth defects, and consigns millions of people in the region to live below their physical and mental potentials.

The Number of Orphans Is High and Is Growing

More than 46 million children in Sub-Saharan Africa—12.3 percent of all children there—were orphans in 2005; 26 percent were orphans because of AIDS.[4] About 23 million children in the region had lost their mothers (more than a third from AIDS), 28.2 million had lost their fathers (more than a quarter from AIDS), and 7.7 million had lost both parents (more than half from AIDS). In 2005 alone, 5 million African children became orphans.

The proportion of orphans is higher here than in any other region of the world. Moreover, the number of orphans is increasing, largely because of the high incidence of AIDS (see figure 1.6). Unless antiretroviral therapy

Figure 1.6. Sub-Saharan Africa Is the Only Region in the World Where the Number of Orphans Is Growing

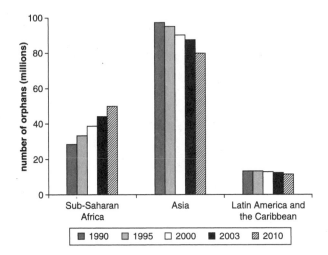

Source: UNAIDS, UNICEF, and USAID 2004.

is made available on a very large scale, the number of orphans in the region might reach 18.4 million by 2010 (UNAIDS, UNICEF, and USAID 2004). (See figure 1.7.)

Seventeen countries in Sub-Saharan Africa are expected to have more than 1 million orphans each by 2010. In 13 countries, at least 15 percent of all children are projected to be orphans by 2010 (UNAIDS, UNICEF, and USAID 2004). The greatest increases in the proportion of orphans are projected to occur in Swaziland (from 18 percent in 2003 to 24 percent in 2010), Namibia (from 12 percent to 18 percent), and—more ominously, because of the larger number involved—South Africa (from 13 percent to 19 percent), where the number of orphans is projected to grow from 2.2 million in 2003 to 3.1 million in 2010. The situation is also alarming in the Democratic Republic of Congo, where the number of orphans is projected to rise from 4.2 million in 2003 to 4.9 million in 2010, and in Ethiopia, where the number of orphans is projected to rise from 3.9 million to 4.7 million.

The number of orphans declined in The Gambia and Rwanda. In The Gambia the number fell from 48,000 in 1990 to 45,000 in 2003, and the proportion of orphans fell from 12 percent to 9 percent of all children. In Rwanda the number fell from 830,000 in 2000 to 810,000 in 2003, after increasing from 550,000 in 1990. The proportion of orphans fell

Figure 1.7. The Number of AIDS Orphans in Sub-Saharan Africa Skyrocketed between 1990 and 2003 and Is Projected to Continue to Do So

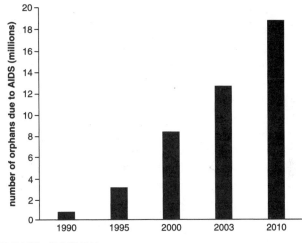

Source: UNAIDS, UNICEF, and USAID 2004.

from 19 percent in 2000 to 17 percent in 2003 and is projected to drop to its 1990 level of 14 percent by 2010.

Among the larger countries, Uganda seems to hold the most promise, with the number of orphans projected to drop from 2 million in 2003 to 1.9 million in 2010, with the percentage of orphans dropping from 14 percent to 11 percent of all children. In Sudan the number of orphans remained at 1.3 million between 1995 and 2003, but it is projected to rise to 1.5 million in 2010. The percentage of orphans out of the total child population will probably remain at 9 percent through 2010.

Too Few African Children Attend Preschool

Just 12 percent of Sub-Saharan Africa's preschool-age children between ages 3 and 6 enrolled in preschool in 2004, which is a third of the rate in East Asia and South Asia (UNESCO 2006). The gross preprimary school enrollment rate has grown by 2 percentage points between 1999 and 2004, increasing from a total enrollment of 5.1 million children to 7.4 million. This large increase in absolute numbers, however, was not matched by the ratios because of the region's high population growth rate during that period. The gaps between high- and low-performing countries are greater in SSA than in any other region; the low-performing countries have the worst indicators in the world (see table 1.1). Countries with high preprimary gross enrollment ratios (GERs) included Mauritius and Seychelles, which had universal enrollment, Kenya (44 percent), Ghana (40 percent), Liberia (41 percent), and Equatorial Guinea (31 percent). These rates contrast markedly with the low enrollment in Mali of 3 percent, in Côte d'Ivoire of 2 percent, and in Senegal of 1 percent. More than half (64 percent) of all preprimary school enrollment was accounted for by private institutions including nongovernmental organizations (NGOs), neighborhood associations, churches, mosques, and private providers.

Preprimary school life expectancy (the average number of years of preprimary education a child expects to receive if current participation rates remain constant) is very low, at just 0.3 years. Children in the region's high-performing countries (Liberia, Mauritius, and Seychelles), however, stay in preschool longer than children in many other countries in the world, including Canada and Greece, indicating a wide variety of conditions in early education in the continent.

During the 1990s preprimary gross enrollment ratios grew at an average of 5.2 percentage points in Sub-Saharan Africa. In the poorest countries (countries with per capita GNP of less than \$695), the ratio rose just 1.4 percentage points (Jaramillo and Mingat 2006, p. 8), while in the region's richest countries, the ratio grew 33 percentage points. If enrollment continues to grow this rapidly, these latter countries would become the first group of countries in the world to achieve universal preprimary education by 2015. For the region as a whole, only 4 out of 36 low-income countries and 4 out of 8 higher-income countries are on track to reach the target of 25 percent preprimary gross enrollment ratio by 2015 (Jaramillo and Mingat 2006, p.11). The preprimary gross enrollment ratio would have to increase by at least 2 percentage points a year in every country for all countries to reach the target.

Primary completion rates stand at only 58 percent in Sub-Saharan Africa—far lower than the 74–96 percent in other developing regions. Moreover, more children repeat primary grades than in all other regions except Latin America and the Caribbean (see table 1.2.).

Investing in Young Children Increases Primary Completion Rates

National data from 47 Sub-Saharan African countries shown in figure 1.8 reveal a strong association between early childhood factors and success in primary school. Average primary completion rates are strongly associated with the level of preprimary enrollment and with children's health and nutrition status in their early years. While the association is positive, the

Table 1.2. Gross Enrollment Rates in Preschools Grew in Sub-Saharan Africa, but the Rates Are Far Below the Rest of the World

	Preschool gross enrollment ratio (%)		Total preschool enrollment		Change in total preschool enrollment between 1999 and 2004 (%)
	1999	2004	1999	2004	
Sub-Saharan Africa	10	12	5,219,000	7,359,000	+43.5
South and West Asia	23	32	22,186,000	31,166,000	+40.5
East Asia	40	40	36,152,000	32,831,000	−9.2
Latin America	55	61	15,720,000	18,154,000	+15.5
Developing Countries	28	32	80,070,000	91,089,000	+13.8
Developed Countries	73	77	25,386,000	25,482,000	+0.4
North America/ West Europe	76	78	19,151,000	19,408,000	+1.3

Source: UNESCO 2006.

Figure 1.8. The Association Is Positive between Preprimary Enrollment and Primary Completion Rates

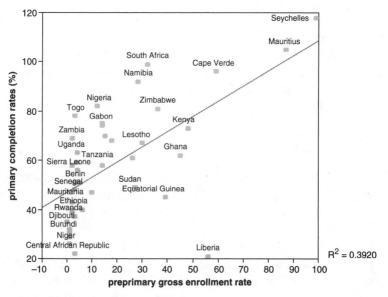

Source: Calculated by the authors from UNESCO 2006 data.

spread around the regression line varies widely particularly for African countries, indicating the influence of other factors. Namibia's preprimary enrollment rate of only 29 percent achieved 75 percent completion in primary grades, whereas a roughly similar preprimary enrollment of 31 percent in Lesotho achieved roughly 55 percent primary completion

Table 1.3. Higher Preprimary Gross Enrollment Rates Are Associated with Lower Repetition Rates

	Preschool gross enrollment rate (%)						
	0	*10*	*20*	*30*	*40*	*50*	*60*
Repetition rate							
All African countries	20.4	19.2	17.9	16.7	15.5	14.2	13.0
Francophone countries	22.7	21.5	20.3	19.0	17.8	16.6	15.3
Anglophone countries	15.3	14.0	12.8	11.6	10.4	9.1	7.9
Survival rate to Grade 5	65.3	68.5	71.6	74.8	78.0	81.2	84.3

Source: Jaramillo and Mingat 2006.

rates. These results occur even after controlling for incomes, suggesting that preprimary schooling (formal or informal) is likely to increase the chance of these children remaining in primary school.

In a separate analysis, Jaramillo and Mingat (2003, 2006) find similar results (see table 1.3). In countries with preschool gross enrollment rates of 60 percent, 84 percent of children reached fifth grade. In contrast, in countries where the gross enrollment rate was just 10 percent, less than 69 percent of students did so. Overall, these are in line with the main findings from longitudinal studies elsewhere in the world. Improvements in primary school performance for those who attended preprimary schooling and had good nutrition in the early years have been reported in many countries (Alderman et al. 2001, Fogel 1994, Grantham-McGregor et al. 1997).

Investments in Young Children

Cross-national data on the status of young children in Africa highlight the dire conditions and the urgent need to improve nutrition, health, and early childhood conditions in nearly all of the countries. The region has the highest rates of absolute child poverty in the world, affecting more than half of all the young children.

The findings from the cross-national data presented in this chapter confirm earlier research that investing in young children would likely improve the chances of these children to succeed later in life. The completion rates in the primary years, as well as the primary gross enrollment rates, are positively affected by the level at which countries invest in the early years in nutrition, health, preschools, and childhood care. Because improvement in education improves lifelong human capital, investments in the early years would contribute to the longer-term economic development of Sub-Saharan African countries.

Notes

1. Data on preprimary enrollment are guesstimates at best, because they include over- and underage children and are based on different definitions of preprimary children. Net preprimary enrollment rates are better indicators of educational participation, but these data have not yet been compiled for Sub-Saharan African countries.

2. The human development index is "a composite index measuring average achievement in three basic dimensions of human development—a long and healthy life, knowledge, and a decent standard of living" (Watkins 2005, 357).

3. For national data for most Sub-Saharan African countries, as well as other developing countries, see Gordon et al. (2003).

4. Unless stated otherwise, this section is based on UNAIDS, UNICEF, and USAID (2004), which defines orphans as "any child under age 18 who has lost one or both parents."

References

ACC/SCN and IFPRI (International Food Policy Research Institute). 2000. *4th Report on the World Nutrition Situation*. Geneva: ACC/SCN and IFPRI.

Alderman, H., J. Behrman, V. Lavy, and R. Menon. 2001. "Child Health and School Enrollment: A Longitudinal Analysis." *Journal of Human Resources* 36 (1): 185–205.

Fogel, R. W. 1994. "Economic Growth, Population Theory, and Physiology: The Bearing of Long-Term Processes on the Making of Economic Policy." NBER Research Working Paper W4638. National Bureau of Economic Research, Cambridge, MA.

Gordon, D., S. Nandy, C. Pantazis, S. Pemberton, and P. Townsend. 2003. *Child Poverty in the Developing World*. Bristol, U.K.: Policy Press.

Grantham-McGregor S. M., S. P. Walker, S. M. Chang, and C. A. Powell. 1997. "Effects of Early Childhood Supplementation With and Without Stimulation on Later Development in Stunted Jamaican Children." *American Journal of Clinical Nutrition* 66: 247–53.

Jaramillo, A., and A. Mingat. 2003. *Early Childhood Care and Education in Sub-Saharan Africa: What Would It Take to Meet the Dakar Goal?* Washington, DC: World Bank.

———. 2006. "Early Childhood Care and Education in Sub-Saharan Africa: What Would It Take to Meet the Millennium Development Goals?" Paper presented at the Association for the Development of Education in Africa's Biennale on Education in Africa, Libreville, Gabon. March 27–31.

Mills, A., and S. Shillcutt. 2004. *Summary of Copenhagen Consensus Challenge Paper: Communicable Diseases*. Retrieved November 6, 2006, from http://www. copenhagenconsensus.com/Default.aspx?ID=220.

UNAIDS (Joint United Nations Programme on HIV/AIDS). 2006. *2006 Report on the Global AIDS Epidemic*. Geneva: UNAIDS.

UNAIDS, UNICEF (United Nations Children's Fund), and USAID (U.S. Agency for International Development). 2004. *Children on the Brink 2004: A Joint Report of New Orphan Estimates and a Framework for Action*. New York: USAID.

UNESCO (United Nations Educational, Scientific, and Cultural Organization). 2006. *Strong Foundations: EFA Global Monitoring Report 2007*. Paris: UNESCO.

UNICEF. 2004. *The State of the World's Children 2005*. New York: UNICEF.

———. 2006. *The State of the World's Children 2007*. New York: UNICEF.

van der Gaag, J., and E. Dunkelberg. 2004. *Measuring Child Well-Being in the Mediterranean Countries—Toward a Comprehensive Welfare Index*. Genoa: MedChild Institute.

Watkins, K. 2005. *International Cooperation at a Crossroads: Aid, Trade, and Security in an Unequal World*. Human Development Report 2005. New York: United Nations Development Programme.

WHO (World Health Organization). 2005. *Health and the Millennium Development Goals*. Geneva: WHO.

———. 2007. *The World Health Report 2007*. Geneva: WHO.

World Bank. 2005. *World Development Indicators 2005*. Retrieved November 6, 2006, from http://www.worldbank.org/data/wdi2000/.

———. 2006. *World Development Indicators 2006*. Washington, DC: World Bank.

———. 2007. *World Development Indicators 2007*. Washington, DC: World Bank.

CHAPTER 2

Positioning ECD Nationally: Trends in Selected African Countries

Agnes Akosua Aidoo

"We recognize that the future of Africa lies with the well-being of its children and youth. The prospect of socioeconomic transformation of the continent rests with investing in the young people of the continent. Today's investment in children is tomorrow's peace, stability, security, democracy, and sustainable development."

—*Africa Fit for Children: The African Common Position*
(Organization of African Unity 2001, para. 6)

Early childhood development (ECD) is the foundation of human development. A focus on the young child and holistic ECD provides an opportunity for sustainable human development, economic growth, social change, and transformation in Africa. To that end, countries need to develop ECD policies that will guide strategic decision making and resource allocation.

Nearly all countries in Sub-Saharan Africa (SSA) have developed and implemented various forms of sectoral ECD activities since at least the 1960s in support of young children and their families. A few countries have developed, or are in the process of developing, specific national

ECD policies that integrate the various sectoral activities. The integrated approach aims at the holistic development of the child. It encompasses health, nutrition, water and sanitation, basic care, stimulation, learning, social protection, and family and community empowerment so that children can develop to their fullest potential. The time is opportune to expand and accelerate a holistic ECD policy process as a central focus in Africa's development.

This chapter suggests a critical link between the early development of Africa's children and the successful implementation of international conventions and commitments. The chapter also makes recommendations on how best to provide policy supports for young children and their families within the context of current challenges and opportunities.

The first section below summarizes the situation of Africa's young children, indicating progress and key challenges. The second section summarizes the recent evolution of ECD policy. The third section links ECD and the relevant international and regional conventions that influence national development policies and plans. The fourth section discusses the need for a specific national ECD policy and the challenges of a unified policy. The fifth section describes essential policy development and implementation processes as well as lessons learned in the region. The final section draws conclusions and proposes key actions for the supportive policy environment to accelerate ECD in Africa.

Africa's Young Children

African societies value children and place them at the center of their family life and communities. The African Charter on the Rights and Welfare of the Child (ACRWC) states that "the child occupies a unique and privileged position in the African society" (Organization of African Unity 1999, Preamble, para. 4). Over many decades, governments have declared the importance of children in their development efforts and have devoted considerable resources to child development, especially in education and health. They affirmed their commitment in *Africa Fit for Children: The African Common Position* (Organization of African Unity 2001) at the Pan-African Forum for Children in Cairo in May 2001. That position was endorsed by the heads of state and government of the Organization of African Unity (now African Union [AU]) in Lusaka in July 2001. *The African Common Position* became Africa's input into the United Nations Special Session on Children held in May 2002.

Children and young people constitute more than half of Africa's population (African Union et al. 2003). Despite significant efforts over the past 10 years to ensure the rights of children, most children in SSA have a difficult start in life, due mainly to deepening poverty, national debt, inadequate policy support and services, political and civil conflict, and, in some cases, harmful cultural practices. Countries in SSA also face serious challenges as the child population is growing faster than services can be provided.

The enormous challenges most African children face affect the capacity of their families to take adequate care of them. Changing work patterns for parents and high HIV/AIDS prevalence among women and young people render more and more families and communities unable to take adequate care of their children. Therefore, governments must be called upon as duty bearers in human rights–based development to ensure quality services for all children, protection, and support systems for their families.

Evolution of ECD Policy

Before 1990 young children, especially from birth to 5 years, were nearly invisible in most African policy documents, except in sectoral health and nutrition policies and strategies. The international impetus given to children and ECD in 1990 in the World Declaration on Education for All (UNESCO 1990) stimulated official action in Sub-Saharan Africa. From their quick signature of the Convention on the Rights of the Child (CRC; United Nations 1989) and active participation in the Education for All (EFA) conferences and the World Summit for Children, African countries began to integrate children's issues more clearly in sectoral policies. Ghana, Malawi, Mauritius, Namibia, and Uganda established ministries or national commissions responsible for children. Other countries focused on children under ministries of family or social affairs.

In 1998, the Seventh Conference of Ministers of Education of African Member States (MINEDAF VII; UNESCO 1998) expressed a specific political commitment to promote ECD policies. The conference accepted recommendations of the Regional Consultation of African nongovernmental organizations (NGOs), among which was the key recommendation that all African countries formulate clear policies to promote early childhood education and development (UNESCO 1998). The challenges for the countries included capacity to formulate culturally appropriate and effective integrated ECD policies and funding.

The engagement of key donor or development partners such as the United Nations Children's Fund (UNICEF) and the World Bank in ECD promotion and funding were important to secure government commitment in different countries. UNICEF-supported programs for children's rights and ECD intensified in virtually all SSA countries. From the mid-1990s, the World Bank provided credit funding in countries such as Eritrea, Kenya, and Uganda. With overwhelming research evidence on the positive returns to investments in ECD, the Bank substantially increased its funding for child care, health, nutrition, and education. As Mary Eming Young, a senior World Bank ECD specialist, has noted, the Bank recognizes that "children must prosper before economies can grow" (Young 2005, 2). Thus, as of February 2005, the World Bank lending portfolio of ECD had reached $1.5 billion for projects in all regions of the world (Young 2005).

The Working Group on Early Childhood Development (WGECD) of the Association for the Development of Education in Africa (ADEA), established in 1997, has made a significant contribution to ECD policy development. In 1999, the WGECD identified support to policy development as a major way in which the partners could contribute and make a difference collectively to sustainable programs for holistic child development in Africa (Torkington 2001). The WGECD Policy Projects combined assessments and capacity building. The first project activity involved case studies of ECD policies in Ghana, Mauritius, and Namibia as well as a survey of ECD policy issues in 2000/1 (see Torkington 2001). The second project activity provided extensive technical support to national ECD policy planning in Burkina Faso, Mauritania, and Senegal in 2002/3 (see Vargas-Barón 2004). The relevant lessons learned from these valuable experiences will be discussed later.

Further support for ECD resulted from Africa-wide meetings—held in Kampala (1999), Eritrea (2002), and Ghana (2005)—of African and international specialists, policy and decision makers, and funding agencies that have helped to galvanize interest in ECD in the continent, which led to more comprehensive policies and programs. Already, Angola, Eritrea, Ghana, Malawi, Mauritius, and Namibia have developed and adopted national ECD policies. Other countries, including Burkina Faso, Burundi, The Gambia, Kenya, Mauritania, Senegal, Swaziland, and Uganda are in the process of developing policies.

ECD Links with International and Regional Conventions and African Development Policies

The links are critical between the achievement of the best start in life for Africa's children and the successful implementation of the human rights conventions such as the Convention on the Rights of the Child (United Nations 1989), the African Charter on the Rights and Welfare of the Child (Organization of African Unity 1999), and the Convention on the Elimination of All Forms of Discrimination Against Women (CEDAW; United Nations 1979) as well as international development policies and strategies such as Education for All, Poverty Reduction Strategy Papers (PRSPs), the Millennium Development Goals (MDGs), sectorwide approaches (SWAps), and the New Partnership for Africa's Development (NEPAD). African leaders emphasized the links in 2001 when they stated in *Africa Fit for Children*: "The socioeconomic transformation of the continent rests with investing in the young people . . . responding to the needs of Africa's children is imperative. Children should be the core of priorities for policy makers" (Organization of African Unity 2001, paras. 6–7).

The Human Rights Imperative: CRC, ACRWC, and CEDAW
CRC, ACRWC, and CEDAW give the human rights, moral, and ethical rationale for the links between ECD and national development. ACRWC, which was adopted less than a year after the adoption of CRC and came into force in November 1999, shares the key human rights principles with CRC. However, ACRWC gives further direction on some ECD issues pertinent to Africa. For example, it calls for measures "to eliminate harmful social and cultural practices affecting the welfare, dignity, normal growth, and development of the child and, in particular, the girl child" (Organization of African Unity 1999, art. 21). It also prohibits child marriage and betrothal of girls and boys. ACRWC highlights the roles and responsibilities of parents, the extended family, and other caregivers; it also makes a strong call on the state parties to assist families in need and working parents with necessary basic services and child care facilities (Organization of African Unity 1999, arts. 18–20).

CEDAW provides the ethical imperative from the gender perspective. However, its influence is not fully felt in ECD and other development policies. Difficulties incorporating the gender dimension and ensuring gender equality in childhood are partly a reflection of the sociocultural and political problems in different countries worldwide that led to delays in signing and ratifying the convention. Thus, while CRC came into force only 10 months after its adoption in 1989, CEDAW, which had been adopted 10 years earlier in 1979, came into force only on September 3, 1981 and is still not universally ratified. Nevertheless, both the EFA goals and MDGs insist on gender equality in child development, and so reflect the CEDAW links. ECD must be seen as the starting point for children to learn and for families and communities to practice gender equality. Effective and well-integrated ECD policies and programs that involve parents also free women to participate in community decision making and development activities as well as in gainful employment and production as recommended by CEDAW.

Development Instruments: PRSPs, MDGs, and SWAps

Prior to the ascendancy of Structural Adjustment Programs (SAPs) in the mid-1980s, most independent African countries produced coordinated national development plans or frameworks. These provided a vision for the overall development of the countries and identified overarching social and economic policies and strategies for the short, medium, and long term. With the SAPs, most countries abandoned such comprehensive national planning or strategy formulation. The focus shifted to short-term macroeconomic stability and export-oriented growth, which was achieved at great cost to human and social development. An important consequence through the 1990s was that most African countries were unable to develop coherent national social policies that could have incorporated ECD. Social change, including holistic ECD, takes longer to achieve than the SAPs and their successor PRSPs proposed. The loss of long-term vision and planning in Africa is reflected in the PRSPs, which have become the substitute "national development plans" for many countries.

The PRSPs, SWAps, and MDGs pose a challenge. They are highly focused and have strong sectoral approaches, rather than the multisectoral approach that is necessary for holistic child development. In the first generation of PRSPs, social development focused mainly on policies in health and education. The tendency was to regard children according to their diseases or the health regimes they required, or to see ECD as a downward extension of the primary education system to "preschool" children from 3 to 6 years old, leaving out children from 0 to 3 years old. The sectoral policies generally missed the whole child.

It is worth noting, however, that the PRSPs have contributed significantly to focusing national attention on poverty. They have deepened the understanding of poverty through participatory poverty assessments and overall poverty analysis at the country level. The PRSPs have also given needed priority to health and education—social sectors that faced decline in many SSA countries in the socioeconomic crises of the 1980s and early 1990s. Nevertheless, from the perspective of ECD, the PRSPs generally have no child focus, analysis of child poverty and deprivation, or attention to families. Early childhood care and education are generally missing, and women and gender are marginalized, except as regards girls' education. This shortcoming is serious if structural poverty in Africa is to be reduced. Women's poverty directly affects their children's deprivation; women's income greatly improves child welfare and development and helps to break the poverty cycle.

As of March 31, 2005, 21 African countries had full PRSPs approved by the World Bank, and 9 others had interim PRSPs. Countries including Ghana, Tanzania, Uganda, and Zambia are developing the second generation of PRSPs; it is hoped they will incorporate holistic child development. Ghana, Uganda, and Zambia are attempting to integrate ECD into revised versions of their PRSPs. The adoption and pursuit of the MDGs has created a favorable opportunity to intensify this process of child-focused PRSP development. According to the World Bank, many SSA countries have aligned their PRSP goals and targets with the MDGs (Jaramillo and Mingat 2003). However, the *Millennium Project Report* has criticized the PRSPs for not being comprehensive or sufficiently long term to achieve the MDGs (United Nations Millennium Project 2005).

SWAps, developed mainly in health and education, provide another opportunity to promote ECD. The advantages of SWAps include their detailed sector analysis, policy reform orientation, and strategic planning linked to PRSPs and national budgets. On the positive side, SWAps cover sectoral aspects of ECD such as immunizations, maternal health, and kindergartens, but SWAps need to cover the whole child and adopt the life-cycle approach more systematically for children from birth to 8 years. Disadvantages to overcome include weak cross-sectoral links and the absence of focus on the whole child and the family.

Burkina Faso, The Gambia, Ghana, Niger, São Tomé and Principe, Uganda, and Zambia have SWAps in health and education; Burkina Faso, Mali, and Niger have SWAps in water and sanitation. More opportunities could also be identified to promote integrated SWAp/ECD activities at district and community levels. The link between ECD and HIV/AIDS prevention and care provides a major opportunity to strengthen the SWAp/ECD links and to access additional resources, such as the Multicountry HIV/AIDS Program (MAP) funds. These links are being pursued in Uganda and Zambia. Uganda is also promoting emergency obstetric care within the health SWAp for the reduction of maternal mortality and is incorporating ECD in the Education Sector Strategic Plan 2004–15 so that the sectors will budget for ECD (UNICEF 2005).

The African Union has come to the same conclusion on the need to link ECD and long-term development with respect to NEPAD (African

Union 2001). In partnership with the Economic Commission for Africa (ECA) and UNICEF, in September 2003 the AU published *The Young Face of NEPAD: Children and Young People in the New Partnership for Africa's Development*, which called for African leaders to take bold and radical actions in favor of Africa's children, starting with ECD: "Early childhood care for survival, growth, and development is . . . not just an obvious humanitarian action, but an action at the center of the long-term development and evolution of society" (African Union et al. 2003, 14).

National ECD Policies: Needs and Challenges

What is a policy? According to the *Concise Oxford English Dictionary* (1990), a policy is "a course or principle of action adopted or proposed by a government, business, party, or an individual." At the national level, a policy represents a philosophy or guiding principles, goals, and objectives of the government with respect to key issues of the country and its citizens, to which it will commit resources in a strategic course of action to be taken at different levels in different areas of development. Political will and an underlying vision are important starting points for policy development. A policy must receive high-level endorsement or approval from the cabinet or parliament and, in some cases, legal and constitutional backing, to be able to provide national direction.

Two different approaches have been taken to develop national policies for young children and their families: creating a policy framework to which all sectors have to respond and creating a stand-alone ECD policy.

Policy Framework

There is no doubt that countries with adequate and robust social policies, integrated sectoral policies and strategies, and well-defined children's policies may not need to engage in the long process of ECD policy development. What may be necessary is an integrated framework or plan of action to ensure coordination, intersectoral priority setting, and effective implementation, and to fill notable gaps. South Africa has chosen this path. It engaged in a process to develop an integrated national strategy to increase understanding and commitment to ECD by policy and decision makers at national and local levels. The country now has a national integrated plan for ECD, 2005–10, as well as national guidelines on ECD for all stakeholders (UNICEF 2005).

An ECD Policy

Countries that show a weak understanding of ECD principles, accord low priority in sectoral and other national policies to vulnerable children from prenatal to 8 years old, and have low levels of intersectoral coordination on issues of children and women, would find national ECD policies important and useful. The urgency of the social challenges facing Africa's children and women, as noted, makes specific ECD policies advisable. Countries including Burundi, Kenya, Rwanda, and Zambia have noted that the absence of national policies constitutes a major constraint to priority and resource allocation to ECD.

A national ECD policy not only envisions the best interests of all young children, but also indicates the modalities to provide for that reality. Such a policy must be multidisciplinary, multisectoral, and developed strategically to give priority to the well-being of young children (prenatal to 8 years), their families, communities, and society as a whole. In many African countries there is scarcity of information and lack of knowledge about young children—especially those aged 0–3 years old—and the needs and practices of their families. Therefore, ECD policy development needs to incorporate a situation analysis and other appropriate studies of all young children—especially the most vulnerable ones—and their families. It should also include information on parenting and child care practices in rural and urban areas, disadvantaged and privileged communities, and different cultural groups.

A national ECD policy would be rights-based and nondiscriminatory and would promote the best interests of the child. It would reflect a holistic and integrated approach as well as address issues of the different age cycles and levels of development through good quality social and basic services supported with effective human and financial resources of government and a broad partnership of parents, communities, NGOs, the private sector, and international agencies.

Some challenges to having a specific national ECD policy need to be overcome. The most fundamental challenge relates to government commitment and political will. Is the government—or can the government become—committed not only in vision and principle, but also in resource allocation and mobilization of all its concerned branches for ECD? Faced with competing development priorities and serious limitations on financial resources, will the government and its partners accord high priority to an ECD policy? Solutions to these problems to a large extent can come through advocacy and social mobilization.

Another fundamental challenge comes from the structure of government. While ECD policy is holistic and follows an integrated approach to promote links and synergies to support the whole child, government is organized sectorally. Planning and budgetary allocations are generally done sectorally for the same population groups and communities. More recently, greater emphases appear to be placed on *systems* and their reform, particularly in health and education SWAps, than on all the categories of *people* who are the subjects and beneficiaries of sectoral development. This situation makes multisectoral coordination for ECD difficult. Sectoral priorities and activities often override ECD needs. Many countries (such as Eritrea, Ethiopia, Kenya, Zambia, and Zimbabwe) that are implementing ECD activities or are beginning to implement newly adopted policies face constraints in the lack—or limited nature— of intersectoral coordination and cooperation at different levels (UNICEF 2005).

There may also be challenges in defining the scope of a national ECD policy. To be a good and effective policy, it should address the rights and needs of all children. This may seem daunting considering the large child population in African countries, the huge problems of children affected by HIV/AIDS, and the increasing numbers of orphans and children with special needs who must all be covered, as their right, with limited financial and human resources.

The experiences of ECD policy making in the region reveal that capacity for policy development can be a major challenge, as illustrated by cases in Burkina Faso, Mauritania, Namibia, and Senegal (Torkington 2001; Vargas-Barón 2004). While national expertise exists in various child-related sectors, experience in planning policies across sectors appears to be quite limited. Also, sectoral experts may require capacity building to appreciate and apply new concepts—such as the holistic and integrated approach to ECD—and to plan for 0–3-year-olds and for vulnerable children and families.[1]

ECD policy making is ultimately a political choice. Governments must choose, among all the competing socioeconomic priorities, to give children the best start in life. Resources, particularly financial, are a significant influence. Thus, even where the idea of holistic and universal ECD has been accepted, low-income African countries face the problem of choosing the types of ECD delivery systems for child care, health, nutrition, early education, and family support. The choice is mainly either family- and community-based ECD programs, which are less expensive to the state and are often more effective, or the more costly formal, institution-based approaches characterized by preschools. The dilemma relates also to quality and equity between the community-based programs, which reach more underprivileged children, and the formal, elitist, institution-based system that politically might attract more public finances.

Policy Development Process

The experiences of policy development in Africa indicate that the process takes time (at least two years) and needs flexibility and sensitivity. Four key "lessons learned" are the need for (1) broad consultation and participation by all stakeholders, (2) alignment of the ECD policy with major national and sectoral development policies and strategies, (3) availability of technical and institutional capacity for cross-sectoral policy planning, and (4) strategic structures to host and promote the policy and its implementation.

Consultation and participation—Consultation among all concerned groups and institutions on ECD and their active participation in the policy development process help to build consensus on key issues and fundamental concepts and place the child's interest above specific groups or sectoral focus. Consultation and stakeholder participation also promote transparency, synergy, and cost-effectiveness in the shared roles and responsibilities for the well-being of the child. Above all, they ensure national ownership of the policy. The quality of the participatory process has an impact on the quality of the policy itself and the effectiveness of its implementation.

Burkina Faso, Ghana, Malawi, Mauritania, and Senegal have launched their policy development process with national stakeholders' conferences and workshops that were supported strongly by UNICEF. In Burkina Faso and Senegal, prior to the national workshops, the policy development country teams conducted local and regional consultations in different parts of the countries using local languages. This strategy enabled the communities and local people to provide culturally pertinent input. Initial stakeholders' consultations promoted collective visualization to capture the ideas of a better future for all the young children in that particular society. They also helped to identify existing relevant policies, strategies, and programs for children that need to be taken into account in the comprehensive ECD policy, such as in Ghana and Malawi. Such related policies and programs might be focused on orphans and vulnerable children (OVC), children with special needs, HIV/AIDS-affected children, preschoolers, child nutrition, and child protection.

ECD policy alignment—It is important for the broad consultations to continue throughout the policy development process to ensure sustained interest and commitment. It is essential that the ministries of finance and economic planning be involved at an effective level. The ministries responsible for overall policy formulation and implementation of the PRSPs, MDGs, and, to varying extents, SWAps, have a key role in ensuring the link or alignment of the ECD policy with those national policies and strategies. Their advice and input are crucial on the costs and financing of the ECD policy and programs. Institutions for national statistics also need to participate and provide technsical input into the policy to facilitate needed research and monitoring.

The United Nations Millennium Project report *Investing in Development* (2005) proposes major changes to development planning that may open up new opportunities for ECD policies. In the absence of overall national development plans and strategies in most countries, every opportunity should be taken to incorporate child welfare and holistic ECD into the proposed long-term national development strategy. The report, discussed by the UN General Assembly in 2005, strongly recommended a revision of PRSPs to make them ambitious enough that countries would be able to achieve the MDGs (ibid.). The PRSPs are to be reorganized into 3- to 5-year programs within 10-year poverty and MDG-based national development strategies. The revised PRSPs would focus on, among other things, human rights, which must start with children's rights. It should be noted, however, that serious country-level advocacy and technical work are needed to ensure that the proposed priority public investments and, particularly, the suggested "quick wins" would more adequately cover prenatal to 8-year-old children and their families (UN Millennium Project 2005).

Capacity for cross-sectoral policy planning—The broad strategic partnerships of the national government, civil society, NGOs, and development partners have helped several countries to mobilize the multisectoral capacity needed for ECD policy development. For example, experts and specialists from the government, NGOs, the national university, UNICEF, and the Consultative Group on Early Childhood Care and Development (ECCD) generated the required capacity to develop a progressive and model ECD policy in Namibia (Namibia Inter-Ministerial Task Force on Early Childhood Development 1995). Similar groups working with Early Childhood Development Virtual University (ECDVU) participants accomplished a similar objective in Malawi in 2001 (see Pence 2004). In West and Central Africa, UNICEF has played a major role in regional training and capacity building for national partners and UNICEF ECD staff. For example, UNICEF strongly supported and facilitated three regional training workshops for national ECD policies in Burkina Faso, Mauritania, and Senegal between September 2002 and July 2003 as part of the WGECD project. The Mauritania policy is in final draft, while those of Senegal and Burkina Faso are in draft.

Strategic structures—Another important lesson from the countries that have engaged in the ECD policy development process is the need to have strategic national structures to host and promote the policy and its implementation. These structures are particularly necessary to ensure smooth and expeditious transitions between policy formulation and policy adoption and between policy adoption and policy implementation. Several factors, including national emergencies, can influence the important process. For example, Ghana experienced an unusually long 11-year delay from the consensus-building national ECD seminar in 1993, to the finalization of the policy in 2001, and cabinet approval and the policy launch in August 2004. Causes of the delay included changes in government, debates over which ministry or institution would lead the ECD process, and lack of quick resolution and decision on the issues.

By contrast, Mauritius took only two years (1996–98) to prepare and receive cabinet approval of its ECD policy for children ages 0–3 years under the leadership of the Ministry of Women, Family Welfare, and Child Development, which had primary responsibility for the age group. In Namibia, good leadership, competent internal and external expertise, and wide ownership helped to produce a model integrated ECD policy for children ages 0–8 years; it received cabinet approval in four years (1992–96). However, institutional change in the host structure in 2000, from the original Ministry of Regional and Local Government and Housing to a newly created Ministry of Women's Affairs and Child Welfare, impacted the implementation, which affected capacity-building programs at the district level and intersectoral collaboration (Pence 2004; Torkington 2001).

Senegal had a similar change in host ministry. At the start of the policy development, the Ministry of Family, Social Development, and National Solidarity had responsibility for ECD. This responsibility was later transferred to the Delegated Ministry for Early Childhood and Case de Tout-Petits (Learning Centers for Young Children). The impact of the change on the ongoing policy development process is yet to be assessed (Vargas-Barón 2004).

Policy Implementation

Most SSA countries have been implementing specific sectoral aspects of ECD, such as prenatal care, immunization, supplementary feeding, early learning, and preschools. Mauritius and Namibia have had the longest implementation periods; their policies were reviewed in 2005–06, and suggestions were made for changes. Policy implementation in Ghana began with the establishment of the ECD Steering Committee in April 2005. Experiences so far indicate some of the critical elements for successful policy implementation, which include (1) steering committee; (2) action or operational plan and guidelines; (3) funding; (4) advocacy, social mobilization, and information; (5) networking; and (6) monitoring and evaluation.

Steering committee—Effective implementation after policy adoption requires a dynamic, high-level structure or mechanism for follow-up. Botswana, Ghana, Malawi, Namibia, South Africa, and Tanzania have established high-level national interministerial steering or coordinating committees, assisted in some cases by technical working groups or task forces. The main tasks of the committees include high-level advocacy, promotion of intersectoral coordination, and monitoring and evaluation of the policy and programs. Such committees face challenges of consistent, high-level participation and funding for their activities. The early development of action or operational plans with funding strategies, as well as high-level political support by government, would alleviate some of the problems.

Plan and guidelines—The Namibia case study showed that the absence of an action plan after adopting the policy had a negative impact on implementation (Torkington 2001). The experience in Malawi showed that action plans, in addition to policies, are critical to advancing ECD (Pence 2004). Action plans identify implementation strategies and time frames for coordination and partnership building, links with existing child care (for example, OVC and prevention of mother-to-child transmission), sectoral and national development policies, funding, capacity building, advocacy, social mobilization and networking, monitoring and evaluation of program activities, as well as the entire policy. Action plans must be monitored and updated in the light of new challenges and opportunities. Some countries, including South Africa and Uganda, have developed guidelines to facilitate policy implementation by multiple partners.

Funding—A funding strategy is essential for successful policy implementation. Every effort must be made to ensure that funds are available to implement the policy and its component programs. The strategy should identify diversified funding sources and potential contributions from communities, local and national governments, civil society, NGOs, private sector, and international partners. The strategy should also indicate the accountability criteria and modalities. Given the multiple partnerships, transparency is crucial for success. Case studies and other experiences show that the funding issues are some of the major bottlenecks to policy implementation. South Africa has had positive experiences that increased access to ECD services. It developed a broad partnership for funding that involved all levels of government, employers, community organizations, parents, and donor agencies. When holistic ECD is incorporated into sectors such as health, education, water, and sanitation through transparent intersectoral cooperation, those sectors should contribute to financing these activities (Jaramillo and Mingat 2003).

Advocacy, social mobilization, and information—Continuous advocacy is necessary at all levels for policy implementation. A well-developed research- and knowledge-based advocacy, social mobilization, communications, and information strategy would facilitate reaching policy makers, local government, community leaders, and parents for their support and input. It would also help to generate public demand for ECD services. Often policies remain at the national level with little dissemination to districts and communities. Eritrea, a rare exception, successfully translated the ECD policy and program materials into eight official local languages, which proved crucial in gaining local support for ECD implementation at district and community levels (Pence 2004).

Cameroon has had a successful experiment since 2003 in implementing a convergence model to promote services for holistic child development in one province. The approach coordinates five entry points for children and their families for nutrition and health, education, water and sanitation, protection, and the fight against HIV/AIDS. A key factor for the success of the program was social mobilization that led to the active participation of traditional leaders and communities in microplanning. The program has witnessed, among other things, increased birth registration and schooling for girls (UNICEF 2004a).

Networking—Many countries, especially Tanzania and Uganda, have used networking as an effective strategy to promote ECD policies and implementation. Through effective sensitization and information sharing, an ECD network was developed at both national and district levels between

2000 and 2004. The Tanzania ECD Network has played a key role in organizing national meetings to promote an ECD/EFA Action Plan for 2003–15 and ECD and HIV/AIDS strategies (Pence 2004). Tanzania highlighted the importance of national and international organizations appreciating critical points in capacity building that are achieved and are then prepared to act quickly to support such local efforts. When capacity is relatively thin, the timing of support becomes critical if solid advances are to be stabilized and progress is to continue.

Monitoring and evaluation—Finally, national ECD policies need well-designed and adequately funded plans for monitoring and evaluation. Policy monitoring and evaluation should be an essential part of the ECD policy so that appropriate revisions can be made to respond to new challenges and opportunities. Quantitative and qualitative indicators for ECD should be used in cross-sectoral programs to influence the orientation, scope, and coverage of major development policies and plans. Strong links between the national planning department, statistical services, and universities are recommended to obtain the necessary capacity and to develop appropriate expertise (Vargas-Barón 2004).

Conclusion and Key Actions

All the human rights instruments confirm the value that societies place on children. In Africa, this value is particularly highlighted in the ACRWC. The instruments and recent international and regional development policies provide a conducive environment and framework for governments to act to reduce and eliminate the serious challenges to the survival, growth, safe development, and protection of all children. As expressed by Mary Eming Young (2005, 2), "children must prosper before economies can grow."

African governments must recognize that the critical situation of children, especially the youngest and most vulnerable, is unacceptable. Radical and sustained action is needed to secure the best start in life, continuous healthy growth, and safe development for all children between the ages of 0 and 8 years, who are the foundation of Africa's human capital. Governments need to act with urgency because Africa's youngest and most vulnerable children cannot wait.

The time is opportune to expand and accelerate the development of comprehensive ECD policies in Africa. But ECD policy making is ultimately a political choice. Governments must choose among all the competing development priorities to give all children the best start in life. A focus on the youngest children of Africa (from the prenatal stage to age 8) through holistic ECD policies and programs, provides a real chance for sustainable, gender-equal human development, economic growth, social change, and transformation. As the African Union and NEPAD Secretariat and their partners, ECA and UNICEF, have concluded, "the ultimate test of our success [in development] will be the well-being of children" (African Union, et al. 2003, 3).

The following summarizes some of the key actions to be considered to accelerate ECD in Africa.

Demonstrate Political Will, Vision, and Courage

Governments at the highest levels need to translate the commitments in CRC, ACRWC, CEDAW, NEPAD, national constitutions, and laws for the rights and well-being of children into policies for the holistic development of all children. In the face of competing priorities and pressures, it requires political will, clear vision, and courage of governments to

- take ownership of the well-being of all children, starting with the youngest and most vulnerable;
- use the expanding democratic processes to focus on, and give priority to, children's and women rights as part of human rights;
- decide to develop or strengthen holistic ECD policies for children from the prenatal stage to age 8;
- enact necessary legislation on ECD and ensure enforcement;
- designate the most strategic mechanisms in the government structure to promote the ECD policies;
- ensure necessary investment in ECD and allocate human and financial resources from government budgets; and,
- oblige all concerned government sectors and partners to give priority to ECD and to support and fund its activities, separately, through the pooling of resources for children, or both.

Promote Advocacy, Social Mobilization, and Information on ECD

Governments, NGOs, and other partners need to

- engage in continuous advocacy for human rights–based, holistic ECD policy development and implementation at all levels;
- develop and implement a culture-sensitive social mobilization, communications, and information strategy to facilitate acceptance of the ECD

policy; secure implementation commitments by central, regional, and local government agencies, NGOs, other partners, communities, and parents; and generate and sustain public demand for ECD services;
- translate ECD policy and other relevant documents into local languages in an efficient and appropriate manner for the country; and,
- involve national media and public relations people in policy formulation, advocacy, and monitoring.

Conduct Research for ECD Promotion

Governments, statistical services, research institutes, and partners need to

- undertake research to fill gaps in knowledge, such as on the importance of ages 0 to 3 in holistic child development, traditional care practices, basic data on children's status (such as infant mortality rates by geographic region), and the situation of especially vulnerable young children, particularly orphans, children with special needs, and those affected by HIV/AIDS; and,
- collaborate on monitoring and evaluation of ECD policies and use the findings for policy advocacy, review, and revision.

Build and Strengthen Technical Capacity for ECD Policy and Implementation

Governments and their partners need to

- use and coordinate in-country expertise in multisectoral policy planning and development (for example, as may exist for PRSPs, MDGs, and SWAps) for ECD policy development;
- ensure adequate capacity in the focal ministry or structure for ECD policy as well as program coordination, advocacy, and monitoring; that ministry or structure should actively engage in cross-sectoral and cross-institutional dialogue and technical cooperation to promote ECD and to avoid its isolation;
- develop and implement a strategy for capacity building and retention in the ECD field in partnership with national institutions, universities, international organizations (especially members of the WGECD), ECDVU, and appropriate experts; and
- use available capacity and resources of partners to build and enhance national capacity for ECD at the national, regional, local, and community levels.

Build and Sustain Broad Partnerships to Accelerate ECD Policy Development and Implementation

Governments must

- ensure that ECD partnerships reach and include parents and communities whose contributions at the household and community levels are critical and indispensable for the survival, development, and protection of young children;
- ensure that quality basic services reach all children—especially the youngest and most vulnerable—and their families, who must also receive empowering and poverty-reducing socioeconomic support including parent enrichment and income-generating activities; and,
- adopt strategies of coordination and participation by all partners that would reduce costs in ECD policy development and program implementation, monitoring, and evaluation.

Ensure Effective Links of ECD Policies and Programs with Major National Development Policies and Frameworks

Governments, ECD advocates, and partners must

- engage in constant proactive processes to link ECD policies to the formulation, planning, and revisions of national development plans and visions, where they exist, and especially the PRSPs, MDGs, SWAps, and NEPAD;
- use expertise and capacity for multisectoral analysis and planning in Ministries of Finance and Economic Planning and Statistical Services to support integrated ECD policy formulation and planning; and,
- develop guidelines for multisectoral and integrated policy planning with ECD to share with—or to train—related sectoral, civil society, and other partner personnel.

Invest in and Allocate Adequate Resources to ECD

Governments and partners urgently need to

- ensure adequate national budgetary resources and investments in ECD;
- leverage resources—for child care for the young, development, and protection—from PRSPs; MDGs; SWAps; other sectoral plans; NEPAD; MAP; the Global Fund to Fight AIDS, Tuberculosis, and

Malaria; and other bilateral, multilateral, and NGO funds; funds are particularly needed for critical care and developmental programs for the prenatal period, emergency obstetric care, children 0–3 years, parent education and support, and poverty alleviation for women; and

- earmark heavily indebted poor countries (HIPC) and other debt relief funds to purchase vaccines, insecticide-treated bed nets, supplies for emergency obstetric care, community-based child care centers and preschools, and activities targeted to high-risk poor and vulnerable children and their families to ensure equity.

Note

1. Two valuable tools for such capacity building are UNICEF's *Early Childhood Resource Pack: Young Child Survival, Growth, and Development* (2004b) and the Consultative Group's *Early Childhood Counts: A Programming Guide on Early Childhood Care for Development* (Evans, Myers, and Ilfeld 2000).

References

African Union. 2001. *The New Partnership for Africa's Development* (NEPAD). Abuja: African Union.

African Union, Economic Commission for Africa, NEPAD Secretariat and UNICEF. 2003. *The Young Face of NEPAD: Children and Young People in the New Partnership for Africa's Development* (NEPAD). New York: UNICEF.

Concise Oxford English Dictionary. 1990. Oxford: Oxford University Press.

Evans, J. L., with R. G. Myers, and E. M. Ilfeld. 2000. *Early Childhood Counts: A Programming Guide on Early Childhood Care for Development.* Washington, DC: World Bank.

Ghana (Ministry of Women and Children's Affairs). 2004. *Early Childhood Care and Development Policy.* Accra: Ministry of Women and Children's Affairs.

Jaramillo, A., and A. Mingat. 2003. *Early Childhood Care and Education in Sub-Saharan Africa: What Would it Take to Meet the Millennium Development Goals?* Washington, DC: World Bank.

Malawi (Ministry of Gender, Youth, and Community Services). 2001. *National Policy on Early Childhood Development.* Lilongwe: Ministry of Gender, Youth, and Community Services.

Namibia Inter-Ministerial Task Force on Early Childhood Development. 1995. *National Early Childhood Development Policy in Namibia.* Windhoek: Government of Namibia.

Organization of African Unity. 1999. *African Charter on the Rights and Welfare of the Child.* Retrieved November 5, 2006, from http://www.africa-union.org/.

————. 2001 *Africa Fit for Children: The African Common Position*. Pan-African Forum for Children, Cairo, Egypt, May 28–31. Retrieved November 5, 2006, from http://www.unicef.org/specialsession/documentation/documents/africa-position-forum-eng.doc.

Pence, A. R. 2004. *ECD Policy Development and Implementation in Africa*. UNESCO Early Childhood and Family Policy Series, 9. Paris: UNESCO.

Torkington, K. 2001. *WGECD Policy Project: A Synthesis Report*. Paris: ADEA/ Netherlands Ministry of Foreign Affairs.

UNESCO (United Nations Educational, Scientific, and Cultural Organization). 1990. *World Declaration on Education for All and Framework for Action to Meet Basic Learning Needs*. World Conference on Education for All, Meeting Basic Learning Needs, Jomtien, Thailand. March 5–9. Retrieved November 5, 2006, from http://www.unesco.org/education/information/nfsunesco/pdf/JOMTIE_ E.PDF.

————. 1998. *Report of the Seventh Conference of Ministers of Education of African States (MINEDAF VII)*. Durban. April 20–24.

UNICEF (United Nations Children's Fund). 2004a. *Annual Report* (Cameroon). Yaoundé: UNICEF.

————. 2004b. *Early Childhood Resource Pack: Young Child Survival, Growth, and Development*. New York: UNICEF.

————. 2005. Analysis of Regional Integrated Early Childhood Development (IECD): Country-by-Country Annual Reports–2004. East and Southern Africa Regional Office. Nairobi: UNICEF.

United Nations. 1979. *Convention on the Elimination of All Forms of Discrimination Against Women*. Retrieved November 5, 2006, from http://www.un.org/ womenwatch/daw/cedaw/cedaw.htm.

————. 1989. *Convention on the Rights of the Child*. Retrieved September 5, 2006, from http://www.unicef.org/crc/.

————. Millennium Project. 2005. *Investing in Development: A Practical Guide to Achieve the Millennium Development Goals—Overview*. New York: United Nations Millennium Project.

Vargas-Barón, E. 2004. *Final Report: Project to Support National Policy Planning for Early Childhood Development in Three Countries of West Africa*. The Hague: Association for the Development of Education in Africa, Working Group on ECD (ADEA-WGECD).

Young, M. E. 2005. Statement delivered at UNICEF WCARO Regional Workshop on ECD, Dakar, Thailand. March.

CHAPTER 3

Early Childhood Care and Education in Sub-Saharan Africa: What Would It Take to Meet the Millennium Development Goals?

Adriana Jaramillo and Alain Mingat

The importance of the link between children's health, education, and well-being and poverty reduction is gaining recognition by policy makers working in international development. An example of this recognition is the fact that five of the eight Millennium Development Goals (MDGs) adopted by the United Nations in 2000 relate to the health, nutrition, and education of young children. These goals include halving the percentage of children who suffer hunger, reducing by two-thirds the rate at which children under age 5 are dying, decreasing by three-quarters the ratio of maternal deaths to live births, providing all children the opportunity to complete primary education, and eliminating gender disparities in schooling opportunities. Recognition of the importance of the early years is also reflected in the first of the six goals set at the Dakar World Forum on Education for All (EFA) in April 2000: "to expand and improve comprehensive early childhood care and education, especially for the most vulnerable and disadvantaged children" (UNESCO 2000). At the country level, the emphasis that African governments are placing on improving the health and education of children is seen in national Poverty Reduction Strategy Papers (PRSPs), which set goals and targets aligned with the MDGs.

In essence, poor children are likely to grow up to become poor adults and to give birth to children who are poor, perpetuating the poverty cycle. In contrast, children are more likely to go to school and to perform well if they have support during the earliest years and if their parents are educated and supported in providing appropriate care. The health of the mother is also of concern. Healthy, well-nourished mothers have healthy newborns who, if a healthy trajectory is followed, become healthy children and adolescents, increasing the possibility of a healthy next generation. Research backs up the link between a supportive environment for the young child and poverty reduction. The economic, private, and social returns on investments in nutrition, health, and education early in life have been demonstrated by van der Gaag and Tan (1998), Myers (1998), and Schweinhart, Barnes, and Weikart (1993). Meeting the basic health, nutrition, and education needs of young children is key to breaking the poverty cycle.

The objective of this chapter is not to advocate that early childhood care and development (ECCD) is an important objective to pursue; this is already known.[1] Rather, the purpose is to examine the status of ECCD provision in countries in Sub-Saharan Africa (SSA) and to determine if current support for preprimary activities will lead to the achievement of MDGs. This chapter is organized in three sections. Section 1 examines how African countries are positioned to meet the MDGs and EFA Goal 1. The section analyzes current preschool coverage in SSA; it compares SSA with other regions and analyzes preschool coverage in individual African countries. An analysis of the evolution of ECCD provision looks at the progress during the 1990s and projects the current trend to the year 2015. Section 2 provides arguments to support the extension of ECCD in Africa. Section 3 discusses the choices and trade-offs needed to design a strategy toward reaching the internationally established Millennium Development and *Education for All* early childhood goals.

Can the World's Goals for Children Be Met?

It is important to analyze how the early childhood development goals are positioned when universal completion of five years of primary education remains the priority. This priority, which is both an EFA objective and an MDG for the year 2015, is not easily reached.

ECCD Goals in SSA and Other Regions

Table 3.1 shows how Sub-Saharan Africa lags behind in achieving early childhood goals in relation to other regions and all developing countries. For example, in 2000, the prevalence of malnutrition in children under age 5 in SSA is more than twice that in East Asia and almost four times that in Latin America and the Caribbean (LAC). The under-5 mortality rate is more than twice the rate for all developing countries, more than four times higher than LAC, and more than three times

Table 3.1. Status of Millennium Development Goals by Region

	Africa 1990	Africa 2000	All developing countries 2000	Latin America and the Caribbean 2000	East Asia 2000
MDG 1					
Population with income below $1 a day (%)	47.1	48.1	—	12.1	14.7
Prevalence of child malnutrition (% of children <5)	—	26.5	—	7.6	12.2
MDG 2					
Primary school completion rate (%)	49.0	54.0	77.0	85.0	84.0
Cohort reaching grade 5 (%)	—	67.2	—	85.4	95.4
Youth literacy rate (% ages 15–24)	67.7	78.0	85.6	93.9	97.3
MDG 3					
Ratio of girls to boys in primary and secondary education (%)	78.6	79.9	86.5	98.7	89.2
Ratio of young literate females to males (% ages 15–24)	79.8	88.7	91.8	100.8	97.9
Share of women employed in the nonagricultural sector (%)	—	—	—	41.2	—
MDG 4					
Under-5 mortality rate (per 1,000)	158.5	161.2	77.8	36.7	45.3
Infant mortality rate (per 1,000 live births)	102.5	91.2	53.8	29.0	36.0
Immunization, measles (% of children <1)	64.2	52.9	72.6	93.0	85.0

Source: World Bank 2001; UNICEF 2000.

Note: — = not available.

higher than East Asia. The infant mortality rate has a similar pattern; the immunization rate for children under 1 year of age is almost half that in LAC and 20 percentage points lower than the average for all developing countries. For some indicators, the situation has deteriorated; for example, African immunization levels were lower in 2000 than in 1990.

Health in Africa has not been improving at the same pace as other regions. The improvement rate for infant mortality, for example, has been much lower than in East Asia, the only region with comparably poor health indicators (UNICEF 2000; World Bank 2001).

Even when country income and health expenditures are accounted for, international comparisons systematically underscore the relatively lower level of performance of SSA countries when compared with other low-income countries. Africa also scores lower in access to professional services, health staff per capita, and use of low-cost technology (UNICEF 2000; World Bank 2001).

A Focus on Preschool Participation

ECCD activities are not confined to preschooling but are concerned with the total well-being and development of the child—emotionally, physically, and intellectually—in the crucial period from birth to age 6. The two main objectives of early interventions in SSA are to prepare children for entry into primary school and to unburden families from their child care duties during the workday hours. The scope of ECCD goes beyond these main objectives and concerns every child's right to survival, protection, care, and optimal development from conception onward. Nonetheless, the following discussion focuses on preschool participation.

In the SSA region, the overall enrollment rate for preschool in 1999 was 16.3 percent (9.9 percent for International Development Association [IDA] countries[2]); in most cases, parent contributions pay for preschool. Table 3.2 presents aggregate figures by world regions for the gross enrollment ratio (GER) for preschool for 1990 and 1999, as well as the primary education completion rate for 1999.

Countries in SSA lag behind countries in other parts of the world in preschool coverage as measured by GER. In 1999, the average preschool GER of countries in the Middle East (28.8 percent) is more than 12 percentage points higher, Asia's GER (36.5 percent) is more than twice that observed in SSA, and enrollment in both Eastern Europe and Central Asia (59.5 percent) and Latin America and the Caribbean (62.8 percent) is almost four times higher than in SSA.

Table 3.2. Preschool, Primary Education, and Proportion of Children Underweight by World Region (Country-Weighted Averages)

Regions	GER in preschool education (%)				Primary education (%) 1999			Children <5 underweight (%) 1995–2000
	Girls 1999	Boys 1999	Together 1990	1999	Completion rate	Survival to grade 5	Repetition rate	
Sub-Saharan Africa	16.6	16.0	11.1	16.3	54.0	67.2	17.8	26.5
IDA countries	9.8	10.0	8.5	9.9	45.6	66.0	19.3	28.6
Non-IDA countries	51.6	54.7	20.3	53.2	90.6	73.3	11.9	17.9
Non-Sub-Saharan Africa developing countries								
Middle-East and Northern Africa	27.4	30.2	21.3	28.8	77.2	92.3	7.2	16.1
Eastern Europe and Central Asia	58.8	60.2	61.4	59.5	93.4	98.0	1.4	6.1
South Asia, East Asia and Pacific	36.5	36.5	25.7	36.5	85.8	78.8	7.9	30.3
Latin America and the Caribbean	62.4	61.0	46.3	62.8	86.0	85.4	7.6	8.9
IDA countries	22.6	22.8	26.0	22.7	76.4	70.2	8.0	29.5
Non-IDA countries	52.7	53.4	42.2	53.0	88.0	89.3	5.6	12.3
OECD countries	78.7	78.7	71.8	78.7	100.0	100.0	1.3	—

Source: UNESCO statistics; UNICEF 2000.
Note: IDA countries have a per capita GDP below $755.
— = not available.

On average and as expected, preschool coverage tends to be greater in countries that have both a higher level of economic development and a greater enrollment in primary schooling. This trend holds within the Africa region (see tables 3.2 and 3.3). The average GER for preschool is estimated at only 10 percent in the African IDA countries with the lowest income (average per capita GDP of $355 and primary completion rate of 45.6 percent), while the average preschool GER is 53 percent in the few non-IDA countries of the region (average per capita GDP of $2,880 and primary completion rate of 90.6 percent).

Interestingly, when considering countries within a limited range of per capita GDP, such as the IDA countries, no clear relationship exists between preschool and primary school coverage and level of economic development. Within this group there is virtually no such relationship; preschool coverage has wide variations across countries (see table 3.3). For example, the neighboring countries of The Gambia and Senegal have very different figures for preschool coverage, with 28 percent in the former and only 3 percent in the latter. Similarly, Sudan has a preschool GER of 22 percent, while in its neighbor Ethiopia, it is only 1.7 percent. The comparison between Kenya (38 percent) and Uganda (2.9 percent) demonstrates this point. Variance is determined by political will, rather than other contextual factors.

Among the different regions of the world, the African continent is far from achieving the EFA Goal 1. (Note that to make an accurate assessment, the goal needs to be defined operationally, a point addressed later in this section.) For the poorest SSA countries—those that are eligible for IDA credits—the average GER at the preschool level was estimated to be only 10.3 percent in 1999, so there is far to go to reach 100 percent by 2015. If the trend between 1990 and 1999 is projected to 2015, the situation is bleak. Table 3.4 provides data on improvement in the preschool GER from 1990 to 1999 and these trends if projected to 2015.

If we go beyond regional averages and focus on individual countries throughout the world, we find wide variation, which is true to a lesser extent across Sub-Saharan African countries. The specific target rate for preschool coverage was not made explicit in the EFA goal statement to "expand and improve comprehensive early childhood care and education, especially for the most vulnerable and disadvantaged children." For the purpose of simulation, table 3.5 illustrates different levels of coverage in 2015 for preschool GER of 25, 40, 70, and 90 percent. The table indicates the distribution of the 133 developing countries with available data, according to their likelihood of reaching these coverage levels by 2015 based on their GER in 1999 and progress since then.

Table 3.3. Gross Enrollment Ratio (GER) in Standard Preschool, Proportion of Children Under 5 That Are Underweight, and Under-5 and Infant Mortality in Sub-Saharan African Countries (1999)

	Per capita GDP 1999 (1995 US$)	GER in standard preschool (%)			Children <5 underweight (%)	Mortality rate (per 1,000)	
		Girls	Boys	Total		<5	Infant
Angola*	523	—	—	2.0	42	295	172
Benin*	402	7.1	6.7	6.9	29	156	99
Botswana**	3,909	—	—	—	17	59	46
Burkina Faso*	253	1.6	1.7	1.6	36	199	106
Burundi*	143	0.9	0.8	0.9	37	176	106
Cameroon*	662	9.6	10.8	10.2	22	154	95
Cape Verde**	1,466	—	—	—	14	73	54
Central African Republic *	335	—	—	1.0	27	172	113
Chad*	222	—	—	1.0	39	198	118
Comoros*	452	1.6	1.8	1.7	26	86	64
Congo, Dem. Rep. of*	113	—	—	2.0	17	207	128
Congo, Rep. of**	802	2.2	3.2	2.7	26	108	81
Côte d'Ivoire*	777	2.8	2.7	2.7	24	171	102
Equatorial Guinea**	1,405	29.3	30.7	30.0	—	160	105
Eritrea*	173	5.7	5.3	5.5	—	105	66
Ethiopia*	113	1.8	1.7	1.7	47	176	118
Gabon**	4,406	—	—	—	—	143	85
Gambia, The*	362	29.8	26.8	28.3	26	75	61
Ghana*	408	57.3	56.9	57.1	25	101	63
Guinea*	605	—	—	2.0	—	181	115
Guinea-Bissau*	199	3.8	4.0	3.9	23	200	128
Kenya*	337	37.1	39.7	38.4	22	118	76
Lesotho*	538	20.3	23.3	21.8	16	134	93
Liberia*	—	—	—	—	25	235	157

(continued)

Table 3.3. Gross Enrollment Ratio (GER) in Standard Preschool, Proportion of Children Under 5 That Are Underweight, and Under-5 and Infant Mortality in Sub-Saharan African Countries (1999) (continued)

	Per capita GDP 1999 (1995 US$)	GER in standard preschool (%)			Children <5 underweight (%)	Mortality rate (per 1,000)	
		Girls	Boys	Total		<5	Infant
Madagascar*	242	3.3	3.4	3.4	40	156	95
Malawi*	169	—	—	2.0	30	211	132
Mali*	291	1.9	2.9	2.4	40	235	143
Mauritania*	487	—	—	1.0	23	183	120
Mauritius**	4,043	95.2	97.0	96.1	16	23	19
Mozambique*	192	—	—	2.0	26	203	127
Namibia**	2,370	60.2	69.3	64.7	26	70	56
Niger*	209	0.9	1.0	0.9	47	275	162
Nigeria*	250	—	—	2.0	36	187	112
Rwanda*	234	—	—	2.0	27	180	110
São Tomé and Principe*	338	—	—	—	16	76	59
Senegal*	592	2.9	3.0	3.0	22	118	68
Sierra Leone*	146	3.9	4.2	4.0	29	316	182
Somalia*	—	—	—	—	26	211	125
South Africa**	3,954	21.8	21.8	21.8	9	69	54
Sudan*	300	23.0	21.5	22.2	34	109	67
Swaziland**	1,488	—	—	—	10	90	62
Tanzania*	186	—	—	2.0	27	141	90
Togo*	339	2.2	2.3	2.2	25	143	80
Uganda*	345	2.9	2.9	2.9	26	131	83
Zambia*	388	2.1	2.5	2.3	24	202	112
Zimbabwe*	665	—	—	—	15	—	—
Country-weighted average*	**343**	**10.1**	**10.0**	**9.9**	**28.6**	**173**	**107**

Source: Authors' calculations.

Note: *IDA countries; **non-IDA countries.

— = not available.

Table 3.4. Evolution in Preschool GER by Region (1990–99) and Projection of the Trend (to 2015)

| | GER at the preschool level (%) | | | |
	1990	*1999*	*Gains 1990–99*	*Projected 2015*
Sub-Saharan Africa	11.1	16.3	+5.2	25.5
IDA countries	8.5	9.9	+1.4	12.4
Non-IDA countries	20.3	53.2	+32.9	111.7
Non-Sub-Saharan Africa developing countries				
Middle East and North Africa	21.3	28.8	+7.5	42.1
Eastern Europe and Central Asia	61.4	59.5	−1.9	(56.1)
South Asia, South East Asia and Pacific	25.7	36.5	+10.8	55.7
Latin America and the Caribbean	46.3	62.8	+16.5	92.1
IDA countries	26.0	22.7	−3.3	(16.8)
Non-IDA countries	42.2	53.0	+10.8	72.2
OECD countries	71.8	78.7	+7.1	91.0

Source: Authors.

Table 3.5. The Prospects for Achieving Various Target Levels of Preschool Coverage in 133 Developing Countries, Given Current Trends (by 2015)

| | Target preschool GER in 2015 | | | |
	25%	*40%*	*70%*	*90%*
Countries that have already reached the target in 1999	65	48	25	10
Countries that are likely to reach the target in 2015, based on current trends	5	12	13	16
Countries with a positive trend that will not reach the target in 2015	43	51	66	75
Countries with a negative trend that will not reach the target in 2015	20	22	29	32
Total developing countries	133	133	133	133

Source: Authors.

We distinguish four cases: (1) countries that had already reached the target figure in 1999; (2) countries that had not reached the target in 1999, but that will reach it by 2015 provided that the progress registered between 1990 and 1999 continues; (3) countries that had not reached the target in 1999, that registered a positive trend during the 1990s, but that will fall short of reaching the target if the observed trend is maintained; and (4) countries that had not reached the target in 1999 and are characterized by a negative trend over the previous decade.

Obviously the more ambitious the target for the year 2015, the less likely countries are to achieve their objectives, given current trends. Of the 133 developing countries, 52 percent (65 + 5) have—or will have in 2015—coverage of at least 25 percent. However, if the target for preschool coverage in 2015 is 40 percent, the percentage of countries that will reach that GER objective declines to 45 percent (60/133). If the GER target is 70 percent, the percentage of countries drops further to 29 percent (38/133); only 20 percent (26/133) have the probability of achieving a target of 90 percent preschool coverage. These figures suggest that for most countries, and to some extent irrespective of the degree of ambition in relation to the goal for 2015, strong actions need to be taken between now and 2015 to reach the desired objectives for preschool coverage.

Arguments to Support the Extension of ECCD Activities in Sub-Saharan Africa

In Africa, data are scanty on the benefits of early childhood interventions. However, data are available to assess the extent to which better performance in primary education can be associated with better levels of preschool development. To this end, a bivariate and graphic perspective was adopted by plotting the GER at the preschool level against repetition and survival rates in primary education, using country-level data. Figure 3.1 relates preschool GER to the grade repetition rate in

Figure 3.1. Grade Repetition Rate in Primary Education and Preschool Coverage

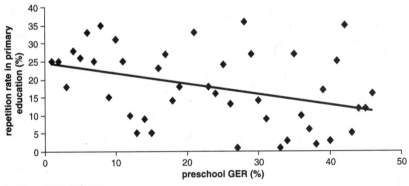

Source: Authors' calculations.

primary education. Figure 3.2 relates preschool GER to the survival rate to grade 5 among students entering primary grade 1. Figure 3.3 relates preschool GER with the proportion of children under age 5 who are underweight.

The three figures present interesting and expected associations. All cases have a substantial variance on both sides of the overall relationship, but there is also a clear pattern of association between the variables on both axes.

The frequency of grade repetition in primary education tends to decline as the proportion of the children who attended preschool increases. The magnitude is substantial: The estimated figure for a preschool

Figure 3.2. Survival Rate to Primary Grade 5 and Preschool Coverage

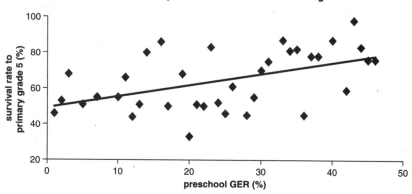

Source: Authors' calculations.

Figure 3.3. Proportion of Underweight Children Under 5 and Preschool Coverage

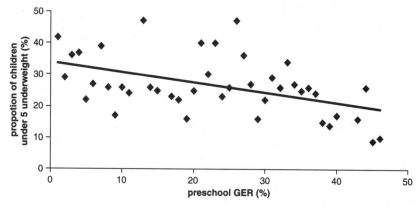

Source: Authors' calculations.

GER of zero would be about 25 percent repetition; this figure declines to about 12 percent repetition in countries where preschool enrollment is 45 percent.

The pattern is similar for the impact of preschool on completion of grade 5 among students entering grade 1. The trend is again quite positive: The completion rate for grade 5 is better when a greater proportion of the age group attended preschool. Again, the magnitude of the impact is quite noticeable, from a completion rate of about 50 percent in the absence of preschool, to about 80 percent completion when half of the age group has benefited from preschool.

Finally, the proportion of children under age 5 that are underweight tends to decline as the preschool coverage in a country increases. Here again, even with the overall variance, the bivariate impact is relatively substantial: 33 percent of children are underweight in countries where there is no preschool, while less than 20 percent of the children are underweight when nearly half of the school-age population benefits from preschool.

Caution is needed, however, not to draw conclusions too rapidly from these graphs. Other factors, such as the level of economic development, may influence both of the variables, resulting in erroneous correlations and conclusions. Therefore, an econometric analysis with control for the influence of other factors, such as per capita GDP, is recommended to assess the impact of preschool upon the identified outcomes.

The three relationships on two samples of countries were analyzed: all countries with relevant data (40 countries) and all SSA countries (24 countries). The results are clear and similar for both sets of countries. Concerning the impact of preschool on both the repetition and survival rates, controlling for per capita GDP makes virtually no difference because the per capita GDP variable is not statistically significant. The repetition rates are about 30 percent and the preschool variable is significant at the .05 level or, more often, the .01 level of confidence.

However, when analyzing the proportion of children under age 5 that are underweight, the impact of per capita GDP is very significant, leaving the preschool variable without a statistically significant impact. There is no direct relationship between preschool and being underweight, which is not surprising, because feeding programs in preschools are not common. Yet, these results support the point that some structural relationship indeed exists between preschool and primary education. This relationship is expected, but it is not trivial to support the anticipated relationship with factual results.

It may not be adequate, however, to suppose the existence of flat or direct relationships between preschool coverage and frequency of repetition or survival in primary education. The reality may be better described by using a structure such as the one in figure 3.4.

In this framework, preschool is supposed to have a positive impact on learning in the course of primary education; learning has a negative impact on grade repetition; and lower levels of repetition imply better survival in primary education. Parents often see repetition as a signal that the child is not fit for school, so should stay home to contribute to the household economy. However, in addition to the impact of preschool on primary school survival (through an assessment of student learning and repetition rates), a direct impact of preschool enrollment on primary school survival rates is associated with the fact that children (and their parents) have developed more positive attitudes toward schooling and have created a stronger demand.

The data analyzed for this study concern only the rates of preschool enrollment, repetition, and survival; comparative data on student learning were not available. Therefore, we focus on a reduced form of the previous framework, with a "short circuit" between preschool and repetition. This framework has been tested on the sample of 24 SSA countries that had relevant data; the results for the 40 lowest-income countries of the world are similar. Figure 3.5 shows the results of the estimates, which are summarized in figure 3.6.

The estimates show that preschool has a negative effect on grade repetition (that is, greater preschool coverage implies lower levels of repetition), with one additional percentage point in preschool GER implying an average reduction of 0.12 percentage point in the primary repetition rate. This estimate also shows that, for a given level of preschool GER, Anglophone African countries are characterized by significantly lower repetition (7.45 percentage points) than their Francophone counterparts. The estimates also show that repetition has a negative impact on

Figure 3.4. The Hypothesized Relationship between Preschool, Learning Repetition, and Survival to Primary Grade 5

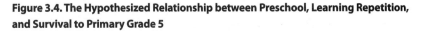
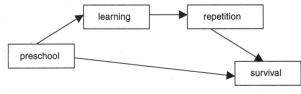

Source: Authors.

Figure 3.5. The Effect of Preschool on Repetition Rates (R^2) and Survival (Using Bivariate Data Analysis)

Impact of preschool on repetition

repetition = 20.56 – 0.123 × preschool GER + 0.37 ln (pcGDP) – 7.45 × anglophone   (R^2 = 0.509) (*) (**)

Impact of repetition on survival

survival = 82.87 – 0.875 × repetition   (R^2 = 0.280)   (**)

Impact of preschool on survival
total effect:
survival = 65.35 + 0.317 × preschool   (R^2 = 0.268)   (**)
direct net effect:
survival = 65.35 + (0.317 – (0.123 × 0.875)) × preschool = 65.35 – 0.209 × preschool

---

Source: Authors' calculations.
Note: *Significant at 5 percent; **Significant at 1 percent.

Figure 3.6. Direct and Indirect Effect of Preschool upon Repetition and Survival in Primary Education in 24 SSA Countries

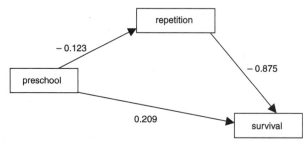

Source: Authors.

primary school survival, with an elasticity of –0.875, implying that a reduction of one percentage point in the repetition rate in primary school commands, on average in African countries, an increase of 0.875 percentage points. The total effect is substantial: An increase of one percentage point in preschool GER creates, on average, an increase of 0.317 percentage points in the rate of survival to grade 5.

This effect results from two sources: (1) an indirect effect through the combined impact of preschool on repetition and of repetition on survival; and (2) a direct effect (that may represent the impact of preschool on the demand for schooling), which is estimated here at 0.209, implying that an increase of 1 percentage point in preschool GER would yield an increase of 0.209 percentage points in the survival rate to grade 5. Table 3.6 presents these results more concretely through numerical simulations.

As table 3.6 indicates, preschool enrollment has a positive impact on student flow in primary schooling. From an initial context of very low preschool coverage (most African countries were in such circumstances in 2000) to circumstances in which the preschool GER could reach, for example, 40 percent in 2015 (a goal that seems reachable), the anticipated benefits are substantial: Repetition rates could go down from 20 to 15 percent, while the proportion of primary grade 1 students that reach grade 5 could increase from 65 percent in 2000 to 78 percent in 2015. This result would have two implications: (1) the objective of universal completion of six years of primary education has better chances to be met and (2) the efficiency of resource use in primary education would be improved.

To get a sense of what these figures imply in terms of potential efficiency gains in primary education as a consequence of preschool investments, it is straightforward to simulate the pattern of student flow in primary education of a hypothetical country that currently has no preschool coverage (with a projected survival rate to grade 5 of 65.3 percent and a grade repetition rate of 20.4 percent) and that of the same country with a preschool coverage set at 40 percent (with a projected survival rate to grade 5 of 78.0 percent and repetition rate of 15.5 percent). For each of the two student flow patterns, we can calculate an input-output ratio, defined as the ratio of the effective number of pupil years to produce one graduate given the existing pattern of repetition and dropout and the optimal number of pupil years in the absence of repetition and dropouts to produce the same graduate. In an ideal case (with neither repetition nor dropout) the input-output ratio is equal to 1.

Table 3.6. Simulation of the Grade Repetition Rate and Survival Rate to Grade 5, according to Preschool Coverage in 24 SSA Countries

Preschool GER (%)	0	10	20	30	40	50	60
Repetition rate (%)							
All African countries	20.4	19.2	17.9	16.7	15.5	14.2	13.0
Francophone countries	22.7	21.5	20.3	19.0	17.8	16.6	15.3
Anglophone countries	15.3	14.0	12.8	11.6	10.4	9.1	7.9
Survival rate to grade 5 (%)							
Total effect	65.3	68.5	71.6	74.8	78.0	81.2	84.3
Indirect effect	65.3	67.4	69.5	71.6	73.7	75.8	77.8
Direct effect	65.3	66.4	67.5	68.5	69.6	70.7	71.8

Source: Authors' calculations.

The results show that the numerical value of the coefficient of student flow efficiency in primary education is 1.67 in the case with no preschool coverage, while it is 1.37 when calculated with a preschool GER of 40 percent. This result means that in the first case the country needs to spend 67 percent more resources than necessary, while the second country needs only 37 percent. The savings associated with 40 percent preschool coverage can therefore be estimated to amount to 17.5 percent [(1.67–1.37)/1.67] of spending on primary education, which represents substantial resources. These savings are real because the quality of primary education is not compromised (as would be the case with an increase in class size or a reduction in pedagogical materials). In this case, the savings are not at the expense of quality; rather the savings represent policy measures directly related to strengthening the quality of education outcomes.

Policy Implications for Reaching ECD Goals

Governments must make important policy decisions if they are to have a realistic chance of achieving early childhood MDGs and the first EFA goal. These decisions involve (1) defining the specific ECCD activities that could be undertaken within the social context, (2) designing a strategy that maximizes the mix of formal structures and community-based activities, (3) developing ECCD programs that match the needs of the 0–3 and 4–6 age groups, and (4) setting priorities among populations to be served by ECCD activities.

Defining Specific ECCD Activities

It is widely accepted that young children benefit from a healthy, safe, and enriched environment—conditions that are not in place in most of SSA. It is also advocated that the ECCD activities for young children be guided by an integrated framework. ECCD does not evolve in a vacuum; it needs to find its place within or in addition to existing structures. It might be useful to distinguish between the activities that are specifically targeted to young children—such as parental education, child care, and preschool—and the factors that are important or even essential for young children but that are not child-specific—such as environmental elements including access to safe water and sanitation. Given these distinct categories, the ECCD strategy is two-fold: (1) Identify specific activities, design their implementation, and secure their financing; and (2) coordinate the different bodies and structures in charge of the factors to maximize their impact on young children.

Designing a Strategy to Maximize the Mix of Activities

Most of the activities undertaken for young children in SSA countries are organized in formal structures, in particular, preschools. Scarcer, community-based (informal) services are generally organized with the support of nongovernmental organizations (NGOs) or United Nations Children's Fund (UNICEF). Experience shows that formal structures are more often in urban settings, often (but not only) operated with private financing. Formal structures are characterized by relatively high unit costs per child[3] and they benefit better-off children disproportionately. By contrast, community-based activities are more often in rural settings and are characterized by either relatively low or high costs per child, depending on whether all costs are included in the calculations.

In designing the ECCD strategy, it is useful to document the respective merits of using formal or informal (community-based) structures to implement the types of activity under consideration. Costs and outcomes must be considered. The following questions need answers: What is the balance between the cost incurred and the impact on outcomes? To what extent is preschool a cost-effective strategy, given the alternatives, to improve educational outcomes in primary education?

Designing ECCD Programs to Match the Needs of Age Groups

Among the different modalities, programs can be roughly divided by age group: those that target 0- to 3-year-olds and those that are aimed at 4- to 6-year-olds.

Programs for 0- to 3-year-olds are more focused on parental education, health and nutrition, and psychosocial development. These types of programs are rarely center-based. Parents are the main audience and, in most cases, trained community leaders are the key providers.[4]

The center-based approach, however, is better suited to meet the needs of the 4- to 6-year-olds. Preschool programs focus on socialization (such as cooperating in a group, following discipline and rules), fostering cognitive development (such as spatial and psychomotor abilities, language), and supporting the child's healthy physical development.

These approaches are not exclusive. It has proven to be effective to continue to work with parents when children are in the older age group. Often parents of 4- to 6-year-olds have toddlers or infants at home; parental education and outreach programs conducted out of the center can be more focused and make monitoring easier. In practical terms, the same caregivers can teach the 4- to 6-year-old children and provide relevant education to parents on how to adopt the behaviors that are most appropriate for the harmonious development of their 0- to 3-year-old children.

Setting Priorities in Service Provision

The need to set priorities and make strategic choices about who will receive early childhood programs is a crucial theme in the development of ECCD programs in the years ahead in the Africa region. The need to prioritize applies to two complementary issues. First, the expansion of ECCD coverage that is called for will, by necessity, be gradual. Given that coverage is less than 5 percent in most countries of the region, universal coverage can be envisaged only in the long run. For a large proportion of countries, reaching preschool enrollment of 25 to 30 percent by 2015 or 2020 would be a positive achievement. In such circumstances, it will be difficult to determine who will be included and who will be excluded from the interventions.

Based on the experience of health and education systems, where this issue of selectivity has oftentimes been dealt with implicitly, services are first put in place to serve populations where demand is high and the logistics are easy. Consequently, services have often been provided first to better-off urban children. In the next phase, systems have been expanded to benefit progressively less-advantaged populations. In 2005, the rural and poor populations constituted the majority of those who were still excluded from health and education services (or who had access only to low-quality services). The actual geographic and social distribution of preschool in most countries is an example of such implicit selectivity in service delivery.

The EFA Goal 1 states that ECCD should be targeted "especially for vulnerable and disadvantaged children." If this goal is to be taken seriously, ECCD programs need to explicitly address prioritizing and selectivity, setting criteria transparently and positively, then implementing activities accordingly.

The second issue of prioritizing concerns the comprehensiveness, quality, and cost of the services. For example, some countries might decide on a common core of services for all children, with additional services provided for a certain segment (such as those who are living in especially difficult conditions). Another option would be to focus on specific kinds of interventions (such as nutrition).

Similarly, the services provided might be the same, but the subsidy might differ according to particular circumstances. For example, some communities might be asked to contribute (in kind or in money) to the financing of goods or services (for example, construction of a preschool or remuneration of a teacher or caregiver), while some other (poorer) communities may get these goods and services at a subsidized rate.

Another issue that determines what a government does to expand its early childhood provision relates to the costs of various programs. (See chapter 23 for a discussion of these issues.)

Conclusion

Given the current levels of preschool provision across Sub-Saharan African countries, it is probable that MDG and EFA goals will not be met by the year 2015. What will make a difference? Political will reflected in the adoption of education policies that include ECCD programs. Governments (of the majority of African countries) whose education budgets are unlikely to substantially increase in the coming years must carefully analyze their choice of education policies. Shifting a percentage of their current budget structure to support quality preschool programs should be a priority. While in the short term this shift might decrease funding for some areas of education—although not necessarily, as efficiency gains are not a result of decreased funding—in the long term this shift will increase the efficiency and effectiveness of their education systems.

Notes

This chapter was excerpted from Adriana Jaramillo and Alain Mingat, *Early Childhood Care and Education in Sub-Saharan Africa: What Would It Take to Meet the Millennium Development Goals?* (Washington, DC: World Bank, Africa Region, October 2003).

1. For a review of the literature on the subject, and in particular in developing countries, see *Early Childhood Counts* (2000) by Evans, Myers, and Ilfeld; *ECD: Laying the Foundation of Learning* (1999), a UNESCO publication; Practice and Reflection Series (1992–2000), Bernard van Leer Foundation; or *The Coordinators' Notebook*, published quarterly by the Consultative Group on ECCD.

2. Low-income countries that have a per capita GDP below $775 are eligible for IDA credits.

3. The average unit cost of preschool is about 50 percent higher than that of primary education. The costs vary widely across countries because the child-personnel ratio may vary from 15 to 1 to 47 to 1 across countries of the region.

4. Soucat (2003) argues that 15 years of experience with Minimum Package of Activities in countries such as Mali or Guinea have demonstrated that actions taken at the household level (such as exclusive breastfeeding and proper feeding practices, home care for common illness including diarrhea and acute respiratory infections, safe sexual behavior, and use of bed nets) have a significant impact on outcomes such as under-5 mortality or nutritional development of children.

References

Bernard van Leer Foundation. 1992–2000. Practice and Reflection Series. Retrieved September 8, 2006, from http://www.bernardvanleer.org/.

Consultative Group on Early Childhood Care and Development. (n.d.). *The Coordinators' Notebook.* Retrieved September 8, 2006, from http://www.ecdgroup.com/coordinators_notebook.asp.

Evans, J. L., with R. G. Myers, and E. M. Ilfeld. 2000. *Early Childhood Counts: A Programming Guide on Early Childhood Care for Development.* Washington, DC: World Bank.

International Monetary Fund. (n.d.). *Poverty Reduction Strategy Papers.* Retrieved September 6, 2006, from http://www.imf.org/external/np/prsp/prsp.asp.

Myers, R. G. 1998. *The Parent Education Project in Mexico.* Consultative Group on ECCD. Washington, DC: World Bank.

Schweinhart, L. J., H. V. Barnes, and D. P. Weikart. 1993. *Significant Benefits: The High/Scope Perry Preschool Study through Age 27.* Ypsilanti, MI: High/Scope Press.

Soucat, A. 2003. *Mauritania Case Study: Poverty Reduction.* Washington, DC: World Bank.

UNESCO (United Nations Educational, Scientific, and Cultural Organization). 1999. *Laying the Foundation of Learning.* Paris: UNESCO.

———. 2000. *The Dakar Framework for Action. Education for All: Meeting Our Collective Commitments.* Adopted by the World Education Forum, Dakar, Senegal, April 26–28. Paris: UNESCO.

UNICEF (United Nations Children's Fund). 2000. *The State of the World's Children 2000.* Retrieved November 21, 2006, from http://www.unicef.org/sowc00/.

United Nations. 2000. *United Nations Millennium Declaration.* Retrieved September 6, 2006, from http://www.un.org/millennium/declaration/ares552e.pdf.

van der Gaag, J., and J.-P. Tan. 1998. *The Benefits of Early Child Development Programs: An Economic Analysis.* Washington, DC: World Bank.

World Bank. 2001. *World Development Report Indicators.* Washington, DC: World Bank.

CHAPTER 4

Brain Development and ECD: A Case for Investment

Mary Eming Young and Fraser Mustard

Established and emerging evidence about brain development in the early years reinforces that quality early childhood development programs are a key societal imperative. Scientists have shown definitively that brain development is experience-based and has long-lasting effects; these two findings have serious implications for early child development (ECD).[1] We now know that a child's environment and experiences—beginning in utero—not only affect brain development, but also physical and mental health, learning, and behavior for a lifetime. These effects span much more than early learning or education. This key period affects well-being and health for life.

Countries can no longer ignore this evidence. Developing and industrialized countries must give priority to investing in the development of their populations; this investment must begin in early childhood.

ECD programs, involving parents and key care providers, are essential to improve the quality and capacity of populations. These interventions can improve the health, nutrition, and stimulation of all children, rich and poor. ECD programs tap into critical and sensitive windows of opportunity and periods of brain development: early, preschool years (ages 0–6). ECD programs that are available and accessible help to ensure that all children are well nurtured, healthy, and able to learn efficiently. The impact is lifelong and is magnified in populations and nations.

The Economics of ECD

Many studies show that attendance in ECD programs correlates with increased enrollment and retention in primary and secondary school, improved behavior, and better academic performance (Myers 1995). Each year of schooling benefits the child and society. Early interventions lead to increased earnings and promote social attachment. The financial return on investment is as high as 15 to 17 percent (Heckman 2006).

The cost-benefit of ECD programs outweighs that of other investments. Van der Gaag and Tan (1998) project cost-benefit ratios of 1.38 to 2.07 (for a preschool program in Bolivia), based on the estimated increases in lifetime productivity expected from attending an ECD program. If the corollary benefits of the program such as later age of motherhood (that is, reduced birthrate) are included, the ratios increase to 2.38 to 3.06. Nobel laureate James Heckman notes that early child development is more productive in improving human development than is the formal school system. Waiting even until kindergarten or primary school may be too late to improve learning and education. Heckman has concluded that ECD is far more effective and promises greater returns than remedial training later (Heckman 1999).

Clearly, economists' estimates of the benefits of ECD programs demonstrate that investments in ECD programs can outperform investments in more traditional development efforts later in life. In fact, the high economic returns on investments in education—a key component and benefit of all ECD programs—are the main reason for the global emphasis on *Education for All* (EFA). Improving human development in the early years is the surest way out of poverty because it has a very high economic rate of return. ECD is the first step in this process, as reflected in the priorities that emerged from the Dakar EFA meetings (UNESCO 2000).

To be competitive in the world marketplace, now and in the future, nations must develop, adopt, and support local, regional, and national policies that provide ECD programs. Countries that have recognized the importance of investing in ECD to improve the competence, health, and well-being of their populations include Cuba, the Scandinavian countries, and several Asian countries (such as Japan, Singapore, and South Korea). The ECD focus in these countries is exemplary for others throughout the world.

Africa Today

As the data in chapter 1 notes, the situation for Africa's children is alarming. Lancet (2007) estimates that 117 million children under 5 live in Sub-Saharan Africa; 61 percent of these children are stunted, living in poverty, or both. These children are at risk of delayed or poor development because of a complex of factors that includes poverty, malnutrition, disease, social strife, displacement, and lack of access to (or unavailable) schooling. One-third of Africa's children under age 5 are stunted from malnutrition. More than 95 percent of the continent's 5- to 6-year-olds do not have access to preschools, early stimulation, or good child development facilities. An astounding 45.4 million of the 115.3 million children worldwide who do not attend any primary school are in Africa (UNICEF 2005). Furthermore, many of those children who enter primary school drop out.

Moreover, HIV/AIDS has created a crisis of orphans in Africa (see chapters 5 and 15). The number of children who are orphaned by HIV/AIDS in Africa is expected to rise from 14 million in 2005 to 25 million by 2010. The total number of orphans, including those from war and civil strife, is even greater and will rise higher. By 2010, 15 percent of all children under age 15 in 12 African countries will be orphans (UNAIDS, UNICEF, and USAID 2004).

ECD is essential for all children everywhere, yet the challenges for mandating and supporting ECD programs in Africa are daunting. Sickness and death of parents and caregivers from HIV/AIDS are major problems. Very young children are left without a support structure and are placed in orphanages that are typically poorly equipped to offer the nurturance and stimulation that children need. Throughout Africa, a high priority must be given to the organization of comprehensive ECD programs that provide quality environments (physical and social) for children, as well as appropriate and effective care, nurturing, and stimulation.

The crisis of orphans is compounded by other major challenges on the continent. Many countries and regions have inadequate infrastructures for public health (such as vaccination, clean water, sanitation). Some countries are suffering from widespread and continuing wars or civil strife, which disrupt social structures and displace individuals and communities. Disease and poor nutrition are endemic in many areas. Quality health care (including needed immunizations) is often not available or accessible.

ECD programs depend on—and, importantly, can foster—improvements in a community's infrastructure, social stability, health, and well-being. ECD programs bring communities together to address the basic needs of children and families. The challenges for ECD interventions in Africa are great, and so are the rewards: hope and new possibilities for the future.

Why ECD?

ECD programs are necessary for two reasons: brain development during the first years of life is experience-based and it has significant, lifelong effects.

Brain Development and Function: The Science

The human brain can be grouped into four key components: (1) the brain stem, which is responsible for regulating core functions such as respiration, body temperature, heart rate, and blood pressure; (2) the midbrain, which works with the brain stem to mediate the state of arousal, appetite control, and sleep; (3) the limbic area, which is responsible for aspects of emotion, including regulation and attachment; and (4) the cortex, which is responsible for abstract cognition and language systems. Although each component is responsible for different functions, there are many interacting and interconnected systems composed of neural networks. The network systems work together to carry out specific functions, such as sensing (vision, hearing) and responding (arousal, emotion, and thinking) in different areas of the brain.

The billions of neurons in the brain have the same genetic coding. The differentiation of neurons is influenced by the stimulation (experience) in early life, including in utero, which influences whether the genes are turned off or on. Experience also affects the development of connections between neurons, that is, the synapses. The formation of the connections among neurons establishes pathways that govern our intellectual, emotional, psychological, and physical response to stimuli and biological pathways that affect our physical and mental health.

Experience-Based Brain Development

The human brain has at least four key periods of development: (1) in utero; (2) infancy, toddler, and early childhood; (3) adolescence; and (4) adulthood and aging. The body's genetic structure fundamentally controls basic development of the brain and the peripheral nervous system in utero. Experience—as sensed by the body's sensing systems such as touch, vision, and hearing—has significant effects on the development, structure, and function of the brain in early life, which, for certain pathways, can last throughout the life cycle. The brain's plasticity, however, is such that there are regions where further developments in the structure and function can occur at later stages in life. The question is essential: Which parts of the brain have critical or sensitive periods and which remain plastic throughout life?

The parts of the brain and neurological pathways that influence health, learning, and behavior are all substantially influenced by experience and brain development early in life. Thus, for example, competence in language and literacy in adulthood is strongly influenced by the environment in one's early life, which correlates with early child development and health as measured by life expectancy. Although we do not know the relationships among all these neurological and biological pathways in brain development, many pathways have critical and sensitive development periods that are influenced by the conditions in utero and in early life.

An important biological consideration is how external stimuli picked up through the body's sensing systems affect gene expression in the neurons in different parts of the brain leading to differentiation in the neuron functions and the development of the neural pathways and their synaptic connections that are key for the effects of the brain on behavior, health, and capacity to learn. In terms of brain development, it is as important to understand how the various genes (DNA) are turned on and off. Normally genes can be deactivated more or less permanently by processes that affect gene function or the histone proteins around which the genes are coiled. This process is referred to as epigenetics. We now know that when a cell whose genes have been affected by epigenetics replicates as it divides, the pattern of suppressors (the epigenome effect) is often replicated with them.[2]

In the brain, all the neurons have the same gene information but through epigenetic processes, the genes in different parts of the brain are regulated and activated differently, according to the function. In other words, expression of genes is dependent on and modified by the environment. The connections between neurons (synapses) that establish neuron pathways are also strongly influenced—in terms of the strength—by activation of genes in the nucleus of the receptive neurons. The strength of the synapses influences the function of neuronal pathways. Thus, it is not surprising that learning a skill such as playing a musical instrument, swimming, or playing tennis is influenced by the age at which it is started. This skill acquisition is also true for other activities such as skiing and skating, which require highly integrated motor and sensing brain circuits to execute the skills effectively. Thus, it is not surprising that language, learning, and behavior show the same significant effects of early brain development on these functions.

Language and reading are an excellent example of how brain development in the early years affects literacy and understanding competence in later life. For language and reading to develop, both the vision and the sound sensing pathways have to be appropriately stimulated in the critical and sensitive periods in early development. We know that the vision pathways have a critical development period: the early years (Chiu 2003; Ellemberg et al. 2000; Hubel and Weisel 1998; Zhou, Tao, and Poo 2003). If the stimuli received from the retina are not transmitted to the occipital cortex in the early years of development, the absence, because of poor differentiation of the neurons, can lead to visual dysfunction. Hearing also appears to have a critical period when the sounds from the ear have to reach the temporal cortex for full differentiation of those neurons (Loeb 1996).

Studies of birdsongs have shown that birds do not learn their vocalizations easily at all phases of development. If birds do not pick up the songs of their parents when they are very young, they are defective in their songs. For young children, if they are exposed to the sound of two languages as infants, they will become proficient in both languages with no accent as they grow older. It appears that the period from birth to age 7 or 8 months is when the differentiation of the neurons for hearing takes place in humans. Thus, it is more difficult to learn a second language later in life and, interestingly, individuals who acquire two-language capability early in life are also able to easily learn more languages later in life. It is therefore not surprising that studies have shown that the extent of language exposure to young children has a significant effect on their verbal skills by age 3; the extent of verbal skills at age 3 correlates with language capability at age 9.

In the American Abecedarian study (Campbell et al. 2002; Ramey et al. 2000), a group of African-American children whose mothers had intelligence quotients (IQs) ranging from 74 to 124 (average 85) were randomized initially into two groups. One group of 4-month-old children was put into a preschool center-based ECD program involving parents and compared with the control group that was not placed in a specific program. The children who had been in the preschool program later showed better cognitive performance in reading at the time of school entry than the children in the control group. At the time of school entry, each of the two groups was again randomized: one half of each group went into a special three-year program in the school system and the other half went into the regular school program. At age 21, the best performance in math and language was in the group given the preschool program plus the special three-year education program. They also had the highest IQs. The group given only the special education program showed small improvement in the early years of schooling but, by age 21, the effect was largely lost. The group given the preschool program but no special education program showed improvement in language and math in the school system, but the effect was not sustained at the same level as the group given both the preschool program and the school three-year program. This evidence is consistent with the neuroscience data that brain development in the early years sets the foundation for later performance in school. Other studies show the long reach between early development and performance and behavior in the school system.

Early Child Development and Behavior

In this discussion, behavior includes antisocial behavior as well as attention deficit disorder and mental health conditions such as depression. All of these behaviors are strongly influenced by ECD conditions including the in-utero period. This particular neurological pathway is usually referred to as the limbic hypothalamus pituitary adrenal (LHPA) axis and includes the hippocampus and frontal brain. Studies in rats and monkeys show that caregiving in the very early years has major effects on how these pathways are established and their function later in life. These pathways, often referred to as the stress pathways, control how we respond to everyday challenges. The amygdala is the key part of the brain that picks up sensory stimuli and affects the response of the hypothalamus, which influences the action of the pituitary gland and the secretion of ACTH, which causes the adrenal gland to produce cortisol, which affects most of the tissues in the human body, including the brain. This pathway also stimulates the autonomic system, leading to the release of adrenaline from the adrenal gland, which is often referred to as the quick stress response. McEwen (2002) has referred to the effect of these pathways on the body as *allostasis*, which can be considered as the maintenance of stability through change. The burden that this pathway places on the human body can be referred to as the allostasis load. It can be too high or too low. Too little cortisol can be as bad as too much, and underproduction can lead to, among other health problems, chronic fatigue syndrome. Too much stimulation of this pathway can lead to depression, alcoholism, drug addiction, obsessive-compulsive disorders, cardiovascular disease, type II diabetes, and other health problems.

The development of the stress pathway and its performance is strongly influenced in rats, monkeys, and humans by the degree of caregiver interaction in early life. Touch appears to be an important sensing pathway in setting up how this pathway responds to stimuli. In rats it has been shown that if the mother neglects the pups by not licking and grooming them at birth, they have a poorly regulated LHPA pathway, which can have major effects on brain development, including cognition and behavior in adult life. In detailed studies of the parts of the rats' brain LHPA system, neglect has been shown to be associated with increased methylation of the genes in this pathway (epigenetic effect). In these studies, female rats brought up without good maternal care will look poorly after their infants. Pups of high-licking mothers who were raised by low-licking mothers will tend to have the same abnormality as pups of low licking mothers. Infant rhesus macaque monkeys brought up separated from their mothers, if they are genetically vulnerable, show impulsive or inappropriate behavior in stressful situations (Suomi 1997). These animals will also excessively consume alcohol. In this study it appears that the vulnerable animals are those with the short gene promoter structure for serotonin transport. Serotonin levels have a major effect on the frontal brain, which affects behavior. In these studies, it appears that rhesus macaque monkeys brought up in adverse circumstances have methylation of the serotonin transporter gene, which reduces serotonin function in the frontal brain (Habib and Suomi 2000).

In humans, evidence is compatible with epigenetic effects on gene expression. A gene for monoamine oxidase (MOA) oxidizes the monoamines serotonin, dopamine, and norephrenephrine, all of which affect the frontal brain and behavior. It is interesting in humans that individuals with low MOA activity tend to be associated with impulsive behavior and conduct disorders. This gene has a functional gene polymorphism in the transcriptional control region for the gene. Individuals with high levels of MOA expression (who possibly have the long gene structure) did not show the proportion of conduct disorders as did individuals with low MOA activity (possibly short gene structure). Individuals with low MOA activity, maltreated when young, had a substantial increase in conduct disorders.

Studies of the 1970 Dunedin birth cohort (Caspi 2003) found that children with the short allele (gene structure) for polymorphism of the serotonin transporter gene who were raised in neglectful, adverse, abusive environments during early childhood were at risk for depression in adult life. Those with the short gene structure who were brought up in good environments during early childhood were not at risk. The subjects most at risk were those with two short alleles for the serotonin transporter gene, while those with two long alleles were resistant (resilient) to the adverse effects of poor early childhood development. In the rhesus monkey studies, it appears that those brought up in poor environments when young show increased methylation of the serotonin transporter gene. Again it appears that those with the short gene are most vulnerable. It appears that adverse maternal or caregiver behavior can lead to poor protein synthesis from DNA in these neurons because of epigenetic effects on the gene promoter function. Because the epigenetic effect on gene structure is difficult to reverse, this mechanism is responsible for the long-term environmental effects of maternal interaction with young children on gene expression. This modification in gene function can be carried into adult life.

In studies of brain development in infants and young children exposed to physical and sexual abuse and violence, Martin Teicher (2002) found substantial changes in brain structure and function. He concluded that severe stress in early life leads to an indelible effect on brain structure and function (Teicher 2003). He found that the result in adult life could appear as depression, anxiety, posttraumatic stress, aggression, impulsiveness, delinquency, hyperactivity, or substance abuse. In a Kaiser Permanente study (Felitti et al. 1998), researchers found a strong correlation between child abuse and neglect and addiction to alcohol and drugs in adult life.

Because the brain is most plastic and sensitive to experience during its development in the early years, it is perhaps not surprising that there are effects on many of the brain's functions during this period that influence health, learning, and behavior. A Swedish longitudinal study (Stattin 1993) found that the language development in the first two years of life could be related to literacy performance and antisocial behavior when the children were teenagers. About 25 percent of these teenagers who show poor language development in the first two years did poorly in language and literacy in their school years and were involved with the criminal justice system as teenagers as a result of their antisocial behavior. Because language skills are heavily influenced by the degree of language exposure in early life and it is difficult to talk or read to a child without holding it (touch), it is perhaps not surprising that infants and toddlers who are talked to or read to have good language skills and normal behavior. It is not surprising, therefore, that good ECD programs involving parents in the early years of life have a profound effect on cognition and behavior in later life.

Health

Increasing evidence shows that the conditions of early child development affect the risk of physical and mental health problems in adult life. The findings from a Swedish longitudinal study (Lundberg 1993) show that children brought up in environments where there was neglect and abuse had an increased risk for poor health in adult life. In this study the risk for heart problems for adults who had been in adverse early child development circumstances, compared with those adults brought up in a good environment, was 7 to 1. The risk for mental health problems was 10 to 1. This evidence is compatible with the biological evidence previously discussed in respect to early child development and depression. Those with the short serotonin transporter gene who were brought up in adverse circumstances were at increased risk for depression as adults. A series of studies over 15 years (Barker 1989, 1998; Gluckman and Hanson 2004) has shown that conditions in utero and infancy have a significant effect on health problems throughout the life cycle. These studies show an increased risk for coronary heart disease and high blood pressure as well as an increased risk for type II diabetes and mental health problems such as schizophrenia.

The immune system is another system that is influenced by the LHPA pathway and brain development in the early years. In animal experiments, it appears that the development of the LHPA pathway has a major effect on the function of the immune system. The LHPA axis, through its regulation of cortisol secretion, can result in a hyperactive immune system. As Sternberg (2000) notes in *The Balance Within*, cortisol has a double-edged effect on the immune system: too much cortisol can suppress the immune function and make us more vulnerable to bacterial and viral infections. All of us have experienced our vulnerability to colds when we are responding to demanding and continuous challenges and then are freed from them. Thus we remember, however, that a short burst of increased cortisol can help the immune system respond to infection or injury. Some immune conditions, such as allergies and asthma, are related to underproduction of cortisol. Some autoimmune disorders can be related to an underproduction of the LHPA axis.

Literacy and Health

Population-based assessments of health and literacy in developed countries show a strong correlation between literacy competence and life expectancy (OECD 2000; see figure 4.1). One of the striking

Figure 4.1. The Relationship between Life Expectancy and Proportion of the Population at Low Literacy Levels in Developed Countries

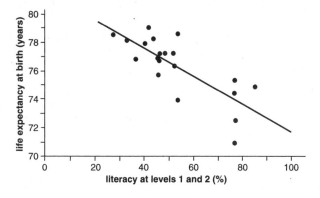

Source: Adapted from *Literacy in the Information Age: Final Report of the International Adult Literacy Survey* (OECD 2000, 82).
Note: See the note for table 4.1 for the OECD definition of literacy levels 1 and 2.

features of this study is that countries with a higher performance in literacy tend to have healthy populations. The key countries that show this correlation are the Scandinavian countries, which have robust ECD programs. In the assessment of literacy in the developed world and Latin America, literacy levels of the population are plotted against the parents' level of education (those low on this socio-economic status measure are most deficient).

It is interesting that Latin American countries such as Chile performed less well than developed countries such as Canada, the Netherlands, and Sweden (see figure 4.2). These studies by the Organisation for Economic Co-operation and Development (OECD 2000), found that 42 and 48 percent of individuals in Canada and the United States, respectively, performed poorly (levels 1 and 2) on the literacy assessments, whereas in Chile and Mexico, more than 80 percent of the population functioned at these low levels (see table 4.1). The overall literacy performance of the Scandinavian countries is high. High-quality ECD programs are universal for their population. The Scandinavian countries have well-established cultures with good social programs and homogeneous populations, so it is not surprising that they have good ECD programs and that their literacy performance is better than other countries. However, Cuba has a very heterogeneous population (African, Spanish, and Aboriginal) and also has impressive

Figure 4.2. Socioeconomic Gradients for Literacy Scores

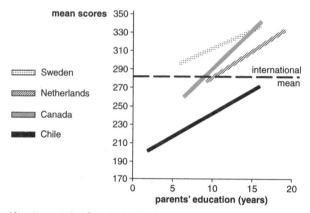

Source: Adapted from *Literacy in the Information Age: Final Report of the International Adult Literacy Survey* (OECD 2000, 32).

Table 4.1. Literacy Rates, Ages 16–65, 1994–98

	Levels 1 and 2 (%)	Levels 4 and 5 (%)
Sweden	23	34.0
Canada	42	23.0
Australia	43	17.0
United States	48	18.0
Chile	85	3.0
Mexico	84	1.7

Source: OECD 2000.

Note: Literacy Performance Scale 1–5, defined by OECD:

Level 1: Individuals can answer questions from familiar contexts where all relevant information is present, questions clearly defined. Able to identify information and carry out routine procedures in explicit situations. Can perform obvious actions from the given stimuli.

Level 2: Individuals can interpret and recognize situations of direct inference. Can extract relevant information, employ basic procedures, and are capable of direct reasoning. Can make literal interpretations of the results.

Level 3: Individuals can execute clearly described procedures, including sequential decision making. Can select and apply simple problem-solving strategies. Can use representations based on different sources. Can develop short communications.

Level 4: Individuals can work with explicit models for complex concrete situations that involve making assumptions. Can select and integrate different representations with real world situations. Can use their well-developed reasoning skills to communicate explanations.

Level 5: Individuals can conceptualize and use information based on their investigations and models (advanced thinking and reasoning). Can apply insight to novel situations. Can formulate and precisely communicate their actions and reflections to the original situation.

literacy performance values and health statistics. Cuba has much better health, education, and literacy values than other Latin American countries. In tests of language and math at grade 3, the mean value for the Cuban student population was two standard deviations higher than other Latin American countries. In terms of behavior, aggression—as measured by the number of fights in the school systems in Cuba—was one-quarter that in other Latin American countries. Thus, based on population evidence, countries with good ECD programs that invest in mothers and children do better in language, literacy, and health than countries that do not have universal high-quality programs for early child development.

Turning Around Poor Development in the Early Years

Does the age for support of early child development matter? One line of evidence about the importance of the early years comes from studies of children in orphanages. Studies by Frank and Earls (1996) showed that the children placed in orphanages had poor development and that this is not easily reversed in later life. Also most children placed in orphanages were at risk for infection, poor language development, and poor health in later life.

There have been some important findings from studies of children adopted from Romanian orphanages into middle-class British homes. Rutter and O'Connor (2004) examined the development of these children compared with 52 nondeprived British-born children placed into adopting families before the age of 6 months. There was a strong relationship between cognitive development and the age at which the Romanian children were adopted into British homes. The earlier the adoption, the better the outcome. Although there was some recovery for all children after adoption into British homes, substantial deficits in development persisted for many of the children adopted after many months in the orphanages. Rutter and O'Connor concluded that some form of early biological programming or neural damage stemmed from the effect of institutional deprivation on the vulnerable children adopted after time in the orphanage that could not be substantially changed by the families who adopted them.

These findings are in agreement with those of Ames (1997) and Le Mare (2005) in their studies of Romanian orphans adopted into middle-class Canadian homes in British Columbia. Both studies compared children adopted within the first 4 months after birth with those who lived in the Romanian orphanages beyond the age of 8 months. Both groups were compared with Canadian-born middle-class children raised within the birth-family structure. When the children reached age 10, the group who had lived in an orphanage beyond the age of

8 months (late adoptees) had lower IQs than both the children who were adopted early and the Canadian children of British Columbian families. This result is consistent with the finding that IQ is influenced by the quality of early child development (Klebanov 1998; Wickelgren 1999). The late adoptees had lower school achievement scores, more attention deficit disorders, and more behavioral problems. It is interesting that parents who adopted children who lived in a Romanian orphanage beyond the age of 8 months reported far greater parenting stress than the parents who had adopted Romanian children soon after birth. In terms of attention deficit hyperactivity disorder, 34 percent of the late adoptees had a clinical diagnosis, while only 3 percent from the British Columbian group and 9 percent of the early adoptees had this problem. All of these observational studies are compatible with the evidence that the quality of support and care given to infants in the early months has a significant effect on brain development and behavior and learning later in life. The results also show that while late adoptees can be helped to develop, they do not reach the same performance level as early adoptees. This evidence is also consistent with the biological data that there are critical and sensitive periods for the development of the brain and related biological pathways that set functions that are difficult to change later in life.

Vulnerability and Cognition

The national example of Cuba has relevance at local community and family levels. Analysis of data from the *National Longitudinal Survey of Children and Youth* in Canada (Willms 2002) shows that socioeconomic gradients are not the whole story and that they are complex phenomena. At first glance, the data indicate a clear socioeconomic gradient for children's vulnerability and families' socioeconomic position. Approximately 40 percent of the children in the lowest socioeconomic class were considered vulnerable (as defined in the study) at the time they entered school, compared with only 10 percent in the highest socioeconomic class. On further analysis, however, there were no socioeconomic gradients for cognition or behavior for children who had been read to or had experienced good social support before entering school, regardless of their social class (Willms 2002). These results indicate that gradients for children are not caused by purely economic factors, but also by the quality of interactions with young children, regardless of their families' socioeconomic position. This finding has major implications for public policies regarding ECD.

The Benefits of ECD for Africa

Data regarding the long-term impact of ECD programs have now been collected for more than 40 years. Early childhood programs have been shown to benefit society and are a boon to the economies of both developing and industrialized countries (Kagitcibasi, Sunar, and Bekman 2001; Myers 1995; Ramey et al. 2000; Reynolds et al. 2001; Schweinhart et al. 2005). For Africa, ECD programs are essential for improving the quality and capacity of populations, increasing adult productivity, and mitigating the effects of poverty, disease, and civil strife.

The many benefits of ECD programs have been proven over time and in different countries. Three main benefits that are germane for Africa are (1) enhanced school readiness, enrollment, and completion; (2) later age of motherhood for young women (that is, reduced birthrate); and (3) improved family situations, including the empowerment of women.

ECD programs enhance children's readiness for school and increase enrollment in and completion of primary and secondary school. Numerous authors have documented the effects of model preschool programs in the United States in reducing rates of grade retention and grade repetition (Campbell et al. 2002; Karoly et al. 1998; Reynolds et al. 2001; Schweinhart et al. 2005). A follow-up study of participants in the Perry Preschool Project at age 40 (the longest running evaluation of a pilot ECD program in the United States) shows that the graduation rate from high school for those who participated in the program was 66 percent, compared with only 45 percent for the control group (Schweinhart et al. 2005).

Myers' (1995) review of 19 evaluations of ECD programs in developing countries confirms that early education correlates highly with improved school readiness, probability of on-time enrollment in primary school, lower grade repetition and dropout rates, and improved academic performance overall. Aldaz-Carroll (1999) reported a study in Peru in which nearly 60 percent more of the poor children who had participated in preschool completed primary school than did poor children who had not participated in preschool. Similar results have been documented in Brazil (Paes de Barros and Mendonça 1999; World Bank 2001). In Bolivia, children who had participated in a home-based day-care program attended primary school on time, compared with those who had not participated in the program (Young 1996).

Early education also has a long-term effect on reducing fertility rates. Analysis of data from Brazil's *Living Standard Measurement Survey* (Paes de Barros and Mendonça 1999; World Bank 2001) shows that the incidence of early motherhood for girls ages 10–18 who had attended preschool as children is less than half that for girls of the same age who had not attended preschool.

For families, ECD programs involving parents can improve parent-child relationships, "free up" older siblings from caregiving responsibilities to attend school, and enable mothers to participate in the paid workforce and increase the family's income. For families to benefit, it is essential to assure that ECD services are affordable as well as accessible.

A study in Kenya demonstrates the effects of affordable ECD programs. The researchers found that (1) a high cost for child care discourages households from using formal child care facilities and has a negative effect on mothers' participation in the marketplace; (2) the cost of child care and the level of mothers' wages affect the enrollment of older children in school, although the effect is different for boys and girls (an increase in the mothers' wages increases boys' enrollment and depresses girls' enrollment); and (3) higher child care costs have no significant effect on the number of boys in school, but significantly decrease the number of girls in school (Lokshin, Glinskaya, and Garcia 2000).

Based on the studies cited, we can summarize that young children exposed to ECD do better in school than do children without early education. Young children exposed to ECD have the following benefits:

- *Improved nutrition and health.* ECD programs help to ensure that children receive health care and they offer psychosocial stimulation that enhances the programs' effects. Children participating in Colombia's Community Child Care and Nutrition program or in Bolivia's Integrated Child Development projects, for example, are required to complete their immunizations within 6 months of entering the programs. ECD staff can also monitor growth, provide food supplements and micronutrients, and direct children to public health programs.
- *Higher intelligence.* ECD programs encourage young children to explore and they facilitate the social interaction that promotes cognitive development. Children who participated in Jamaica's First Home Visiting Program, Colombia's Cali Project, Peru's Programa No Formal de Educación Inicial (PRONOEI), and the Turkish Early Enrichment Project in low-income areas of Istanbul averaged higher scores on intellectual aptitude tests than did nonparticipants.
- *Higher school enrollment.* Colombia's ECD program PROMESA reports significantly higher enrollment rates in primary school for children participating in the program, compared with children not participating in the program.

- *Less grade repetition.* In Colombia's PROMESA program, the Alagoas and Fortaleza PROAPE study of Northeast Brazil, and the Argentina ECD study, children who participated in the programs repeated fewer grades and progressed better through school than did nonparticipants in similar circumstances.
- *Fewer dropouts.* In three out of four studies, dropout rates were lower for children participating in an ECD program than for children not participating in these programs. In India's Dalmau program, attendance of children ages 6–8 in primary school increased by 16 percent for children who had participated in the program. In Colombia, the grade 3 enrollment rates for children who participated in the PROMESA program increased by 100 percent, reflecting their lower dropout and repetition rates. In addition, 60 percent of the children who participated in the ECD program attained grade 4, compared with only 30 percent of the comparison group (Young 1996, 9–11).

In Brazil, affordable child care also "freed up" mothers to work. In Rio de Janeiro, poor women who used free child care services outside the home were able to increase their income by as much as 20 percent (Deutsch 1998). Studies in Brazil, Guatemala, and Mexico further show that access to child care also "frees up" older siblings—usually girls—to return to school or go to work (Deutsch 1998).

Some ECD interventions target mothers in particular. Reporting on the Turkish Early Enrichment Project, a highly successful intervention in semi-urban, low-income, squatter housing areas, Kagitcibasi (1996) documented that, compared with a control group, mothers who participated in a program of cognitive training and mother enrichment (1) significantly improved their mother-child interactions; (2) said they read or told stories to their children more; and (3) had higher expectations for their children, especially in school. These effects benefit both mothers and children, improve family situations, and underpin the quality of a nation.

Conclusion

Healthy brain development is critical to the realization of human potential. Brain development sets trajectories for learning, behavior, and emotions that last a lifetime and that cannot be overcome later by the formal education system. Children's social and physical environments affect their growth and development in early childhood and their competence, health, and well-being in adulthood.

Mandating and supporting well-designed ECD policies and programs is a national imperative for all countries. By investing in children at the earliest ages (beginning in utero), a nation builds quality and capacity to evolve into a stable and prosperous society.

Countries that do not invest sufficiently in the development of their young children cannot reach their potential because literacy is essential for participating in the global economy and well-adapted behavior is far less costly to societies than are juvenile delinquency, criminality, and violence. For especially poor countries, investing in ECD can overcome the major deficits caused by poverty, disease, and social disruption. In Africa the challenges, which may seem daunting, must be met with a clear vision of possibilities for the future—for peaceful, tolerant, equitable, educated, and democratic societies within which children can strive to reach their full potential and to build sustainable and healthy lives.

Notes

1. The authors of this chapter use the acronym ECD to refer to "early child development."

2. Epigenetics has languished in the shadow of the work of the human genome project, but the importance of this field in brain development is leading to advocacy for a human epigenome project.

References

Aldaz-Carroll, E. 1999. *The Intergenerational Transmission of Poverty: Significance for Latin America and the Inter-American Development Bank (IDB)*. Washington, DC: IDB, Sustainable Development Department, Social Development Division.

Ames, E. W. 1997. *The Development of Romanian Orphanage Children Adopted to Canada: Final Report*. Ottawa, ON: Human Resources Development Canada.

Barker, D. J. P. 1989. "Growth in Utero, Blood Pressure in Childhood and Adult Life, and Mortality from Cardiovascular Disease." *British Medical Journal* 298: 564–67.

————. 1998. *Mothers, Babies, and Health in Later Life*. Edinburgh: Churchill Livingstone.

Campbell, F., C. Ramey, E. Pungello, J. Sparling, and S. Miller-Johnson. 2002. "Early Childhood Education: Young Adult Outcomes from the Abecedarian Project." *Applied Development and Science* 6 (1): 42–57.

Caspi, A. 2003. "Influence of Life Stress on Depression: Moderation by a Polymorphism in the 5-HTT Gene." *Science* 301: 386–89.

Chiu, C. 2003. "Synaptic Modification by Vision." *Science* 300: 1890–91.

Deutsch, R. 1998. "Does Child Care Pay? Labor Force Participation and Earnings Effects of Access to Child Care in the Favelas of Rio de Janeiro." Working Paper 384. Inter-American Development Bank, Office of the Chief Economist, Washington, DC.

Ellemberg, D., T. L. Lewis, D. Maurer, and H. P. Brent. 2000. "Influence of Monocular Deprivation during Infancy on the Later Development of Spatial and Temporal Vision." *Vision Research* 40: 3283–95.

Felitti, V. J., R. F. Anda, D. Nordenberg, D. F. Williamson, A. M. Spitz, V. Edwards, M. P. Koss, and J. S. Marks. 1998. "Relationship of Childhood Abuse and Household Dysfunction to Many of the Leading Causes of Death in Adults. The Adverse Childhood Experiences (ACE) Study." *American Journal of Preventive Medicine* 14 (4): 245–58.

Frank, D. A., and F. Earls. 1996. "Infants and Young Children in Orphanages: One View from Pediatrics and Child Psychiatry. *Pediatrics* 97: 569–78.

Gluckman, P. D., and M. A. Hanson. 2004. "Living with the Past: Evolution, Development, and Patterns of Disease." *Science* 305: 1733–36.

Habib, K. E., and S. Suomi. 2000. *Oral Administration of a Corticotropin-Releasing Hormone Receptor Antagonist Significantly Attenuates Behavioral, Neuroendocrine, and Autonomic Responses to Stress in Primates.* Proceedings of the National Academy of Sciences of the United States of America, Washington, DC. 97 (11): 6079–84.

Heckman, J. 1999. "Policies to Foster Human Capital." National Bureau of Economic Research Working Paper 7288. National Bureau of Economic Research, Cambridge, MA.

———. 2006. "Catch 'Em Young." 2006. *The Wall Street Journal.* January 10, A14.

Hubel, D. H., and T. N. Weisel. 1998. "Early Exploration of the Visual Vortex." *Neuron* 20 (3): 401–12.

Kagitcibasi, C. 1996. *Family and Human Development across Cultures: A View from the Other Side.* Hillsdale, NJ: Lawrence Erlbaum.

Kagitcibasi, C., D. Sunar, and S. Bekman. 2001. "Long-Term Effect of Early Intervention: Turkish Low-Income Mothers and Children." *Applied Developmental Psychology* 22: 333–61.

Karoly, L. A., P. W. Greenwood, S. S. Everingham, J. Hoube,, M. R. Kilburn, C. P. Rydell, M. Sanders, and J. Chiesa, eds. 1998. *Investing in Our Children: What We Know and Don't Know about the Cost and Benefits of Early Childhood Interventions.* Santa Monica, CA: RAND.

Klebanov, P. K. 1998. "The Contribution of Neighborhood and Family Income to Developmental Test Scores over the First Three Years of Life. *Child Development* 69 (5): 1420–36.

Lancet. 2007. "Developmental Potential in the First Five Years for Children in Developing Countries." 369: 60–70.

Le Mare, L. 2005. "Romanian Adoption Project." Retrieved August 24, 2006, from http://lucy.viper.ca/.

Loeb, G. E. 1996. "An Information Highway to the Auditory Nerve." *Seminars in Hearing* 17: 309–16.

Lokshin, M., E. Glinskaya, and M. Garcia. 2000. "The Effect of Early Childhood Development Programs on Women's Labor Force Participation and Older Children's Schooling in Kenya." Gender and Development Working Paper 15. World Bank, Washington, DC.

Lundberg, O. 1993. "The Impact of Childhood Living Conditions on Illness and Mortality in Adulthood." *Social Science and Medicine* 36 (8): 1047–52.

McEwen, B. S. 2002. *The End of Stress as We Know It.* Washington, DC: Joseph Henry Press.

Myers, R. 1995. *The Twelve Who Survive: Strengthening Programmes of Early Childhood Development in the Third World.* 2nd ed. London: Routledge.

OECD (Organisation for Economic Co-operation and Development). 2000. *Literacy in the Information Age: Final Report of the International Adult Literacy Survey.* Paris: OECD.

Paes de Barros, R., and R. Mendonça. 1999. *Costs and Benefits of Preschool Education in Brazil.* Rio de Janeiro: Institute of Applied Economic Research.

Ramey, C. T., F. A. Campbell, M. Burchinal, M. L. Skinner, D. M. Gardner, and S. L. Ramey. 2000. "Persistent Effects of Early Intervention on High-Risk Children and Their Mothers. *Applied Developmental Science* 4: 2–14.

Reynolds, A. J., J. A. Temple, D. L. Robertson, and E. A. Mann. 2001. "Long-Term Effects of an Early Childhood Intervention on Educational Achievement and Juvenile Arrest." *Journal of the American Medical Association* 285 (18): 2339–45.

Rutter, M., and T. G. O'Connor. 2004. "Are There Biological Programming Effects for Psychological Development? Findings from a Study of Romanian Adoptees." *Developmental Psychology* 40 (1): 81–94.

Schweinhart, L. J., J. Montie, Z. Xiang, W. S. Barnett, C. R. Belfield, and M. Nores. 2005. *Lifetime Effects: The High/Scope Perry Preschool Study through Age 40.* Ypsilanti, MI: High/Scope Educational Research Foundation.

Stattin, H. 1993. "Early Language and Intelligence Development and Their Relationship to Future Criminal Behavior. *Journal of Abnormal Psychology* 102 (3): 369–78.

Sternberg, E. M. 2000. *The Balance Within*. New York: W.H. Freeman.

Suomi, S. J. 1997. "Early Determinants of Behavior: Evidence from Primate Studies." *British Medical Bulletin* 53 (1): 12–15.

Teicher, M. H. 2002. "Scars that Won't Heal: The Neurobiology of Child Abuse." *Scientific American* (March) 68–75.

————. 2003. "The Neurobiological Consequences of Early Stress and Childhood Maltreatment." *Neuroscience and Biobehavioral Reviews* 27: 33–44.

UNAIDS (Joint United Nations Programme on HIV/AIDS), UNICEF (United Nations Children's Fund), and USAID (U.S. Agency for International Development). 2004. *Children on the Brink: A Joint Report of New Orphan Estimates and a Framework for Action*. Washington, DC: USAID.

UNESCO (United Nations Educational, Scientific, and Cultural Organization). 2000. *The Dakar Framework for Action. Education for All: Meeting Our Collective Commitments*. Adopted by the World Education Forum, Dakar, Senegal, April 26–28. Paris: UNESCO.

UNICEF (United Nations Children's Fund). 2005. *Progress for Children: A Report Card on Gender Parity and Primary Education*. Retrieved August 24, 2006, from http://www.unicef.org/progressforchildren/2005n2/PFC05n2en.pdf.

van der Gaag, J., and J.-P. Tan 1998. *The Benefits of Early Child Development Programs: An Economic Analysis*. Washington, DC: World Bank.

Wickelgren, I. 1999. "Nature Helps Mold Able Minds." *Science* 283 (5409): 1832–34.

Willms, D. 2002. *Vulnerable Children*. Edmonton, AB: University of Alberta Press.

World Bank. 2001. "Brazil: Early Child Development—A Focus on the Impact of Preschool." Report 22841-BR. World Bank, Washington, DC.

Young, M. E. 1996. *Early Child Development: Investing in the Future*. Directions in Development. Washington, DC: World Bank.

Zhou, Q., H. W. Tao, and M. Poo. 2003. "Reversal and Stabilization of Synaptic Modifications in a Developing Visual System. *Science* 300: 1953.

CHAPTER 5

New Threats to Early Childhood Development: Children Affected by HIV/AIDS

Jodie Fonseca, Chloe O'Gara, Linda Sussman, and John Williamson

By the year 2003, AIDS had killed one or both parents of an estimated 12 million children in Sub-Saharan Africa. About one out of every eight of those millions of children was under 6 years of age. The survival of these young children is precarious, and they face other devastating consequences from the loss of parents or from being infected with HIV, yet they have too often been left off the world's HIV/AIDS agenda. This omission is strikingly evident in Sub-Saharan Africa, where the number of young orphans of AIDS is greatest. The pandemic is increasing infant and child mortality figures that are already the highest in the world and is further undermining fragile economies and societies.

Despite the lack of attention to young children on the HIV/AIDS agenda, the humanitarian and development communities are increasingly aware of the depth of the problem for children under 6, and of the benefits of efforts that include a deliberate focus on early childhood development (ECD). This chapter presents the case that this focus on young children is an essential part of the response to the HIV/AIDS pandemic in Sub-Saharan Africa.

HIV/AIDS and Young Children: The Problem

The HIV/AIDS pandemic has had dire consequences for affected children and their families and communities; Sub-Saharan Africa has been particularly hard hit. The total number of orphans due to AIDS in the region, which was more than a half million in 1990, is projected to rise to approximately 18.4 million by 2010 (UNAIDS, UNICEF, and USAID 2004). These figures do not include the vast number of other children who have been made vulnerable by HIV/AIDS or who are themselves HIV-positive.

These absolute numbers paint a stark picture, but the proportion of orphaned children is even more startling. In the average Sub-Saharan African nation, for example, 12.3 percent of children were orphans due to AIDS and other causes in 2003, nearly double the percentages of orphans in other developing regions of the world. In 11 countries, 15 percent or more of all children are orphans (UNAIDS, UNICEF, and USAID 2004). One out of every five households with children in southern Africa was caring for one or more orphans in 2003 (UNICEF 2003).

Children affected by HIV/AIDS are often viewed as a single group, but in reality there is great diversity in their ages, circumstances, and degrees of vulnerability. Of the millions of young people in Sub-Saharan Africa who have been orphaned by the pandemic, about 16 percent are under 6 years of age (UNAIDS, UNICEF, and USAID 2004). This age group is already at elevated risk of illness and death in developing countries even without the effects of HIV/AIDS, but the pandemic has added a layer to the intrinsic vulnerabilities of early childhood. Two out of every three HIV-positive people in the world live in Sub-Saharan Africa; nearly all of the nations in the region have the worst infant and child mortality indicators (UNAIDS 2004). In 2002, HIV/AIDS caused roughly 3.6 percent of childhood deaths globally, but in southern Africa that figure was nearly 8 percent. In countries such as Botswana and Zimbabwe, which have among the highest HIV prevalence in the world, more than half of all childhood deaths are caused by AIDS (Global Health Council 2006; WHO 2003). Families in heavily affected countries are bearing an increasing burden of the care of children left behind by AIDS patients. In Uganda, for example, about one out of every three households was hosting at least one orphan in 2001. Over both the short and long terms, this fostering had considerable negative impacts on the economic status of the households as well as the nutritional and educational status of the children involved (Deininger, Garcia, and Subbarao 2002).

Children affected by HIV/AIDS experience the same challenges as those who lose a parent or whose parent is chronically ill due to other causes, but they also face difficult circumstances that are specific to HIV/AIDS, such as stigma and discrimination. Furthermore, the impact of HIV/AIDS is exacerbated by poverty. One study in Zambia, for example, found that when school enrollment rates for orphans in the richest 20 percent of households were compared with rates for the poorest 40 percent, the enrollment was lowest among the poor (Ainsworth and Filmer 2002). Another study in Kenya determined the negative impact of parental death to be concentrated in households that had fewer assets before the parent's death (Evans and Miguel 2004). Thus HIV/AIDS often hits hardest where there is least resilience to shocks.

The Effects of Parental Illness and Death on Young Children

When the caregivers of young children are also caring for someone who is chronically ill with AIDS—or are chronically ill themselves—they are often unable to provide adequate support, which can, therefore, lead to neglect of the special needs of young children for proper nutrition, immunizations, treatment of common infections, and the stimulation they require for healthy development. Children face the additional trauma of witnessing a loved one's protracted illness, which, combined with all these factors can lead to poor physical and emotional health and even early mortality among children. Because of the nature of HIV transmission, if one parent has the virus, the likelihood is strong that the other parent has also been infected and will eventually develop AIDS and die, resulting in a series of shocks to the children.

Prolonged illness can also have grave economic and social consequences for children and their families. Adults living with HIV/AIDS often lose their ability to work, and other household members can be pulled away from their normal livelihood and child care activities to care for the sick. Children—especially girls—whose parents are ill or who are busy caring for someone who is HIV-positive may be kept out of school to provide care for younger siblings or other young children (Steinberg et al. 2002; Yamano and Jayne 2004).

Costs for antiretroviral therapy (ART) and treatment for the opportunistic infections that are part of AIDS, which typically require frequent travel to health clinics, can further drain already stretched household resources. In addition, many families desperately seek care from many sources over the course of a parent's AIDS-related illness, often spending money on ineffective or inappropriate care. The families of people living with HIV/AIDS can accumulate unmanageable debt due to a continuous and expensive search for a cure; the entire family pays the price over the short and long term because their household assets are depleted and they are increasingly beholden to others (Béchu 1998). Loss of inheritance, property, and assets due to property grabbing after the death of an adult is likely to further impoverish the survivors.

After being orphaned, children are often left in the care of the remaining parent—who may also be sick—or a grandparent, extended family member, or foster family. In some cases, when both parents have died and other adult caregivers are not available, orphaned children live in a child-headed household (CHH). While global numbers of CHHs are difficult to obtain, some country-specific data are available. In Rwanda, for example, a reported 100,000 children are living in CHHs, due in large part to conflict and HIV/AIDS (UNICEF New Zealand n.d.). Swaziland has an estimated 15,000 CHHs countrywide (National Emergency Response Council on HIV/AIDS n.d.). A 2004 study in the Rakai District of Uganda tells us more about the composition and circumstances of that nation's CHHs: The study found 969 CHHs in the district with an average of 2.3 children each. About 31 percent of those children were between the ages of 0 and 9 (Luzze and Ssedyabule 2004).

Orphans may also be taken in by orphanages or other institutions, or they may be forced to live on the streets. *In these circumstances, young children are less likely to receive the quality of stimulation, social connection, and support they would have received from family-based care.*

Because of their age and vulnerability, young children are at a specific disadvantage when the burden of orphan care is shared after the death of their primary caregivers. Whereas older children may be taken into households because they are considered an asset based on their ability to contribute to housework or income, young children might be considered more of a liability because they need a great deal of care with little immediate return to the caregiver (Lusk and O'Gara 2002).

Regardless of their age, all children cared for by adults who are not the biological parent may be at risk of discrimination due to differential care provided to nonbiological and biological children (Case, Paxson, and Ableidinger 2004). Moreover, a high level of stigma is associated with the epidemic, which, in many places, affects the care that families and societies provide to the children of people with HIV/AIDS (McGaw and Wameyo 2005). For example, the foster family might have negative attitudes and assumptions about the HIV serostatus of the child, such as the fear of HIV infection spreading to others, even if the child is not actually infected. If so, that child is likely to be segregated from other family members and neighbors and be given inadequate care.

Effects on Communities and Societies

The direct effects of HIV/AIDS on individual children are many, but the indirect burden placed on families and communities by the pandemic has also been significant. Extended family structures that traditionally care for the sick and absorb orphans after the death of parents are being stretched beyond their capacities (Ntozi and Zirimenya 1999; UNICEF n.d.). Reciprocal assistance between close relatives has in some cases been replaced by exploitative economic transactions with strangers for survival, including transactional sexual relationships as a last resort for women and girls who are desperate to provide for their families (Bryceson and Fonseca 2004). Agrarian households in Africa have been hit hard by the loss of agricultural labor due to AIDS-related illness and death (de Waal and Whiteside 2003), contributing to chronic and sometimes acute malnutrition for millions of children. The loss of adults in their most productive years has caused the population pyramid to thin out in the middle in heavily affected countries (Heaton et al. 2004), increasing the burden of child care on surviving adults including the elderly—or on other children.

Health and education systems are also being stretched beyond their capacities in many areas. The majority of inpatients at hospitals in the most heavily affected countries are suffering from AIDS-related illness (Buvé 1997) and some education systems have lost teachers faster than they can be replaced (see, for example, Malawi 2003). Students in families affected by HIV/AIDS can be at increased risk of dropout and poor achievement due to reduced household resources and increased time demands (Steinberg et al. 2002; Yamano and Jayne 2004).

HIV in Newborns and Infants

Newborns and infants in a world of HIV/AIDS face the double threat of transmission of HIV from their mothers and the stigma and discrimination that result from real or perceived HIV serostatus.

The transmission of HIV from mother to baby—which can occur before or during birth or through breastfeeding—is by far the most likely way for children under 6 to contract the virus in Africa and multiplies the intergenerational effects of the pandemic. The transmission risk is as much as 10 percent during pregnancy, 20 percent during labor and delivery, and an additional 20 percent during breastfeeding. The total risk that a child born to an HIV-positive mother in Africa will also be infected, therefore, can be as high as 50 percent (Tindyebwa et al. 2004). In contrast, the risk of transmission of each act of unprotected heterosexual intercourse between healthy adults has been estimated at far less than 1 percent (Gray et al. 2001).

Breastfeeding is key to the optimal physical, psychological, and cognitive development of babies. Because HIV is transmissible through breast milk, however, an infected mother faces an agonizing choice between the benefits of breastfeeding and the threat of HIV infection to her child (Fowler, Bertolli, and Nieburg 1999; LINKAGES Project 2004). UN agencies recommend that HIV-positive women avoid breastfeeding if replacement feeding meets the criteria of *acceptable, feasible, affordable, sustainable, and safe* (AFASS; WHO 2001). However, the AFASS criteria can not often be met in resource-poor settings in Africa, because replacement feeding products are usually too expensive and the risk of malnutrition and diarrheal disease among bottle-fed babies is unacceptably high, particularly in areas with limited access to clean water (WHO 2004). In addition, replacement feeding in a society where breastfeeding is the norm can mark a mother as HIV-infected and lead to stigma and discrimination (HIV/AIDS Survey Indicators Database n.d.).

If an HIV-positive mother does breastfeed, either because she prefers to do so or has no other choice, then she can face additional difficult choices between exclusive breastfeeding or mixed feeding. Exclusive breastfeeding with abrupt weaning is much safer than mixing breastfeeding with solid foods, although it still carries some risk of HIV infection (WHO 2004). This feeding technique can be difficult for new mothers to maintain, however, because it requires good breast health and proper understanding of the dangers of mixed feeding and the need for abrupt weaning. Local practices may, in fact, promote mixed feeding at an early age (Sellen 1998; Shapiro et al. 2003), which carries a higher risk of HIV transmission than exclusive breastfeeding (Coutsoudis et al. 2001).

HIV-positive mothers and their newborns must negotiate the perils of vertical transmission through birth or breastfeeding, but the challenges do not end there. The chances of abandonment and neglect can be elevated when HIV infection is confirmed or suspected in the child. An HIV-positive mother may mistakenly believe that her baby will automatically also have the virus and, consequently, may abandon or neglect the baby or leave it with relatives, because she believes she will not be able to meet the special needs she assumes her child will have.

In turn, caregivers—relatives, friends, orphanage staff, or others—may fear caring for an HIV-positive baby, expect the child will soon die anyway, or believe that the child's care is beyond their financial, medical, and emotional abilities (UNICEF and International Social Service 2004). Therefore, without external support to teach caregivers how to look after HIV-positive children and provide medical and other support, these children are at risk of being further abandoned or neglected. Even medical professionals can be reluctant to care for children who are HIV-positive due to the fear of being infected, the absence of postexposure prophylaxis to treat accidental exposure to the virus, the lack of information about how to care for the special medical needs of infected children, or the belief that these children are a lost cause or a waste of resources because they will inevitably die of AIDS (Letamo 2005; Reis et al. 2005).

In many places, babies without parental care are placed in orphanages or other institutions, such as hospitals, where they may be cared for temporarily before being adopted. However, few adopting parents are willing to accept a baby whom they know or suspect is HIV-positive and testing technology to ascertain the serostatus of babies is far from straightforward. The most commonly used HIV tests in developing countries identify HIV antibodies rather than the virus itself, but the mother's HIV antibodies, passed through the placenta, may persist in the baby for as long as 18 months and cause false-positive tests during that time (De Cock, Bunnell, and Mermin 2006). HIV testing methods that identify the presence of the virus itself and therefore eliminate the possibility of a false antibody test can be used immediately after birth, but these methods are expensive and generally unavailable outside of developed countries. Therefore, mothers and medical professionals in these countries are left in limbo for 18 months until the serostatus of the babies can be ascertained with the available test.

In some places, special centers or orphanages are being established for children who are known to be HIV-positive. These orphanages can "pull" children from families into an institutional setting because caregivers assume that they cannot provide support to HIV-positive children, a belief that is reinforced by the existence of facilities specifically for children with HIV/AIDS. Caregivers believe that the child will receive better care in such places (Powell et al. 1994) or may see orphanages and other centers as an option to relieve them of the overwhelming responsibility of caring for an additional child who may be ill. Outreach and support to such families has proven to be effective and much less costly than orphanages in caring for infants and young children who test positive for HIV

(World Bank 1997). This approach also has the major developmental benefit of keeping the child within a family environment.

AIDS in Young Children

The progression of HIV infection to AIDS-related illness after a child's birth is strikingly rapid. With no intervention, the majority of African children infected from their mothers develop HIV-related symptoms by 6 months of age, and fully half die of AIDS-related causes by age 2 (Luo 2005; Tindyebwa et al. 2004). African adults, for purposes of comparison, often live with HIV for six years or more with no symptoms. Treatment with pediatric formulations of ART, as well as prophylaxis or treatment of AIDS-related opportunistic infections, is imperative but is rarely provided to young children experiencing rapid and severe progression to AIDS. Children respond well to ART and cotrimoxazole prophylaxis of opportunistic infections, which, along with prevention of mother-to-child transmission (PMTCT) interventions, has the potential to avert more than a million deaths of African children in the near term (Luo 2005).

The Rationale for a Response

Although the world has not acted systematically or on an adequate scale to address the needs of young children affected by HIV/AIDS, years of experience in ECD programming demonstrate why a response for this age group can help bring about significant, long-term benefits and, conversely, why failure to provide for their needs will have long-term negative consequences.

Lack of Attention to Young Children Affected by HIV/AIDS Can Have Long-Term Negative Consequences

Early childhood is a critical period for development toward adulthood. According to the Consultative Group on Early Childhood Care and Development, damage in the early years cannot be undone, and children under the age of 5 need targeted programming (Lusk and O'Gara 2002). Even if young children manage to survive the vulnerable early years, impaired cognitive function and stunting in late childhood are often the ripple effects of malnutrition, isolation, and deprived environments in early childhood. Rapid brain development in young children results in intense psychosocial and cognitive needs, the satisfaction of which defines—or limits—one's potential for a lifetime.

These impacts in the first six years of children's lives can have long-range consequences, not just for individual children and their families, but also for entire communities and societies. For example, poor care in early childhood can lead to lower academic achievement and school completion later in life (Griffin and Lundy-Ponce 2003). The likelihood of such children growing out of poverty and contributing to the prosperity of their societies is thus lowered.

In the context of HIV/AIDS, ECD is even more critical—and more at risk. Inadequate coverage of PMTCT programs will result in growing numbers of very young children who suffer consequences such as poor neurological development, lowered physical growth, and motor impairment as a result of infection with the virus, even before they develop AIDS (Sherr 2005). Failure to make pediatric treatment widely available will mean that pediatric AIDS, which is increasingly a manageable chronic illness in wealthier countries, will continue to be a sure death sentence for children in poor countries.

Even if children are HIV-negative—or are HIV-positive but overcome the odds to survive past the age of 2—the AIDS-related illness and death of their adult caregivers can have undeniable consequences for achievement later in life. For example, in a study from Kagera, Tanzania, of the long-term effect of orphanhood during early childhood on adult health and educational attainment, the authors found that if a child was not yet enrolled in school at the time his or her mother died, that child can be expected to complete about 54 percent less schooling by adulthood, while the death of the father would result in about 33 percent less schooling by adulthood (Beegle, De Weerdt, and Dercon 2005). This implies that orphanhood is a stronger shock, at least in terms of long-range educational attainment, for children who are affected at young ages.

Another study from Tanzania confirms that recent adult death delayed the enrollment of young children in primary school, but did not have an effect on the eventual enrollment of younger children (Ainsworth, Beegle, and Koda 2002). When children orphaned by HIV/AIDS manage to attend school, they are less likely to be in the correct grade for their age (UNICEF 2004).

The material and psychosocial impact of HIV/AIDS on young children can also be severe. A study in Uganda showed that 70 percent of children born to HIV-positive mothers are older than 5 before their mother dies (Nakiyingi et al. 2003), meaning that many children are likely to witness the slow and painful death of their mothers in addition to suffering from the decreased care their chronically ill mothers would have been able to provide.

After the death of parents, new caregivers may not be able to provide for the child's emotional, physical, and cognitive development. Indeed, the extended family that often takes in children has been described as a "safety net with holes in it," leading to a high risk of multiple placements for orphans (Adnopoz 2000) and the resulting loss of familiar surroundings, including siblings. In some cases, children are separated from relatives and sent to orphanages, where they may grow up divorced from the local culture and lose the benefits of family life, although their material needs may be met. Care in orphanages has been proven detrimental because of the fundamental need of young children to be raised and form attachments in a family setting in order to thrive optimally (Bowlby 1951; Chapin 1926; Mead 1962).

Although evidence of the psychosocial effects of HIV/AIDS on young children is hard to obtain, it is well documented that psychosocial trauma can have troubling consequences for children's education. A UNAIDS case study of the psychosocial needs of children affected by HIV/AIDS in Tanzania and Zimbabwe, for example, found that school performance was negatively affected by unaddressed psychological trauma (Fox 2001). A similar study in Uganda in 1999 examined the impact of parental illness on a child's performance. The study reports that,

> when researchers asked older children of [people living with HIV/AIDS] what impact parental illness had on their education, 26 percent of children reported that their attendance declined and 27.6 percent reported that their school performance declined as a result of parental illness. They say that this is a result of staying home to care for sick parents, an increase in household responsibilities (including caring for younger children), emotional distress (worry, sadness, or declining motivation), and being unable to pay school fees. The impact of parental illness on schooling is especially important in light of findings that, when asked what makes them happy, children are very likely to report "being in school" and "being with other children." Conversely, missing school and doing poorly in school are associated with feelings of sadness and social isolation (Gilborn et al. 2001).

The costs of not providing children with adequate emotional, medical, cognitive, and social support at a young age are long term. Resiliency, self-efficacy, and the ability to establish positive relationships are vital characteristics, contributing to healthy survival in a society that has been severely affected by HIV/AIDS. The importance of fostering these characteristics should not be underestimated, especially where poverty exacerbates conditions that are already harsh. Furthermore, the increase in vulnerability and risk behavior that poorly socialized children may experience can help fuel a vicious cycle of HIV transmission in future generations.

ECD Programs Lead to Significant, Long-Term Gains in Child Well-Being and Have a High Rate of Return

While a lack of attention to ECD can have devastating effects, the reverse is fortunately also true: Studies show that higher levels of physical, cognitive, and emotional well-being and increased lifetime learning and earning are associated with good early childhood care (Lusk and O'Gara 2002). Despite the many challenges to early childhood survival and growth in Africa, interventions to support young children can be an effective way to help societies stabilize and flourish into the future. These interventions are typically inexpensive, and, moreover, the cognitive and emotional development they promote in the early years of life result in tangible economic returns later in life. Conversely, the damage of inadequate attention to ECD cannot easily or inexpensively be undone. According to the World Bank (n.d.),

> early interventions yield higher returns as a preventive measure compared with remedial services later in life. Policies that seek to remedy deficits incurred in the early years are much more costly than initial investments in the early years. Nobel Laureate Heckman . . . argues that investments in children bring a higher rate of return than investments in low-skill adults (para. 5).

The adage that prevention is better than a cure holds true for interventions in early childhood versus remediation later in life. Accumulated knowledge about ECD demonstrates that not only is it a sound investment in and of itself, but early interventions can also enhance the efficacy of other investments in children. For example, the World Bank (n.d.) notes that "early childhood interventions in health and nutrition programs increase children's chances of survival" (para. 4). In addition, the benefits of ECD are often most visible as children transition into the early primary school grades with reduced dropout and repetition, more appropriate age for grade, and improved academic achievement than children who did not participate (Save the Children 2003).

ECD programs are good for all children in developing countries, but they have been shown to be especially beneficial in terms of educational outcomes for the most disadvantaged children (Save the Children 2004), which can include children affected by HIV/AIDS.

Support to children in their homes and communities is more cost-effective for the donors and governments than care in orphanages. While costs vary from country to country and among programs, comparisons have found consistently that several children can be supported in family care for the cost of keeping one child in an institution. For example, the World Bank found that the annual cost for one child in residential care in the Kagera region of Tanzania was more than US$1,000, about six times the cost of supporting a child in a foster home (see table 5.1).[1] A study in South Africa also found residential care to be up to six times more expensive than providing care for children living in vulnerable families, and four times more expensive than foster care or statutory adoption.[2] In eastern Africa, a third study found residential care to be 10 times more expensive than community-based forms of care.[3]

HIV-prevention activities are an inexpensive means to help families and communities avoid losses due to AIDS in the long run. Adults and young people must have access to effective HIV prevention interventions to reduce their risk of becoming infected. They must also have access to information and resources to determine when they will have children and when they will not. Family planning should be made available to people living with HIV/AIDS, as well as to those who are not HIV-positive.

Prevention efforts also have great benefits, with a very low price tag, for pregnant, HIV-positive women. After years of research, the medical community knows how to reduce the likelihood of mother-to-child transmission dramatically through simple interventions, such as antiretroviral drugs and safer breastfeeding practices. PMTCT through single doses of Nevirapine for a mother and her baby, for example, can cost as little as $1.30 and can save as much as $1,300 per infection averted and $2,600 per child death averted (Uganda National AIDS Commission 2003; USAID 2004).

Table 5.1. Annual Costs of Programs to Mitigate the Household Impacts of AIDS in Kagera, Tanzania

Type of program	Annual cost
Orphanage care	$1,063 per child
Foster care	$185 per child
Educational support	$13 per child

Source: Adapted from World Bank 1997.

For as little as $300 per year in many African nations that are scaling up AIDS-related treatment, an adult with the syndrome can receive generic antiretroviral medication that will prolong the productive and healthy period of life, perhaps indefinitely (UNAIDS 2004). This cost is small compared with the price paid by young children who lose their parents to AIDS and the others who must pick up that burden of care.

Unfortunately for children with HIV, marketing of low-cost pediatric treatment options in poor countries has lagged behind the marketing of options for adults, although inexpensive prophylaxis for opportunistic infections is available to help postpone the need for treatment. As UNICEF (2005) reports, the antibiotic cotrimoxazole has been shown to reduce mortality in children living with HIV/AIDS (in some settings) by more than 40 percent, all for less than a dollar a month.

Young Children Affected by HIV/AIDS: The Way Forward

The impacts of HIV/AIDS on young children are unique in many ways; consequently, their needs for prevention, treatment, care, and support differ from those of older children and adults. A response that considers these multiple and devastating effects of AIDS-related orphanhood and vulnerability for young children in Sub-Saharan Africa is imperative. Yet, over the past three decades of humanitarian and development assistance, the early childhood period has received little attention. The growth of HIV/AIDS since the early 1980s has added to the burden for this already neglected age group in dramatic fashion, but with a less-than-dramatic response from the world.

Perhaps the most important challenge in raising the profile of young children affected by HIV/AIDS is that they lack a "voice" to call attention to their situation or ask for help, making them dependent on others to advocate for their needs. Even when children are old enough to express themselves, they must rely on others to provide them with the opportunity to do so. This lack of voice for young children occurs at all levels, from the local to the global. In communities, younger children are likely to be less visible and are therefore more difficult for service providers to identify. Schools are often a primary focus of interventions and a means to identify children in need, but the youngest children are not yet in school and therefore do not have access to school-related responses.

Globally, young children also lack a voice. International declarations and guidelines on HIV/AIDS have few references to young children. The United Nations General Assembly Special Session on HIV/AIDS in

2001 made no specific reference to the very youngest children in its *Declaration of Commitment on HIV/AIDS* (United Nations 2001). At the national level, only 17 countries with generalized epidemics reported having a national policy to guide strategic decision making and resource allocation for orphans and vulnerable children—let alone for younger children—at the end of 2003 (UNAIDS, UNICEF, and USAID 2004).

Resource expenditures have followed the same trend. While funding for children affected by AIDS has grown in recent years, it remains small when compared with other HIV/AIDS expenditures (UNAIDS, UNICEF, and USAID 2004). The U.S. response of $15 billion for global HIV/AIDS over five years, for example, designated only 10 percent for such interventions, none of which was specifically for the needs of young children affected by HIV/AIDS.

Programs have taken only small steps to promote ECD in the growing HIV/AIDS pandemic. For example, despite effective, low-cost interventions for PMTCT, less than 10 percent of pregnant, HIV-positive women in Sub-Saharan Africa have access to the services they need to keep their babies virus free (Luo 2005).

Drugs for HIV/AIDS treatment have been on the market for years, but the unique treatment needs of very young children receive little attention. Pediatric HIV/AIDS formulations are vastly more expensive than many of those for adults. For example, while UNICEF is purchasing antiretroviral fixed-dose combination treatment for adults for as little as $140 per person per year, comparable formulations for infants cost four to eight times more, depending on the infant's age and weight (UNICEF 2005). Pediatric fixed-dose combinations[4] have only recently emerged on the market and are not yet widely available, while more readily available pediatric drug formulations are difficult for health professionals to handle and the bad taste can be unacceptable to children. As a result, caregivers often break and crush adult pills to administer the drugs to children, raising the risk of improper dosing (UNICEF 2005).

In addition, although much of the world agreed to the World Health Organization (WHO) target of three million people on treatment by 2005, pediatric treatment has no internationally established subtarget. Fewer than 5 percent of young children around the world who need treatment for AIDS are receiving it (UNICEF 2005). One region has been hit disproportionately hard by this neglect: Out of the estimated 270,000 children ages 0–8 months in need of antiretroviral therapy worldwide in 2005, 89 percent lived in Sub-Saharan Africa (Luo 2005).

The lack of information about how and when to include younger children in programming and funding is both a cause and a symptom of the neglect of this age group. Policy makers, donors, and program planners know little about the best practices and the resource needs to help young children affected by HIV/AIDS, and so they take little action. Yet action is the key that leads to improved understanding of the best responses. Increased advocacy and information is urgently needed to help decision makers appropriately consider the needs of young children in their efforts.

Advocating for increased attention to young children affected by HIV/AIDS would be counterproductive, however, if the reaction were to result in further vertical efforts, which are overabundant. A vertical effort stands alone and/or creates new systems when it could be part of an integrated package to reinforce existing systems. For example, providing pediatric treatment to young children without addressing the treatment, care, and support needs of the child's mother and larger household would make little sense for the long-term well-being of the child. Similarly, creating a stand-alone clinic to provide that pediatric treatment, rather than working within and bolstering national government systems, may work well in the short run, but places long-run sustainability in jeopardy. Increased awareness and attention to this often forgotten population of children should facilitate their inclusion within existing systems and efforts.

Now is an opportune time to focus greater programmatic attention on HIV/AIDS and young children. The increasing attention to adult diagnosis, treatment, and care that is driven by national and donor governments creates an opportunity to identify and respond to young children in the same households. In addition, adult ART and PMTCT interventions effectively increase the well-being of young children: ART improves the health and well-being of children's caregivers, and PMTCT interventions result in fewer HIV-positive babies, which helps to prevent the medical and social impacts of HIV/AIDS on young children.

Support for programming to benefit children affected by HIV/AIDS is on the rise with the help of funding through donors such as the U.S. and U.K. governments and the increasing efforts of faith- and community-based organizations. In the past few years, greater advocacy and attention to younger children on the part of multiple actors, and strengthened networks among agencies concerned with orphans and vulnerable children, have created opportunities for information dissemination and exchange that are necessary to increase appropriate responses.

Finally, implementing agencies have taken strides in developing interventions that meet the unique needs of young children affected by HIV/AIDS in a comprehensive manner, including attention to health, nutrition, education, and psychosocial issues. ECD efforts already supported by donors, governments, and communities provide an opportunity to integrate children affected by HIV/AIDS into existing systems and resources for young children. Many communities have spontaneously responded to the growing burden of young children affected by HIV/AIDS, drawing on their own local child care traditions. The potential is great for donors and implementing agencies to provide support to strengthen and increase the scope of those homegrown efforts and to reach more children with better care.

Notes

1. *Confronting AIDS: Public Priorities in a Global Epidemic* (Washington, DC: World Bank and Oxford University Press, 1997) p. 221 and personal communication with Mead Over, of the World Bank. The text actually reports that institutional care was 10 times as expensive as foster care, but a subsequent review of the data indicated that the ratio was closer to 6 to 1.

2. Chris Desmond and Jeff Gow, "The Cost Effectiveness of Six Models of Care for Orphans and Vulnerable Children in South Africa," prepared for UNICEF South Africa (Durban, South Africa: University of Natal, 2001).

3. Diane M. Swales, *Applying the Standards: Improving quality Childcare Provision in East and Central Africa* (U.K.: Save the Children, 2006), 108.

4. Fixed-dose combinations contain two or more drugs in one tablet, greatly simplifying the drug regimen. Inexpensive fixed-dose combinations for adults are available in many African countries.

References

Adnopoz, J. 2000. "Relative Caregiving: An Effective Option for Permanency." *Child and Adolescent Psychiatric Clinics of North America* 9 (2): 359–73.

Ainsworth, M., and D. Filmer. 2002. "Poverty, AIDS, and Children's Schooling: A Targeting Dilemma." Policy Research Working Paper 2885. World Bank, Washington, DC.

Ainsworth, M., K. Beegle, and D. Koda. 2002. "The Impact of Adult Mortality on Primary School Enrollment in Northwestern Tanzania." Africa Region Human Development Working Paper 3. World Bank, Washington, DC.

Béchu, N. 1998. "The Impact of AIDS on the Economy of Families in Côte d'Ivoire: Changes in Consumption among AIDS-Affected Households." In *Confronting AIDS: Evidence from the Developing World: Selected Background Papers for the World Bank Policy Research Report*, ed. M. Ainsworth, L. Fransen, and M. Over, 341–48. Brussels: European Commission.

Beegle, K., J. De Weerdt, and S. Dercon. 2005. *Orphanhood and the Long-Run Impact on Children*. Washington, DC: World Bank, DANIDA, and UK Economic Research Council.

Bowlby, J. 1951. *Maternal Care and Mental Health*. Geneva: World Health Organization.

Bryceson, D. F., and J. Fonseca. 2004. *Social Pathways from the HIV/AIDS Deadlock of Disease, Denial, and Desperation in Rural Malawi*. Lilongwe: CARE International in Malawi.

Buvé, A. 1997. "AIDS and Hospital Bed Occupancy: An Overview." *Tropical Medicine and International Health* 2 (2): 136–39.

Case, A., C. Paxson, and J. Ableidinger. 2004. "Orphans in Africa: Parental Death, Poverty, and School Enrollment." Princeton, NJ: Center for Health and Well-Being, Research Program in Development Studies, Princeton University.

Chapin, H. D. 1926. "Family vs. Institution." *Survey* 55 (January): 485–88.

Coutsoudis, A., K. Pillay, L. Kuhn, E. Spooner, W. Y. Tsai, H. M. Coovadia, et al. 2001. "Method of Feeding and Transmission of HIV-1 from Mothers to Children by 15 Months of Age: Prospective Cohort Study from Durban, South Africa." *AIDS* 15 (10): 379–87.

De Cock, K., R. Bunnell, and J. Mermin. 2006. "Unfinished Business: Expanding HIV Testing in Developing Countries." *New England Journal of Medicine* 354 (5): 440–42.

de Waal, A., and A. Whiteside. 2003. "New Variant Famine: AIDS and Food Crisis in Southern Africa." *The Lancet* 362 (October): 1234–37.

Deininger, K., M. Garcia,, and K. Subbarao. 2002. *AIDS-Induced Orphanhood as a Systemic Shock: Magnitude, Impact, and Program Interventions in Africa*. Washington, DC: World Bank.

Evans, D., and E. Miguel, E. 2004. "Orphans and Schooling in Africa: A Longitudinal Analysis." Working Paper 56. Bureau for Research in Economic Analysis of Development, London.

Fowler, M. G., J. Bertolli, and P. Nieburg. 1999. "When Is Breastfeeding Not Best? The Dilemma Facing HIV-Infected Women in Resource-Poor Settings." *Journal of the American Medical Association* 282: 781–83.

Fox, S. 2001. *Investing in Our Future: Psychosocial Support for Children Affected by HIV/AIDS. A Case Study in Zimbabwe and the United Republic of Tanzania.* Geneva: UNAIDS.

Gilborn, L., R. Nyonyintono, R. Kabumbuli, and G. Jagwe-Wadda. 2001. *Making a Difference for Children Affected by AIDS: Baseline Findings from Operations Research in Uganda.* Washington, DC: Horizons Program and Makerere University.

Global Health Council. 2006. *Child Health.* Retrieved November 3, 2006, from http://www.globalhealth.org/printview.php3?id=226.

Gray, R. H., M. J. Wawer, R. Brookmeyer, N. K. Sewankambo, D. Serwadda, F. Wabwire-Mangen, et al. 2001. "Probability of HIV-1 Transmission per Coital Act in Monogamous, Heterosexual, HIV-1-Discordant Couples in Rakai, Uganda." *The Lancet* 357 (9263): 1149–53.

Griffin, D., and G. Lundy-Ponce. 2003. "At the Starting Line: Early Childhood Education in the 50 States." Retrieved November 3, 2006, from http://www.aft.org/pubs-eports/american_educator/summer2003/startingline.html.

Heaton, L. M., T. B. Fowler, B. G. Epstein, T. Mulder, and P. O. Way. 2004. "The Demographic Impact of HIV/AIDS in 15 Developing Countries." Washington, DC: United States Census Bureau. Retrieved November 3, 2006, from http://www.census.gov/ipc/www/slideshows/hiv-aids/TextOnly/index.html.

HIV/AIDS Survey Indicators Database. n.d. "Program Areas: Stigma and Discrimination." Retrieved November 3, 2006, from http://www.measuredhs.com/hivdata/prog_detl.cfm?prog_area_id=3.

Letamo, G. 2005. "The Discriminatory Attitudes of Health Workers against People Living with HIV." *PLoS Medicine* 2 (8): 715–16.

LINKAGES Project. 2004. *Infant Feeding Options in the Context of HIV.* Washington, DC: Academy for Educational Development.

Luo, C. 2005. "Scaling Up Pediatric HIV Care in Low-Resource Settings: Programming Considerations." Presentation to Save the Children staff, Washington, DC, September 10.

Lusk, D., and C. O'Gara. 2002. "The Two Who Survive: The Impact of HIV/AIDS on Young Children, Their Families, and Communities." *Coordinator's Notebook.* 26: 3–21. Washington, DC: Consultative Group on Early Childhood Care and Development.

Luzze, F., and D. Ssedyabule. 2004. *The Nature of Child-Headed Households in Rakai District, Uganda.* Geneva: Lutheran World Federation, Concern Worldwide, Orphans Community-Based Organization, and Medecins du Monde.

Malawi. 2003. *National HIV/AIDS Policy: A Call for Renewed Action.* Lilongwe: Office of the President, National AIDS Commission.

McGaw, L., and A. Wameyo. 2005. *Violence against Children Affected by HIV/AIDS: A Case Study of Uganda*. Nairobi: World Vision International.

Mead, M. 1962. "A Cultural Anthropologist's Approach to Maternal Deprivation." In *Deprivation of Maternal Care: A Reassessment of Its Effects*, ed. M. D. Ainsworth. Geneva: World Health Organization.

Nakiyingi, J., M. Bracher, J. A. G. Whitworth, A. Ruberantwari, J. Busingye, S. M. Mbulaiteye, et al. 2003. "Child Survival in Relation to Mother's HIV Infection and Survival: Evidence from a Ugandan Cohort Study." *AIDS* 17 (12): 1827–34.

National Emergency Response Council on HIV/AIDS. n.d. *Young Heroes*. Retrieved November 3, 2006, from http://www.youngheroes.org.sz/.

Ntozi, J. P., and S. Zirimenya. 1999. "Changes in Household Composition and Family Structure during the AIDS Epidemic in Uganda." In *The Continuing African HIV/AIDS Epidemic: Responses and Coping Strategies*, ed. I. O. Orubuloye, J. Caldwell, and J. P. Ntozi, 193–209. Canberra, Australia: Health Transition Centre.

Powell, G. M., S. Morreira, C. Rudd, and P. P. Ngonyama. 1994. "Child Welfare Policy and Practice in Zimbabwe." Study of the Department of Pediatrics of the University of Zimbabwe and the Zimbabwe Department of Social Welfare. Harare, Zimbabwe: UNICEF Zimbabwe.

Reis, C., M. Heisler, L. L. Amowitz, R. Scott Moreland, J. O. Mafeni, C. Anyamele, et al. 2005. "Discriminatory Attitudes and Practices by Health Workers toward Patients with HIV/AIDS in Nigeria." *PLoS Medicine* 2 (8): 743–52.

Save the Children. 2003. "What's the Difference? An ECD Impact Study from Nepal." Retrieved November 3, 2006, from http://www.unicef.org/media/files/Nepal_2003_ECD_Impact_Studty.pdf.

————. 2004. *Early Childhood Development: A Positive Impact*. Westport, CT: Save the Children.

Sellen, D. W. 1998. "Infant and Young Child Feeding Practices among African Pastoralists: The Datoga of Tanzania." *Journal of Biosocial Science* 30 (4): 481–99.

Shapiro, R. L., S. Lockman, I. Thior, L. Stocking, P. Kebaabetswe, C. Wester, et al. 2003. "Low Adherence to Recommended Infant Feeding Strategies among HIV-Infected Women: Results from the Pilot Phase of a Randomized Trial to Prevent Mother-to-Child Transmission in Botswana." *AIDS Education and Prevention* 15 (3): 221–30.

Sherr, L. 2005. "Young Children and HIV/AIDS: Mapping the Field." Working Papers in Early Childhood Development, Young Children and HIV/AIDS 33. Bernard van Leer Foundation, The Hague.

Steinberg, M., S. Johnson, G. Schierhout, and D. Ndegwa. 2002. *Hitting Home: How Households Cope with the Impact of the HIV/AIDS Epidemic.* Cape Town: Henry J. Kaiser Foundation and Health Systems Trust.

Tindyebwa, D., J. Kayita, P. Musoke, B. Eley, R. Nduati, H. Coovadia, et al., eds. 2004. *Handbook on Pediatric AIDS in Africa.* New York: USAID; African Network for the Care of Children Affected by AIDS.

Uganda National AIDS Commission. 2003. "Draft Memo to Uganda ARV Finance Sub-Committee: Preliminary Results from ATC in Uganda." Kampala: National AIDS Commission.

UNAIDS. 2004. *Report on the Global AIDS Epidemic.* Geneva: UNAIDS.

UNAIDS, UNICEF, and USAID. 2004. *Children on the Brink: A Joint Report of New Orphan Estimates and a Framework for Action.* Washington, DC: USAID.

UNICEF (United Nations Children's Fund). 2003. *Africa's Orphaned Generations.* New York: UNICEF.

———. 2004. *Girls, HIV/AIDS, and Education.* New York: UNICEF.

———. 2005. *A Call to Action: Children, the Missing Face of AIDS.* New York: UNICEF.

———. n.d. *Protection and Support for Orphans and Families Affected by HIV/AIDS.* Retrieved November 4, 2006, from http://www.unicef.org/aids/index_orphans.html.

UNICEF and International Social Service. 2004. *Care for Children Affected by HIV/AIDS: The Urgent Need for International Standards.* New York: UNICEF.

UNICEF New Zealand. n.d. *Child-Headed Households.* Retrieved November 4, 2006, from http://www.unicef.org.nz/school-room/hivaids/childheaded households.

United Nations. 2001. *Declaration of Commitment on HIV/AIDS.* Retrieved November 4, 2006, from http://data.unaids.org/publications/irc-pub03/aidsdeclaration_en.pdf.

USAID (U.S. Agency for International Development). 2004. *Adding Family Planning to PMTCT Sites Increases the Benefits of PMTCT.* Retrieved November 4, 2006, from http://www.usaid.gov/our_work/global_health/pop/publications/docs/familypmtct.html.

WHO (World Health Organization). 2001. *New Data on the Prevention of Mother-to-Child Transmission (PMTCT) of HIV and Their Policy Implications.* Geneva: WHO.

———. 2003. "Surviving the First Five Years of Life." In *World Health Report 2003.* Retrieved November 4, 2006, from http://www.who.int/whr/2003/chapter1/en/index2.html.

————. 2004. *Prevention of Mother-to-Child Transmission of HIV Generic Training Package: Participant Manual.* Geneva: WHO; Atlanta: U.S. Department of Health and Human Services, Centers for Disease Control.

World Bank. 1997. *Confronting AIDS: Public Priorities in a Global Epidemic.* Washington, DC: World Bank.

————. n.d. *Why Invest in Early Child Development?* Retrieved November 4, 2006, from http://www.worldbank.org/.

Yamano, T., and T. S. Jayne. 2004. "Working-Age Adult Mortality and Primary School Attendance in Rural Kenya." Policy Brief 4. TEGEMEO Institute for Agricultural Development and Policy, Egerton University, Nairobi.

Sociohistorical Contexts

CHAPTER 6

ECD in Africa: A Historical Perspective

Larry Prochner and Margaret Kabiru

This chapter presents an overview of the history of formal early childhood development (ECD) programs in Africa, drawn mainly from examples from British colonial Africa. European preschool initiatives (including infant school, kindergarten, and nursery school) are contrasted with indigenous childrearing practices and postindependence developments in Kenya and other nations. This chapter highlights broad ECD historical themes that are relevant now. History is often used as a context for current policy or as a set of negative lessons to teach us how not to proceed; we can also better understand the limits and potential of current reform agendas by taking into account the social and historical context of educational policy and practice. Current ECD programs, like past efforts, are formed and reformed in relation to the dominant discourse surrounding social concerns. Missionary schools established in Africa in the 19th century, for example, reflected and supported Western ideas concerning race, childhood, education, and religion. European missionary societies aimed to convert and "civilize" young African children through the study of Christian scripture and the adoption of a European worldview, for example, by stressing individualist as opposed to collectivist values. Missionary teachers brought ideas for infant schools (for ages 2–6) to Africa that reflected the dominant ECD program of the time.

Various current concerns guided our thinking as the authors considered the history of ECD. How have reformed ECD programs—those intended to prepare African children for schooling and for life in as full a manner as possible—built upon preschool models originally developed to promote independence among children from their families, communities, and culture? How have these models been changed or adapted to fit local circumstances? Have new indigenous models replaced imported models? Is the stress on quality assurance in ECD models that is prevalent in Western thinking (Goffin and Wilson 2001) relevant for African ECD?

ECD in the Colonial Era

Program and policy borrowing have a long history in early childhood education and can be traced to ECD programs as they developed from the early 1800s to the 1960s—from the infant schools in the earliest period to the "Head Start" initiatives of the latter.

Infant school—In the 1820s the popular form of early childhood education for poor children was the infant school, a British model that was transported to the colonies (Kaur 2004; May 2005; Prochner 2004). The schools—developed by Robert Owen and popularized by Samuel Wilderspin—combined child care with an introduction to the skills that would prepare children for a laboring life. Infant schools were promoted as "agents of moral and social rescue and training, and emphasized rote learning of reading, writing, and numeracy; sewing and manual dexterity activities in the classrooms; and physical training in the playgrounds" (Anning 1991, 2). Few materials were required other than slates, some pictures for the wall, and a Bible. Younger children practiced their lessons by tracing numbers and letters in sand. The schools were efficient and economical; the largest expense was the teacher's salary. In many schools, a single teacher managed up to 250 pupils aged 2–7, with assistance from older students. Although according to theories about infant schools this schooling should occur in a manner consistent with what was believed to be children's natural proclivity, to play—or through "amusements" in the terminology of the time—in general practice, the schools were highly regimented and teaching was mainly through recitation. The teaching methods, drawn from the monitorial system, were designed for large class sizes: smaller numbers of pupils reduced the economy of the school and efficiency of the method.

The value of time was a fundamental principle of the monitorial system. Because many children attended school for only a few years before leaving to watch over younger siblings or for paid employment, their time in school could not be spent in idle pursuits, such as playing. Working-class parents favored private preschools, called dame schools, where children learned by rote and did not play at all (Roberts 1972). When compulsory school-starting age was debated in the British Parliament later in the 19th century, the same sentiment prevailed: "The difficulty was to obtain education without trenching on the time for gaining a living: begin-ning early and ending early would present a solution" (National Education Union 1870, as cited in Anning 1991, 3). Thus pragmatism—rather than developmental considerations—reigned.

Early Childhood Programs for African Children in the 19th Century

Infant schools established in the colonies for poor settler and indigenous children functioned similarly to those in Britain; basic academic and subject knowledge were offered alongside religious instruction (Berman 1975). The schools for indigenous children were further influenced by British principles concerning education and the management of relation-ships with indigenous peoples (Select Committee on Aborigines 1837): These principles concerning education—the conversion and civilization of indigenous children—reflected race theory, Protestant evangelism, and British imperialism. Civilization was to be attained through knowledge of Western literature and science, a process that involved the denigration and eventual elimination of local heritage (Macaulay 1935).

This view of colonial education was evident in Samuel Wilderspin's estimation of the value of an infant school in Cape Town established for the children of slaves in 1830:

> [In the infant school] the children of barbarous tribes start with the advan-tages of those of civilized man, and instead of being retarded in their progress by the ignorance and imbecility of a people only rising above the savage state, they raise up to cultivate and humanize their parents, and become the elements of a society that will soon be able to supply its own wants, advocate their own rights, and diffuse the blessings of civilization among the tribes in the interior of Africa (Wilderspin 1832, 16–17).

In 1833, a class for poor European children was added to the Cape Town school, and in its early years it was not segregated. A missionary,

George Champion (1968, 5), elaborated on the role infant schools could play by teaching children in English as a means of assimilation:

> There is an opinion prevalent here among those interested in missions, that those entering new missionary fields should sit down immediately, [and] in the infant school teach the children the English Language, in order that in the course of two or three generations the native language may be extirpated. The English introduced, [and] thus that all the stores of literature, science, and religion that there are in the English tongue may be laid at their feet. Thus you save translations, [and] you have a language adapted to civilized [and] Christian men. The language then will not cramp their minds as those minds expand under the influence of Christianity.

Such a view reflected the idea that children's minds were blank slates, and that indigenous children merely needed proper instruction to be remade as Europeans. Mission teachers and colonial government officials disagreed on this point. Officials considered a short, basic education sufficient; this position was tied to race theory that held Africans to be intellectually deficient and unable to benefit from a more extensive curriculum (Lyons 1975). This view also reflected the colonial administration's unwillingness to create an African intellectual elite and a desire to produce and maintain a laboring class (Woodhead 1996). Work, rather than education, led to "civilization." When industrial (or vocational) education was introduced for Africans in the 1860s, preschool education was abandoned, apart from a few mission schools.

Early Childhood Programs for Settler Children in Africa

The schools for settler children also functioned as a means to socialize and tame the "wild colonial child" (May 1997), who might otherwise turn "savage," into the colonial order. The preschool model for settler children varied over time, beginning with the infant school and later adding ideas from the kindergarten and, in the 20th century, the nursery school.

Kindergarten—The kindergarten was developed in Europe by Friedrich Froebel as a nonacademic approach to early education, an antidote to the rigid British infant school. Froebel shared Rousseau's vision of the innocence of childhood and, with Pestalozzi, he believed in the importance of connecting learning to real-life experiences (Pestalozzi's "object lessons") but Froebel used "materials" for a more symbolic purpose (Froebel 1897). A key element of the kindergarten was that education must follow a child's lead. Froebel believed children's minds to be fully formed at birth and capable of reason. A teacher's sensitive guidance could bring a child's inner reason to full flower by introducing materials known as "gifts" and activities, called "occupations." The ritual use of these materials easily assimilated into infant school practice; kindergartens used these materials as "building blocks" to develop work skills, manual dexterity, and perseverance.

Nursery school—Margaret Macmillan (1919) developed the nursery school as a compensatory program for socially and economically disadvantaged children in England. Its focus was on the physical and emotional health of children, with attention to sensory development and literacy. Macmillan, like her contemporary Maria Montessori in Italy, based her approach to education partly on the theories of Edouard Sequin of France, stressing sensory education and motor skills training. While Sequin began with the intellectually handicapped child, Macmillan applied the same learning principles to the typically developing but economically destitute child. An active education was the nursery school tonic for the "deadness" of kindergarten work (p. 331). The nursery school was intended to be similar to the day nurseries found in the homes of wealthy families, a child's space where joy could be found "in the beauty of childhood" (p. 30). Susan Isaacs (1949) added a psychoanalytic purpose to nursery school practice in England, in which psychological well-being was believed to develop through social relations. The nursery school was envisioned as a quasi-domestic setting to improve on home life: healthier and more stimulating of the imagination, in the company of peers, and under the direction of a trained teacher.

Three types of early childhood programs—The infant school, kindergarten, and nursery school had different receptions within the public school. The first two prepared children for schooling with a focus on academics and work habits (in the future), while the nursery school was a bridge to school with a focus on the home and a child's emotional life (in the past and present). In Isaacs' (1949, 28) view, nursery school was "to make a link between the natural and indispensable fostering of the child in the home and the social life in the world at large." For this and other reasons (such as differences in teacher preparation and school-starting age) nursery school methods were less easily brought into public school systems.

Infant school methods were easily assimilated into colonial school systems, but the kindergarten was less enthusiastically received; it was not broadly promoted as a distinct program in British colonial Africa. This resistance followed the experience in England, where kindergarten exercises were incorporated into some infant classes but otherwise had a modest effect on public schools. It is interesting to note that while some educators in England were concerned that the kindergarten model needed to be adapted to local culture and conditions (Brehony 2000), Afrikaners in South Africa resisted kindergarten as too English (Jansen et al. 1992, 425). The German colonial administration also exported kindergarten to Southwest Africa (Namibia) in the years prior to World War I. These kindergartens were only for the children of German colonists, but, in some instances, were for "colored" children, until the latter were barred in about 1905 (Smith 1998). The Woman's League of the German Colonial Society believed the kindergartens would provide employment for "surplus" women in Germany and help settlers by "removing their children from the 'danger' that African nannies and servants supposedly posed" (Wildenthal 2001, 162). Overall, the British nursery school, with its focus on play, health, and hygiene, had a far greater influence on African ECD than the kindergarten.

Colonial governments in the 20th century largely neglected preprimary school programs for black African children. A survey of preschools in South Africa in the 1950s listed just four private nursery schools for African children; none were subsidized by the government (International Bureau of Education 1961). The situation was different for child care institutions: about 30 crèches were in one township near Johannesburg in the mid-1960s (Kahn 1968). Most of these crèches were privately funded and operated as feeding programs for children under the supervision of untrained staff, reflecting a health or pediatric orientation (Cleghorn and Prochner 2003).

Norrel A. London (2002) observed that there was a lag between the development of educational ideas and their adaptation in colonial settings. In relation to curriculum changes in Trinidad and Tobago, he concluded, "regardless of the original provenance of particular ideologies, [curriculum] planners could harness from a given doctrine those orientations that appeared to suit their purpose best" (p. 67). In Africa, infant schools were part of the early wave of missionary activity, arriving on the continent soon after their development in Europe. Infant schools were a good fit for the colonies; the monitorial system developed by Andrew Bell in India was one influence.

The infant school curriculum included moral and religious lessons taught mechanically to large numbers of mixed-age classes. In a colonial setting with indigenous children, religious training was emphasized more than literacy. This was unsatisfactory for those African parents who desired a broader education for their children: it meant that access to a

Western education and related social and economic benefits were never really possible. The school administrators in turn blamed parents, considering the home culture to be a barrier to the children's education, as accounted by a missionary in an infant school in Sierra Leone in 1828:

> So long as the children are allowed to be running wild about the streets, and even joining the nightly yelling and dancing, of which there is very little cessation the year round—so long as they are not trained to any habits of order—it is not to be expected that they will make much progress in learning, which necessarily requires thought, application, and restraint—exercises to which they have never been trained (Church Missionary Society 1828, 284–85).

Similar arguments were made about working-class children and their parents. In a colonial context, however, the arguments were tied to race theory and the priorities of colonial administration.

Indigenous ECD in Historical Perspective

Children were—and remain—highly valued in African communities. They played a vital role in the family and the community. Marriage legitimacy was sealed through parenthood. A barren woman was considered a stigma. Both men and women desired children, because children gave their parents a new status. Kenyatta and Kariuki (1984, 87) observed:

> A childless marriage among the Gikuyu communities is practically a failure, for children bring joy not only to their parents, but also to their *mbari* (clan) as a whole. In Gikuyu society the rearing of a family brings with it rise in social status.

Parents valued children for their assistance in carrying out family chores and responsibilities. Children were viewed as an investment when parents grew old (Kenyatta and Kariuki 1984; Kilbride and Kilbride 1990; Mwamwenda 1996). They were seen as a source of joy and received with pride. Parents shared the joy of the newborn with relatives and friends (Kenya Institute of Education 1984; Kenyatta and Kariuki 1984; Kilbride and Kilbride 1990; MOEST and UNESCO 2005; Swadener, Kabiru, and Njenga 2000). Children had a spiritual significance, linking the creator and generations, past and present. According to Behamuka (1983, 101), "having children is a religious duty, which links not only the individual but also the creator, the ancestors, and the biological parents."

The expectations of families and communities and the values they placed on children influenced how children were cared for and educated. In the traditional society, education of the child was governed by family and community traditions and by social structures. Each community had its own education system to socialize children into its culture, values, and traditions. The child's education began at birth and continued through various stages and age groups, with a system of education defined for every stage. Children were prepared to contribute to strengthening the community. Children were expected to acquire skills essential for protection, food production, and mastery of the environment. Early education transmitted important aspects of culture and values, such as sharing, social responsibility, belonging, mutual dependence, mutual respect, continuity, obedience, respect for elders, cooperation, fear of God, and ability to relate with other people (Dembele 1999; Kenyatta and Kariuki 1984; Kilbride and Kilbride 1990; Mwamwenda 1996). Children learned social etiquette and conduct (for example, how to greet, sit, eat, and not interfere with adult conversation). Misbehavior was punished through caning, denial of food, verbal threats, or being locked out in the dark for some time. In addition, children were taught the history and traditions of the family, clan, and the whole community.

Children learned and were taught as they participated in the daily living activities in the home, through ceremonies, direct instructions, observation, and apprenticeship. Beginning in infancy, children were taught through lullabies, songs, and games, mainly by their mothers, although other caregivers such as grandparents, aunts, and older siblings assisted. As children grew older they received direct instructions and were tested through questioning. Stories and legends were used to instill morals and to teach the community's history and traditions. Oral literature was also used to teach abstract philosophical attitudes toward life, beliefs, practices, and taboos (Mbithi 1982). Fathers, elders, and neighbors participated in the education and socialization of older children. Grandparents played a special role of teaching children sensitive topics (such as sexuality) and of passing on morals, values, history, and traditions through stories, legends, and conversations. Children began to be assigned major responsibilities from the age of 7 years and were expected to gain skills for generating a livelihood. At this age, children were socialized into what the society considered to be gender-appropriate roles. Boys usually ran errands, looked after livestock, or took part in farmwork. Girls took care of younger siblings and undertook household chores (such as cooking, sweeping, and cleaning dishes) and also worked in the farm alongside their mothers. Children also acquired intellectual and social skills while they played among peers in the neighborhood. Parents left children to freely indulge in play and games. Kenyatta and Kariuki (1984, 61) cited, "anyone observing children at their play will no doubt be impressed by the freedom which characterizes the period of childhood among the Gikuyu." Lenaiyasa (1999) observed that Samburu children had a common play area where they participated in games during the day and also at night when there is moonlight.

In some cases, young children were brought together in a group to a community-based early childhood center. Such centers continue today, for example in Kenya and Mali. In Mali, according to Dembele (1999) this *garderie traditionnelle* is a spontaneous organization of child care during periods of intense community activities that take place mainly during the rainy season. An elderly woman (*denminenaa*) is responsible for the care and is often assisted by elder siblings (*denmineden*). Older children organize the play and report food and discipline problems to the elderly caregivers. Community members ensure that the caregiver is supplied with food, water, firewood, and other requirements. Similar care arrangements, known as *loipi*, were also found among the Samburu in Kenya. Children were left in a group under the care of grandmothers, aunties, or neighbors when the mothers were away. The caregivers ensured that when hungry, the children took their milk from the gourds left by their mothers. They also told children stories and supervised them as they played (Lenaiyasa and Kimathi 2002).

Islamic education, which originated from outside the continent, has a long history in Sub-Saharan Africa. The Koranic school prepares Muslim children to know and practice Islam as a way of life. In East Africa children are enrolled in Koranic schools from the age of 4 years. According to Dembele (1999, 5), in the Sahel region, "when a child can count from 1 to 10, it is sent to the Koranic teacher who hosts as many as 50 children aged from 4 to 15 years. Memorizing the Koran and learning to act as a Muslim are central musts." In the Sahel region, the Koranic teacher is the most learned person in a rural community and the most influential in both urban and rural areas.

Similar institutions abound in East Africa, where they are referred to as *madrasa* or *dugsies*. In parts of East Africa and Morocco, Muslim communities—in collaboration with governments and development agencies, especially the Aga Khan Foundation—have initiated projects that incorporate secular aspects of the broader national curriculum into the Koranic education (Hyde and Kabiru 2003). According to the *Integrated*

Islamic Education Programme, its aim is "to ensure that the Kenyan Muslim child is properly molded in his faith as well as prepared to fit into the Kenyan society as a useful citizen" (NACECE 1993, 6).

Over the last few decades, social and economic changes have influenced child care and socialization. Older children attend school while young fathers move to towns or commercial agricultural areas to seek wage employment. Mothers are left to take care of children and undertake other responsibilities with inadequate assistance. They are often overburdened by these responsibilities. Some mothers also take up wage employment or trade to supplement the family income. Grandmothers, neighbors, or hired maids (known as *ayahs*) assist with child care when the mother is away (Kipkorir 1993; Weisner et al. 1997). Despite these changes, traditions remain strong in many areas. Many children are still cared for and socialized by strong networks of caregivers. Mothers are the major caregivers of infants and very young children, but other caregivers such as grandparents, siblings, and neighbors assist them. Fathers do not traditionally participate actively in the care of infants, though today young men can be seen holding, feeding, and taking care of infants. Men are expected to provide security and to ensure that the family has sufficient resources (Gakuru and Koech 1995; Swadener, Kabiru, and Njenga 2000; Woodhead 1996). The well-being of African children is, however, threatened by interrelated factors including armed conflicts, natural disasters, food shortages, increasing poverty, and HIV and AIDS (World Bank, UNICEF, and WGECD-ADEA 2002).

A Contemporary Community-Based ECD Model: Kenya's Harambee Preschools

Formal preschools serve children ages 4 to 6 in the majority of African countries, however, the enrollment rate is typically less than 10 percent. Most preschools are found in the urban areas; the lowest access rates are in remote rural areas and urban slums. Enrollment rates are low, yet teacher-child ratios are relatively high. Most African governments do not employ preschool teachers; a large proportion of the teachers are not trained. Preschool curricula are often based on models from the West or are downward extensions of primary education (Gakuru 1992; Hyde and Kabiru 2003; Kabiru 1993; Myers 2001). African governments and communities have shown increased concern for early education in response to international agreements such as the Convention on the Rights of the Child, Children's Summit, Dakar Framework for Action Education for All,

UN Special Session for Children, and the Millennium Development Goals. Recent ECD conferences have also have emphasized that early care and education are essential to achieve basic education goals and to develop human resources. It is evident that governments have to increase resources for this sector. Comprehensive programs meeting holistic needs of children and involving parents and communities should be developed and made accessible; curricula should be indigenized, training be made more relevant and accessible, and early care and education partnerships be strengthened (World Bank, UNICEF, and WGECD-ADEA 2002). The following case study describes a current national example of early care and education in Kenya and how the country improves the service.

Before independence in 1963, preschool education and care services in Kenya were racially segregated. The first preschools were established in urban areas to serve European and Asian children. Beginning in the 1940s, plantation owners established daycare centers for African children on agricultural plantations. These centers provided custodial care for children while their mothers worked. Later, local authorities started some centers in African residential areas in towns to meet nutritional and medical care needs for poor children. Many more daycare centers were established in rural central Kenya during the Mau Mau struggle for independence (1953–60) to provide custodial care while parents were engaged in forced labor by the colonial government. Missionaries provided milk and medical care to children enrolled in these centers (Bernard van Leer Foundation 1994; Gakuru 1992; Kabiru 1993; MOEST and UNESCO 2005; Woodhead 1996). For centuries, young Muslim children have also attended Koranic schools, which emphasized faith-based learning.

After Kenya's independence in 1963, preschool centers expanded rapidly. Their growth was stimulated by Kenyan President Jomo Kenyatta's popularization of the *Harambee* motto, meaning "pulling and pushing together." Harambee encompasses the principles of community initiatives based on joint efforts, mutual assistance, social responsibility, and community self-reliance. Even immediately after independence people were hungry for education, believing in the importance of preschool education and expecting that preschools would prepare their children for the highly competitive education system (Gakuru 1992; Kabiru 1993). Parents and communities responded positively to the Harambee call and immersed themselves in fundraising and resource mobilization to establish preschool institutions ranging from daycare centers, nursery schools, and Koranic schools to kindergartens attached to primary schools.

In some cases nursery schools previously established by nongovernmental organizations (NGOs) or missions were part of this movement. The Ngecha Nursery School, founded by the International Red Cross in 1952, became a Harambee school 10 years later (Whiting et al. 2004).

Harambee preschools are managed by committees that are elected by the local community. The committee is responsible for organizing the community to acquire land and building materials. Every member of the community is expected to contribute toward the project through money, labor, or materials. The land is either bought or donated by an individual, extended family, clan, or local authority. The committee mobilizes parents to enroll their children, usually those 3–6 years old. In agricultural plantations and low-income urban areas, younger children are enrolled because mothers work outside the home and the families cannot afford to employ child minders. The committee organizes consultative meetings through which the community determines the fees, identifies the teacher—who, in most cases, is a member of the community—and the salary. Most preschool teachers are women. The committee is expected to supervise and support the teacher. The teacher's salary depends on the fees paid and the quality of the management provided by the committee, though, on the whole, preschool teachers receive extremely low and irregular salaries. The government registers community preschools; it inspects and supervises the schools, though irregularly. The government also offers subsidized training for the teachers.

Today preschools are found even in the most remote parts of Kenya. In 2005, more than 1.5 million children aged 3–6 years old enrolled in preschools, representing about 35 percent of the children in this age group (MOEST and UNESCO 2005). Parents and local communities manage and run these centers with limited financial resources and inadequate materials. Many parents are poor and are not able to pay even the minimal fees to pay the teacher, buy basic materials to construct and maintain adequate buildings, or provide appropriate teaching/learning materials.

The focus of the preschools is to prepare children for school by introducing basic numeracy and literacy in as many as three languages (mother tongue, Kiswahili, and English). Parents also expect children to gain social skills, while working parents also need custodial care for their children. To satisfy the expectations of parents and primary schools, preschool teachers often pressure children to learn skills beyond their ability and development. The teachers often revert to rote methods rather than individualized, active, child-centered methods. About 45 percent of preschool teachers are not trained and therefore easily succumb to external pressures.

Despite these challenges, parents and communities have made a major contribution to making preschool education accessible to many children. They respond positively to the guidance provided by the government and other partners. For example, parents have contributed to the integration of local culture and traditions by offering stories, poems, riddles, and such to be incorporated in the curriculum. Many communities have introduced feeding programs and growth monitoring to improve the health and nutrition needs of children (Kenya Institute of Education 1987; MOEST and UNESCO 2005).

Local involvement has created a unique feature of the Kenya preschool program that is largely community based. Community participation ensures that formal preschool education serves a cross-section of children from different social, economic, and cultural backgrounds, unlike many parts of Africa where preschools are for the privileged elite in urban areas (MOEST and UNESCO 2005). The Kenyan government encourages innovations by communities and different organizations to develop other ways of delivering early care and education. Home-based and informal community-based models, for example, are noted to increase quality, relevance, and access and to ensure equity, particularly for the most marginalized groups such as pastoral and urban slum communities.

Since 1970, the Kenyan government has recognized and appreciated the contribution of parents and local communities and has made efforts to improve the quality of preschool education. Between 1972 and 1982 the Ministry of Education and the Bernard van Leer Foundation implemented a project to develop curricula and training programs. Formal responsibility for the management and regulation of preschool education was vested in the Ministry of Education in 1980. The ministry undertakes the formulation of policy; training of preschool trainers, supervisors, and teachers; empowerment and support to communities; registration of preschools; coordination of partners and stakeholders; development of the curriculum and learning materials; and quality assurance. The professional development of preschool education involving training and curriculum development is vested in the National Center for Early Childhood Education (NACECE) and its network of 71 District Centers for Early Childhood Education (DICECE). In 1988 a policy of partnership to provide early childhood education and care services was adopted to mobilize and coordinate resources from local communities, faith-based organizations, nongovernmental organizations, welfare organizations, the private sector, and bilateral and multilateral bodies (MOEST and UNESCO 2005).

Conclusion

Our brief review of preschool history suggests priorities for the future of ECD in Africa that build on strengths and address gaps. These priorities include the need to support parents and communities to cope with the changing social and economic situation and the need to focus on policy development. The wealth of the traditional knowledge and methodologies needs to be incorporated in ECD curricula and practices while considering the changes traditional knowledge will undergo in this process (Coe 2005). Robert Myers (2000, 3) noted a "tendency for programs in Minority World countries to be taken as the template or standard for development of ECDC in the future." Programs developed elsewhere cannot fully meet the needs of African families. At the same time, colonial-era models—such as the kindergarten and nursery school—have been shown to be amenable to indigenization. As indicated by the example of community-based programs in Kenya, ECD programs are strengthened when they are reconceptualized from an African standpoint.

References

Anning, A. 1991. *The First Years at School: Education 4 to 8*. Buckingham, UK: Open University Press.

Behamuka, J. M. 1983. *Our Religious Heritage*. Nairobi: Thomas Nelson and Sons.

Berman, E. H. 1975. "Christian Missions in Africa." In *African Reactions to Missionary Education*, ed. E. H. Berman, 1–53. New York: Teachers College Press.

Bernard van Leer Foundation. 1994. *Building on Peoples' Strengths: Early Childhood in Africa*. The Hague: Bernard van Leer Foundation.

Brehony, K. 2000. The Kindergarten in England, 1851–1918. In *Kindergartens and Cultures: The Global Diffusion of an Idea*, ed. R. Wollons, 59–86. New Haven: Yale University Press.

Champion, G. 1968. *The Journal of an American Missionary in the Cape Colony 1835*, ed. A. R. Booth. Cape Town: South African Library.

Church Missionary Society. 1828. *Missionary Register*. June. London: Seeley.

Cleghorn, A., and L. Prochner. 2003. "Contrasting Visions of Childhood: Examples from Settings in India and Zimbabwe." *Journal of Early Childhood Research* 1 (2): 131–53.

Coe, C. 2005. *Dilemmas of Culture in African Schools: Youth, Nationalism, and the Transformation of Knowledge*. Chicago: University of Chicago Press.

Dembele, N. U. 1999. "What for Our Young Ancestors Back on Earth?" Paper presented at the international conference "Early Childhood Care and Education," Kampala. September.

Froebel, F. 1897. *Friedrich Froebel's Pedagogics of the Kindergarten, or, His Ideas Concerning the Play and Playthings of the Child.* Trans. J. Jarvis. London: Edward Arnold.

Gakuru, O. N. 1992 "Class and Preschool Education in Kenya." Unpublished doctoral dissertation, University of Nairobi.

Gakuru, O. N., and B. G. Koech. 1995. "The Experience of Young Children: A Conceptualized Case Study of Early Childhood Care and Education in Kenya." Final report to Bernard van Leer Foundation. The Hague: Bernard van Leer Foundation.

Goffin, S., and C. Wilson. 2001. *Curriculum Models and Early Childhood Education: Appraising the Relationship.* 2nd ed. Upper Saddle River, NJ: Prentice-Hall.

Hyde, A. L., and M. Kabiru. 2003. *Early Childhood Development as an Important Strategy to Improve Learning Outcomes.* Paris: WGECD-ADEA.

International Bureau of Education. 1961. *Organization of Pre-primary Education.* Geneva: International Bureau of Education.

Isaacs, S. 1949. *The Educational Value of the Nursery School.* London: The Nursery School Association of Great Britain and Northern Ireland.

Jansen, C., E. Calitz, L. Du Toit, H. Grobler, A. Kotzé, and M. Lancaster. 1992. "Preschool and Primary Education in South Africa." In *The International Handbook of Early Childhood Education,* ed. G. Woodill, J. Bernhard, and L. Prochner, 425–39. New York: Garland.

Kabiru, M. 1993. *Early Childhood Care and Development: A Kenyan Experience.* Nairobi: UNICEF Eastern and Southern Africa Regional Office.

Kahn, E. J., Jr. 1968. *The Separated People: A Look at Contemporary South Africa.* New York: W.W. Norton.

Kaur, B. 2004. "Keeping the Infants of Coolies out of Harm's Way: Raj, Church, and Infant Education in India, 1830–51." *Contemporary Issues in Early Childhood* 5 (2): 221–35.

Kenya Institute of Education. 1984. *Guidelines for Early Childhood Education in Kenya.* Nairobi: Jomo Kenyatta Foundation.

———. 1987. *Early Childhood Education in Kenya: Implications for Policy and Practice.* Report presented at "Jadini Seminar," Nairobi. August–September.

Kenyatta, J., and J. Kariuki. 1984. *Facing Mount Kenya.* Nairobi: Heinemann.

Kilbride, P. L., and J. C. Kilbride. 1990. *Changing Family Life in East Africa.* Nairobi: Gideon S. Were Press.

Kipkorir, L. I. 1993. "Kenya." In *International Handbook of Child Care Policies and Programs,* ed. M. Cochran, 333–52. Westport, CT: Greenwood.

Lenaiyasa, S. 1999. *The Samburu Community ECD Project in Northern Kenya.* Paper presented at the international conference "Early Childhood Care and Development," Kampala. September.

Lenaiyasa, S., and H. Kimathi. 2002. *Samburu Community-Based ECD Project*. Paper presented at the regional conference "Early Childhood Development," Mombasa. February.

London, N. A. 2002. "Curriculum Convergence: An Ethno-Historical Investigation into Schooling in Trinidad and Tobago." *Comparative Education* 38 (1): 53–73.

Lyons, C. H. 1975. *To Wash an Aethiop White: British Ideas about Black African Educability, 1530–1960*. New York: Teachers College Press.

Macaulay, T. 1935. *Speeches by Lord Macaulay, With His 'Minute on Indian Education.'* London: Oxford University Press.

Macmillan, M. 1919. *The Nursery School*. New York: F. P. Dutton.

May, H. 1997. *The Discovery of Early Childhood*. Auckland: Auckland University Press/Bridget Williams Books.

———. 2005. *School Beginnings: A 19th-Century Colonial Story*. Wellington: New Zealand Council for Educational Research.

Mbithi, P. M. 1982. *Early Childhood and Society: An Overview*. Paper presented at the Kenya Institute of Education national seminar "Preschool Education and Its Development in Kenya," Nairobi.

MOEST (Ministry of Education, Science, and Technology) and UNESCO (United Nations Educational, Scientific, and Cultural Organization). 2005. "Policy Framework on Early Childhood Development." Discussion paper. MOEST and UNESCO, Nairobi.

Mwamwenda, T. S. 1996. *Educational Psychology: An African Perspective*. Durban: Heinemann.

Myers, R. G. 2000. *Education for All, 2000 Assessment. Thematic Studies: Early Childhood Care and Development*. Paris: UNESCO.

———. 2001. "In Search of Early Childhood Indicators." *Coordinators Notebook* (25): 4–49.

NACECE (National Center for Early Childhood Education). 1993. *Integrated Islamic Education Programme*. Nairobi: NAECE.

Prochner, L. 2004. "Early Education Programs for Indigenous Children in Canada, Australia, and New Zealand: An Historical Review." *Australian Journal of Early Childhood* 29 (4): 7–16.

Roberts, A. F. 1972. "A New View of the Infant School Movement." *British Journal of Educational Studies* 20 (2).

Select Committee on Aborigines. 1837. *Report from the Select Committee on Aborigines. British Parliamentary Papers*. Vol. 3, Anthropology: Aborigines. London: House of Commons.

Smith, H. W. 1998. "The Talk of Genocide, the Rhetoric of Miscegenation: Notes on Debates in the German Reichstag Concerning Southwest Africa,

1904–1914." In *The Imperialist Imagination: German Colonialism and Its Legacy*, ed. S. Friedrichsmeyer, S. Lennox, and S. Zantop, 107–24. Ann Arbor: University of Michigan Press.

Swadener, B. B., with M. Kabiru, and A. Njenga. 2000. *Does the Village Still Raise the Child? A Collaborative Study of Changing Childrearing and Early Education in Kenya*. Albany, NY: State University of New York Press.

Weisner, T. S., C. Bradley, P. L. Kilbride, A. B. C. Ocholla-Ayayo, J. Akong'a, and S. Wandibba, eds. 1997. *African Families and the Crisis of Social Change*. Westport, CT: Bergin and Garvey.

Whiting, B. B., J. Whiting, J. Herzog, and C. Edwards, with A. Curtis. 2004. "The Historical Stage." In *Ngecha: A Kenyan Village in a Time of Rapid Social Change*, ed. C. P. Edwards and B. B. Whiting, 53–90. Lincoln: University of Nebraska Press.

Wildenthal, L. 2001. *German Women for the Empire*. Durham, NC: Duke University Press.

Wilderspin, S. 1832. *Early Discipline Illustrated, or, The Infant System Prospering and Successful*. London: Westley and Davis.

Woodhead, M. 1996. *In Search of the Rainbow: Pathways to Quality in Large-Scale Programs for Young Disadvantaged Children*. The Hague: Bernard van Leer Foundation.

World Bank, UNICEF (United Nations Children's Fund), and WGECD-ADEA (Working Group on ECD, Association for the Development of Education in Africa). 2002. "Declaration, Overview, and Synthesis Statements." Presented at the conference "Asmara Child Development," Asmara, Eritrea. October.

CHAPTER 7

(Mis)Understanding ECD in Africa: The Force of Local and Global Motives

A. Bame Nsamenang

The mission of this chapter, to borrow from Rose (1999, 20), is a "matter of introducing a critical attitude toward those things that are given to our present [African] experience as if they were timeless, natural, unquestionable: to stand against the maxims of one's time, against the spirit of one's age, against the current of received wisdom." This chapter contributes a modest voice to the discourse on developing culturally sensitive approaches in early childhood development (ECD). This critical voice is meant to extend the dialogue and substantiate the importance of cultural conceptualizations of childhood by introducing child development theories and practices that follow from African ways of acting in—and understanding—the world. This chapter reasons with Smale (1998, 3) that this work might support "the need for changes in attitudes, approaches, methodologies, and service provision" in ECD.

This chapter emerges from experiences of belonging to a derided continent "whose distinctive culture is little appreciated" (Ellis 1978, 1) and a culture that seems targeted for systematic replacement instead of enhancement. The objective is to inject a critical spirit to both indigenous and imported ECD services in Africa.

Whose Interests Are Addressed in ECD Programs?

Interest and investment in children 0–8 years has increased around the world. Any service, such as ECD, that can give "a good start in life involving nurturing, care, and a safe environment" (African Ministers and Representatives of Ministers 2005) to children—the future hope of any society and nation—deserves support and encouragement to work out appropriate policies and programs, build effective capacity, and enhance networking (Pence 2004; Pence and Marfo 2004). But what image will those programs take? Will they emerge from within, or from outside, Africa?

When Euro-American ECD programs are applied as the gold standards by which to measure forms of Africa's ECD, they deny equity to and recognition of Africa's ways of provisioning for its young, and thereby deprive the continent a niche in global ECD knowledge waves (Nsamenang 2005b). Surprisingly, "important interest groups, nation states themselves, and powerful international organizations such as OECD [Organisation for Economic Co-operation and Development], UNICEF [United Nations Children's Fund], and the World Bank" (Moss and Petrie 2002, 1), and other UN organizations, sustain and proselytize throughout the world forms of ECD that are functional in Europe and North America as the "right" way to make progress with young children.

The dominant ECD narrative assumes that children can learn a universal culture; it has introduced an insidiously destructive force in the field—acquiescence to the institutionalization of ECD (Dahlberg, Moss, and Pence 1999)—as a socioeducational service that is a right of all children and their families (Rinaldi 2005), regardless of their circumstances. As Prochner and Kabiru noted in chapter 6, such an approach has a long history in Africa and in other parts of the world. ECD as a globalizing, universalizing, institutional force is increasingly debated (Canella and Viruru 2004; Dahlberg, Moss, and Pence 1999; Swadener and Mutua forthcoming), joining earlier and continuing critiques of universal approaches in child development (Cole 1996; Kagitcibasi 1996).

The motivation behind ECD planners and implementers is based on whose interests are addressed in policy development and implementation and the suitability of services in Africa: the interests of the development community or the interests of children and their communities. This compelling issue determines positioning for program status, control of or access to ECD resources, and which of Africa's children benefits from the ECD largess. The last point is easily noticeable in the parts of Africa that donors prefer to focus development cooperation.

The prevailing attitude and orientation is inconsistent with and intolerant of cultural diversity and is contrary to evidence "that alternative patterns of care based on different moral and practical considerations can constitute normal patterns of development that had not been imagined in developmental theories" (LeVine 2004, 163). This evidence is consistent with the finding that experienced Sub-Saharan African mothers understand infant care and development in ways that contrast "sharply with expert knowledge in the child development field" (p. 149), a point that reinforces the value of culturally appropriate approaches. The gap between African children's conditions and the theories that interveners apply to them persists because the field relies more on scripted new conceptualizations than on embedded contextual realities of childhood. Culture determines the nature of many dimensions of children's developmental niches—including daily routines and settings, parenting, and childrearing arrangements—and it must be incorporated into policy development and service provision in Africa and in other parts of the world.

One expectation is that ECD experts and practitioners understand and endeavor to move children and their families forward from acceptance of their current circumstances. However, instead of drawing strength from the wisdom of African traditions, which the people have preserved for centuries, a Eurocentric or Western frame of reference encourages a detachment to the indigenous worldview, values, and practices. Those identified as "expert" typically have different perceptions from the people in the community for whom their work or support is intended. It is as if they have been educated to discount the stark realities and contexts of Africa's ECD. In South Africa, Callaghan (1998, 31) keenly recorded "a blindness and inability to see and value Africans in the African context." It is thus not difficult to detect a modernity index professed by experts, rather than the beneficiary community, that is tacitly imposed on African governments as a condition for financial and technical support (Nsamenang 2005b). Accordingly and arguably, an influential but veiled motive in ECD work internationally could be employment, rather than the desire to establish genuinely relevant functional services that strengthen existing community structures to reach children in the cultural contexts in which their community would fully participate (Lanyasunya and Lesolayia 2001).

Recognizing that everything is not bad, but that everything is potentially dangerous (Foucault 1980), appraisal of ECD policy and program development should extend to scrutinizing even the best intentions of researchers and the development community. For example, ECD workers, including native-born staff, often use labels and radiate attitudes that range from cultural superiority to contempt (Bram 1998; Creekmore 1986). When interveners portray interventions as neutral, they work against Africa because this portrayal devalues Africa's rich cultures and dependable, albeit un-Western, traditions; they distort and fail to acknowledge Africa's capacity and accomplishments. They do not see in Africa any lesson for progress.

In consequence, there is tension, apprehension, or hesitation in accepting imported understandings of ECD. What is the source of failure, for example, in the 20-year effort to integrate San children of Botswana into formal schooling, with an outcome that has not been "very positive" (le Roux 2002, 33)? Should the ECD agenda be pushed forward with the San by working from an understanding of the cultural or environmental sources of program failure? Or should the San experience be reported as one of the "many hints and lessons that can be applied in other situations involving work with indigenous or other minority groups" (Cohen 2001, 6)? This state of the field reinforces the need for a more focused search for culturally appropriate investments in children in their early years and to commitments of fewer resources to uprooting heritages that have served groups successfully and within which they understand the world. With the high cost and suspect sustainability of ECD, it is rational to follow Sharp's (1970, 20) warning "against destroying too abruptly the traditional background of the African," which is still "the best guarantee of the child's welfare and education."

How aware are those involved that the approach to ECD advocated by the development community can bring African parents into a "web of cultural transition where there are no longer clearly defined values and moral codes of behavior that should be instilled in children and young people" (Cohen 2001, 6)? ECD stakeholders in general, and African policy planners, researchers, and practitioners in particular, need to open up creatively to the reality that African parents raise culturally competent infants and toddlers "according to a different set of standards" (LeVine 2004, 159), most of which have not been theorized or formulated into ECD policy. Children so raised and who have "ventured outside their ethnic niches have adapted remarkably well and have excelled in alien contexts" (Nsamenang and Lamb 1994, 137). The stories of top African athletes and football stars in Europe, who were groomed in "impoverished" Africa and are among the best in Europe, are examples of achievement from adversity. Can their success cast a liberating light on such "different sets of standards" for ECD in Africa?

Systematic research into the wealth of ECD practices of the Turkana and Samburu of Kenya and other early childhood traditions may offer theoretic insights and policy reorientations. More important, research on indigenous approaches to child rearing, which "fit well into the modern situation in terms of child stimulation and play materials, songs, lullabies, [and] poems" (Lanyasunya and Lesolayia 2001, 4), are too often ignored or obscured in the effort to respond to donor-identified needs and service development.

The remainder of this chapter will outline indigenous African systems of ECD that have survived. Although indigenous African ECD programs produce child outcomes that are culturally valued and capable of global achievement, they are community based, not institutional.

Fundamentals of Indigenous African ECD

This section sketches elements and briefly clarifies core principles of ECD within an African perspective, which diverges from Eurocentric views of ECD. This African view permits children to enter into adult roles early and to manage their own learning and development within the peer culture. Socialization and education are organized to target children with core cultural (that is, developmental) tasks at various stages, therefore it is important to understand social ontogenesis to discern the (ethno) theories and pedagogic strategies beneath Africa's indigenous ECD services.

African Social Ontogeny: Phases of Personhood

Discourse on Africa's indigenous ECD is best undertaken within its own worldview, which inspires a circular path to human ontogenesis in three phases, identifiable more by cultural imperatives than by the biological markers that trigger them. *Social selfhood*, an experiential reality that begins with conception, connects the two metaphysical phases of *spiritual* and *ancestral selfhood* to substantiate the concept of human life cycle. Social selfhood, or the existential self, develops through seven periods: prebirth/neonatal, social priming, social apprenticing, social entrée, social internment, adulthood, and old age/death (see Nsamenang 1992b, 144–48).

Social ontogeny draws on African life journeys (Serpell 1993) to recognize the transformation of the human newborn from a biological imperative into a viable cultural agent of a particular community en route to adulthood. As children develop, they gradually and systematically enter into and assume different levels of personhood, identity, and being (Nsamenang 2005a). Accordingly, we can interpret child development as the acquisition and growth of competencies in the physical, cognitive, social, and emotional domains and the moral maturity required to competently engage in family and society. *Social transformation* in the individual is brought about by participation in family and societal life (Rogoff 2003). The guidance of child development as a process of gradual and systematic social integration rather than sovereign individuation "differs in theoretical focus from the more individualistic accounts proposed by Freud, Erikson, and Piaget" (Serpell 1994, 18).

Developmental Learning
African developmental and educational thought is represented in garden metaphors to reflect a gradual unfolding of social ontogenesis, human abilities, and selfhood. The stages of development are framed by conception of the unborn as "buds of hope and expectation" (Zimba 2002, 98), "entirely geared toward the future" (Erny 1973, 23). This classic developmental perspective connotes keen awareness that today's adults are a product of their childhoods (Lanyasunya and Lesolayia 2001, 4).

Children are not born with the knowledge and cognitive skills to make sense of and to engage the world; they learn or grow into them as they develop (Nsamenang 2004). Based on perceived child states and milestones of human ontogenesis, Africans assign sequential cultural tasks to the stages of development they recognize. In this way, they organize child development as a sociogenic process, with cultural beliefs and practices that guide systematic socialization, education, and the expectations required for each ontogenetic stage. Cultural rites such as naming, marriage, initiation, and death rituals are "graduated" to ease social integration and transition points in development.

In African family traditions, education begins in the cradle, if not earlier. For example, "African cultural practices subject pregnant women and their spouses to behavioral taboos that guide sexual intercourse, specific food items, and emotional distress, among others, in order to promote the health of the unborn child and mother" (Zimba and Otaala 1995). The education is wedged into the culture—the daily routines of family and society—and sequenced to fit into the developmental stages of the "school of life" (Moumouni 1968, 29). Children progressively "graduate" from one activity setting or "pivot role" to another, until they attain adulthood. In so doing, children come more under the guidance and supervision of peer mentors than of parents or adult caregivers

(Nsamenang and Lamb 1995). Children follow an unwritten curriculum, which they tacitly learn or "teach" to themselves at different phases that correspond to the developmental stages the culture recognizes.

This socialization is according to children's emerging abilities (Nsamenang 2002). Children are trained from an early age to participate in self-care, routine duties, and family maintenance chores. The normally developing African child is expected to complete his or her basic training in the social, intellectual, moral, and practical sectors of economic and communal life by the end of adolescence (Cameroon 1981). The practical demonstration of acquired competencies is the extent to which a given child notices and responds to the needs of peers or sibling charges. The infant or toddler matures into a child-participant in domestic chores and, thereafter, into an adolescent who graduates into higher order interactional networks and transactional roles.

African Educational Thought and Praxes
Educational provisioning reinforces children's innate abilities to abstract livelihood lessons, sociocognitive competencies, and affective dispositions from their ecocultures. At critical points of social ontogeny, through a sequence of rites, African parents prime readiness through anticipatory socialization and ease transition into the developmental tasks of stages that are expected in the future (Nsamenang 2002, 2004). Sibling caregiving is an inescapable anticipatory role into which most African children are primed from childhood. This involvement eases their transition into the parenting role.

The generativity of Africa's folk developmental learning is consistent with Piaget's (1952) theory of interactional-extractive learning, as African parents focus on children's participation in responsible and productive livelihood activities as the primary principle in their development and learning (Nsamenang 2004). This perspective differs from the dominant Western narrative, which constructs children as "reproducers, to be filled with knowledge and values and made 'ready to learn' and 'ready for school,' and as redemptive agents, appropriate vehicles for solving social and economic problems in society if subjected early enough to effective technical interventions" (Moss and Petrie 2002, 3).

Teaching and Learning Strategies and Techniques
The primary orienting disposition to learning is participatory, not instructional. This disposition derives from the assumption that children are competent and capable of taking on responsible roles, even in their own

development and learning, from an early age (Nsamenang 1992b, 2004). Although Africans may not articulate it as ECD experts expect, a strand of an African ethnotheory disposes African parents into perceiving and acting on socialization as a generative process by which children actively learn or teach themselves. This orientation perhaps explains the ubiquity of the African neighborhood peer group, which may be developmentally more useful and perhaps more influential in child development and learning than is direct parenting or adult socialization (Nsamenang 1992a).

In Africa, caretaking is a social enterprise in which mothers or other adults are available as partial caregivers, while sibling caretakers provide the bulk of the care for children who have been weaned (Nsamenang 1992a). Older siblings nurture or cultivate responsibility by assigning domestic chores and errands to children (Ogunaike and Houser 2002). That is, African parents concede or delegate important child care responsibilities such as cleaning tasks and care of younger siblings to children and their peer group. By Euro-American norms, this childrearing environment is "deviant," however, "research to date has shown no sign of increased risks to child survival or psychological development from sibling care in Africa" (LeVine 2004, 163).

The work that children perform socializes responsible and prosocial values, develops sociocognitive and productive skills, and eases social integration. The moral lessons and skills that children learn working and playing are built into social interactions, cultural life, and economic activities (Nsamenang 1992b, 2004). In general, children are not instructed, but they extract the knowledge, skills, and intelligences that exist in their culture (Ogbu 1994).

The condemnation by international advocates that this mode of cognitive socialization and social integration is child abuse underscores the disjunction between Western-led policies and local realities. Western ECD services initiate Africa's children into an educational process by which children, from one developmental stage to another, increasingly gain unfamiliar knowledge and skills, but sink disturbingly into alienation and ignorance of their cultural circumstances and agrarian livelihoods. These service programs and education curricula are deficient on local content and insensible of national skills demands (Nsamenang 2005b). Thus education, beginning with ECD, transforms Africans into participants who are ignorant of their circumstances. This blindness to local circumstances is ECD's weakest point as a player in Africa's modernization. ECD educational and service programs that are either constructed by a specific cultural community (for example, Kohanga Reo National

Trust [2006]) or coconstructed (Pence and Ball 1999; Ball and Pence 2006) are largely untried in Africa.

The African Neighborhood Peer Culture: Better Together

The guidance of child development is organized to permit children's learning together *as participants in cultural communities* (Rogoff 2003, 3, author's emphasis) within the family and peer group. As such, child development can be understood only in light of the cultural ideas and practices that ordain childhood, which change as children attain different phases of social ontogeny and are assigned appropriate cultural tasks with which to gain in responsible intelligence (Nsamenang 2006).

Much of children's learning in the early years is factored into peer group activities, more so than through adults' interactions. Indeed, from early toddlerhood, most African children are not traditionally raised by adults, except through the school system, but instead spend considerable time with peers, some of whom are mentors. Despite a purported naivety of African life, "liberal" ethnotheories and socialization values permit even infants to engage the world by themselves in order to learn and develop (Nsamenang and Lamb 1995). From their interaction with the environment and with each other, especially within the peer culture, children generate, acquire, and control knowledge and competencies, which is not quite so with schooling. As with the Mayan-Ixil children in Guatemala, "the restrictive and inappropriate pedagogy of the schools" is not only "rigid and mechanical" but also "does not allow laughter and play" (Tzay 1998, 19).

Monitoring and Assessment of Development and Learning

Indigenous mechanisms exist to monitor developmental appropriateness and to check and control child abuse—which is what child rights advocates should focus on rather than undermining and condemning a culture's modes of preparing its next generation. African parents monitor child development by applying "unwritten . . . criteria to assess the extent to which children are thriving" (Nsamenang 1992b, 149). They readily take remedial action to correct any perceived deviation from the expected developmental path. The community has the right to monitor and prevent child abuse and cruelty to children.

Africans use social competence to assess a child's responsibility or "intelligence." They keep a mental record of tasks a child successfully completes as a marker of how *tumikila* (intelligent) the child is (Serpell 1993). In addition, parents use evidence that a child has the ability to give and receive social support and to notice and attend to the needs of others as markers of mental and general development (Weisner 1997).

Cognitive Stimulation

In the settings of the peer culture, children are not prodded into learning by intervention; they undertake self-generated activities, therein engaging in self-motivated learning and interstimulation (Nsamenang 2005a). Due to a lack of commercially prepared toys, most African children create their own playthings from objects available in their environment (Nsamenang and Lamb 1994). Children's creations express ingenuity; recognizing them as "products" enhances their self-esteem. It rouses and reinforces children's abstract and spatial thinking as well as their cognitive and creative abilities (Segall et al. 1999). These creations place primacy on activity-based, rather than the commonplace didactic, ECD curricula.

African parents and peer mentors use tacit cultural techniques and strategies that provoke the cognitive faculties, such as not providing direct answers to children's queries. For example, if a child asked for an explanation of what the parent did, a typical parental response would be "Don't you see?" This reply translates into "You're expected to observe, notice, learn, and understand what and how to do what I've done."

Concluding Thoughts

Africa, like the rest of the "majority world," has suffered not simply cultural capture but, more important, the disregard of its worldview and resourcefulness to care for and educate its offspring on its own terms. African approaches to ECD are withering, but nowhere have they entirely disappeared. Africa's ECD programs have shown unusual resilience in the face of extraordinary measures to suppress them into extinction.

Donors, experts, and advocates who prescribe decontextualized "best practices" condemn and exclude Africa's developmental theories and educational praxes from ECD and school curricula, rather than seeking to understand and improve them. The failure to "modernize" Africa as rapidly as the "civilizing mission" anticipated stems largely from the neglect, if not refusal, to blend Africa's indigenous systems with those imported to "civilize" the continent.

Africa and Africans deserve a niche in the ECD enterprise. A rights-based intervention would not set out to replace and exclude, but to improve and enhance Africa's rich but un-Western ECD programs. Africa's systems are culturally functional and serviceable to their owners; they deserve attention and discovery rather than replacement with whatever "superior" system has been formulated elsewhere. A learning posture, which is about how ECD experts may bring themselves into perceiving and performing their role as "first and always a learner" (Ngaujah 2003), can permit such discovery. It fosters opening up and a flexibility that allows theorists, policy planners, and advocates to gain new visions from the participatory mode of Africa's ECD.

Conceptualizing ECD as a context-bound service for Africa's "buds of hope" can permit and focus research on the different facets of the developmental niche: (1) the physical and social settings of early childhood; (2) the culturally regulated customs and practices of child care and child rearing; (3) the psychology of caretakers, teachers, and peer mentors; (4) the positive or negative elements to improve or replace; and (5) how the developmental tasks of the early years prime children for a futuristic adulthood (ontogenetic development and adaptation; Super and Harkness 1986). Conceptually, such research would benefit from visualizing the human newborn as "nothing but expectation, power in search of actualization" (Erny 1973, 23) in the diversity of childhood ecologies and cultures, instead of assuming ethnotheories that apply universally.

We can acknowledge ECD's diversity by initiating and sustaining respectful discourse on how the latest policies or program designs translate into "best practices" across the messy variety of early childhood situations. Reggio Emilia's innovative ECD (New 2005, 3) prompts such discourse. A diversity paradigm not only recognizes and tolerates variety, but also undertakes to improve the circumstances of people in their differentness, instead of insisting on homogenizing or measuring them against standards alien to their circumstances (Nsamenang 2005b), which is what current ECD efforts do in Africa.

The ECD field in Africa is more complex than has been contemplated or theorized. The complexity stems from "a restive intermingling, like strands on a braid, of Eastern and Western legacies, superimposed on a deeply resilient Africanity" (Nsamenang 2005b). In Africa today, multiple realities live together in the same communities and children, imposing their toll. As such, the success of ECD efforts in Africa devolves on fine-tuning or delicately balancing indigenous African ECD, imported ECD, and various layers of stakeholder motives and the apprehensions they engender, as well as the contextualization of the benefits imagined in institutionalizing and educationalizing childhood.

References

African Ministers and Representatives of Ministers. 2005. "Moving Early Childhood Development Forward in Africa." Communiqué of the 3rd African International Conference on Early Childhood Development. Accra, Ghana. May–June.

Ball, J., and A. R. Pence. 2006. *Supporting Indigenous Children's Development: Community-University Partnerships.* Vancouver, BC: UBC Press.

Bram, C. 1998. "A Culturally Oriented Approach for Early Childhood Development." *Early Childhood Matters* 89: 23–29.

Callaghan, L. 1998. "Building on an African Worldview." *Early Childhood Matters* 89: 30–33.

Cameroon. 1981. *Encyclopedie de la Republique Unie du Cameroun* [Encyclopedia of the United Republic of Cameroon]. Douala, Cameroon: Eddy Ness.

Canella, G. S., and R. Viruru. 2004. *Childhood and Postcolonization: Power, Education, and Contemporary Practice.* New York: Routledge Falmer.

Cohen, R. N. 2001. "Foreword." In *In the Web of Cultural Transition: A Tracer Study of Children in Embu District of Kenya,* by A. Njenga and M. Kabiru. The Hague: Bernard van Leer Foundation.

Cole, M. 1996. *Critical Psychology: A Once and Future Discipline.* Cambridge, MA: Belknap Press.

Creekmore, C. 1986. "Misunderstanding Africa." *Psychology Today* 12: 40–45.

Dahlberg, G., P. Moss, and A. Pence. 1999. *Beyond Quality in Early Childhood Education and Care: Postmodern Perspectives.* London: Falmer/Routledge.

Ellis, J. 1978. *West African Families in Great Britain.* London: Routledge.

Erny, P. 1973. *Childhood and Cosmos: The Social Psychology of the Black African Child.* New York: New Perspectives.

Foucault, M. 1980. *Power/Knowledge: Selected Interviews and Other Writings.* Brighton: Harvester.

Kagitcibasi, C. 1996. *Family and Human Development across Cultures: A View from the Other Side.* Hillsdale, NJ: Lawrence Erlbaum.

Kohanga Reo National Trust. 2006. Retrieved November 14, 2006, from http://www.kohanga.ac.nz.

Lanyasunya, A. R., and M. S. Lesolayia. 2001. *El-barta Child and Family Project.* Working Papers in Early Childhood Development 28. The Hague: Bernard van Leer Foundation.

le Roux, W. 2002. *The Challenges of Change: A Tracer Study of San Preschool Children in Botswana.* The Hague: Bernard van Leer Foundation.

LeVine, R. A. 2004. "Challenging Expert Knowledge: Findings from an African Study of Infant Care and Development." In *Childhood and*

Adolescence: Cross-Cultural Perspectives and Applications, ed. U.P. Gielen and J. Roopnarine, 149–65. Westport, CT: Praeger.

Moss, P., and P. Petrie. 2002. *From Children's Services to Children's Spaces: Public Policy, Children, and Childhood*. London: Routledge.

Moumouni, A. 1968. *Education in Africa*. New York: Praeger.

New, R. S. 2005. *Reggio Emilia: Catalyst for Change and Conversation* (ERIC Digest Report No. EDO-PS-00-15). Retrieved August 24, 2006, from http://www.ericdigests.org.

Ngaujah, D. E. 2003. "An Eco-cultural and Social Paradigm for Understanding Human Development: A (West African) Context. Review of A. B. Nsamenang (1992b) *Human Development in Cultural Context*." Unpublished graduate seminar paper (supervised by Dr. Dennis H. Dirks), Biola University, La Mirada, California.

Nsamenang, A. B. 1992a. "Early Childhood Care and Education in Cameroon." In *Day Care in Context: Socio-Cultural Perspectives*, ed. M. E. Lamb, K. J. Sternberg, C. P. Hwang, and A. Broberg. Hillsdale, NJ: Erlbaum.

———. 1992b. *Human Development in Cultural Context: A Third World Perspective*. Newbury Park, CA: Sage.

———. 2002. "Adolescence in Sub-Saharan Africa: An Image Constructed from Africa's Triple Inheritance." In *The World's Youth: Adolescence in Eight Regions of the Globe*, ed. B.B. Brown, R.W. Larson, and T.S. Saraswathi, 61–104. Cambridge: Cambridge University Press.

———. 2004. *Cultures of Human Development and Education: Challenge to Growing up African*. New York: Nova.

———. 2005a. "Education in African Family Traditions." In *Encyclopedia of Applied Developmental Science*, ed. C. Fisher and R. Lerner, 61–62. Thousand Oaks, CA: Sage.

———. 2005b. "Educational Development and Knowledge Flow: Local and Global Forces in Human Development in Africa." *Higher Education Policy* 18: 275–88.

———. 2005c. "The Intersection of Traditional African Education with School Learning." In *Psychology: An Introduction*, ed. L. Swartz, C. de la Rey, and N. Duncan, 327–37. Cape Town: Oxford University Press.

———. 2006. "Human Ontogenesis: An Indigenous African View on Development and Intelligence." *International Journal of Psychology* 41 (4): 293–97.

Nsamenang, A. B., and M. E. Lamb. 1994. "Socialization of Nso Children in the Bamenda Grassfields of Northwest Cameroon." In *Cross-Cultural Roots of Minority Child Development*, ed. P. M. Greenfield and R. R. Cocking, 133–46. Hillsdale, NJ: Erlbaum.

———. 1995. "The Force of Beliefs: How the Parental Values of the Nso of Northwest Cameroon Shape Children's Progress Towards Adult Models." *Journal of Applied Developmental Psychology* 16 (4): 613–27.

Ogbu, J. U. 1994. "From Cultural Differences to Differences in Cultural Frames of Reference." In *Cross-Cultural Minority Child Development*, ed. P. M. Greenfield and R. R. Cocking, 365–91. Hillsdale, NJ: Erlbaum.

Ogunaike, O. A., and R. F. Houser, Jr. 2002. "Yoruba Toddlers' Engagement in Errands and Cognitive Performance on the Yoruba Mental Subscale." *International Journal of Behavioral Development* 26 (2): 145–53.

Pence, A. 2004. "ECD Policy Development and Implementation in Africa." Early Childhood and Family Policy Series 9. Paris: UNESCO.

Pence, A., and J. Ball. 1999. "Two Sides of an Eagle's Feather: Co-constructing ECCD Training Curricula in University Partnerships with Canadian First Nations Communities." In *Theory, Policy, and Practice in Early Childhood Services*, ed. H. Penn, 36–47. Buckingham, UK: Open University Press.

Pence, A. R., and K. Marfo, eds. 2004. "Capacity Building for Early Childhood Education in Africa" [Special Issue]. *International Journal of Educational Policy, Research, and Practice* 5 (3).

Piaget, J. 1952. *The Origins of Intelligence in Children*. New York: International Universities Press.

Rinaldi, C. 2005. *In Dialogue with Reggio Emilia*. London: Routledge.

Rogoff, B. 2003. *The Cultural Nature of Human Development*. Oxford: Oxford University Press.

Rose, N. 1999. *Powers of Freedom: Reframing Political Thought*. Cambridge: Cambridge University Press.

Segall, M. H., P. R. Dasen, J. W. Berry, and Y. H. Poortinga. 1999. *Human Behavior in Global Perspective*. Boston: Allyn and Bacon.

Serpell, R. 1993. *The Significance of Schooling: Life-Journeys in an African Society*. Cambridge: Cambridge University Press.

———. 1994. "An African Social Ontogeny: Review of A. Bame Nsamenang (1992b) *Human Development in Cultural Context*." *Cross-Cultural Psychology Bulletin* 28 (1): 17–21.

Sharp, E. 1970. *The African Child*. Westport, CT: Negro University Press.

Smale, J. 1998. "Culturally Appropriate Approaches in ECD." *Early Childhood Matters* 89: 3–5.

Super, C. M., and S. Harkness. 1986. "The Developmental Niche: A Conceptualization at the Interface of Child and Culture." *International Journal of Behavioral Development* 9: 545–69.

Swadener, B. B., and K. Mutua. Forthcoming. "Decolonizing Performances: Deconstructing the Global Postcolonial." In *Handbook of Critical, Indigenous Inquiry*, ed. N. K. Denzin, Y. S. Lincoln, and L. T. Smith. Thousand Oaks, CA: Sage.

Tzay, C. 1998. "Guatemala: Working with the Mayan-Ixil People." *Early Childhood Matters* 89: 18–22.

Weisner, T. S. 1997. "Support for Children and the African Family Crisis." In *African Families and the Crisis of Social Change*, ed. T. S. Weisner, C. Bradley, and C. P. Kilbride, 20–44. Westport, CT: Bergin and Garvey.

Zimba, R. F. 2002. "Indigenous Conceptions of Childhood Development and Social Realities in Southern Africa." In *Between Cultures and Biology: Perspectives on Ontogenetic Development*, ed. H. Keller, Y. P. Poortinga, and A. Scholmerish, 89–115. Cambridge: Cambridge University Press.

Zimba, R. F., and B. Otaala. 1995. *The Family in Transition: A Study of Childrearing Practices and Beliefs among the Nama of the Karas and Hardap Regions of Namibia*. Windhoek: UNICEF Namibia and the University of Namibia.

CHAPTER 8

Fathering: The Role of Men in Raising Children in Africa—Holding Up the Other Half of the Sky

Linda M. Richter and Robert Morrell

"It takes a great deal of effort to separate a mother from her newborn infant; by contrast, it usually takes a fair amount of effort to get a father to be involved with his," states Francis Fukuyama (1999, 101). According to Fukuyama, marriage is the social arrangement through which society puts pressure on men to support mothers and children. These sentiments, though true of some fathers, preclude men from child rearing just as declarations of female reproductive and child care destiny cause women to feel excluded from the work world. Such views are easily turned into self-fulfilling prophecies. If we aren't committed to providing affordable, good quality child care to enable women to be economically active, then we ensure that they will have truncated careers. As we shall show in this chapter, men are an essential part of a child's world; men need to hold up half of the child's sky. If we restrict reproductive and child health care, preschool services, and other child-oriented provisions to women, men are unlikely to involve themselves in efforts to improve their children's health and well-being.

Fatherhood is a social role—especially in Africa. In the Western world it is generally accepted that a man becomes a father when he impregnates a woman. This biological criterion of fatherhood, though, is under increasing stress. Some biological fathers don't act like fathers and don't support their children; new technologies make it possible to create human life without impregnation; a man does not become a "father" if his sperm, from a sperm bank, is used to fertilize a woman's ova; and cloning is rapidly becoming a possibility. In contrast, the isiZulu word *Baba*—used also in other languages—both denotes a social definition of fatherhood and connects us to a deeper, more archetypal view of what, in many cultures, is expected of a man called father (Richter and Morrell 2005).

In much of Africa, child rearing is the shared responsibility of the extended family. A man is a father because he has responsibility for a child (Nsamenang 1987). Through collective parenting, a mother's sister is also a child's mother, as is a father's brother also a child's father. These other men are addressed as father and are expected to behave in a manner deserving of being called father (Mkhize 2005).

Collective fatherhood is characteristic of traditional African society, but social fatherhood has become characteristic of life in cities and towns, as well. A man may father a child but never live in the same home with her or him, or he may live with a woman and care for her children from another man while supporting the children of his brother in a different household. In varying circumstances, many men provide father care and support for children who may not be their biological offspring (Mkhize 2004). The African notion of father, then, is a man who enacts the responsibility of caring for and protecting a child.

Patterns of migrant labor in the colonial period and the disruptions and displacements caused by war and famine have made it difficult for many men in Africa and in other developing areas of the world to meet the societal expectation of a father as an economic provider. In some cases the shame of being unable to provide for families has driven men away from their children to seek solace in drink and other women (Ramphele 2002). Among some younger men, respect for fathers, as well as a father's own sense of responsibility for his children, have diminished. It is now tragically common for a young man to turn his back on his pregnant girlfriend and the child they share.

Absent Fathers

Fathers are absent in two ways: for a variety of reasons, they are absent from the homes where their children live; and they are absent from the health, social, and educational services designed to improve the well-being of their children.

Especially in southern Africa, because migrant labor systems have been in place for many generations, a large proportion of men are absent from the households where their children live. In addition, because of injury and violence, men have higher death rates than same-aged women. Figure 8.1 shows the percentage of fathers who are deceased or absent, according to country-specific demographic and health surveys (Posel and Devey 2005). As indicated, fathers are absent from nearly a third of households in several southern African countries and from more than half of all households in Namibia and South Africa. In South Africa, data from the *2005 General Household Survey* (Statistics South Africa 2005) are similar. While the fathers of 14.5 percent of children under 15 years are reported to be deceased, 46.5 percent of fathers are alive but not living in the same household with their children. Many of these absent men live in compounds, shacks, and with other families in the towns and cities to which they have migrated to look for work.

This sort of data does not show the proportion of absent fathers who support their children or the number for whom their absence from the household is an unavoidable consequence of migrant labor. Data from

Figure 8.1. Fathers Absent and Deceased

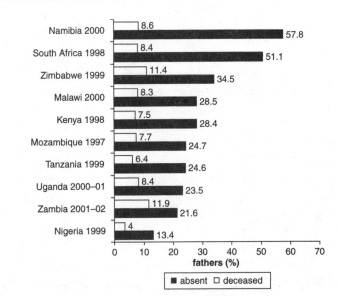

Source: Demographic and health surveys country data in Posel and Devey (2005).

Table 8.1. Fathers Alive and Resident by Expenditure Patterns in South Africa

Expenditure	Fathers in households (%)
R400–R799	37
R800–R1,199	49
R1,200–R1,799	57
R1,800–R2,499	65
R2,500–R4,999	74
R5,000–R9,999	84
R10,000+	93

Source: Desmond and Desmond 2005, based on data from the *2002 General Household Survey.*
Note: $1 = R7 as at July 2006.

the *2002 General Household Survey* (Desmond and Desmond 2005) in table 8.1 shows the relationship between the wealth of a household and the presence of the father. The better off a household as judged by its level of expenditure, the greater the likelihood that a father will live with his family. There is no indication of the direction of effect—that is, households might be poorer because there is no father, or fathers in poorer households might leave home because of poverty, either to look for work or for other reasons.

During interviews with migrant mine workers in Johannesburg, Rabe (2005) found that many men were working far from home to support their families, including their own children. In addition, their conceptions of a father were of a man who cares for and gives financial support to his family, refrains from unacceptable behavior such as beating children, and guides his children and sets a good example for them.

It is also clear that many men, even when they live in the same household as their children, are largely absent from many parts of their children's lives. It is uncommon to see men in well-baby clinics, preschool centers, or schools, either accompanying their children or discussing their children's health, well-being, or education with the relevant authorities. With changing gender roles and men's increasing involvement in home and child care, men are beginning to grumble that the reason for their absence is that they are not made welcome in services for children.

Health providers, program facilitators, and teachers speak to women, report feeling uncomfortable with men, and have failed, up to now, to adapt their approach and materials for male as well as female caregivers (Engle, Beardshaw, and Loftin 2005). The neglect and exclusion of men from programs and services for young children, and the urgent need to include them, has been very evident in the aftermath of AIDS-related deaths and the crisis of care for children associated with high adult mortality (Chirwa 2002; Desmond and Desmond 2005).

Why Is It Important to Involve Men in the Care of Young Children?

Tom Beardshaw of Fathers Direct, an advocacy organization in the United Kingdom, has outlined the dependencies between men and women and how they affect the well-being of children. Beardshaw (2004) asserts that men determine resources and decisions that critically influence the health and education of children, such as whether or not a woman will have health care during pregnancy, whether she breastfeeds, the adequacy of weaning foods she has to give to her child, the timing of a child's entry and retention in school, and the like. Even though most of these decisions rest with men, a man's involvement in the early care of his children, and his continued close engagement with them during childhood, is largely determined by women. Wives, mothers, and other women in the community function as gatekeepers who either invite men in and encourage them to take responsibility for children's care, or close men out and make them feel incompetent in matters of children and less of a man for getting involved (Beardshaw 2004).

In addition to the fact that in many societies, especially in Africa, men make many of the important decisions affecting the health, well-being, and care of young children, the empirical research indicates that men are good for children—and children are good for men. The love and responsibility a man feels for a child who looks up to him can be a strong motivator for him to work hard and to avoid hazards to his health (Richter 2005).

Men bring direct and indirect benefits to children. Direct benefits include decision making and resource allocation in favor of children, as previously described. Households with men also have more resources available for potential allocation to benefit the children. It is almost universally true that two-parent households, where fathers are present, are better off than single-mother households (Jarrett 1994). Not only do men generally earn more than women, and therefore bring more income into the household if they are employed, but they may also be able to access more resources for children in the community because of their prestige and status as men.

Men may also be able to avert harm to children. Guma and Henda (2004) suggest that children in households where men are present are much less likely to be abused or exploited by other men in the community than are children who live only with women. A father who acknowledges and lives with his children may confer social value on them, especially in societies with a very high absence of fathers. Fathers also have indirect effects on children through their support for mothers. For example, women who live with partners tend to report that they are less stressed about child care. The benefits of fathers in children's lives, particularly in their early years, might accrue particularly through the supportive influence of a partner on maternal behavior (Clarke-Stewart 1978; Richter 2005).

Studies show a close relationship between financial resources and the presence or absence of a father, as illustrated in table 8.1. A father's presence or absence has a multiplier effect: if fathers are absent, the household is financially worse off and vice versa.

Children are not invariably better off in male-headed households, because men's decisions about how resources are allocated in a household and between members of the household do not always benefit children. In households with the same level of financial resources, men tend to allocate less money to food, school fees, and clothes than do women who have charge of money (Kennedy and Peters 1992). Townsend (2002, 270) contends that "children are not necessarily disadvantaged by the absence of their father, but they are disadvantaged when they belong to a household without access to the social position, labor, and financial support that is provided by men."

Direct effects are exerted on children by the father's presence, by the amount of time men spend with children, and in the kinds of activities in which men engage children. With respect to men's presence in the household and proximity between men and children, for example, a South African study found that nonbiological resident fathers spent more time with their children, doing activities such as homework, than biological fathers who did not live with their children (Anderson et al. 1999). This difference emphasizes the importance of social, or "responsible," fatherhood in comparison to mere biological fatherhood, as well as the importance of men's presence in the daily lives of their children.

Men are generally characterized as "deficient women," spending less time with children and in child care tasks than women (Population Council 2001). Michael Lamb and his colleagues (1985) have refined the hours-spent approach to looking at men's involvement in children's lives. They propose three categories of fathering behavior: engagement or interaction between father and child; accessibility or availability; and responsibility for the child's care. Responsibility—as opposed to being delegated by mothers to perform child-related activities—is the category where men seem to fall short most often. Women accuse fathers of not planning for and anticipating children's needs, even when they are prepared to take on tasks of child care.

Men are usually defined, and self-defined, as breadwinners and providers; they have generally low levels of engagement in child care, especially when children are young (Lewis and Lamb 2004). An ethnographic study published in the early 1970s summarized results from 186 cultures and found that fewer than 5 percent of the men regularly took care of their preschool children (Barry and Paxson 1971). But gender roles and work patterns are changing, which is affecting the amount of time men spend with children. For example, a man's proportion of child care rises when his woman partner works outside the home. Unfortunately though, this is not necessarily because men spend more time with children, but because working women usually spend less time with children, thus leaving children with less parental time overall (Pleck 1997). Clearly men need to take more responsibility for children: planning, anticipating, responding to, and following up on children's needs.

Despite men's lower levels of involvement with children, substantial literature indicates that men have direct positive psychological and educational effects on children. In summary:

- Father presence contributes to cognitive development, intellectual functioning, and school achievement (Amato 1998). In South Africa, for example, Mboya and Nesengani (1999) found that boys who lived in father-present households had higher academic achievement than boys who lived in father-absent households.
- Father presence also contributes to emotional well-being (Johnson 1996). Children are less likely to manifest emotional and behavioral problems if their father is available to them; father presence shows a strong relationship with higher self-esteem among girls (Hunt and Hunt 1977).
- Father absence or lack of contact with fathers appears to have its most dramatic effects on male children. Father availability tends to have a modulating effect on boys' aggressive tendencies, so that boys who grow up with a father tend to be less aggressive than boys without this male guidance (Seltzer and Bianchi 1988).

The literature on the availability and involvement of fathers is highly consistent with respect to showing benefits for children in school performance, reduced aggressive behaviors in boys, and increased self-esteem in girls (Palkowitz 2002). Some studies suggest that the fathers' psychological care and "emotional generosity" (expressiveness and intimacy) has the greatest long-term implications for children's development (Grossman, Pollack, and Golding 1988).

What Do Children Say about Fathers?

There is very little literature on children's views of fathers, and none in Africa that we could find. A recent South African study among 10- to 12-year-old rural and urban children uncovered some surprising findings (Richter and Smith 2005). Children generally reinforced the customary notion of fathers as providers and protectors, but they also discerned, and appreciated, a role for men and fathers in their lives that goes beyond provision of resources. Children unanimously long for and cherish the time, interest, and energy that men put into them and their activities.

This message is important at a time when many men are unable to provide economic support for children as a result of being unemployed or without a livelihood. It is widely believed that at least one reason men abandon their wives and children is because of the stress, shame, and loss of esteem they experience when they cannot provide financially for their families (Ramphele and Richter 2005).

Children confirmed that many men in the extended family fulfill fatherly functions in their lives, particularly in rural areas. One child said: "Me and my brother (and the rest of the family besides my mother) call him (the man I think of as my father) *Ntata omdala*, which means older father. He is the head of the family, therefore he sees to everyone's problems." Children also observed and valued the domestic work their fathers do in the home and what household and child care tasks men do specifically for their children. For many children, this is their primary confirmation that their father loves and cares for them. For example: "My father's name is Thulani. He is a kind man because every day when he comes from work he helps my mother with dishes and cooking food, if my mother is not well. He earns not much but he can do everything at home for us" (Richter and Smith 2005).

Children also appreciate the support their fathers give to their mothers and the many ways in which fathers make the life of the household better. One child said about his father: "I call him uncle because he is not married to my mother, yet he is a father to me in all respects. He is a nice person to my family. My mother calls him Nicolas. Though he lives in town he supports our family in every possible way. He buys food for us and also gives my mother our transport money. He buys us proper school uniforms. He plays a very important role in my family. When my mother is not okay we just wish father could come. When he comes we can see my mother's smiling face. He is a loving person. When he comes home he hugs and kisses us but not the way he kisses mom, he holds her for a long time. I can see that they are in love. He is a responsible man. He cleans the yard when he is at home and he makes sure that I am there to see how it is done. He teaches me how to say a prayer every night, he says that the prayer is the best way to communicate with God. He helps me with my homework, he is my best friend, I talk, I play, I laugh with him. I will be happy if he marries my mother then builds the house to accommodate the whole family. He is my hero" (Richter and Smith 2005).

Some children also reported neglect and cruelty from their fathers, as well as their father's drunken and sometimes violent, deceitful, and inconsiderate behavior toward their mothers. For example: "I don't like it when my dad smokes, sleeps, watches TV, or doesn't want to go anywhere . . . and when he's lazy and doesn't want to do any work, and also when he goes places that my mom doesn't know about." Another child said: "My father hurt me in my back and I feel unhappy. And he eats meat but we don't eat meat every day. He doesn't want me to hurt anyone, but he hurts me, and I feel very, very worried about him. He doesn't want us to visit other places and I don't want to do anything wrong. My father hurts us and we feel unhappy, and we have started to stay away from him. I feel so very, very sad" (Richter and Smith 2005).

Men's Care and Protection of Young Children

Several articles in the United Nations Convention on the Rights of the Child promote shared parenting. Article 7 proclaims that every child has the right to know and be cared for by his or her parents. Article 18 sets out the obligations that states have to recognize the responsibilities of both parents for the care and socialization of their children and to support both parents in their child-rearing responsibilities (Engle, Beardshaw, and Loftin 2005). In March 2004, the United Nations Commission on the Status of Women made a strong call for increased male involvement in achieving gender equality and in supporting children's growth and development. Statements include the need to "create and improve training and education programs to enhance awareness and knowledge among men and women on their roles as parents, legal guardians, and caregivers and the importance of sharing family responsibilities, and include fathers as well as mothers in programs that teach infant and child care and development" (United Nations Commission on the Status of Women 2004, 2). The International Fatherhood Summit in Oxford in 2003 brought together experts, researchers, program staff with field experience, and fathers to discuss current knowledge and practice on how to support father-child relationships (Brown and Barker 2004). In an overview of work done, Engle, Beardshaw, and Loftin (2005, 295–96) conclude that:

> programs around the world that have made conscious efforts to support father involvement include reproductive health and teen pregnancy prevention, broad-based perinatal services for children, infant and child health and nutrition, early years services, parenting education, and employment programs that support men's relationships with their children. There is an increasing emphasis on involving fathers in children's learning (for example, in schools) and on working with the fathers of young offenders. Increasingly, domestic violence and substance abuse programs are recognizing the value of engaging men in their parenting role. There has been a lot of work with fathers in prison (which is beginning to extend to the resettlement of offenders), as well as work with refugee fathers and some resettlement support for fathers returning from war.

Although the movement to include men and fathers in the care and protection of children has tended to be poorly funded and has operated at the margins of mainstream services, there are signs that it is growing, such as through several national initiatives in South Africa, including the South African Men's Forum and Men as Partners (Peacock and Botha 2005). The United Nations Children's Fund (UNICEF), in particular, has accumulated experience from innovative programs around the world (Engle, Beardshaw, and Loftin 2005). In 2002, 10 of the 73 countries with parenting programs reported activities to enhance the role of fathers in children's care. By 2003, 28 countries reported activities that specifically focused on fathers. Among the African countries, the activities included parenting initiatives operated out of preschools and community-based child care centers (for example, in Burkina Faso, Burundi, Cameroon, and Ghana). Others have collected data through surveys and focus groups on ways to increase father participation and involvement, as has occurred in The Gambia, Namibia, South Africa, and Togo (Engle, Beardshaw, and Loftin 2005). In South Africa, UNICEF is a partner in the Fatherhood Project (Human Sciences Research Council of South Africa n.d.), an action research program that works through advocacy, information dissemination, and research to increase the engagement of men in children's health and well-being.

A variety of approaches have been used to draw men into care for children. For example, in a project in The Gambia, mixed teams of men and women—including community leaders, health workers, and fathers—work together to increase breastfeeding. A community-based health program in Malawi that stresses the role of men in supporting children's survival, growth, and development effected a significant increase in fathers' reported involvement with young children.

What Still Needs to Be Done?

In *Baba: Men and Fatherhood in South Africa*, Tom Beardshaw (2005) lays out an international agenda to advance the issues of fatherhood in research, policy, and programs, particularly in the areas of the labor market, child health and education, law, and social services. Beardshaw argues that health services have a profound impact on fathering behavior, primarily through the inclusion or exclusion of men from reproductive services, which communicates powerful messages about society's expectations of fathering behavior. The birth of a child is one of the best opportunities to engage with a man about being a father, a time when most men have high aspirations for their role as a father and of their child and family. This occasion could provide the opening for a continuum of involvement through which men, as well as women, receive information about child care; hygiene; disease prevention, recognition, and treatment; diet and nutrition; access to health services; and other information that all parents need in order to take responsibility for their children's health.

Education, says Beardshaw (2005), has the potential to influence young people's thinking about the roles of mothers and fathers. In many countries, fathers are the critical decision makers regarding which children receive what length and quality of education. In his view, some important interventions in education would include portraying accurately in all aspects of the curriculum the diversity of fatherhood, including responsible fathers who are active participants in their children's lives; encouraging both boys and girls to enroll in courses on home and child care; and training education staff to include fathers and mothers in all communication and to inform fathers and mothers of the value of their involvement in their children's education—formally at school and informally at home. It is important to realize that involving men in their children's education can also benefit fathers. As an example, for teenage fathers with low educational attainment, their engagement with their child's schooling can be a route into their own adult and further education.

Effort is needed in many areas including programs for health, education, and labor to involve men as they hold up their half of the sky. However, there are encouraging signs from men, and increasingly also from women, of a greater motivation for men to be involved with children. Innovative programs are beginning to show how involvement can be increased, high-level policies are starting to create an enabling environment, and research is showing where—and why—greater effort is required. According to Engle, Beardshaw, and Loftin (2005, 302):

> The barriers to fathers becoming involved, confident, and competent as parents are manifold. These barriers exist within institutions and in virtually all policies that impact on family life. Gender stereotypes of fathers as uninterested, uncaring, and incapable are reflected in the practices of institutions such as health and education programs that target only mothers, even when fathers are present and active in their children's lives and are making key decisions affecting children's futures. Developing strategies to include fathers in such programs, as recommended by the Commission on the Status of Women, constitutes a vital first step in maximizing the potential of fathers to improve the lives of children and to promote the shared responsibility for children between mothers and fathers.

The South African Fatherhood Project advocates a few simple messages to initiate fatherhood activities in countries, in communities, and in programs. These messages include,

- There is no such thing as a fatherless child. Every child had or has a father somewhere, even if the child doesn't live with its father or see him very often. Many men can play the role of father to a child, including grandfathers, uncles, stepfathers, foster fathers, older brothers, cousins, family friends, and men who have responsibility to care for children.
- Children need and want the care of men. Children in all cultures value the idea of a father or a father figure. Children are usually taught to respect men, and children want to spend time with men and learn from them. Children also have great fun with men through adventurous and boisterous play and by being involved in men's work and activities.
- If men can't live with their children, they can still keep in contact with them. Children appreciate hearing from their fathers and knowing that their fathers care about them.
- If men can't support their children or provide materially for their needs, they can still give them love, affection, and support. Fathers are important sources of guidance and help to children.

- Men who live with their children need to be kind to them and not hurt them. Men are so much bigger and stronger than women and children. Their strength should be used to protect children from harm.
- Children need the care and protection of men. A man can make all the difference to a child's life by preventing or stopping neglect or abuse perpetrated by other people. Men need to protect children in the neighborhood, at school, on public transport systems, and in the home.
- Young fathers benefit from staying in contact with their children. They make more effort to protect themselves from harm and to be economically active as a result of knowing that the child they love depends on them.

Men are good for children, and children are good for men. But many fathers abandon their children or fail to provide for their safety or their emotional and financial needs. Efforts to improve the care, protection, and education of children need to acknowledge the many ways that fathers can be involved in their children's lives and the many men who can provide fatherly support and protection for children. It is crucial to adjust services so that they draw men into children's care, health, and education by developing training materials that address men's interests and concerns, by counseling women on the benefits of including men in parenting, and by reaching out with men's forums into the community, where men feel more at ease.

References

Amato, P. 1998. "More Than Money? Men's Contributions to Their Children's Lives." In *Men in Families. When Do They Get Involved? What Difference Do They Make?* ed. A. Booth and A. Crouter, 241–77. Mahwah, NJ: Lawrence Erlbaum.

Anderson, K., H. Kaplan, D. Lam, and J. Lancaster. 1999. "Parental Care by Genetic Fathers and Stepfathers II: Reports by Xhosa High School Students." *Evolution and Human Behavior* 20: 433–51.

Barry, H., and L. Paxson. 1971. "Infancy and Early Childhood: Cross-Cultural Codes 2." *Ethnology* 10: 466–508.

Beardshaw, T. 2004. "From Here to Paternity." Paper delivered at the Fatherhood Conference, Durban, South Africa. November 24. Retrieved November 19, 2006, from http://www.hsrc.ac.za/fatherhood/.

———. 2005. "Taking Forward Work with Men in Families." In *Baba: Men and Fatherhood in South Africa*, ed. L. Richter and R. Morrell, 306–16. Cape Town: HSRC Press.

Brown, J., and G. Barker. 2004. "Global Diversity and Trends in Patterns of Fatherhood." In *Supporting Fathers: Contributions from the International Fatherhood Summit 2003.* The Hague: Bernard van Leer Foundation.

Chirwa, W. 2002. "Social Exclusion and Inclusion: Challenges to Orphan Care in Malawi." *Nordic Journal of African Studies* 11: 93–113.

Clarke-Stewart, K. 1978. "And Daddy Makes Three: The Father's Impact on Mother and Young Child." *Child Development* 49: 466–78.

Desmond, C., and C. Desmond. 2005. "HIV/AIDS and the Crisis of Care for Children." In *Baba: Men and Fatherhood in South Africa,* ed. L. Richter and R. Morrell, 226–36. Cape Town: HSRC Press.

Engle, P., T. Beardshaw, and C. Loftin. 2005. "The Child's Right to Shared Parenting." In *Baba: Men and Fatherhood in South Africa,* ed. L. Richter and R. Morrell, 293–305. Cape Town: HSRC Press.

Fukuyama, F. 1999. *The Great Disruption: Human Nature and the Reconstitution of the Social Order.* New York: Free Press.

Grossman, F., W. Pollack, and E. Golding. 1988. "Fathers and Children: Predicting the Quality and Quantity of Fathering." *Developmental Psychology* 24: 82–91.

Guma, M., and N. Henda. 2004. "The Socio-Cultural Context of Child Abuse: A Betrayal of Trust." In *Sexual Abuse of Young Children in Southern Africa,* ed. L. Richter, A. Dawes, and C. Higson-Smith, 95–109. Cape Town: HSRC Press.

Human Sciences Research Council of South Africa. n.d. "The Fatherhood Project." Retrieved September 8, 2006, from http://www.hsrc.ac.za/fatherhood/.

Hunt, L., and J. Hunt. 1977. "Race, Daughters, and Father Loss: Does Absence Make the Girl Grow Stronger?" *Social Problems* 25: 90–102.

Jarrett, R. 1994. "Living Poor: Family Life among Single-Parent, African-American Women." *Social Problems* 41: 30–49.

Johnson, D. J. 1996. *Father Presence Matters: A Review of the Literature.* Philadelphia: National Center on Fathers and Families.

Kennedy, E., and P. Peters. 1992. "Influence of Gender and Head of Household on Food Security, Health, and Nutrition." *World Development* 20: 1077–85.

Lamb, M., J. Pleck, E. Charnov, and J. Levine. 1985. "Paternal Behavior in Humans." *American Psychologist* 25: 883–94.

Lewis, C., and M. Lamb. 2004. "Fathers: The Research Perspective." In *Supporting Fathers: Contributions from the International Fatherhood Summit 2003.* The Hague: Bernard van Leer Foundation.

Mboya, M., and R. Nesengani. 1999. "Migrant Labor in South Africa: A Comparative Analysis of the Academic Achievement of Father-Present and Father-Absent Adolescents." *Adolescence* 34: 763–67.

Mkhize, N. 2004. "Who Is a Father?" *ChildrenFIRST* 56: 3–8.

———. 2005. "African Traditions and the Social, Economic, and Moral Dimensions of Fatherhood." In *Baba: Men and Fatherhood in South Africa*, ed. L. Richter and R. Morrell, 183–98. Cape Town: HSRC Press.

Nsamenang, B. 1987. "A West African Perspective." In *The Father's Role: Cross-Cultural Perspectives*, ed. M. Lamb, 273–93. Hillsdale, NJ: Lawrence Erlbaum.

Palkowitz, R. 2002. *Involved Fathering and Men's Adult Development: Provisional Balances.* Mahwah, NJ: Lawrence Erlbaum.

Peacock, D., and M. Botha. 2005. "The New Gender Platforms and Fatherhood." In *Baba: Men and Fatherhood in South Africa*, ed. L. Richter and R. Morrell, 281–92. Cape Town: HSRC Press.

Pleck, E. 1997. "Paternal Involvement: Levels, Sources, and Consequences." In *The Role of the Father in Child Development* 3rd ed., ed. M. Lamb, 66–103. New York: Wiley.

Population Council. 2001. *The Unfinished Transition. Gender Equity: Sharing the Responsibilities of Parenthood.* A Population Council Issues Paper. Population Council, New York.

Posel, D., and R. Devey. 2005. "The Demographics of Fatherhood in South Africa: An Analysis of Survey Data, 1993–2002." In *Baba: Men and Fatherhood in South Africa*, ed. L. Richter and R. Morrell, 58–81. Cape Town: HSRC Press.

Rabe, M. 2005. "Being a Father in a Man's World: The Experience of Goldmine Workers." In *Baba: Men and Fatherhood in South Africa*, ed. L. Richter and R. Morrell, 250–64. Cape Town: HSRC Press.

Ramphele, M. 2002. *Steering by the Stars: Being Young in South Africa.* Cape Town: Tafelberg Publishers.

Ramphele, M., and L. Richter, L. 2005. "Migrancy, Family Dissolution, and Fatherhood." In *Baba: Men and Fatherhood in South Africa*, ed. L. Richter and R. Morrell, 73–81. Cape Town: HSRC Press.

Richter, L. 2005. "The Importance of Fathering for Children." In *Baba: Men and Fatherhood in South Africa*, ed. L. Richter and R. Morrell, 53–69. Cape Town: HSRC Press.

Richter, L., and R. Morrell, eds. 2005. *Baba: Men and Fatherhood in South Africa.* Cape Town: HSRC Press.

Richter, L., and W. Smith. 2005. "Children's Views of Fathers." In *Baba: Men and Fatherhood in South Africa*, ed. L. Richter and R. Morrell, 155–72. Cape Town: HSRC Press.

Seltzer, J., and S. Bianchi. 1988. "Children's Contact with Absent Parents." *Journal of Marriage and the Family* 50: 663–77.

Statistics South Africa. 2002. *General Household Survey, 2002.* Pretoria: Statistics South Africa.

————. 2005. *General Household Survey, 2005.* Pretoria: Statistics South Africa.

Townsend, N. 2002. "Cultural Contexts of Father Involvement." In *Handbook of Father Involvement: Multidisciplinary Perspectives,* ed. C. Tamis-LeMonda and N. Cabrera, 249–77. Mahwah, NJ: Erlbaum.

United Nations Commission on the Status of Women. 2004. "The Role of Men and Boys in Achieving Gender Equality: Agreed Conclusions." Retrieved September 8, 2006, from http://www.un.org/womenwatch/daw/csw/csw48/ac-men-auv.pdf.

Policy Development

CHAPTER 9

ECD Policy: A Comparative Analysis in Ghana, Mauritius, and Namibia

J. K. A. Boakye, Stella Etse, Madeez Adamu-Issah, Medha Devi Moti, Juditha Leketo Matjila, and Shamani-Jeffrey Shikwambi

Against a backdrop of renewed international commitment to early childhood development (ECD) as an important part of *Education for All*, the Association for the Development of Education in Africa's (ADEA) Working Group on ECD (WGECD) initiated a study of ECD policy processes and implementation in Ghana, Mauritius, and Namibia under the directorship of Kate Torkington (2001). The three African countries were each at different stages of developing a cross-sectoral policy focused on the holistic development of young children. Namibia's cabinet had approved the policy in 1996 and it was published the same year; Mauritius approved its policy in 1998 and had started implementing it; and Ghana's cabinet had not yet approved the draft policy. This chapter provides an overview of findings from those case studies, the most recent update of the policy developments in each country, and the implications for the evolution of ECD or ECCD (early childhood care and development) policies in other African countries.

The three country reports presented here follow a common outline: a brief history of the situation before the policy was demanded; the factors that prompted its formulation; the policy development/formulation process, including problems encountered and their solutions; the main issues captured in the policy; implementation issues (mechanisms proposed, in place, or used); the current situation; and lessons learned.

Ghana

Brief History: The Situation before the Policy Was Demanded

Ghana, formerly the Gold Coast, gained political independence from Britain in 1957; it was the first member country to ratify the United Nations (UN) Convention on the Rights of the Child (CRC) on February 5, 1990. Though public interest in ECD started in the 19th century when, in 1843, the Basel Missionaries first introduced day nurseries alongside their primary school classes, government directives on ECD were only given after 1960, mainly in the form of acts, reports of special commissions, decrees, and laws that focused more on social welfare and cognitive aspects instead of on the holistic development of young children. The current, holistic national early childhood care and development policy (Ghana 2004) was initiated in 1993 and promulgated in August 2004.

Factors That Prompted Development of a Policy for ECD

Five major factors prompted policy development. The first was increased awareness of the poor situation of young children and the urgent need to address it. For example, about 90 percent of children aged 0–6, especially those from rural and/or poor areas, did not have access to early childhood services. The second factor was the internal obligation to ensure the survival, growth, development, and protection of children, as envisaged in Ghana's 1992 constitution (Ghana 1992), the Children's Act of 1998 (Ghana 1998), and bylaws of metropolitan, municipal, and district assemblies. The third factor was the obligation to meet the tenets of the international conventions and treaties Ghana had ratified, including CRC. The fourth and fifth factors were, respectively, the recognition of ECD as a strategy for poverty reduction and the need for policy to streamline the activities of all ECD stakeholders.

The Policy Development/Formulation Process: Problems Encountered and How They Were Solved

A national seminar on ECD held in Accra in November 1993 with the support of the Ghana National Commission on Children (GNCC), United Nations Children's Fund (UNICEF), the Ghana National Association of Teachers, and the Danish National Federation of Early

Childhood and Youth Education served as the watershed for the current ECCD policy development. The seminar created a national awareness of the poor conditions of young children and the need to correct them. A task force of representatives from relevant sector ministries and stakeholders was appointed immediately to collate ECD information from their organizations. They were trained in policy drafting in a five-day workshop organized by the GNCC and facilitated by Kate Torkington, an ECD consultant. A first draft was eventually produced in 1995.

The problem of deciding on a coordinating body for ECD caused a delay of almost five years, but was solved eventually by placing it under the GNCC in the Office of the President. The draft policy was then subjected to stakeholders' reviews throughout the country. In December 2000, when the final draft was sent to Ghana's cabinet for consideration, the political administration changed. The new government created the Ministry of Women and Children's Affairs (MOWAC) and placed the GNCC under it as a department. Ghana's cabinet studied the draft policy, made the relevant changes, and eventually adopted the policy in August 2004 (Ghana 2004).

The factors that caused the delay in formulating the policy included a rather long preparation time by the task force, frequent draft rewrites, submission of the drafts to stakeholders' reviews throughout the country, protracted indecision over which ministry should coordinate ECCD, and the change in political administration that necessitated a final revision to suit the changes.

Main Issues Captured in the Policy

The major issues captured in the Ghana ECCD policy include an operational definition of ECCD; a rationale; policy goals, objectives, and targets; institutional arrangements; roles and responsibilities; implementation strategies; and costs and financial implications.

Ghana adopted the broad definitions of the Consultative Group on Early Childhood Care and Development, and titled its ECD policy as *Early Childhood Care and Development Policy* (ECCD Policy). ECCD is operationally defined in the policy as the timely provision of a range of services that promote the survival, growth, development, and protection of the young child (0–8). The rationale is to provide a framework for the guidance of government, as well as other relevant sector ministries, district assemblies, companies, families, the private sector, nongovernmental organizations (NGOs), and development partners for investing in, and effective implementation of, ECD programs. The broad goal of the policy is to promote the survival, growth, development, and protection of all children 0–8 years in Ghana, with many specific objectives relating to the holistic development of all young children. An institutional framework with a national ECD coordinating committee is made up of representatives of sector ministries and other stakeholders to translate these objectives into actual programs at the national, district, and community levels. The sector ministries have assigned roles and responsibilities in line with Ghana's decentralization policy. The next sections spell out implementation mechanisms as well as costs and financial implications.

Implementation Issues

The policy's proposed implementation mechanisms include the creation of an institutional framework at national, regional, district, and community levels; the creation of a conducive environment for developing ECD programs; the promotion of integrated services as packages that will take care of the physical, mental, social, moral, and spiritual needs of the child; the establishment of conventional and unconventional ECD systems; broadening of parent participation; assignment of roles and responsibilities to cognate sectors; provision of quality ECD services; mobilization of resources; and organization of regular research, monitoring, and evaluation to improve all aspects of ECD systems.

Some of these mechanisms are in place and are working. A national ECD coordinating committee with a mandate to advise MOWAC on ECD issues has been inaugurated, an ECCD secretariat has been established in MOWAC, and a full-time secretariat has been appointed and is working. Key decision makers, parents, and other stakeholders have been sensitized on ECD issues in 37 of the 138 districts on a pilot basis. With the help of UNICEF's Western and Central Africa Regional Office, integrated ECD is being introduced and an action plan drawn that embraces the issues of health, nutrition and food, water and environmental sanitation, psychosocial stimulation, early learning, and child protection. Agencies providing these services are encouraged to collaborate and complement each other's efforts.

To build capacity, a university, 15 teacher training colleges, the Ghana National Association of Teachers, and private practitioners are giving training in ECD. Cognate ministries, departments, agencies, and civil society organizations have been assigned relevant leading roles in ECD. Research activities include a nationwide early learning standards and indicators project geared toward meeting the current gap in assessing ECD and a nationwide study of care facilities for HIV/AIDS orphans.

Resources are mobilized through cost sharing and pooling of resources from parents, communities, district assemblies, NGOs, private organizations, government, and development partners. The Ministry of Finance will compel all ministries, departments, and agencies to create annual budget lines for ECD activities.

The Current Situation of ECCD Policy in Ghana

After its long incubation period of almost 11 years, Ghana's ECCD policy has been born, and, with the national coordinating committee and secretariat working, the policy is on solid ground. So far, mechanisms that have been proposed for the ECCD policy are being applied modestly; the results are expected to be fruitful.

Lessons Learned from the Policy Development Process and Implementation

The policy development process and implementation to date highlight many lessons. First, the national seminar on ECD created awareness of the poor conditions of young children and served as useful background information for policy development. In addition, it generated collective efforts among diverse stakeholders, allowing them to work toward the common objective of young children's development. Second, though subjecting the draft policy to stakeholders' constant reviews caused some delay, it brought some benefits: The reviews improved policy quality, made the process participatory, and increased a sense of ownership among the stakeholders. Third, Ghana's ECCD policy conforms to the current internationally accepted principles underlying the holistic development of young children, and its implementation is gradually unveiling the practical realization that the young child needs to be cared for from many dimensions.

Finally, the current mainstreaming of ECD into the basic education system, as well as the capitation grant introduced in the 2005/6 school year making basic education free, is reported to have increased enrollment tremendously. This boost will definitely improve the overall development chances of the majority of the country's young citizens, especially those in deprived and rural communities.

Mauritius

Brief History: The Situation before the Policy Was Demanded

In the preindependence decades from 1948 to 1968, ad hoc decisions were taken and implemented by the colonial authorities—under pressure from

local political advocates and backed by health and education professionals—
to ensure the survival of mothers and children. Thus polio and malaria
were gradually eradicated, the birthrate was brought down, child welfare
clinics were set up, and access to primary education was extended.

Factors That Prompted Development of a Policy for ECD

The postindependence decade (1968–78) offered opportunities to consolidate these advances with the support of international agencies such
as the World Health Organization, UNICEF, United Nations Development Program, and the World Food Program. During this period, despite
economic constraints and rising unemployment, maternal and child health
services were developed, immunization coverage was increased, a family
allowance was introduced, and universal access to primary education was
achieved, with free milk, bread, and cheese for children in primary schools.
At the same time, various NGOs emerged to advocate for appropriate
child care and development services. Some local authorities, research
teams, and religious bodies pioneered pilot projects that demonstrated
the positive results of an up-to-date and scientific approach to ECD. The
International Year of the Child, the findings of a UNICEF-sponsored survey on preschool provision (Dalais 1978), the creation of institutions with
specific remits (such as the Pre-Primary Unit in 1978 and the Preschool
Trust Fund in 1984), and effective bilateral and multilateral cooperation
and regional exchanges all created a synergy that called for direction and
official commitment.

Policy statements regarding preschool educational provision can be traced
as far back as the National Development Plan for 1975–80 (Mauritius
1976) but it was only in 1998 that the first national ECD policy focusing
on ages 0–3 was published (Mauritius 1998). The following factors directly
determined the decision to create such a document: a regional workshop
on ECD in Africa (1996), a survey on daycare centers carried out in the
context of a World Bank ECD initiative (1996–98), and UNICEF con-
sultancies of Judith Evans and Sarla Gopalan on ECD policy formulation
(Evans 1997; Gopalan 1997). A further step was taken when that policy
was analyzed two years later as part of the Policy Studies Project of ADEA-
WGECD (consultants Kate Torkington and Margaret Irvine 2000). A new
policy development culture was emerging: the exercise had become
more participative, more open to scrutiny. The policy analysis showed
the need for a comprehensive national policy for children (NPC).
Immediate action was taken in this respect. The NPC (Mauritius 2003) was
officially launched in May 2003 after nearly one year of consultation with

partners and stakeholders. Thus the participatory approach initiated with the national ECD policy (Mauritius 1998) was consolidated.

The Policy Development/Formulation Process: Problems Encountered and How They Were Solved

It took 50 years for the ECD policy formulation and implementation process in Mauritius to progress from top-down, ad hoc decisions and actions to a broad-based, consultative, and participative debate and partnership. The most significant paradigm shifts that occurred during this process were

- from survival to development;
- from needs to rights; and,
- from sectoral to cross-sectoral planning.

Initially, realities in the field and even crises in the health and education sectors triggered the process. Specific commitments amplified the momentum, such as the CRC, Convention on the Elimination of All Forms of Discrimination Against Women (CEDAW), *Education for All*, and the World Summit for Children goals as well as international events such as the International Years of the Child and of Disabled Persons, along with the advocacy campaigns and the research they generated. The driving forces may be summed up as follows: political will; financial commitment; human resource development; and institutional capacity building, networking, and cooperation at local, regional, and international levels. Some of the restraining forces were territorial rivalries and sectoral interests, lack of adequate human and financial resources, bureaucracy, pressures of a highly competitive education system, job tenure insecurity and high staff turnover rate, focus on provision rather than inclusion, and absence of a strong coordinating mechanism. Many of the problems were tackled with varying degrees of success by initiating and pursuing formal dialogue and debate, building up a strong administrative and legislative framework, enhancing professionalism and leadership, defining conditions of work and terms of employment, ensuring budgetary as well as staffing provisions, and catalyzing the policy development and implementation process through external expertise and support.

Main Issues Captured in the Policy

Integrated early childhood development (IECD) is one of the seven core policy areas of the NPC. The term IECD—instead of ECD, as in the 1998 national ECD policy document (Mauritius 1998)—reflects progress in the conceptualization of an integrated approach.

The NPC adopts a cross-cutting methodology inspired by guidelines in the classics on policy planning for IECD (Dalais, Landers, and Fuertes 1996; Evans, Myers, and Ilfeld 2000; Myers 1992; Vargas-Barón 2005). The main issues the NPC addresses include fragmented provision; institutional splitting; the need to train and mainstream private informal caregivers; the need to strengthen the ECD section at the Ministry of Women's Rights, Child Development, and Family Welfare (MWRCDFW); the need to define career paths for trained ECD staff; the need for quality indicators; the need to focus on children with disabilities; a lack of incentives to private promoters; and no government subsidy for children under 4 years old.

The NPC proposes the following strategies to tackle these issues: bring all partners together and establish a coordinating mechanism; develop an integrated, holistic approach and program framework for children 0–8; train practitioners and streamline the training and career structure; reinforce the ECD section at MWRCDFW; apply program guidelines and set up a quality assurance system; focus on disadvantaged children; and provide incentives to private promoters. (The question of a subsidy for children under 4 is not addressed.)

The strategies proposed in the NPC need to be updated and realigned with the new government's program, as formulated in the president's address to Parliament in July 2005 (Mauritius 2005). This document focuses on five key aspects of ECD: the family, children with special needs, health, development, and education. It proposes the following 14 measures:

- review the role and functions of the Preschool Trust Fund;
- create a center for ECD;
- develop an action plan for children with learning difficulties;
- develop an action plan for children with disabilities;
- set up regional health and education centers;
- set up a children's hospital;
- set up intensive neonatal services at Nehru and Jeetoo hospitals;
- adopt a national policy on family;
- set up a family court;
- adopt a national children's policy and plan of action;
- consolidate daycare centers;
- strengthen the mechanisms for protection against domestic violence;

- focus on ECD and Parental Empowerment Program; and
- protect the family against violence and insecurity, and ensure that every family enjoys its right to a house.

Implementation Issues

Implementation issues raised in the NPC are addressed in the National Plan of Action (NPA; Mauritius 2004) published less than a year later. The NPA identifies three main objectives for IECD:

- adopting a holistic approach to ECD;
- promoting continuous dialogue among parents, managers, and child caregivers; and
- establishing standards and norms for staff of child care institutions.

The NPA proposes eight actions: a review of curriculum and pedagogical approaches, preparation of a new pedagogical kit, sensitization, counseling services, referral services, regular visits by ministry officers, psychological testing, and training review.

The Current Situation of ECD Policy in Mauritius

Basic indicators in 2006 on ECD are encouraging but are no cause for complacency: an infant mortality rate of 14.4, a maternal mortality rate of 0.17, immunization coverage of 92 percent, preschool enrollment rates for 4- to 5-year-old children of 95 percent, and universal access to primary health care and basic education. Institutional and legislative/regulatory frameworks are operational. NGOs and civil society are increasingly active and committed. However, the ECD landscape is still dominated by a three-tier structure, segmented horizontally into three age groups (0–3, 4, and 5–8) and vertically between four ministries. This segmentation leads to discrepancies and dispersal of efforts and resources. Moreover, the quality of services varies to such an extent that inequalities are reinforced, and the gap is critical in services for children with special needs. A strong coordinating and monitoring mechanism is imperative if the nation is to have value for money and if the government truly wants to build a republic fit for children. At a crucial time when the country is bracing itself to boost its economy and meet the challenges of globalization, human resource development and, its very foundation, IECD must figure high on its agenda.

Lessons Learned from the Policy Development Process and Implementation

As mentioned, the Mauritius case study illustrates the slow and complex evolution of the policy formulation process from ad hoc, top-down decisions to a broad-based consultative and participatory debate and partnership. Lessons learned include the following:

• Policy development, implementation, and analysis should be ongoing, participatory, and consultative processes sustained by dialogue, consensus building, partnership building, monitoring, and evaluation.
• The end objective of policy formulation should not be just to produce a document. It must be backed up by action that will make a difference to the most vulnerable groups.
• A situational analysis or environment scan must be complemented by a causality analysis.
• The action plan must be clearly and thoroughly formulated if the documents produced are to be useful tools for planning, implementation, monitoring, and evaluation. Monitoring, evaluation, review, and readjustment must be built into the action plan.
• Rushed drafts, decisions, and actions are confusing and counterproductive.
• Research findings, surveys, ongoing studies, and evaluations are indispensable to inform policy development and decision making.
• Building on existing foundations, rather than scrapping them and starting from scratch, is economically and pedagogically sound.
• Constant monitoring and review ensure coherence and direction.
• Policy formulation and implementation are everybody's business and should not be left to the "authorities" alone. Sustained advocacy, open debate, and ongoing dialogue are necessary to ensure progress and viability, equity, and quality.

Namibia

Brief History: The Situation before the Policy Was Demanded

Namibia, a pre-World War I German colony known as South-West Africa, became in 1921 a mandated territory of the League of Nations under the administration of South Africa. Namibia's colonial past left a strong impact on the Namibian people, creating a pattern that entrenched poverty and human deficiency. With the end of the apartheid system in 1990, the newly elected government of Namibia inherited an education system that was characterized by inequalities in the distribution of resources, where access to learning was a priority only for a few whites, and where equality of educational opportunity was not considered.

Factors That Prompted Development of a Policy for ECD

In addressing the inherited education system, the new government declared in article 20 of the country's constitution (Namibia 1990) that all people should have access to education and that basic education shall be free and compulsory. This vision took form in a government policy document entitled *Toward Education for All—A Development Brief for Education, Culture, and Training* (Namibia 1993). Four major goals are at the helm of *Toward Education for All*: access, equity, quality, and democracy. The goals' guiding principle is that the government's first commitment is to provide universal basic education: "Basic education is intended to ensure that by the year 2000 the majority of our citizens will have acquired basic skills of reading, writing, numeracy, and understandings of sociocultural processes and natural phenomena. This is the only way we can march with some hope into the next millennium" (p. 33).

Namibia obtained its independence in the same month and year in which the World Conference on *Education for All* was held in Jomtien, Thailand. The goals and principles embodied in the World Declaration on *Education for All* (UNESCO 2000b) and its *Framework for Action* (UNESCO 2000a) were already key components of the Namibian government's policy on education. During the same year, Namibia became one of the first African countries to complete a national plan of action for children and to ratify the UN CRC. Formulation of a national early childhood policy fit well with the young government's priorities, and a draft was formulated (Namibia 1996) along the guidelines of the CRC and the African Charter on the Rights and Welfare of the Child (Organization of African Unity 1990), both of which require member states to develop national plans of action for children.

The Policy Development/Formulation Process: Problems Encountered and How They Were Solved

After ratifying the CRC, there was an urgent need to put mechanisms and systems in place to regulate and monitor the agreed-upon national plan of action for children. In May 1992, the government, with UNICEF support, organized a national conference on early childhood protection and development. The conference brought together participants from a wide spectrum of government and nongovernmental organizations, kindergartens, parents, and communities. The objectives of the conference were to look at ways to strengthen existing community-based ECD programs, to discuss and agree on what constitutes quality service delivery, to identify and define the role of all sectors, and, most important, to promote the involvement of parents.

In 1994 an interministerial task force was established and led by the Ministry of Education in close cooperation with the Ministry of Regional Local Government and Housing (MRLGH). Of major significance was the task force's recommendation to move responsibility for ECD from the Ministry of Education to the relatively new Directorate of Community Development in the MRLGH. The rationale behind this move was to locate ECD in the environment of the whole child, the community, and the family, rather than ECD being seen as just preparation for education.

In late 1994 a consultant was hired to develop an early childhood policy, incorporating comments from workshops and both task forces. The draft policy was debated nationally at all levels through mini workshops and consultative meetings organized by the government. After long and fruitful consultations, consensus was reached, and Namibia's cabinet adopted the national ECD policy in late 1996 (Namibia 1996).

Efforts to implement the policy ensued from 1996, culminating in a review of the policy in 2004, at which time a draft revised policy was developed. Before describing components of the revised policy, a brief review of the implementation issues faced in the period 1996–2004 will be described.

Implementation Issues

The main shortcoming identified throughout the implementation period and subsequently identified and affirmed during the 2004 national consultative policy review process was the Namibian cabinet's delay in submitting the adopted policy to the national parliament for enactment. This delay, however, created an opportunity to undertake a national review in 2004 regarding the policy implementation and the relevance of the document based on the current status of children and their care and well-being.

Second, the change of lead ministries from the MRLGH to the Ministry of Gender Equality and Child Welfare (MGECW, previously the Ministry of Women's Affairs and Child Welfare) brought about delays in monitoring and evaluating the implementation of the policy.

Although there has been a multisectoral national ECD committee since the cabinet's approval in 1996, junior representation at this committee has affected decision-making actions, which has subsequently led to continued poor quality delivery of the available services, weak coordination at all levels, and a low uptake of these services. Current data indicate an estimated 32 percent of the children are cared for in such services (Namibia 2003), however, based on anecdotal reports, the quality of care provided may be quite poor. In addition, the holistic approach to ECD that integrates health, nutrition, early stimulation, and preschool education has yet to take shape and remains a challenge in terms of interlinked programs and services.

The Current Situation of ECD Policy in Namibia

In 2004 the national ECD committee, under the leadership of the MGECW, called for a review of the national ECD policy. The purpose of the review was "to give cognizance to many of the profound socioeconomic changes that had taken place over the preceding decade as well as highlighting some of the contemporary, emerging issues that have relevance for young children, their families, and communities in Namibia in the 21st century" (Namibia 2004, 2). Following the same process as that of drafting the 1996 policy, consultations took place at all levels with and among a broad range of stakeholders in the ECD sector.

The review of the policy coincided with the review of the guidelines, the development of IECD curriculum/syllabus, and the development of the Education and Training Sector Improvement Program (ETSIP) implementation plans. This timing enabled representatives from the ECD sector to propose to the government, through the ETSIP ECD subcommittee, the need to formalize and subsidize the preprimary phase. The whole ETSIP document was endorsed by the cabinet of Namibia in late 2005. In 2006 the ETSIP was officially launched by the Ministry of Education. A series of regional visits took place where sensitization workshops were held with key education stakeholders (including teachers, educators, and teacher unions). Subsequently, in November 2006 the cabinet announced the incorporation of the preprimary phase as part of formal education in the sector, which means that the Ministry of Education will have to take over responsibilities for preprimary education from the Ministry of Gender Equality and Child Welfare. The envisaged program will be developed in line with ETSIP. The commencement of the program, however, depends on the endorsement of the reviewed IECD policy and the enactment by parliament, which is expected no later than December 2007.

Main Issues Captured in the Draft Revised 2004 Policy

With the understanding that early childhood development begins at home and that the environment in which children live and grow has great impact on the social, emotional, intellectual, and physical development of infants and young children, the revised national IECD policy promotes the development of IECD programs based on the strengths and capacities of communities.

The draft revised policy, entitled *National Integrated Early Childhood Policy*, states as its goal: "To make provision for family and community-based, sustainable, and integrated early childhood programs, which are accessible to all young children, with a focus on the development of IECD programs in rural areas and for very young children living in difficult circumstances" (Namibia 2005, 15, para. 5.1). Overall, the policy promotes the holistic approach to ECD as prescribed in the CRC and other national development indicators. It seeks to ensure delivery of a sound and comprehensive IECD program at all levels.

Lessons Learned from the Policy Development Process and Implementation

Although individual ministries and NGOs continued to make certain contributions to ECD consistent with the original policy statement approved by Namibia's cabinet, no coordinated implementation plans were put in place containing objectives, targets, and activities against which progress could be monitored and plans adjusted. For example, the Ministry of Education has no coordinated plan to train the increasing numbers of ECD caregivers who have opened ECD facilities (which often arise as an individual income-generating activity). Funding mechanisms to support the development of quality community child care programs have not been put in place, which was partly due to a major disruption in 1999 and 2000 when the responsibility for ECD was transferred to a newly created ministry—from the MRLGH to the MGECW. In the previous ministry, ECD had to compete with the government's major decentralization program, but the new ministry was also saddled with the need to establish offices and identify its priorities and resource allocations. In addition, the original policy did not specify the appointment of an ECD coordinator from the Ministry of Health and Social Services; consequently, input from this ministry has lagged behind.

Multisectoral coordination is proving difficult to implement. Agencies implementing the policy have continued to operate sectorally, communicating vertically between national, regional, and local levels within line ministries.

The national ECD committee, given the responsibility of overseeing the development and implementation of the policy, did not have a sufficiently strong secretariat to service the committee. With a tabled budget and no plans to discuss and monitor, most of the ministries sent lower-level managers with no decision-making powers as representatives. The MGECW has now recognized the need to make this committee an effective coordinating body and is now aware that it must play a stronger role in leading and coordinating all stakeholders involved.

Conclusion

In general, the development process and implementation of ECD policies in the three countries have similarities in the situations before the policies were demanded, the factors that prompted policy development and aspects of the development process, the main contents of the policy documents, and issues concerning their implementation. Each country has a somewhat different current status, and some diversity exists among the lessons learned; however, in combination they provide a useful index for other countries.

Historically, the ECD policies were developed as a result of the realization of inadequacies in the inherited systems characterized variously as not holistic but mainly cognitive, ad hoc, and full of inequalities among social groups. This awareness, along with both internal legislation and international obligations geared toward improving the lives of young citizens, prompted initiation of the current policies in the three countries.

The policy development processes were strikingly similar. The organization of a national seminar to create awareness of the plight of young children and the need to ameliorate their situation served as the starting point. This awareness was followed by the appointment of task forces to do the groundwork—seeking the services of consultants for drafting, then subjecting the drafts to stakeholder reviews to ensure quality, participation, and ownership—and, finally, approval by government for implementation.

Countries that plan to develop similar policies should note that the processes were not without hiccups. They will need to overcome prolonged delays caused by such factors as long periods for drafting, indecision on which sector should serve as the coordinating hub of the policy, frequency of stakeholder reviews, paradigm shifts, consensus building and networking, and changes in political administration. As in Mauritius and Namibia, the old policies should be updated from time to time to suit current realities and requirements.

The main issues contained in current ECD policy, as adequately highlighted in the three countries, include the internationally accepted operational definition of the policy in terms of the holistic and integrated development of all young children 0–8. In addition, the institutional framework, roles, and responsibilities of various stakeholding sectors, implementation mechanisms, and costs and financial implications have been stressed.

Implementation of the policies has been started and is ongoing in all three countries. Institutionally, national coordinating committees have been set up with membership from sector ministries, departments, and agencies giving advice and directing the course of ECD. Practical achievements to move ECD forward include building capacity of caregivers, parents, and institutions involved in ECD work; promoting continuous dialogue among stakeholders; developing curricula; conducting research to improve ECD; and monitoring and evaluation.

The state of ECD policy development and implementation in the three countries is encouraging. In Ghana, the policy is now firmly in place, with a national coordinating committee and a secretariat established and efforts underway to promote the policy countrywide. In Mauritius, institutional and legislative frameworks are in place and indicators are encouraging, despite imbalances in the ECD landscape. Namibia has tried its cabinet-approved policy for some time now, identified some areas that require strengthening, and has reviewed and finalized the policy in preparation for enactment by the parliament.

A Ghanaian proverb recounts that when an orphan happens to be at a place where a father is advising his child, the orphan eavesdrops attentively for his own advantage. Countries that would like to develop and implement ECD policies may learn the following lessons, among others, from the experiences of Ghana, Mauritius, and Namibia. First, creating a national awareness of the plight of young children, probably through a stakeholders' seminar, can be an effective starting point for ECD development. Second, involving all stakeholders at all levels of the development process ensures active involvement, ownership, interest, and positive participation in the efforts to sustain it. Third, the use of research findings as a basis for policy development is indispensable. Fourth, it is important to anticipate factors that may cause delays—for example, deciding on a coordinating body, financial support, and departmental changes—and find ways of avoiding them.

In conclusion, most young children in Africa, especially those in disadvantaged communities, have been deprived of improvements in their holistic development for too long. Unfortunately, policies to help change their situation appear to be few and far between. This chapter on the experiences in Ghana, Mauritius, and Namibia may positively contribute to what can be done on the continent.

References

Dalais, C. 1978. *Survey of Needs in the Pre-Primary Sector of Education.* New York: UNICEF.

Dalais, C., C. Landers, and P. Fuertes. 1996. *Early Childhood Development Revisited: From Policy Formulation to Program Implementation.* New York; UNICEF.

Evans, J. L. 1997. *Early Childhood Development: The Formulation of National Policy.* New York: UNICEF.

Evans, J. L., with R. G. Myers, and E. M. Ilfeld. 2000. *Early Childhood Counts: A Programming Guide on Early Childhood Care for Development.* Washington, DC: World Bank.

Ghana. 1992. *The Constitution of the Republic of Ghana.* Accra: Ghana Publishing Corporation.

———. 1998. *The Children's Act. Act No. 560.* Accra: Ghana Publishing Corporation.

———. 2004. *Early Childhood Care and Development Policy.* Accra: Ministry of Women and Children's Affairs.

Gopalan, S. 1997. *Early Childhood Development: Policy, Strategies, and a Program for Action.* New York: UNICEF.

Mauritius. 1976. *National Development Plan 1975–1980.* Port Louis: Government Printer.

———. 1998. "National Early Childhood Development Policy Paper." Ministry of Women, Family Welfare, and Child Development.

———. 2003. *National Policy for Children—A Republic Fit for Children.* Port Louis: Ministry of Women's Rights, Child Development, and Family Welfare.

———. 2004. *National Policy for Children, National Plan of Action.* Port Louis: Ministry of Women's Rights, Child Development, and Family Welfare.

———. 2005. "Government Program 2005–2010." Address to Parliament by the President of the Republic. Port Louis: Government Printer.

Myers, R. 1992. *The Twelve Who Survive: Strengthening Programs of Early Childhood Development in the Third World.* London: Routledge.

Namibia. 1990. *The Constitution of the Republic of Namibia.* Windhoek: Ministry of Information and Broadcasting.

———. 1996. *National Early Childhood Development Policy.* Windhoek: Ministry of Regional, Local Government and Housing (MRLGH).

———. 2003. *Population and Housing Census, 2001.* Windhoek: National Planning Commission.

———. 2004. *Draft Integrated Early Childhood Development Policy.* Namibia: Ministry of Gender Equality and Child Welfare (MGECW).

————. 2005. *National Integrated Early Childhood Development Policy* (Draft). Windhoek: Ministry of Gender Equality and Child Welfare (MGECW).

Namibia. Ministry of Basic Education and Culture. 1993. *Toward Education for All: A Development Brief for Education, Culture, and Training.* Windhoek: Gamsberg MacMillan.

Organization of African Unity. 1990. *African Charter on the Rights and Welfare of the Child.* Retrieved August 27, 2006, from http://www1.umn.edu/humanrts/africa/afchild.htm.

Torkington, K. 2001. *WGECD Policy Project: A Synthesis Report.* Paris: ADEA/ Netherlands Ministry of Foreign Affairs.

Torkington, Kate, and Margaret Irvine. 2000. *Review of Namibia's Early Childhood Development Policy and Its Implementation, A Case Study.* The Hague: ADEA-WGECD.

UNESCO (United Nations Educational, Scientific, and Cultural Organization). 2000a. *The Dakar Framework for Action. Education for All: Meeting Our Collective Commitments.* Adopted by the World Education Forum, Dakar, Senegal, April 26–28. Paris: UNESCO.

————. 2000b. *NGO Declaration on Education for All.* Retrieved August 27, 2006, from http://www.unesco.org/education/efa/wef_2000/cov_ngo_declaration.shtml.

Vargas-Barón, E. 2005. *Planning Policies for Early Childhood Development: Guidelines for Action.* Paris: ADEA, UNICEF, and UNESCO.

CHAPTER 10

Participatory ECD Policy Planning in Francophone West Africa

Emily Vargas-Barón

The challenges and opportunities for early childhood development (ECD) are greatest in Sub-Saharan Africa (SSA). It is universally acknowledged that SSA has devastating statistics regarding ECD. Less often perceived are the impressive strengths of African ECD specialists who are fighting to improve child survival and development in the region. A growing cadre of dedicated African ECD leaders and specialists is emerging in all African countries. The brilliant Tamsir Samb led ECD policy dialogue in Senegal. He was devoted to consultation at the community level where the dramatic needs of children and families are most clearly evident. Increasingly, African leaders are formulating ECD policies or policy frameworks.[1] Although progress has been made, much more work is required to ensure that all African children will fulfill their potential.

This chapter briefly describes a collaborative ECD policy-planning project conducted in Burkina Faso, Mauritania, and Senegal. It offers lessons learned with the goal of assisting planning teams in other nations, and finally, discusses some future challenges for ECD policy planning in SSA.

This paper is dedicated to the memory of Tamsir Samb, Educational Researcher, Senegal.

The Three-Country Project

The field of ECD policy planning in SSA essentially began when Colletta and Reinhold's (1997) study revealed that only four SSA nations budgeted funds for ECD—and those investments were very small. The Seventh Conference of Ministers of Education of African Member States (MINEDAF VII) in 1998 urged SSA nations to formulate ECD policies (UNESCO 1998). The *Dakar Framework for Action* called for all nations to prepare *Education for All* (EFA) action plans, including ECD as an integral part of the EFA plans (UNESCO 2000). However, the following year Torkington's (2001) study found that in SSA, only Namibia and Mauritius had adopted ECD policies. In 2002, the *Asmara Declaration on Early Childhood Development* encouraged SSA nations to formulate ECD policies within national development strategies and to conduct participatory policy-planning processes that are country driven, cross-sectoral, and culturally appropriate (Asmara Declaration 2002). But it was clear that African nations would face major challenges as they sought to develop robust, culturally appropriate, and feasible ECD policies and National ECD Plans of Action (NEPA) (Pence 2004).

Interagency Collaboration

Most international donors that support ECD policy planning in SSA have become increasingly aware that they must work collaboratively to move the field forward. In 1999, the Working Group for ECD (WGECD) of the Association for the Development of Education in Africa (ADEA) decided to focus its activities on ECD policy planning with three main strategies: research, policy advocacy, and capacity building. Concurrently, United Nations Children's Fund (UNICEF) encouraged the WGECD and United Nations Educational, Scientific, and Cultural Organization (UNESCO) to collaborate in responding to requests for technical support for ECD policy planning from three Francophone nations: Burkina Faso, Mauritania, and Senegal. The "Project to Support National Policy Planning for Early Childhood Development in Three Countries of West Africa" extended from June 2002 to November 2003, with informal support into 2004 (UNICEF 2003b). The Netherlands provided a grant to the WGECD for technical support; UNICEF's regional office for West and Central Africa and its country offices supported ECD planning teams, training workshops, national consultants, and consultation and consensus-building meetings. UNESCO provided travel and technical support.

Torkington's (2001) review of ECD policy experiences in Ghana, Mauritius, and Namibia revealed shortcomings in the first ECD policy efforts in SSA, and it offered useful suggestions for future planning projects. (See chapter 9 in this volume.) A review of ECD literature revealed that very little technical guidance existed for this complex intersectoral area of policy planning. Then this author, who was the international consultant for the three-country project, identified lessons from the project and other ECD planning experiences in the Americas, Australia, Europe, and the Middle East, which resulted in the preparation of *Planning Policies for Early Childhood Development: Guidelines for Action* (Vargas-Barón 2005).

Challenges

Burkina Faso, Mauritania, and Senegal face many challenges to achieving good child development, from their ecology to their fragile systems of governance, education, health, sanitation, and economic development. To be effective, ECD policies should embrace education, health, nutrition, sanitation, and social protection sectors, and should extend from pregnancy to age 8. The conceptual and methodological challenges inherent in maximizing ECD investment in situations of extreme scarcity are significant. Under the best of circumstances, consensus is difficult to achieve among advocates for prenatal education and care, parenting programs, integrated services for children from birth to age 3, center- and home-based child care and education, sanitation, preschools, and transition to primary school. Furthermore, in many SSA countries, ECD had come to mean preschool education. Given its perceived costs, low program coverage, and national emphasis on universal primary schooling, many SSA countries had neglected ECD. The care of children from birth to age 3 was considered the responsibility of extended families and their communities; few programs had been developed for this critical period. Although some health and nutrition services targeted this age group, few countries invested in parenting, psychosocial stimulation, and early childhood intervention (ECI) services for developmentally delayed or disabled children. Rates are high for infant and child mortality, low birthweight, and maternal mortality throughout the region. It is not surprising that 35 to 45 percent of the children of West Africa suffer from chronic ill health, endemic diseases, malnutrition, and developmental delays. If developmental delays are not reversed during children's early years, these children usually achieve poorly in school, repeat grades, and ultimately drop out. The incidence of orphans and other children affected by HIV/AIDS, wars, and natural disasters is increasing rapidly.

Family violence, child abuse and neglect, mendicant children, and children with disabilities are prevalent. Inadequate laws and legal structures for ensuring the juridical protection of pregnant women and young children hamper the few child protection services that exist. The region generally lacks adequate training systems for parent educators; health, nutrition, and ECI specialists; preschool teachers; and mid-level ECD managers. To meet these dramatic challenges, significant institutional and program development will be required over many years. ECD policy planning is but a first step on a long trek to improve the development of children living in extreme poverty.

The major project goal was to help nations develop ECD policies or policy frameworks that would lead to expanding resources for quality services for pregnant women and for children from birth to age 8. The policies were to be developed in a participatory manner that would lead to strong local ownership. They were to be comprehensive, culturally appropriate, and equitable while focusing on vulnerable, unserved children. They were to provide a structural framework for good coordination and encourage program integration wherever possible.

Project Objectives and Expected Results

The advisory project was intended to build knowledge and develop new approaches for future use in SSA and other world regions. The project had the following main objectives:

- help countries prepare their policy-planning processes and ECD policies;
- strengthen networking, partnership development, and policy dialogue among practitioners, communities, nongovernmental organizations (NGOs), governments, international partners, and other stakeholders;
- introduce new methodological and analytical skills for ECD policy analysis and development, and strengthen national policy-planning capacity; and
- identify strategic areas for advocacy, mobilizing public and political support, capacity building, and expanding resources for ECD in SSA.

The following program results were to be achieved:

- national teams would prepare comprehensive and integrated ECD policies;
- a subregional network would begin through combined project workshops;

- a final report would be prepared and disseminated widely; and
- ideas would be contributed to formulate guidelines for ECD policy planning.

All objectives and results were met and, regarding planning tools, they were exceeded.

Project Activities and Structures

The consultant usually worked with two countries at a time to help the countries structure their policy-planning process, build broad stakeholder participation, establish planning teams and committees, prepare work plans, develop situation analyses, plan subnational consultations, prepare drafts of ECD policies and NEPAs, and conduct activities for achieving consensus. At three subregional workshops, planning teams presented their progress and challenges, engaged in dialogue and problem solving, received technical training, and revised their work plans.

The situation analyses were detailed and innovative, covering the status and needs of children, ECD resource identification, and policy analyses. In addition to presenting salient statistics, they focused on community strengths, African cultural ideals, and childrearing practices, and also helped to ensure that ECD policies would be rooted in African realities. Salient consultation findings were incorporated into each policy. Major efforts were made to ensure that the policies were carefully aligned with Millennium Development Goals (MDGs), national Poverty Reduction Strategy Papers (PRSPs), EFA plans, and pertinent sectoral policies and plans.

In each of the countries, the president or prime minister supported the establishment of an ECD policy, and a ministry was officially designated to lead the process. None of the countries placed the responsibility for leading ECD policy planning in ministries of health or education. In Burkina Faso, leadership was delegated to the Ministry of Social Action and National Solidarity. Even though this ministry lacked a large budget for children, it initially secured the collaboration of other ministries. This collaboration fell apart after the project ended. In Mauritania, the Division for Family and Child Development of the Secretariat for the Improvement of the Status of Women led policy planning. The participation of other ministries was secured after considerable outreach and consultation. In Senegal, initially the Ministry of the Family and Early Childhood led policy planning, but subsequently its mandate and name changed, and responsibility was passed to the Agence Nationale de la Case de Tout Petits (National Agency for Huts for Young Children) that manages President Wade's national preschool program.

Broad stakeholder participation was achieved through nationwide consultations that included parents, community members, and national specialists in the fields of health, nutrition, sanitation, education, juridical protection, children's and women's rights, national planning, finance, statistics, and other areas, depending upon national priorities. Stakeholders included all governmental and civil society agencies such as community-based organizations, NGOs, institutes, universities, faith-based organizations, unions, businesses, and other private organizations that serve young children and parents. In addition to national-level meetings, 8 to 16 subnational consultations were held in communities and geographical or cultural subregions to identify local problems and needs, gain ideas, and build widespread support for the ECD policy. The convening ministry invited international partners, NGOs, associations, universities, and foundations to support the planning process and especially the subnational consultations. After consultations were concluded, policy drafts were prepared and circulated, and many consensus-building meetings were held.

Each of the ECD policies includes the following elements: a vision for the nation's children; fundamental principles, goals, and objectives for ECD; major strategies and programs; a training plan; a social communications and policy advocacy plan; a policy evaluation, research, and follow-up plan; an organizational structure; and a coordination plan for policy implementation at all levels. Although all countries were encouraged to present a general financial plan, only Mauritania did so. The planning teams included several of the best minds devoted to ECD in each country. Each team member learned a great deal about the status of children and gained new ideas about how to maximize ECD resources. The project motivated ECD specialists to make innovative contributions, and it identified new ECD leaders and promising young professionals. Even before the policies were completed, policy discussions began to affect national ECD strategies and programs. New partnerships were developed between national institutions and international donors that promise to yield positive results for improving the status of young children in West Africa.

Two of the nations successfully completed and officially adopted a comprehensive ECD policy. Burkina Faso has not adopted its ECD policy, and it has continued to revise and downsize its initial draft. In contrast, Mauritania prepared its NEPA at the same time as its policy; however, the NEPA of Senegal has not been completed as of this writing. Mauritania and Senegal have begun policy implementation and many national decision makers now consider ECD to be an essential part of social sector planning. Various promises have been made to increase national investment in ECD, but changes in ECD financing have not been assessed as yet. In future years, it will be important to evaluate policy outcomes and budgetary flows for ECD in all three countries.

Some Lessons Learned about ECD Policy Planning in Africa

At the end of the project, a regional workshop was held to present project activities and share information on policy planning. Recommendations and a general report of the workshop were prepared and widely disseminated.

Flexibility is essential in structuring ECD policy-planning processes— Each nation's ECD policy should fit its unique needs, cultures, and institutions. Traditions for policy planning vary dramatically within West Africa—and even between ministries in the same country—such as differences in policy formats, ideologies, leadership styles, institutional cultures, interministerial relations, meeting procedures, consensus-building methods, and decision-making processes. Even though policy contents and traditions differ from country to country, successful planning processes are similar. Participatory planning processes have been widely replicated across many world regions. As nations begin to prepare their ECD policies, it is valuable to provide planning teams with process guidance and options for structuring their intent. Because policy options are so sensitive and policies must be established flexibly within national contexts, planning specialists should be wary about simply giving countries copies of other ECD policies and NEPAs and recommending that they prepare similar documents. The processes for developing an ECD policy can be more important than the documents themselves.

*Participatory ECD policy planning is successful in Francophone West Africa—*Some people believe that central planning is all that can be expected in the West African region. Until recently, small teams of isolated planning specialists sat in ministerial offices and prepared most policy documents. This project demonstrated that participatory planning, including widespread consultations for ECD policy development, is not only possible in Africa—it is highly successful. West African ECD leaders rapidly learned, applied, and promoted the participatory approach. To achieve this success, the lead ministry agreed to broad stakeholder involvement and convened countrywide consultations.

The integrated approach and policy alignment must be stressed repeatedly—Given ministerial mandates and personal predilections, planning teams at first tended to focus narrowly on certain child and family issues. They needed to be encouraged to include all areas and to align ECD policies with sectoral and cross-sectoral approaches, such as PRSPs, MDG strategies, and EFA plans. To the extent possible, they should reinforce and harmonize existing cross-sectoral and sectoral policies. However, ECD policies do far more than simply reinforce or harmonize sections of other policies and plans. They establish new strategies, programs, coordination processes, and organizational structures to help ensure that vulnerable children will be served.

Phase I is the most critically important period of ECD policy planning—From the outset, if the organizational framework and work plans for policy development are not well structured, the planning team will encounter significant barriers to achieving its goals. Each country team experienced difficulty in selecting its members and ensuring the commitment of all members to the effort. In one case, some members expected to receive remuneration and other benefits, whereas others understood they were conducting planning work as a part of usual professional responsibilities. Unlike some planning projects supported by international donors, high salaries and fees were not provided. Expectations, roles, and financial implications should be clarified at the outset to avoid misunderstandings. Personnel secondment and consultant arrangements should be contractual and transparent.

Situation analyses reveal dramatic needs for children and help build awareness at all levels—Situation analyses provided baseline data essential for policy development and evaluation, and revealed barriers to child development. As the first national studies on the status and needs of pregnant girls and women, as well as infants, young children, and families, they were of great value and merit publication. The analyses helped decision makers and citizens understand the needs of vulnerable children and parents, and they assisted planning teams to select policy objectives, strategies, and indicators.

Sufficient time should be allotted for the ECD planning process—Policy-planning processes using an integrated approach to ECD are valuable, but they are complex and time consuming. Nations inexperienced in dealing with cross-sectoral planning especially face major challenges.

Considerable time is required to plan and conduct effective consultations, draft policy documents, and build consensus and support. Because governmental agencies and national NGOs are seriously stressed by many ongoing challenges, they often lack a sufficient number of highly trained staff members and are torn between conducting policy and program activities. One year to 18 months should be allowed for planning, but this time will not be lost. Participants learn a great deal and apply their new knowledge during policy implementation.

Training for ECD policy planning is essential—Many West African governmental leaders are aware of preschool education, but lack knowledge about the importance of investing in children from birth to age 3, parenting programs, and ECI services. Most of these leaders have not been involved in participatory or cross-sectoral policy planning, and they usually lack information about the needs of vulnerable children. For these and other reasons, significant training is required. At a minimum, training topics should include research results on child development, ECD planning processes, integrated approaches to ECD, and consultation methods.

Policy implementation must begin during the planning period—Only one of the three countries prepared a NEPA, and only one ECD policy contains a financial plan—and that is the country with a NEPA. If nations do not prepare their NEPA during the planning period, policy implementation may be slow. Nations lacking effective NEPAs and broad political agreement regarding the importance of investing in children may also lack resources for policy implementation. Strong political support is also required to establish policy implementation units that will promote, plan, and evaluate cross-sectoral program development.

It is difficult to secure a broad range of donor support for ECD policy planning—A coalition of national institutions for policy planning usually can be created relatively easily, but a great deal of work is required to establish a donor coalition to fund planning expenses. Two of the countries were unable to conduct their consultations according to schedule because they lacked adequate diversified funding. They achieved their consultation goals, but only after pausing to conduct additional fundraising activities. Interagency coalitions can assist nations to conduct planning activities. The ADEA, UNICEF, and UNESCO successfully attracted other international agencies and NGOs as policy partners.

This collaborative approach promoted diversified support for policy implementation. Partnerships also help initiate coordination of ECD donor assistance and promote transparency and accountability. Donor support for planning ECD policies and NEPAs usually helps to overcome donor resistance to investing in ECD.

Beware of pressures to make a national ECD program the ECD policy— Many leaders in West Africa were confused about the difference between policy and program development. They wanted to make program goals and activities the sum total of national ECD policy. Some donors exhibited similar tendencies because they wished to promote the programs they funded. This situation should be anticipated and dealt with through training and coaching at the outset and repeatedly during planning.

*Policy strategies for training, communications, advocacy, and evaluation are essential—*Most ECD policies that were developed before this project lacked plans for training, social communications, policy advocacy, policy evaluation, and the annual revision of NEPAs. A training strategy and plan are essential for ECD capacity building. Communications plans and training for community education and policy advocacy are required to achieve policy objectives. Representatives of national media and public relations groups should be included in planning activities to gain their support for the communications plan and policy implementation. Because evaluation and monitoring systems are required for policy accountability, members of national planning departments, institutes, and universities should be included in the planning team.

*The quality of ECD policies can be enhanced through partnering with other countries—*Important synergies can result from subregional dialogue and exchanges during ECD policy planning. Combined training workshops for country teams reinforced national leadership and strengthened their sense of policy ownership. The countries achieved more because they validated each other's efforts, discussed activities, and helped each other resolve tough problems. The "positive competition" to excel kept each team motivated, and they began new professional relationships. Neighboring countries should be encouraged to pair up as they prepare their ECD policies.

*Nations should be encouraged to observe others' policy planning activities—*In addition to partnering with nearby countries, nations should conduct study visits to countries conducting ECD policy activities.

During the project, Chad and Niger were invited to participate in the Third Regional Training Workshop in Mauritania. This meeting inspired them to reorient some of their planning approaches. The UNICEF conference held in Dakar for 14 nations of West and Central Africa gave them tools and knowledge about other countries' experiences. Regional ECD policy meetings can help to inspire, motivate, and guide nations; however, more in-depth assistance is also required (UNICEF 2003a).

Future ECD Policy Challenges

Due to the planning teams' commitment and hard work, project objectives were exceeded. However, these countries and others in SSA face major ECD challenges. Political uncertainty, famine, disease, and poverty continue to affect them. As yet, investments in ECD do not appear to have increased greatly, but there are hopeful signs that greater attention is being given to improving child development. Unless children's status improves, ECD policy planning will have been futile. The nations require reinforcement; however, follow-up activities were not included in the plan for the project. Creating an ECD policy or policy framework is a first step, but it is only the beginning of a long-term effort to improve and expand services for vulnerable children.

Once ECD policies are established, international partners should continue to provide strong technical and financial support. National ECD forums and Children's Days should be conducted annually, including all governmental and civil society leaders involved in implementing ECD policies. International partners should participate actively in nationally led donor meetings and support the annual revision of the NEPA. Subregional and regional meetings should be convened to encourage increasing national investment in ECD and to ensure accountability. Evaluations of ECD achievements in each country should be conducted annually. International expectations for policy implementation should be mentioned frequently to national leaders, and an annual "ECD Report Card" on policy and program implementation should be issued.

The late Tamsir Samb was devoted to improving the lives of children affected by severe poverty. He worked tirelessly to ensure that community leaders helped plan the systems that would serve those children. Fortunately, many other West African planners are similarly dedicated to ECD movements in their nations. Several outstanding new ECD leaders emerged during our policy-planning process, and I feel confident that, over time, many of them will be successful in helping Africa's children to survive, thrive, and achieve their potential.

Note

1. For countries with a rich array of policy instruments in sectors related to young children, policy frameworks enable them to link and harmonize their policies, plans, and legislation; fill in gaps; and reinforce existing priorities while adding some new ones.

References

Asmara Declaration on ECD. 2002. Retrieved August 10, 2006, from http://www.ecdgroup.com/asmara_declaration_on_ECD.asp.

Colletta, N., and A. J. Reinhold. 1997. *Review of Early Childhood Policy and Programs in Sub-Saharan Africa*. Washington, DC: World Bank.

Pence, A. 2004. *ECD Policy Development and Implementation in Africa*. Paris: UNESCO.

Torkington, K. 2001. *WGECD Policy Project: A Synthesis Report*. Paris: ADEA/Netherlands Ministry of Foreign Affairs.

UNESCO (United Nations Educational, Scientific, and Cultural Organization). 1998. *Report of the Seventh Conference of Ministers of Education of African States (MINEDAF VII)*. Durban: UNESCO.

———. 2000. *The Dakar Framework for Action. Education for All: Meeting Our Collective Commitments*. Adopted by the World Education Forum, Dakar, Senegal. April 26–28. Paris: UNESCO.

UNICEF (United Nations Children's Fund). 2003a. "Dakar Recommendations." Regional Conference on National Policy Planning for an Integrated Approach to Early Childhood Development. October. Dakar: UNICEF/WCARO. Also available in French.

———. 2003b. *Rapport de l'atelier régional: Politiques nationales pour une approche intégrée du développement du jeune enfant*. Dakar: UNICEF/WCARO.

Vargas-Barón, E. 2005. *Planning Policies for Early Childhood Development: Guidelines for Action*. Paris: ADEA, UNICEF, and UNESCO.

Programming

CHAPTER 11

Responding to the Challenge of Meeting the Needs of Children Under 3 in Africa

Kofi Marfo, Linda Biersteker, Jenieri Sagnia, and Margaret Kabiru

In the 1970s Robert LeVine, who is recognized worldwide for his long-running research in Africa, devoted substantial portions of his career to illuminating the importance of cross-cultural differences in the norms, values, and belief systems that shape children's development in the context of parenting and the broader socialization process. He articulated a hierarchy of three universal goals presumed to inform parenting and socialization across cultures (LeVine 1977): (1) promoting and ensuring the physical survival and health of children, (2) fostering in children the capacity to attain economic self-maintenance, and (3) socializing across cultures to prepare children to develop behavioral competencies to internalize and act in accordance with the core values within their culture. Among others, these core values determine concepts of right and wrong (morality), authority, respect, spirituality, and so on, and also shape the relative balance between valuing interdependence, shared interests, and the common good versus valuing individual achievement, personal autonomy, and self-interest. The pursuit of these socialization goals begins in the context of the early parenting and primary caregiving process and finds ecological continuity through various other socialization agents, including the extended family, the community, formal institutions (such as schools, other group care settings, or places of worship), peers, and the myriad other forces in society that affect children's development directly and indirectly.

LeVine's framework might legitimately be viewed as just one perspective on developmental universals; other models of developmental universals are driven more by the biological underpinnings of human development that account for the many similarities in developmental processes and pathways across cultures. As we have learned from the ecological and sociocultural or ecocultural revolutions in developmental psychology (for example, Bronfenbrenner 1979; Nsamenang 1992; Vygotsky 1962), however, biological determinants of human development are themselves shaped or mediated by experiential and contextual variables embedded within cultures.

In using LeVine's framework as our point of departure, we have merely opted to emphasize the contextual forces that shape children's development and its outcomes. In all cultures, an optimal balance among socialization goals gives children the most ideal opportunities for healthy, all-round development. Setting aside the unique developmental tasks and milestones that make it difficult to transfer knowledge on child development across profoundly different cultural contexts (for example, Western versus non-Western), developmental contexts are not equally endowed with the resources necessary to deal effectively with the many threats to physical survival and optimal health in our contemporary world. LeVine's hierarchy of the "universal goals of socialization" thus has profound implications for developmental contexts in which the physical survival and health of children are under significant threat over prolonged periods from endemic conditions of limited infrastructural resources, underdeveloped health and other human services, and widespread poverty.

From the human capital development perspective, severe and endemic threats to physical survival and health jeopardize the social and economic development of entire societies, and they also create conditions under which childrearing tasks at the primary caregiver, family, and community levels can become geared to protective and survival activities or behaviors, a trade-off that compromises the attention given to other socialization goals. From this perspective, early childhood development (ECD) initiatives in Africa may be rationalized, based at least in part, on the need for formal structures and programs to supplement family and community efforts to attend equally to all three socialization goals in LeVine's hierarchy. ECD initiatives that focus exclusively on socialization goals for psychological development, culturally appropriate competencies, and school readiness are likely to attain minimal results if they pay little or no attention to children's physical survival and health needs. Physical survival and health needs are intricately intertwined with optimal growth and development.

In this chapter, therefore, we propose that the population of children under 3 offers the emerging ECD movement a unique opportunity to grasp the imperative to conceptualize programs and services much more broadly for age groups ranging from the unborn to the 8-year-old child. The case examples we present to illustrate promising emerging policies and innovative program initiatives in selected countries highlight the holistic, cross-sectoral approach that must be the hallmark of all ECD programs to ensure adequate attention to the broader range of determinants of optimal development in the early years.

Key Issues: An Overview

The case for attending to the physical survival and health needs of the African child has been made extensively in other parts of this volume. Our starting point in this chapter is that any viable ECD program in the African context must, as a matter of necessity and principle, build on existing assets and initiatives that address the survival, health, and nutritional needs of children. These issues are addressed in other chapters, so we will focus on ECD components pertaining to developmental stimulation in the context of community-based programs set up explicitly for this purpose. We organize our overview of key issues under three sections: (1) grounding programs in community development and capacity building, (2) framing developmental stimulation within appropriate cultural contexts, and (3) programming dimensions for developmental stimulation.

Grounding ECD in Community Development and Capacity Building
The Akan (Ghana) philosophical principle of *san kofa* (widely expressed outside the culture as a single-word dictum, *sankofa*) is perhaps a parsimonious way to introduce this section. Symbolized by the image of a bird that turns to look back while still flying ahead, the principle of sankofa conveys the importance of reaching into the past for valuable lessons, insights, or practices, even as a culture undergoes transformation and its people embrace new ideas and new ways. Two legacies are worth

retrieving from the past as we think about building and implementing ECD programs. Africa's communal and community legacy is highly celebrated, but the legacy's foundations have been rocked by modernity, urbanization, and the social isolation of people from their cultural and ancestral roots. The community as the unit of social organization for the common good remains an important but decreasingly harnessed traditional asset in development planning in much of rural Africa. Tomorrow's ECD programs must take the fullest advantage of this community asset to rebuild the fortunes of the continent through investments in its youngest citizens. One way to accomplish this task is to turn to the second, more modern legacy: community development as a nation-building strategy.

In many African countries, community development initiatives were a signature feature of national development efforts during the immediate postindependence era. These initiatives used multipronged strategies to mobilize villages and townships to assume greater ownership in "modernization" activities initiated and supported with local, regional, national, and international funding. The tempo of these initiatives appears to have waned with increased urbanization and the shifting of governmental priorities toward centralized, expertise-intensive, institution-based services in predominantly urban centers. When planned and delivered with cross-sectoral collaboration and coordination, ECD programs for children under 3 can become a catalyst in the revival and revitalization of community-based programs on the continent. The thinking and planning behind ECD programs must be in the larger context of national development planning policies in which building strong and resourceful communities is a major priority in its own right (see Marfo et al. 2004). Thinking about ECD in this manner paves the way, naturally, for early childhood development to be seen as a holistic process requiring balanced attention to (1) the forces that impinge on the physical survival and health of children, (2) the ecocultural context of development, including the social well-being of families and communities, and (3) children's development of competence.

Framing Developmental Stimulation within Cultural Contexts

Programming for developmental stimulation of children under 3 takes on special importance in light of the widely established knowledge that the biological and sociocultural foundations for optimal development are laid during this pivotal period (Mustard 2002; see also chapter 4 in this volume). Agreement is nearly universal on the importance of this formative period of development, even if such agreement is not readily apparent from priorities reflected in the social and economic policies pursued in different societies. It is also widely acknowledged that the biological heritage that all humans share, regardless of their ecocultural niches, results in identifiable universal development patterns in children across cultures.

However, there is less agreement on the content and methods of developmental stimulation and early care in the formal and semiformal settings typified by ECD programs. We need to be highly circumspect about developmental stimulation in terms of the lessons we choose to draw from traditions, practices, and knowledge bases accumulated in other parts of the world. We live in a world of increased globalization and unprecedented interaction among cultures. Informal and formal socialization agents can no longer exclusively prepare children to function effectively and successfully in their indigenous cultural contexts. Today's children are being prepared through the formal education sectors for job markets that cut cross regional, national, and continental boundaries. One manifestation of the increasing globalization (and of the historical dominance of Western science) is that not even ECD personnel and programs operating in the most remote of Africa's villages are immune to Western notions of, and practices related to, child development.

Yet, no amount of globalization will create a "homogeneous backcloth to our world," to borrow an expression from Richard Shweder (1991, 6) who notes aptly that "we are multiple from the start" and "our indigenous conceptions are diverse." This orientation precludes the tenability of any notion of a single pathway to optimal development. Additionally, cultural practices need to be understood as fluid and changing with social transformation and the shifting demands and expectations within the variety of developmental environments in which children grow.

Ultimately, cultural childrearing practices must be measured by how well they support the development and well-being of children. Practices, routines, and traditions that are central to optimal growth and development are embedded in all cultures. Similarly, across all cultures, there are practices, routines, and traditions with potentially counterproductive influences on development. Good ECD programs for young children need to be embedded in, and work with, local understandings of childhood and also draw on relevant and appropriate insights from other cultures.

Programming Dimensions for Developmental Stimulation
This chapter is not intended to provide a comprehensive discussion of program design and delivery. Nevertheless, it is important to delineate at least

three important dimensions to programming in the form of target groups that are at the heart of any comprehensive effort to design and implement programs and policies: (1) the children; (2) their families, guardians, and primary caregivers; and (3) the staff (paid or volunteer) who provide formal caregiving and developmental stimulation in group care settings.

The children—The case for investing in the earliest years of life has been made on a variety of fronts and with different emphases in different parts of the world. Whatever the logic, optimal development in children is a key objective in most ECD efforts. In the African context, emphasis on holistic development at all age levels is critically important. Comprehensive and holistic programs should capitalize on the social and interpersonal nature of children's earliest engagements with their world as the foundation for all aspects of development, particularly social competence, language proficiency, emotional maturity, life skills, and general cognitive competence. In light of the numerous challenges children face on the African continent, strategies that emphasize a resilience orientation to developmental stimulation are also critically important.

Consistent with the view that development is a process that is intricately embedded in, shaped by, and primed for functional adaptation within specific ecocultural contexts, ECD programs should draw from and build on indigenous traditions, childrearing practices, and material resources within the local environment in the provision of routine care and developmental stimulation. Indigenous traditions of childrearing are rich with practical tools and strategies—for example, stories, songs, lullabies, lap games, and pretend play activities—for stimulating language, social, emotional, intellectual, moral, and spiritual development. For infants, developmental stimulation and routine care are often inseparable activities; ECD programs should strive to keep them so.

Developmental stimulation for young children with special needs (for example, developmental disabilities) often requires strategies, orientations, and resources beyond those needed to support typically developing children (see Thorburn and Marfo 1994). It is particularly important that African ECD programs take an inclusive approach to service delivery and, consequently, provide staff training and education in developmental stimulation and care for children with special needs. To effectively respond to the challenges of children with special needs and their primary caregivers, developmental screening, which can be accomplished through cross-sectoral collaboration with public health and other primary health care programs, should be essential for ECD programs.

Families, guardians, and primary caregivers—In the earliest years of life, the most influential force in children's development is the family, which is itself influenced significantly by the community setting (see Marfo et al. 2004). For the children under 3, some of the most important contributions of ECD programs come from involving primary caregivers and also from enhancing the capacity of primary caregivers and families to provide adequate care and developmental stimulation to support optimal growth and development in enriching environments. To ensure continuity of care and complementary practices across settings, programs should provide a context for building close relationships between ECD staff/volunteers and the primary caregivers with whom the children spend most of their time. For children for whom family care is not the norm, such as children in orphanages and other institutional care settings, ensuring consistency of care by stable caregivers is essential.

We have chosen deliberately to use the referent "primary caregivers" (in place of parents) to emphasize the reality that in many of the communities served by ECD programs, children's primary care might not be provided by a mother or a father. Grandmothers, aunties, siblings, other members of the extended family, or even neighbors often assume primary caregiver roles for a variety of reasons. This reality has profound implications for how ECD programs approach family involvement, support, or capacity enhancement. Family education initiatives need to be structured and delivered differently depending on the diversity among the primary caregivers. For example, specialized programs may need to be developed to meet the unique childrearing needs of children raising their siblings or of elderly relatives in surrogate parenting roles. Lactating mothers may need education not only on child nutrition and health, but also on their own nutrition and health needs. Beyond programming for individual differences, perhaps all education programs should have some common elements for primary caregivers, including attention to the following: environmental health (sanitation and hygiene), indicators of healthy optimal development, support and encouragement in the appropriate use of local resources (such as indigenous cultural assets) to stimulate development, nurturing self-esteem and confidence in the childrearing process, and providing income-generation skills or facilitating links with community-based programs focusing on income-generation activities (such as training initiatives for cottage industries).

A discussion of family involvement, support, or capacity enhancement would be incomplete without attention to the important issues of parity, respect, and mutual recognition of the contributions that both primary caregivers/families and program staff make to the development and well-being of children. In a field characterized by "expert" models of service delivery, it is not uncommon for programs to assume that parents and other primary caregivers are ignorant of children's developmental needs. As Arnold (1998) notes, parental knowledge and expertise tend to be disregarded by professionals. In a study of parent-teacher collaboration in Nigeria, Ibetoh (2004) found that in their relationships with teachers, parents struggled to attain greater transparency and participation in decision making as well as better treatment, respect, and understanding (see also Marfo et al. 2004). Even in the face of poverty and the challenges it poses for coping with childrearing, primary caregivers bring to the ECD setting unique expertise and insights on their children's development. If families and primary caregivers can be welcomed as partners who are collectively capable of making substantive contributions to programs and their own children's development, then the resulting parity and mutual respect should provide a solid foundation for the common goals that families and ECD programs share.

Program staff—The selection and preparation of personnel are two crucial factors upon which the future of ECD in Africa hinges. Economic realities and the low priority accorded to ECD initiatives pose fundamental challenges to staffing programs with adequately trained grassroots personnel. ECD programs for older preschool-age children that are administered by ministries of education are more likely to benefit from established institutional infrastructures for personnel training, and the hope is that African nations will progress in making training a priority in policies and budgets. Programs for children under 3 are less likely to have systematic structures for personnel training, unless they are operated or supported fiscally by donor agencies or nongovernmental organizations (NGOs) with reasonable funding support from private sources. As African countries embrace the ECD movement and develop national policies to support programs on a large scale, training and ongoing technical support must receive as much attention as the creation of ECD spaces for children within community-based settings.

Training for ECD staff to carry out their responsibilities within the narrower context of individual program sites must at least include the following topics: (1) early childhood development, including typical and atypical development; (2) personal and environmental health, hygiene, and sanitation; (3) nutrition in early development; (4) strategies to develop relationships and collaborate with primary caregivers and community groups; (5) skills to convert local materials into developmentally enhancing objects and activities for children; and (6) strategies to effectively use indigenous cultural knowledge and practices, including community expertise in "curriculum" development and delivery.

An equally important aspect of personnel education is preparation in reflective processes that enable personnel to appreciate the implications of complexity and diversity in the delivery of human services. ECD staff must be helped to anticipate and deal with potential tensions and conflicts that often result from competing values. Caregivers guide their children's development based on values and traditions embedded within their culture (Casper et al. 2003). Children's behaviors in the ECD setting often reflect both child-level developmental idiosyncrasies and the influence of caregiving values and practices at home. This situation is complicated by the reality that even within the same cultural setting childrearing styles vary greatly. Openness and professional astuteness are required to acknowledge and deal effectively and sensitively with the broad range of differences in behaviors, expectations, and orientations emanating from such diversity.

A second, different type of tension is also worth noting. In an environment characterized by limited resources and growing demands for accountability, ECD programs and their staff are likely to find themselves caught between the practical need to develop truly authentic and contextually sensible strategies for fostering the longer term development of children and their families and the pressure to respond to accountability requirements imposed on programs to demonstrate short-term "evidence-based" outcomes (Casper et al. 2003). Responding reasonably to such accountability demands calls for critical reflection, prudence, and creativity, especially when the valued outcomes imposed externally happen to reflect narrow conceptions about developmental stimulation.

Case Studies: Exemplary and Innovative Approaches to Policy and Program Delivery

Increased recognition of the inadequate attention given to the population of children under 3 in ECD programs (Bernard van Leer Foundation 1994) is resulting in greater advocacy to expand programs and policies to address this important missing link (see, for example, Colletta and Reinhold 1997). One objective of this book is to identify and present examples of exemplary and innovative approaches to policy formulation and program delivery around the African continent. Thus, in this final major section, we present promising initiatives in three countries: South Africa, The Gambia, and Kenya.

Policy Initiatives in South Africa

The population of children under 3 in South Africa was approximately 2.66 million in 2001 (Statistics South Africa 2001). More than half the population of young children live in rural areas where poverty is most prevalent. A national survey of ECD provision commissioned in 2000 (South Africa 2001a) found that while more than a quarter of 5- and 6-year-olds were enrolled in ECD facilities, only 5.4 percent of children under 3 had access to either community child care facilities or services offered in homes. Male and female children had equal access, but given South Africa's apartheid history, access is still skewed by population group, with a higher percentage of white children having access to services than black children. Children with disabilities require early identification and intervention, but only 0.6 percent of the ECD enrollment of children is made up of children with special needs under age 3, including specialized facilities. Developmental screening as part of primary health care is not routine in all provinces.

With these realities, South Africa is now taking an integrated approach to serving children 0–4 years.[1] As with other social sector initiatives, vulnerable young children are the major target for the plan, which aims to reduce the adverse effects of poverty on this age group. Large programs already available for this age group in South Africa include free health care for children under 6 and for pregnant and lactating women, as well as child support grants to primary caregivers of children who have less than a specified income level. Accessing these benefits is often difficult, especially in rural areas, due to distances, lack of infrastructure (in the form of roads and means of transportation), transport costs, difficulty getting identity documents, and lack of information.

In May 2004 South Africa's cabinet mandated that the social sector cluster (the Departments of Health, Education, and Social Development) develop an integrated ECD plan for 2005 to 2010. Each of these departments already had policies prioritizing young children with several common features, but implementation has been fragmented. The plan aims at greater integration for ECD through a comprehensive approach to policies and programs, networking to improve the use of resources, and intersectoral collaboration across government, NGOs, and communities. The plan includes the following components: Integrated Management of Childhood Illnesses (IMCI; including developmental screening and promotion of healthy pregnancy, birth, and infancy), immunization, nutrition, facilitation of birth registration, referral services for health and social security grants, supporting children affected by HIV/AIDS and their caregivers (parents as well as substitute care providers), development and implementation of psychosocial programs, and early learning stimulation.

Many of these programs exist, but operate in isolation. Recognizing that service delivery is at the local level, community development workers will be key agents in implementation. Each province will contextualize the program for its own circumstances to ensure local and cultural relevance. The plan gives welcome expression to the policy principle that multiple approaches are needed, including direct services for children and services targeted at parents, families, and communities. Intervention sites will include homes, ECD centers of all kinds, prisons, and orphanages. The plan will be piloted in a selection of rural areas and one informal settlement, then it will be progressively implemented until it reaches the target of 4 million children.

Supporting primary caregivers in South Africa: The family and community motivator (FCM) approach—The family motivator, the foot soldier in ECD service delivery, is gaining momentum as a mechanism for reaching young children in families in areas that lack developed physical infrastructure and services. These volunteers work with young children in families who do not have sufficient access to services necessary to support their early development and are in danger of falling through the cracks. The FCM approach was developed and used in the 1980s by the Early Learning Resource Unit (ELRU), a long-standing ECD NGO, as an ECD intervention strategy for children in subeconomic housing areas and informal settlements[2] around Cape Town, taking on different forms depending on the needs in each area (Majola 1999). Since then, it has also been established with local NGO partners in deep rural areas in the Eastern Cape and Northern Cape Provinces and piloted in areas of Gauteng Province (Nene and Newman 2005; Newman et al. 1999; Newman, Uys, and Noko 2003). Now many NGOs in other parts of South Africa deliver family outreach activities in different forms to reach the large numbers of children outside the network of services.

The assumption is that families are the primary caregivers and duty bearers for young children, and that families may need support to ensure that children access all the rights that foster their development, as guaranteed in the South African Constitution (Newman 2002). Because this approach targets families, the focus is not specifically on children under 3. However, because access to ECD services is generally low, with poor and very young children least likely to participate, many of the children reached by the program are under 3.

The family and community motivators, as documented by Newman and Dlangamandla (2004), are catalysts and child advocates working mainly in communities characterized by unemployment, poverty, crime, and violence. They support young children and families by providing information and psychosocial support and by assisting families to seek ways to identify and increase their access to resources. The FCM approach is to work with the primary caregiver, who may be a mother, grandmother, foster parent, older sibling, or, more rarely, a father or grandfather. Key components include home visits, in which FCMs can identify and respond to the needs of children and caregivers, as well as regular larger workshops. The workshops bring together a group of caregivers and children for input on topics they have identified or to engage in specific activities, such as improvising play materials from local resources or learning how to make a food garden.

During the home visit, the FCMs demonstrate an activity to do with the child, talk to caregivers, and provide other assistance, such as helping families to access identity documents and grants or referring them to health services, as a way of extending the safety net for vulnerable children. FCMs also advocate for placing young children's rights on the local agenda.

The FCM program needs to be embedded in the local community to generate trust and sustainability and to facilitate the integration of indigenous knowledge. The start-up process has to be careful, and it takes time. Typically, ELRU is invited by a local organization (NGO, community-based organization, or local development committee) to talk about the needs of young children, to present the possibilities of the FCM program, and to assist with the development of a plan.

All planning is linked to existing local initiatives, such as the Provincial Plan of Action for children. In some cases ELRU is contacted again after the initial consultative meetings to provide training. Participants in the training program are selected by the local structures and the FCMs are selected from this group. Each FCM is responsible for a minimum of 10 families in a village or area. In some urban areas the FCMs reach more families for a shorter period. The vulnerable families and children the program targets are identified by the local leadership (traditional and/or elected) in each village or by local authority services, such as clinics, in some of the designated areas. Priority is given to families with the youngest children.

These programs operate differently depending on the infrastructure in the area, but they all depend on volunteers who may receive a small stipend. In some areas where there is no infrastructure, the program operates through local development committees. In others with existing preschool or community centers or NGO programs, outreach services have been extended to children and families who do not need a full-time program or who cannot afford to pay the fees. The focus of FCMs working in other parts of South Africa has included mobilizing people for access to clean water and sanitation, clean-up campaigns, health programs (IMCI, immunization, and medicines), nutrition (food aid), and space for play areas.

Various training programs for FCMs, as well as the ELRU *Masithethe* (Let's Talk) series, aim to get people talking about what parents and caregivers can do to enhance the active learning capacity of babies and young children. The series promotes sensitivity and awareness of cultural differences on a range of issues, including the impact of HIV/AIDS. The approach is picture-based and nonprescriptive, using appreciative enquiry. Unlike traditional problem-solving approaches that focus on problems and weaknesses, the Masithethe materials and approach focus on caregivers' strengths. The approach looks at what works in caregivers' homes and the community and explores how caregivers can build on existing traditions, beliefs, and practices of childrearing.

Barriers to scaling up the FCM program—Although the FCM program costs less to run than typical ECD centers (both because of its reliance on volunteers and its part-time nature), funding for stipends and administrative and support costs has been dependent, for the most part, on donor sources, which are not always systematic or sustained (Biersteker 1997). For this reason, it has not been possible to deliver the program widely. In one Eastern Cape project the district social services agency provided funding for a year. In 1998, the provincial Department of Education in Gauteng took up the FCM model in a pilot family ECD program and tested it with 300 caregivers from a range of poor communities as an example of an integrated and economically viable model for ECD provision (Gauteng Department of Education 1999; Newman et al. 1999). Caregivers reported very positively on how the program had supported them and their young children. UNICEF profiled the program in its 2000 *State of the World's Children* report (UNICEF 2000). Although the results were used to draft provincial policy, the program was unfortunately discontinued within 18 months. Notwithstanding these challenges, provincial authorities in the Western Cape and in KwaZulu Natal are interested in family outreach work to young children through a local government partnership with an NGO. In particular, the provision for family programs in the integrated ECD plan for South Africa and in a large social sector public works program suggests that there is at last sufficient support to scale up the FCM program.

The Gambia's Baby Friendly Community Initiative (BFCI)

The Gambia, a very small country in West Africa covering 10,689 square kilometers, has a population of 1.5 million people, 27 percent of whom are children under 8, according to the 2003 census (The Gambia 2003b). Children under 3 years constitute about 8 percent of the population. The economy is based on agriculture; women contribute 49 percent of the total agricultural produce. Poverty is increasing and had risen to about 58 percent by 2003; urbanization is also increasing (reaching 50 percent by 2003), fuelled by rural-urban migration; and unemployment in the public sector is increasingly becoming a major problem (The Gambia 2003a).

At 96.6 deaths per 1,000 live births (The Gambia 2003b), the infant mortality rate is very high. The highest rate of infant mortality in rural communities occurs during the neonatal period, attributable mainly to infections, premature births, and malnutrition. Maternal deaths (estimated in the 1990s at 73/10,000) multiply the tragedy because the chances for survival of motherless infants are limited.

Breastfeeding is an important survival strategy, but optimal breastfeeding is rarely practiced in The Gambia. As in many other countries in Sub-Saharan Africa, many mothers initiate breastfeeding later than the delivery day and give water and other fluids to their newborns. Complementary foods are also introduced as early as 3 months after birth. In 1985 The Gambia adopted an innovative initiative that combines optimal breastfeeding with health, maternal health and nutrition, and water and environmental sanitation to support the survival and development of children under 3. The Baby Friendly Community Initiative (BFCI) is an adaptation of the World Health Organization (WHO)/United Nations Children's Fund (UNICEF) Baby Friendly Hospital Initiative (BFHI), which was launched in 1991. The BFHI initiative aims to protect, promote, and support breastfeeding in health facilities, with the presupposition that most deliveries will occur in health facilities. The WHO and UNICEF developed 10 steps to successful breastfeeding and supported their implementation in

14,584 health facilities globally that were designated as Baby Friendly Hospitals (WHO 1989; WHO and UNICEF 1990).

In The Gambia, as in many other African countries, most deliveries unfortunately do not take place in health facilities but in homes, which means that traditional and cultural care practices of mothers during delivery and immediately after birth are the norm. Some traditional and cultural practices have been found to be a major cause of many maternal and infant deaths. To address such practices and to promote better health care and nutrition for infants, the BFCI was introduced in 1993 in a number of rural Gambian communities where poverty is endemic and access to basic services is poor. The initiative consists of infant feeding (exclusive breastfeeding up to 6 months after delivery, complementary feeding, and young child feeding), maternal health and nutrition (child spacing, food and nutrition effect on pregnancy, disease control, vaccination programs), personal hygiene (hand washing, regular bathing of children, and clean environments for toddlers), and water and environmental sanitation (pit latrines, control of domestic animals, clean surroundings, and clean water in the home).

A major strength of the BFCI is the development of messages in all its components based on traditional knowledge and practices within local communities. The program is caregiver- and parent-focused as well as community based. It targets parents as the primary caregivers as well as other family members within the extended family system. Parenting is seen as everybody's business, including the men's. The initiative develops messages on a variety of issues based on traditional knowledge derived from interviews with community members. This localization strategy has made the initiative most successful, by influencing attitudinal changes and providing knowledge for caregivers on improved early childrearing practices.

Training is important for transmitting messages and is provided for village support groups (VSGs) made up of five women and three men. The training methodology consists of a combination of tools: village meetings, village ceremonies, discussions, drama and roleplay, and fun groups locally known as *Kanyelengo*, which usually are groups of nonchildbearing women well known and respected for their skills in transmitting important educational messages through entertainment. Peer-to-peer education and opinion leaders are also used to maximize information sharing and behavior change.

The approach is monitored monthly through short questionnaires on the 10 steps, performance of the community health nurses as supervisors and the VSGs as implementers, community participation, and mothers' knowledge and practices of infant feeding. The visits also use observation and discussion techniques to assess the constraints and further training needs of the VSGs. An initial evaluation in 1997 interviewed 405 persons in 12 villages. The results indicate unanimous support for the initiative by both religious and traditional leaders who previously preached against exclusive breastfeeding. Nearly 91 percent of the mothers had administered the first milk to their babies. Of the 313 mothers who had babies by 1997, all had initiated breastfeeding within the first 24 hours. Most of the communities saw the following benefits of the approach: a cleaner environment, healthier children, healthier pregnant women, and, above all, unity in the communities as a result of shared involvement and commitment to the initiative.

Despite these positive outcomes, challenges include the sustainability of the voluntary service provided by the VSG members who are mainly young people, the persistent negative attitudes of some religious leaders toward exclusive breastfeeding, and difficulty in sustaining the training and integrating BFCI as part of an overall community development strategy. For any country interested in the initiative, the major challenge would be the willingness of the communities to create VSGs who are prepared to spend a lot of time serving their communities without any compensation.

The BFCI emphasizes infant and maternal nutrition and, because it already contains specific elements of the holistic ECD approach, it provides a real opportunity for a smooth implementation of a more comprehensive ECD approach. For this reason, the initiative was used to implement community-based ECD in The Gambia. The training program for the VSGs has been expanded to include early stimulation and learning, the importance of interaction between other family members and children, ensuring birth registration, promoting clean and safe environments for children, and protecting against abuse and exploitation.

The number of BFCI communities sensitized on the ECD approach increased from 39 in 2002 to 68 in 2004. More than 10,000 caregivers, the majority of whom were women (mothers and grandmothers), have been sensitized on ways to actively assist in the survival and development of their children. As of 2005, more than 20,400 children were benefiting from the BFCI approach in these rural communities. The impetus already created by the BFCI approach for the promotion of early stimulation, emotional development, and child protection has indeed enhanced the smooth implementation of the ECD approach at the community level. The willingness of the communities to embrace new ideas to promote early stimulation and emotional development for very young children is astonishing. This interest and willingness, more than any other factor, will underlie the success and sustainability of the ECD approach, especially for the under-3 population in these communities.

Program Design and Delivery in Kenya

The majority of Kenya's estimated 3 million children under 3 are cared for in the family and not in institutions (Gakuru and Koech 1995; Hyde and Kabiru 2006; Kipkorir 1994; NACECE 1997; Swadener, Kabiru, and Njenga 2000). Traditional caregiving practices still persist in many areas, where mothers are the primary caregivers assisted by older children, grandparents, other relatives, and neighbors. Increasingly, paid caregivers are essential to many families as more women become engaged in wage employment or businesses that take women outside the home for extended periods. Parents and communities are struggling to find alternative suitable and affordable care for their youngest children. The problems of children under 3 have been acknowledged for some time, and a number of forums have made recommendations.

A review of surveys, research, and conference reports between 1992 and 2005 (Bali and Kabiru 1992; Gakuru and Koech 1995; Hyde and Kabiru 2006; Kenya Institute of Education and Bernard van Leer Foundation 2002; Kenya and UNICEF 1999; NACECE 1993, 1995, 1997; and Swadener, Karibu, and Njenga 2000) identified recommendations to improve care for children under 3, including the following:

- Family enhancement and educational programs should be mounted and supported by the government and NGOs to affirm parents' positive caregiving practices and to sensitize both parents and policy makers to the critical importance of providing quality care for children under 3.
- Future policies should emphasize family-centered programming that takes into account the needs and wishes of parents and communities.
- Because the community is the custodian of care, all members of the community, including children, elders, and young people, both men and women, should play a role in educating young children.
- Communities should be mobilized to provide suitable, safe, and healthy learning environments for children, and community-based groups such as women's groups and youth groups should be motivated to participate more in supporting the family in the care of the youngest children.

- Traditional knowledge should be tapped to legitimize and enrich programs for young children, and strategies should be developed to empower communities and professionals to identify traditional strengths and to assess how such strengths and the related traditional knowledge can be recaptured and integrated into contemporary services for young children.
- The government, NGOs, and the private sector should provide grants for community-based services that support families with young children.
- Research on the care of children under 3 should be intensified.

Most of these programs combine several complementary components and approaches. Examples include child-to-child activities that promote the involvement of older siblings and youth as well as home visits by lead parents who are identified by the community and trained as the community's own resource persons (CORPs) by the NGOs. These CORPs organize training workshops for parents and provide one-to-one support and counseling during home visits. In some programs, the CORPs are trained as community health workers; they weigh and monitor the growth of young children and sell essential pharmaceutical drugs that are approved by the Department of Health. The involvement of the family and the community is crucial to the acceptability, quality, and sustainability of such interventions. Parents are encouraged to form support groups based on geographical or social affinity and to cooperate and help one another when in need. The programs endeavor to empower families to build democratic ways of managing their community affairs, mobilizing and managing resources, and generating income to improve the care of children and the welfare of their families and communities (Kenya Institute of Education and Bernard van Leer Foundation 2002; Kenya and UNICEF 1999).

The Mwana Mwende Child Development Center conducts parent enhancement and educational programs that target teenage and young parents, as well as elderly grandparents who are taking care of orphans (Kabiru, Njenga, and Swadener 2003). About 3,000 children are affected by these programs. The center works with the community to mobilize parents and elderly caregivers to form support groups to facilitate mutual support and learning. Information and training workshops are offered on topics such as child care, discipline, parent-child interactions, nutrition, health, income generation, and group management. Group members are supported and trained to start income-generating activities such as growing tree and vegetable seedlings, raising chickens and milk goats, or engaging in small-scale businesses. Those with leadership qualities who are acceptable to their communities are given further practical and on-the-job training to prepare them to serve as community health workers, home-based care providers, or community motivators. After training, the workers organize more workshops for parents and do home visits to counsel and advise parents on a one-to-one basis. The communities form village committees to support these workers to advocate for the rights of the child, identify the most vulnerable children, and find resources to support these children. In some communities the village and community workers have mobilized their villages to establish community pharmacies and resource centers where young children are weighed and their growth is monitored (Kabiru, Njenga, and Swadener 2003).

The regional office of the African Network for Prevention and Protection Against Child Abuse and Neglect (ANPPCAN) exemplifies an innovative approach that can be scaled up, with more support, to improve services for children under 3 who live in slums or congested areas, such as large agricultural plantations. ANPPCAN runs a network of more than 120 home-based daycare centers that cater for children from birth to 6 years. Each mother enrolls 10–15 children in the program that she operates from her one- or two-room home. ANPPCAN trains mothers on child rights, nutrition, health, hygiene, child care and stimulation, as well as income generation. Mothers have learned how to enrich flour to improve the nutrition program that is provided at the centers. By training other mothers in nutrition and child care, a larger market for the enriched flour produced by the ANNPCAN-trained mothers is created (Kenya Institute of Education and Bernard van Leer Foundation 2002). Of the children served by ANPPCAN, about 500 are under 3.

While the combined efforts of the multiple agencies and communities are commendable, the majority of children under 3 are yet to be reached. In recent years, the Kenyan government has collaborated with UNICEF and United Nations Educational, Scientific, and Cultural Organization (UNESCO) to initiate a process to develop an integrated ECD policy to improve quality, increase access and equity, and harness more resources for children from government and other stakeholders. Policy discussion papers containing recommendations for improving the care of children under 3 have been developed. The documents recognize and recommend that care for children under 3 be supported in a variety of settings and approaches including the family, home-based care and community-based group care, mobile center preschools, as well as parent education, home visiting, and child-to-child programs. Recommendations to support the family include extending maternity leave, providing support grants to the most disadvantaged families, training a cross-section of caregivers, and mobilizing communities to support families and create environments that promote the total well-being of children. The documents also provide guidelines and regulations for running the services that cater to children under 3 and define the roles of different partners (Kenya and UNICEF 2004; Kenya and UNESCO 2005).

Summary and Concluding Comments

This chapter has attempted to frame ECD for the under-3 population around a cross-sectoral perspective calling for closer integration of programs, services, and initiatives with direct relevance for children's development and well-being that are currently delivered under the auspices of different governmental agencies and bureaucratic jurisdictions. We have made a case for using existing infrastructures for primary health care, nutrition supplementation, and immunization initiatives as both a foundation and a bridge to programs dedicated specifically to routine care and developmental stimulation in community contexts. We have emphasized family and community capacity enhancement as fundamental to ECD programming, and we have offered perspectives and suggestions on program implementation issues affecting three key target groups: the children, families and primary caregivers, and ECD personnel.

Embedded within our approach to ECD is the value of programming for all children, including those with developmental disabilities and other health conditions. Among the lessons we should learn from the industrialized world is one that is particularly timely, given the emergent nature of the African ECD movement: It is counterproductive to build innovative programs around exclusionary or segregated models only to turn around in the future to struggle toward inclusiveness. Building ECD programs around an inclusion philosophy makes sense both morally and economically.

Finally, we have presented case examples of innovative initiatives in both the policy and service delivery arenas. In addition to other exciting developments highlighted throughout this volume, the case examples of innovative policy and program approaches presented in this chapter provide assurance that ECD programs in Africa are moving in the desirable direction of holistic programming and cross-sectoral policy development. However, the emerging movement is not without its challenges; in these closing paragraphs we draw attention to several issues that demand serious consideration on the part of ECD leaders at all levels: policy, program development, and practice. At the macro level, Africa faces a daunting challenge with regard to economic resources to support ECD activities at a significant level of penetration. ECD initiatives depend largely on funding from donor agencies, philanthropic establishments, and indigenous NGOs, which often depend on foreign sources as well for their operations. These initiatives, by their very nature, serve only small segments of the population of children for whom ECD services can make a dramatic difference in developmental well-being. Governmental involvement in the design and delivery of ECD policies and programs has largely been made possible through international loan programs, such as those offered by the World Bank.

While recognizing the realistic resource constraints many African nations face, it is nevertheless important to raise awareness, at the governmental level, about the dangers of continuing to count on the outside world for support for ECD initiatives. If these initiatives are to thrive to the point of making a real difference in the quality of life for generations of citizens, as well as in the quality of human capital development for the continent as a whole, there must be a conscious shift from long-term dependency on external inputs toward national budgetary planning that reflects clear indigenous valuing of investments in the early years of children's development.

On the other side of the resource constraints issue, ECD advocates and professionals need to be realistic about what is feasible and attainable. Much of the appeal of ECD programs emanates from successful outcomes demonstrated in some of the world's most resource-rich nations. In recognizing and promoting the benefits of ECD programs for Africa, we cannot lose sight of the stark reality that the state of the economy in much of Africa calls for a realistic, incremental, strategic approach in which program design, implementation, and outcome choices are based on what is workable and realistic for the continent. It is unrealistic to expect the outcomes commonly associated with ECD programs in other parts of the world when many of the emerging programs in Africa depend on the poorest of the poor to support service delivery, with little or no remuneration.

Finally, and of direct pertinence to both the resource constraints issue and the issue of contextual relevance, the evolving ECD movement must guard against resorting to transport models of service delivery (Marfo 1998) in which program frameworks and content that have been proven to work in the resource-rich nations are transplanted into the African context with little regard for the ecocultural realities of African communities.

Notes

The authors wish to thank Dr. Cecilia A. Darko for her suggestions on an earlier draft of the manuscript.

1. This particular age group is targeted because children are being phased into a reception year as the first year of primary schooling in the year they turn 5. Interventions planned for children 0–4 years will be differentiated according to developmental stage (South Africa 2001b).

2. Informal settlements are overcrowded large settlements of informal housing that have grown on the margins of cities and towns, mostly housing economic migrants from rural areas. Basic infrastructure (such as water and sanitation) might be lacking, unemployment is widespread, and supportive social networks are limited.

References

Arnold, C. 1998. "Early Childhood: Building Our Understanding and Moving Towards the Best of Both Worlds." Paper presented at the international seminar "Ensuring a Strong Foundation: An Integrated Approach to Educational Development," Aga Khan University, Karachi, Pakistan, March.

Bali, S., and M. Kabiru. 1992. *Development Needs and Early Stimulation of Children under Three Years: Building on People's Strengths*. Nairobi: NACECE (National Center for Early Childhood Education).

Bernard van Leer Foundation. 1994. *Building on People's Strengths: Early Childhood in Africa*. The Hague: Bernard van Leer Foundation.

Biersteker, L. 1997. "An Assessment of Programs and Strategies for 0–4 Year Olds." South African Case Study Report—Africa Regional Integrated Early Childhood Development Services Initiative. Cape Town: Early Learning Resource Unit.

Bronfenbrenner, U. 1979. *The Ecology of Human Development*. Cambridge, MA: Harvard University Press.

Casper, V., R. M. Cooper, C. D. Finn, and F. Stott. 2003. "Caregiving Goals and Societal Expectations." *Zero to Three* 23 (5): 4–6.

Colletta, N. J., and A. J. Reinhold. 1997. "Review of Early Childhood Policy and Programs in Sub-Saharan Africa." World Bank Technical Paper 367, Africa Region Series, World Bank, Washington, DC.

Gakuru, O. N., and B. G. Koech. 1995. "The Experience of Young Children: A Conceptualized Case Study of Early Childhood Care and Education in Kenya: Final Report to Bernard van Leer Foundation." Unpublished report available through Bernard van Leer Foundation, The Hague.

Gambia, The. Department of Central Statistics. 2003a. *Household Economic Survey Report*. Banjul: Department of State for Finance and Economic Affairs.

————. 2003b. *National Population and Housing Census*. Banjul: Department of State for Finance and Economic Affairs.

Gauteng Department of Education. 1999. *Impilo: A Holistic Approach to Early Childhood Development*. Johannesburg: Gauteng Department of Education.

Hyde, A. L., and M. Kabiru. 2006. *Early Childhood Development as an Important Strategy to Improve Learning Outcomes*. Paris: ADEA (Association for the Development of Education in Africa).

Ibetoh, C. A. 2004. "A Guide for Effective Collaboration between Schools and Parents: A Cooperative Development and Delivery Approach." Unpublished master's major project report, University of Victoria, British Columbia, Canada.

Kabiru, M., A. Njenga, and B. B. Swadener. 2003. "Early Childhood Development in Kenya: Empowering Young Mothers, Mobilizing a Community." Unpublished report available through Margaret Kabiru, Director, Mwana Mwende Child Development Center, Nairobi, Kenya.

Kenya Ministry of Education and Human Resource Development, and UNICEF. 1999. *Developing Alternative, Complementary Approaches to Early Childhood Care for Survival, Growth, and Development in Kenya*. Nairobi: Kenya Ministry of Education and Human Resource Development.

Kenya Ministry of Education, Science and Technology, and UNESCO. 2005. "Policy Framework on Early Childhood Development." Discussion Paper, Kenya Ministry of Education and Human Resource Development, Nairobi.

Kenya Ministry of Education, Science and Technology, and UNICEF. 2004. "Draft Policy Concept Paper on Integrated Early Childhood Development." Kenya Ministry of Education, Science and Technology, Nairobi.

Kenya Institute of Education and Bernard van Leer Foundation. 2002. "Report of the Early Childhood Development Regional Conference, Mombassa." Kenya Institute of Education, Nairobi.

Kipkorir, L. 1994. *Childcare: Mother's Dilemma*. Nairobi: Kenya Institute of Education.

LeVine, R. A. 1977. "Child Development as Cultural Adaptation." In *Culture and Infancy: Variations in the Human Experience*, ed. P. H. Leiderman, S. Tulkin, and A. Rosenfeld, 15–27. New York: Academic Press.

Majola, N. 1999. "From Surviving to Thriving." *Children First* 3 (25): 24–26.

Marfo, K. 1998. "Conceptions of Disability in Cultural Contexts: Implications for Transport Models of Service Delivery in Developing Countries." Invited paper presented at the "Expert Meeting on Disability and Culture," Bonn, Germany, June.

Marfo, K., F. K. Agorsah, W. W. Bairu, A. Habtom, M. R. Muheirwe, S. Ngaruiya, and E. M. Sebatane. 2004. "Children, Families, Communities, and Professionals: Preparation for Competence and Collaboration in ECD Programs." *International Journal of Educational Policy, Research, and Practice* 5 (3): 31–60.

Mustard, J. F. 2002. "Early Child Development and the Brain—The Base for Health, Learning, and Behavior Throughout Life." In *From Early Child Development to Human Development*, ed. M. E. Young, 23–62. Washington, DC: World Bank.

NACECE (National Center for Early Childhood Education). 1993. *Partnership and Networking in the Care and Development of Under Threes: A Report of the Conference Held at Nyeri, UNICEF and Ministry of Education*. Nairobi: NACECE.

———. 1995. *Who Takes Care of Children Under Three Years? A Report of a Survey Carried Out in Kericho, Nairobi, Narok and Siaya*. Nairobi: NACECE.

———. 1997. *Early Childhood Development: End-of-Term Report for the Aga Khan-Supported ECD Project (1993–1996)*. Nairobi: NACECE.

Nene, N., and M. Newman. 2005. "Masikhule Family and Community Motivators Case Study." Presentation at the Masikhule ECD dialogue for provincial government and NGOs, Mthatha, South Africa, August.

Newman, M. 2002. "A Children's Rights Focus to Strengthening Indigenous Community and Family Participation in Early Childhood Development." Paper presented at the "Organisation Mondiale pour l'Education Prescolaire (OMEP) World Council and Conference," Durban, South Africa, October.

Newman, M., J. Carr, S. de Beer, P. Goliath, and B. Ngwenya. 1999. *The Qala Ekhaya/Lapeng Kathorus Family-Based ECD Project: Final Report to Gauteng Education Department*. Johannesburg: Kathorus Consortium.

Newman, M., and L. Dlangamandla. 2004. "Family and Community Motivators." Presentation at an ECD dialogue for government and NGOs at the Early Learning Resource Unit/Cape Town, South Africa, October.

Newman, M., T. Uys, and T. Noko. 2003. "Implementers' Report: A Re Direng." Unpublished report, Early Learning Resource Unit/Thusano, South Africa.

Nsamenang, A. B. 1992. *Human Development in Cultural Context: A Third World Perspective*. Newbury Park, CA: Sage.

Shweder, R. A. 1991. *Thinking Through Cultures: Expeditions in Cultural Psychology*. Cambridge, MA: Harvard University Press.

South Africa Department of Education. 2001a. *The Nationwide Audit of ECD Provisioning in South Africa*. Pretoria: South Africa Department of Education.

———. 2001b. "Early Childhood Development." White Paper 5, ECD Directorate, Pretoria.

Statistics South Africa. 2001. *Population Census 2001*. Pretoria: Statistics South Africa.

Swadener, B. B., with M. Kabiru, and A. Njenga. 2000. *Does the Village Still Raise the Child?* Albany, NY: State University of New York Press.

Thorburn, M. J., and K. Marfo. 1994. *Practical Approaches to Childhood Disability in Developing Countries: Insights from Experience and Research.* Tampa, FL: Global Age.

UNICEF (United Nations Children's Fund). 2000. *State of the World's Children.* New York, NY: UNICEF.

Vygotsky, L. 1962. *Thought and Language.* New York: John Wiley.

WHO (World Health Organization). 1989. *Protecting, Promoting, and Supporting Breastfeeding: The Special Role of Maternity Services: A Joint WHO/UNICEF Statement.* Geneva: WHO.

WHO and UNICEF. 1990. *The Innocenti Declaration on the Protection, Promotion, and Support of Breastfeeding.* Florence: Innocenti Center.

CHAPTER 12

Introducing Preprimary Classes in Africa: Opportunities and Challenges

Linda Biersteker, Samuel Ngaruiya, Edith Sebatane, and Sarah Gudyanga

The *Education for All* (EFA) initiative—commencing with the 1990 World Declaration that "learning begins at birth" (UNESCO 1990, art. 5) and continuing through the follow-up meeting in Dakar in 2000, where the first EFA goal was identified as "expanding and improving early childhood care and education" (UNESCO 2000)—has provided a level of commitment to the well-being of preprimary age children not evident before these conferences. Such commitments take place in the context of limited resources, however, and inevitably discussions emerge regarding what kinds of services and for what age children (see chapter 11 for a discussion of services for children 0–3). In the context of limited resources, many countries in Africa (and internationally) look closely at what services might be developed, at what cost, and for what expected benefit for children immediately prior to their entry into primary school. In commenting on the implementation of early childhood rights, the United Nations Committee on the Rights of the Child (2006, para. 28) "recognizes with appreciation that some States parties are planning to make one year of preschool education available and free of cost for all children."

Transition into primary school from home or early childhood development (ECD) service is recognized as a critical period for children's development and learning (for example, Myers 1997; Sylva and Blatchford 1996). Historically, specific approaches to care and education have been developed for this transition from a home environment to a school environment. Kindergartens are one such program found throughout much of the Minority World and parts of the Majority World. As its name (children's garden) implies, the kindergarten philosophy is more one of nurturing the "budding" child than of teaching or providing direct instruction. The kindergarten philosophy has found its way into the broader early childhood education literature leading to a child-centered, interactive play environment approach deemed most appropriate for preprimary learning and development (Bredekamp 1987). In Africa, such an approach to learning and development is no less relevant but, to a considerable degree, and particularly in the private sector, preprimary programs are modeled on a primary instructional approach, which many parents see as the most appropriate approach to prepare the child for later schooling. This reality, largely the result of the limited availability of early childhood care and education training, is just one of the many challenges facing African countries in implementing preprimary programs.

Many countries in Africa are considering, and some have initiated, state-supported preprimary education or bridging programs. This action is most often motivated by a concern to increase schooling success and reduce dropout rates and repetition by, for example,

- creating a transition from the informal to the formal system;
- ensuring that children enter formal education based on readiness rather than chronological age;
- allowing for intervention and remediation before formal schooling is introduced; and
- easing the task of teachers in lower primary grades by ensuring that they have a more homogeneous group to teach (South Africa 1983).

Lowering the age for state-supported education programs to include a preprimary year creates access for potentially large numbers of children in contexts where the majority of young children have not had access to ECD programs. Careful targeting to ensure the inclusion of children disadvantaged by poverty or with special needs, and to ensure that boys and girls have equal access, can maximize the benefits of such interventions.

Yet, introducing a preprimary year presents challenges, especially with regard to the provision of appropriate curriculum, teacher training, financing, supervision, and related supports.

This chapter provides a brief account of the experiences of four Sub-Saharan African countries—South Africa, Kenya, Zimbabwe, and Lesotho—that are in the process of introducing a preprimary class as part of the primary education system.[1] The key areas described include policy and provision of services, financing, curriculum and program elements, and teacher training. In the final section, the authors reflect on the issues and challenges experienced.

South Africa

During the apartheid regime, provision of ECD services was very limited and served mostly white children and children in urban areas. Because of the lack of state involvement in ECD, communities and nongovernmental organizations (NGOs) shouldered most of the burden of providing ECD services and training for other children, including those of colored (mixed origin) and Asian descent. In 1994 the democratic African National Congress government identified ECD as a key area in the process of reconstruction and human resource development and in promoting the rights of young children.

Policy and Provision of Services

The *White Paper on Education and Training* (South Africa 1995) defined the government's commitment to young children, including their intention to phase in a "reception year" as part of compulsory schooling. This commitment was followed in 1996 by an interim ECD policy and a national pilot project to investigate phasing in a reception year and the accreditation of teachers and training providers. The pilot project contributed to the 2001 *Education White Paper 5* on ECD (South Africa 2001a), which provides for the phasing in of a national reception year system (grade R) for children aged 5 years, with a priority for the poorest of the poor. It is intended that all 5-year-olds will be in grade R classes by 2010.[2] Grade R is intended to be universally available but attendance is not compulsory.

Three types of grade R are provided for—programs within the public primary system, programs at community-based ECD centers, and programs that are independent (private)—all of which must register with provincial departments of education. Some community-based centers will, in the short term, become part of the public system of grade R, but only if the public primary school option is not available or is not available within a reasonable distance from the child. By 2004 about 40 percent of approximately 877,500 5-year-olds were in grade R classes in public, community-based, and independent schools. However, provincial variations in access were wide, ranging from 8 percent to 73 percent of the eligible child population. In the 2004 school year, 42 percent of grade R programs were in community-based sites (Wildeman and Nomdo 2004).

Financing
From a curriculum perspective, grade R is the first year of the foundation phase of primary schooling, but it is differently financed and staffed. Government funds it two ways. First, provincial governments fund grants to community-based ECD centers on a per-learner basis. Second, a direct grant in aid from provincial departments of education to school-governing bodies that employ the teachers finances grade R in public primary schools. Subsidization of the reception year is poverty targeted. Children in the poorest 40 percent of schools are intended to receive the highest per capita level of grants. Children in targeted public primary schools also benefit from a primary school nutrition program.

The modest grant—which varies across provinces from R 2 to R 6 per learner per school day for up to 30 learners—is spent on part of the teacher costs, learner support materials, training, furniture, nutrition, and educational equipment. For 2005/6, the nine provincial education departments have allocated R 489 million in grants to grade R. Grade R funding lags substantially behind funding for other grades in the same school, and is approximately 7 times less than for a grade 1 learner.[3] Most grade R teachers receive very low salaries, which negatively affects their motivation. A national norms and standards policy for grade R is being finalized (South Africa 2005). After the policy is accepted, it will bring ECD to 5-year-old children into the government formal funding program, and aims to increase per capita funding for grade R to 70 percent of that for grade 1.

Curriculum and Program Elements
Curriculum for 5-year-olds is part of the *Revised National Curriculum Statement* (South Africa 2002). It forms part of the foundation phase of schooling, which includes grades R, 1, 2, and 3 (approximate ages 5–9 years). The focus is on literacy, numeracy, and life skills. Principles for programming include holistic development of the child, contextually

and developmentally appropriate activities, a focus on human rights and values in the curriculum, and opportunities to play and learn informally through experience in a nurturing environment. In practice, however, location of grade R in primary schools can result in pressure for a more formal approach, which is a challenge being addressed by additional training for grade R teachers. The prescribed teacher-child ratio is 1 to 30, but there is provincial discretion to reduce this ratio by using assistants.

Teacher Training

Prior to the late 1990s, the majority of black ECD teachers were trained by NGOs (South Africa 2001b; Short and Pillay 2002) and their qualifications were not formally recognized. Accredited education and training now falls under the South African Qualifications Authority (SAQA), set up in 1995. ECD qualifications can be obtained from a range of providers: private, nongovernmental, further education and training colleges, as well as universities that are accredited by a quality assurance body appointed by SAQA. Teacher training for primary schooling requires a four-year degree as a minimum (level 6), but the minimum required to teach grade R in this phase-in period is level 4 (equivalent to a further education and training certificate at the completion of high school). The Department of Education has made some funding available through conditional grants and through Department of Labor–funded "learnerships"[4] to train grade R teachers to bring them to level 4. Large-scale upgrading to level 5 is planned (Biersteker and Dawes 2007).

The development of grade R is the largest-ever public commitment to ECD in South Africa, and it has significantly increased access. However, there are challenges. The decision to locate most subsidized grade R programs in public primary schools has severely affected the community-based centers, which mostly rely on parent fees, though some received subsidies for 5- to 6-year-old children. Fees in public primary schools are minimal or nonexistent, and a further attraction is the feeding program, which is only for public schools (Biersteker and Dawes 2007). Between 2000 and 2004, the number of children in public primary grade R schools nearly doubled; many of them were drawn from community-based centers. However, public schools do not offer full-day child care services that provide care and protection for many children. Another concern is that while it is easier for the Department of Education to manage reception classes in public schools, there is a tendency toward a more formal approach to the curriculum when grade R is located there. Finally, it is important to note that grade R is only one of a range of strategies required to address ECD needs, including interventions for younger children and their caregivers, and it attempts to improve the quality of the early years of schooling.

Kenya

In Kenya, there has been a remarkable expansion in the provision of early childhood education (ECE) since the country attained independence in 1963. The impetus is attributed to socioeconomic changes that have affected traditional childrearing systems, as well as increased parental perception of the potential for a cognitive head start for children who attend ECE centers before formal schooling. Thus, institutionalized child care has become a significant alternative to traditional approaches for child care.

Policy and Provision of Services

The establishment of the National Center for Early Childhood Education (NACECE) and its decentralized networks of District Centers for Early Childhood Education (DICECEs) in 1984 and 1985 respectively was a landmark event for the Kenyan government's support to ECE programs (Njoroge 1994). Government commitment to the Early Childhood Development and Education (ECDE) subsector is also articulated in subsequent national development plans and *Sessional Papers No. 6 of 1988* and *No. 1 of 2005* (Kenya 1988; 2005). These statutory documents provide a broad policy framework for the provision of ECDE. Basically, the government encourages a policy of partnership in the provision of ECDE services in which the government collaborates with parents and local communities, faith-based organizations, the private sector, and development partners (Kamunge 1988). *Sessional Paper No. 1 of 2005* (Kenya 2005) on education, training, and research commits Kenya to integrating 4- to 5-year-olds into the primary education cycle by 2010.

In Kenya, attending preprimary class (at an ECDE center) is neither compulsory nor a prerequisite for joining primary school. However, 70 percent of the 17,000 public primary schools in the country have established a preprimary class. There are more than 28,000 ECDE centers, of which 74 percent are linked to public primary schools (Kenya 2003). In 2003, the enrollment in these centers was 1,528,596, with more than 44,000 ECDE teachers, of whom 46 percent are professionally trained. The national gross enrollment rate (GER) is 35 percent and the net enrollment rate (NER) for the 4- to 5-year-olds is 32 percent (both private and public ECDE centers). However, there are wide regional disparities in GER and NER, with lowest enrollments in the arid and semiarid lands and in urban slums where the GER is as low as less than 10 percent (Kenya 2003).

Financing
Government financial support is used for the development of curriculum and curriculum support materials, salaries for program coordinators and managers, and for curriculum developers. The government also subsidizes ECDE teacher training and meets the trainers' training allowance and community mobilization costs. There is no direct government funding to the child except for feeding support in some targeted districts. Lack of direct government funding results in many children going directly to primary school without passing through preprimary.[5]

Curriculum and Program Elements
In 1995, the government expanded the scope of ECE to embrace a holistic, integrated approach to child development with a view of incorporating early learning, health, and nutritional care to all children aged 0–8 years (Ngware 2004). However, *Sessional Paper No. 1* (Kenya 2005) on a policy framework for education training and research, underscores the Ministry of Education, Science, and Technology's focus on children 4–5 years (preprimary) with a view to providing a holistic and integrated program that meets the child's cognitive, social, moral, spiritual, emotional, and physical needs. It is expected that other government ministries, including Health and Social Services, will strengthen their ECD components and carry the load for children outside this age focus, especially for children under 3 years old.

Teacher Training
Capacity building of teachers is crucial to ensuring the quality and efficiency of the ECD subsector. The government supports two years of in-service training of ECDE teachers at both the certificate and diploma levels. One of the main issues facing ECDE teacher training is the low academic qualification of the teachers joining the training. An attempt by the ministry to raise entry grades has resulted in a shortage of teacher trainees, especially in the arid and semiarid regions of Kenya. Also, there is a high turnover of trained teachers from public ECDE centers (Ngware 2004), which are community established and managed and

often have inadequate resources, to private, for-profit centers, which offer better terms.[6] Alternatively, teachers often leave the profession for better opportunities.

The training curriculum focuses on imparting knowledge and skills to the teachers to be able to provide holistic care for the child. In addition to ensuring quality care, nutrition, safety, and health care, the training emphasizes methodologies to ensure early stimulation and learning through the use of play; learning materials and active learning methods such as exploration, experimentation, and observation; and discussions with children to enhance school readiness.

Because primary school teacher training does not include training in early childhood education and the primary school curriculum is not harmonized with that of ECDE, there is a disconnection between primary schooling and ECDE. The majority of primary schools do not embrace a child-centered, activity-oriented learning environment (Nyamweya and Mwaura 1996). This approach not only results in serious transitional challenges, but it also contributes to dropouts from primary school.

Academically focused assessments of children's achievements and abilities are used for placement in primary schools, especially in urban areas. These assessments have resulted in pressure for an academic orientation in the ECD centers and put stress on the children.

The lack of a well-articulated service structure and nongovernment employment of teachers have resulted in low morale among ECDE teachers. Other challenges facing preprimary education include inadequate management, even where preprimary classes are located within primary schools. Factors such as cost, distance to centers, and ignorance by some parents and communities who do not value education affect participation in ECD. Among the poor communities, participation is therefore very low; children from these communities will enter primary school disadvantaged in terms of their school readiness.

Zimbabwe

During the colonial era, provision of ECD services in Zimbabwe was limited. The services were established and run by parents' associations and were thus exclusive to the minority elites who had the resources to run them. In essence, the centers were mostly confined to urban areas and mission centers.

After independence in 1980, the new government endeavored to promote child development and education and encouraged the establishment of community-based ECD centers, especially in rural areas, to cater to children 0–6. The campaign resulted in the mushrooming of ECD centers across Zimbabwe. These centers were developed at health centers, community centers, churches, schools, and clubs. According to Zvobgo (1996), the initial driving force for the establishment of these centers by the Ministry of Community Development and Women's Affairs was to take responsible care of children for a number of hours so that women would be free to work. However, the quality of services was compromised by the shortage of qualified personnel to staff the centers.

In 1988 the ECD program was officially transferred to the Ministry of Primary and Secondary Education. Provision, however, was through partnerships among various line ministries, including the Ministries of Public Service, Labor and Social Welfare, and Health and Child Welfare.

Policy and Provision of Services

The Zimbabwe government, through the Ministry of Education, Sports, and Culture, announced an initiative to provide access to early childhood education to all children 0–8 years starting in January 2005, with services to be provided through an integrated ECD framework. This initiative indicates the Zimbabwe government's commitment to providing children 0–8 years with a good start in life. *Statutory Instrument No. 72* (Zimbabwe 1999b) embraces a holistic approach to ECD programming.

In line with the 1999 Presidential Commission of Inquiry into Education and Training recommendations on preschool (Nziramasanga 1999), the government developed a two-phase, 10-year program to establish a preschool and 2 years of ECD at every primary school in the country.

The *Secretary's Circular No. 14 of 2004* clearly states,

PHASE ONE (FIRST FIVE YEARS)

Every primary school is expected to attach at least one ECD class of 4- to 5-year-olds. The class will be known as ECD "B." This group of children will then proceed to grade 1 the following year.

PHASE TWO (SECOND FIVE-YEAR PROGRAM)

In this phase, another ECD class of 3- to 4-year-olds will be attached to every primary school. The class will be known as ECD "A." This group of children will proceed to ECD "B" class the following year.

The *Director's Circular No. 12 of 2005*, on implementation of the program, states,

The operations of the ECD centers are regulated by the Education Act of 1996 as amended and the Statutory Instrument 106 of 2005. ECD centers are expected to operate on a teacher-pupil ratio of 1 to 20, appropriately, qualified teachers will eventually teach these classes and they will be on a full government salary. Meanwhile paraprofessionals will continue to be engaged receiving allowances from the state. Heads of primary schools, education officers, and ECD district trainers are expected to provide essential professional advice on how to best deliver ECD services. Nursery schools will continue to operate but will have to link up with the head of the nearest school. The nursery schools will have to comply with the Education Act and instruments governing the running of all Early Childhood Education and Care institutions.

To date, Zimbabwe has been working to broaden ECD provision by incorporating community-based programs and upgrading the quality of ECD personnel through the in-service training of paraprofessionals. The purpose of training paraprofessionals is to provide technical support, encourage a more holistic approach, and target parent support. Observations based on monitoring visits include the following:

- An increasing number of teachers employed have some knowledge of ECD and have had some teaching experience of the ECD classes.
- In general, class sizes are too large. The teacher-pupil ratio of 1 to 20 is not being adhered to; in some cases ratios are as high as 1 to 50.
- Accommodation for programs remains a problem. It ranges from storerooms and halls to nothing at all. Equipment also requires investment.
- One particular program, St. Mary's Early Learning Center, is experiencing enrollment problems. While the center has quality services, it has proved to be too expensive for parents, hence parents have opted for the ECD "B" classes offered by local government feeder primary schools.

Nevertheless, given these problems, the program has overwhelmingly taken off and stakeholders are very supportive. The number of centers attached to primary schools has reached 3,316. The figures keep rising.

Financing

The Zimbabwe government provides grants to support ECD services, including salaries for ECD district trainers. Trainers are full government employees responsible for monitoring and supervising ECD activities at the districts and for developing ECD syllabi, handbooks, and teacher training manuals. In 2005, a total of Z$20 million was allocated to each of the 10 provinces for the upgrading of one ECD program to serve as a model center for the region.

Curriculum and Program Elements

To improve the quality and standards of ECD services, the government has developed an ECD curriculum and initiated a training program for ECD teachers, caregivers, and play leaders who staff community-based ECD programs. The *Education Act* (Zimbabwe 1987) and the *Statutory Instrument No. 72* (Zimbabwe 1999b) stipulate the regulations for ECD centers with regard to registration, curriculum, and service provision.

The curriculum provides experiences and activities appropriate for children within each age group. The aim is the development of social skills, sensory awareness, problem-solving skills, language skills, and motor skills.

The two years of ECD A and B are preparation for formal schooling. Primary schools will continue with the current curriculum, with the only difference being additional classes for 4- to 5-year-old children.

The Ministry of Education intends to ensure that every child has exposure and access to ECD programs before formal schooling. The classes are expected to provide intellectual stimulation, interaction opportunities, and activities that promote learning, as well as a stimulating environment that enables children to explore and develop in order to reach their full potential for school and lifelong learning.

ECD is part of a basic education in the education system, and ECD encompasses nursery schools, day care, day mothers, and preschool; hence, one curriculum that embraces all ECD programs should be provided to ensure uniformity in the provision of education to young children in Zimbabwe. The current curriculum followed by nursery schools and ECD centers is as stipulated in *Statutory Instrument No. 72* (Zimbabwe 1999b).

Teacher Training

Following the recommendations of the Nziramasanga Commission (1999), government put in place initiatives to strengthen early childhood teacher training; since then, 1,081 teachers with specialization in ECD and infant education have graduated from Seke Teachers' College (Zimbabwe 2000). Following the commission's recommendation that primary teacher colleges offer ECD teacher training, four primary teachers' training colleges, including Seke Teachers' College, started offering training for ECD teachers in 2004 and 2005 (see table 12.1 for 2004 and 2005 enrollment). The training is geared toward preparing the teachers to

Table 12.1 Students Training to Be ECD Teachers in Zimbabwe

	Students training to be ECD teachers	
College	2004	2005
Seke Teachers' College	150	150
Gwanda ZINTEC	—	100
Mary Mount	—	60
Mkoba	—	60

Source: Zimbabwe 2000.
— = not available.

teach in preprimary and primary grades 1 to 3. The training takes three years and is structured in three phases: a one-year residential session, a one-year practicum, and a one-year final residential session. The minimum entry requirement is possession of an ordinary-level certificate of education with a grade of C in five subjects including mathematics and English. This requirement is the same for primary teacher training.

Additional colleges started training ECD teachers in 2006. For example, the University of Zimbabwe enrolled 43 students to undertake the Bachelor of Education in ECD in 2006, and about 10 students are currently enrolled in the Master's degree program in ECD.

Lesotho

Lesotho's experiences with early childhood provision date to the 1970s. The Lesotho National Council of Women was the first to put in place some form of organized early childhood provision. In the early 1980s, the Bernard van Leer Foundation took over the ECD program as a project; UNICEF joined later to support and fund the program when Bernard van Leer wound up its operations. In 1985, the Lesotho Preschools and Day Care Association, which was formed to be an umbrella body for all preschools in Lesotho, made its main objective to advocate for recognition and absorption of the ECD programs under government auspices. Finally in 1995 the association was successful and the ECD program was absorbed into the Ministry of Education.

Policy and Provision of Services

The right to education for every Mosotho is enshrined in Lesotho's constitution. The government has the responsibility to adopt policies aimed at ensuring that "education is directed to the full development of the human personality and sense of dignity and strengthening the respect for human rights and fundamental freedoms" (Lesotho 1993, para. 28). The government's commitment to early childhood education is expressed in the *Education Act* (Lesotho 1995), which recognizes preprimary schools, providing up to three years of early childhood education, as the first category of schools. Further, in 2004, the Ministry of Education and Training started to incorporate early childhood care and development (ECCD) data into the Lesotho annual education statistics.

As noted, the ECCD program was officially absorbed into the Ministry of Education and Training in 1995, and that led to the establishment of the ECCD Unit. The unit was mandated with planning, regulating, and monitoring the ECCD program nationwide. To this end, the unit was responsible for developing regulations and guidelines for ECCD to enable the unit to monitor all activities taking place within ECCD programs, such as ensuring safety, appropriate hygiene, and nutrition. Subsequently, the unit took on an added responsibility of providing training for ECCD teachers and other stakeholders as it became apparent that safe and appropriate care was compromised in many parts of the country.

ECCD policy development was initiated in 1998 and was completed in 2000. The draft policy was reviewed and modified in 2004 to incorporate the concept of integration in ECCD provision, which would involve putting into practice a multisectoral approach to ECCD service provision, as well as enlisting the commitment of other stakeholders in ECCD. The final draft policy was being incorporated into other policies of the departments of the Ministry in preparation for one consolidated policy embracing all of its subsectors. This is viewed as a positive step toward final official approval of the ECCD policy by end of 2007. The Ministry of Education commissioned various consultancy studies (Lefoka and Matsoso 2001; Lefoka and Swart 1995; Sebatane and Motlomelo 2001) to determine the needs of the ECCD program and to develop recommendations for improvement.

In 1998, 800 ECD centers in the country were catering to 10,000 children aged 3–6 years, or 18 percent of children in this age group (Lefoka and Swart 1995). Many young children were left out of the ECCD program because their parents could not afford the fees charged by the centers. In 2002 the Ministry of Education, responding to this challenge, mobilized, guided, and assisted the needy communities to set up a home-based approach that targets children from poor and needy families, including orphans.

According to the 2004 education statistics, about 36,350 children were in 1,225 ECCD centers and home-based facilities, served by 1,452 teachers and 200 caregivers (Lesotho 2004). As of 2005, ECCD access stands at 33 percent (Lesotho 2005). There are initiatives to improve data collection and the availability of data on ECCD through workshops organized by the Ministry of Education. It is anticipated that more accurate data will in turn provide support for the expansion of services. Preliminary assessment indicates that this approach is helping to expand services.

In response to the World Declaration on *Education for All* and to address challenges of access to ECCD and the smooth transition of children from ECCD into primary schooling, the Ministry introduced a training program for a preprimary class of 5-year-old children (reception class) into primary schools in June 2007. The student-teachers began the two-year certificate course in January 2006, with a one-month residential period, after which they received assignments to complete at their workplaces. A pilot project is intended to start in 10 government primary schools (1 in each of the 10 districts of the country) and will be scaled up gradually. The ministry provided a budget for this initiative and plans to develop the capacity of all personnel, including caregivers involved in the reception phase, standard 1 teachers, principals, and management committees, who will be involved in the preprimary phase of ECCD, to enable them to handle the project effectively.

Financing
Currently, the ECCD program receives funding from government recurrent funds, the United Nations Children's Fund (UNICEF), and the World Bank. To ensure the introduction of the preprimary phase, the budget allocation for the ECCD program rose from M 1,222,000 in the 2004/5 financial year to M 2,712,110 in 2005/6, and increased further to M 3,063,413 in 2006/7.

Unlike primary education, whose free provision began to be phased in in 2000, the preprimary phase is not free; however, the Ministry has ensured that the needs of children will be catered for in order to make it possible to enroll in the project. The 10 primary schools in which the reception year is piloted will receive subvention from the ministry to support their project needs in the preprimary phase. For example, there are specific budget lines for a feeding program for children, school fees for orphaned children, training of personnel, maintenance of buildings, and the purchase of teaching-learning and other materials.

Curriculum and Program Elements
The preprimary curriculum approach is centered on learning through play. The topics taught are planned to expose children to key learning

experiences that involve active learning through exploration, discovery, manipulation, the development of thinking and physical skills, and, most important, engagement in a school readiness program to start preparing children for transition from ECCD to primary schooling.

Teacher Training

In 1998 there were 335 ECCD teachers in Lesotho, most of whom were unqualified or untrained. Prior to 2007, ECCD teachers and caregivers in Lesotho did not have any formal training to prepare them for their jobs. The teachers only receive in-service training, which is not structured but is based on the needs of the teachers at the time. For example, training might concentrate on materials development and do little on thematic teaching and learning.

The strongest recommendations of consultants in the policy development process have been for a training program leading to certification for ECCD teachers as well as improving the standards and the quality of the ECCD program. Faced with this challenge, in June 2007 the Ministry of Education and Training, through the ECCD Unit, introduced a two-year ECCD teacher education program at the Lesotho College of Education.

The Ministry of Education and Training still faces many challenges in the effort to implement the project effectively. One challenge is that ECCD teachers in Lesotho do not have teaching qualifications in either ECCD or teaching, because there is still no institutionalized ECCD teacher training. Another challenge is improving access into ECCD in an environment where primary education is free but where ECCD provision, including the reception year, is not free. Nonetheless, the Ministry of Education and Training hopes to learn valuable lessons from this pilot project that should enable it to make positive adjustments before scaling up the preprimary (reception) phase nationwide.

Opportunities and Challenges: What Have We Learned?

In this chapter we have briefly sketched how a preprimary year is developing in four African countries. In two of them, Kenya and South Africa, a substantial proportion of the eligible children already access the intervention. In this section we reflect on common experiences of these four countries and relate them to the issues most often raised by those advocating the expansion of appropriate ECD services to significant numbers of young children. These themes include access; quality, particularly of the type of program and curriculum; and teacher qualifications.

The United Nations Educational, Scientific, and Cultural Organization (UNESCO) released a policy brief discussing the focus that many countries place on the preprimary phase in meeting their EFA commitments for young children, even though the World Declaration asserts that "learning begins at birth" (UNESCO 2006b, 1). This preprimary focus is particularly the case for countries with limited resources, but even in developed countries, "universal provision starts with the last year of early childhood and moves downward" (UNESCO 2006b). Adding a preprimary class in existing schools is less of a burden on the education sector's capacity, because a network of primary schools and some administrative and physical infrastructure are often in place.

Placing a single year of preprimary in the primary school system has been the route preferred in Kenya, South Africa, and Zimbabwe, although in South Africa there are still significant numbers of grade R classes in community schools. Lesotho, where one-third of 3- to 6-year-olds are in some form of preprimary program, is also piloting a one-year program based in primary school. In Kenya and South Africa, where access to a preprimary year is substantial (32 percent and 40 percent of the eligible populations respectively), it is not yet compulsory. Both these countries face large regional and district disparities in access; poorer children as well as those living in areas that are sparsely populated or that have very little infrastructure tend to have lower access.

Young children disadvantaged by poverty have the most to gain from a preprimary year, but their inclusion is only possible when the service is free, which requires a substantial commitment of public funding. In South Africa, there are poverty-targeted subsidies for children in grade R classes (which will substantially increase). In addition, children benefit from a feeding scheme if they are in grade R classes at public primary schools, which facilitates poor children's access to the system. However, a significant number of grade R classes are in community schools that, though subsidized, have to charge fees to cover food and maintenance costs. In Lesotho, preprimary class students are no longer charged these fees; the ministry realized that fees posed an access challenge for many needy families. In the other two countries, fees are payable, which is a serious access challenge for children from poor families. Feeding schemes in some areas of Kenya and in Lesotho provide some support.

While locating a preprimary year in the primary schooling system has administrative and some infrastructural advantages, this location can have considerable impact on the program. It has been suggested that when preprimary education "is concentrated on 5-year-olds, it is likely to become a crash course for children who are about to enter formal schooling, rather than a gradual process of building a foundation for lifelong learning, focusing on children's holistic development" (UNESCO 2004, 2). This tendency to formalization is especially so when the preprimary program is located at a primary school. How applicable is this location in the cases of the countries we are considering?

First, in each of the four countries the preprimary year falls under an education ministry, while in Kenya and South Africa other ministries are concerned with younger age groups. In Lesotho, South Africa, and Zimbabwe, many key services for young children fall under other ministries, which is a policy concern for integration. Education governance and a national curriculum in three of the four countries tend to prioritize academic aspects of the program, particularly if there is not a cadre of teachers well grounded in early childhood care and education methods, which is the case if primary school teachers take on the preprimary class. The experience in Kenya and South Africa is that, despite a curriculum that is intended to be based on active learning experiences, there is pressure in many primary schools for a more formal approach and a focus on preacademic skills rather than on holistic child development. In South Africa the fact that the grade R curriculum is the first year of the curriculum for the foundation phase of primary schooling is positive for continuity in this period; it was hoped that locating grade R in the foundation phase would influence the methodology of the lower primary classes to be more child centered, rather than formalizing the reception year. Even though the same curriculum is used in the community schools and in most public primary schools, there are striking differences in its interpretation in the more traditional ECD approach. The programmatic approach adopted for preprimary programs is also influenced, as noted in two of the countries, by parent expectations that preprimary education should adopt an instructional, primary curriculum approach.

A common issue for all four countries is the lack of appropriately qualified ECD teachers for the preprimary year; staff members are less academically qualified than primary school staff. This difference in qualifications comes from a legacy in which early childhood services were relatively informal, developed and staffed by parents and community members, and supported by the donor community with little public funding. In the four countries, opportunities have been made available for upgrading teacher qualifications through in-service training, much of this with state or donor funding. Training is still very ad hoc and informal in Lesotho, however with the recent introduction of the ECCD teacher education program, training of ECCD teachers will begin to improve. In South Africa and Zimbabwe, to bring ECD teacher qualifications into line with the qualifications for primary school teachers, the reception year program is part of the training for teachers of children up to the third grade. This qualification certainly raises the status of reception year teachers, but there is often a focus on teaching skills for the early grades of formal schooling, which reinforces a more formal approach.

Upgrading and increasing professionalization of staff for the preprimary year will only be sustainable if teacher salaries offer a reasonable incentive. Until then the numbers of trainees for preprimary will be limited, teacher turnover will be high, and morale will be low, which will continue to be a serious concern, as has been commented on in relation to Kenya and South Africa.

As ECD services scale up in fulfillment of the EFA goals, there is a serious need for improvements in the data environment. We need to move beyond service access measures to service quality measures and beyond tracking inputs to serious consideration of child outcomes. As well as the gross enrollment rate and information on whether girls and boys have equal access to the preprimary year, further information is required to assist in targeting services where they are most needed. For example, how many children who might be considered particularly at risk have access to services? These children—children with disabilities, children affected by disaster, conflict, and HIV, children who are absolutely poor—are the primary target of the EFA ECD goal. We need to know how children are affected by access to the programs. There are encouraging trends—for example, in Lesotho the gathering of education statistics, including those for preprimary, is getting high-level support, and an awareness-raising campaign is underway. South Africa's draft norms and standards provide for tracking inputs (for example, budgets, ratios, learner support materials, and teacher qualifications) and outputs in the form of child progress. Existing information systems that monitor key ECD indicators in each country could be extended for additional data collection.

Conclusion

The impetus for the development of ECD services in each of the countries discussed in this chapter has been development of potential—a strategic response to realize children's education rights, meet the needs of changing economies, and build democracy. In each country parents and communities have made, and continue to make, a significant contribution to ECD services. The introduction of a preprimary class as part of the schooling system is an exciting and significant commitment toward the development of ECD services. Challenges remain to be addressed, however, including the following:

- finding ways to make the preprimary class freely accessible to all eligible children;
- ensuring a holistic, developmentally appropriate program;
- providing teachers with training, support, encouragement, and sustainable salaries; and
- developing systems to monitor the impact of the program on the transition to formal schooling and on child outcomes.

Significant progress has been made despite the challenges, and there is awareness of what needs to be done to address them. Priority is being given to training and consideration to broader issues, such as health, standards, and feeding programs, as well as academic concerns. Most encouragingly, given that "learning begins at birth," the preprimary year is part of a range of other ECD initiatives targeting young children in each of the countries discussed in this chapter.

Notes

1. Terms used for ECD differ in the four countries; the terminology used in official documents from each country has been retained in this chapter.

2. For children younger than 5, the Departments of Education, Social Development (Welfare), and Health have developed an integrated service delivery plan involving government at all levels and community initiatives.

3. Calculations from Wildeman and Nomdo (2004) and the *Government Gazette* (South Africa 2005).

4. A learnership is a vocational education and training program combining theory and practice and culminating in a nationally recognized qualification registered on the National Qualifications Framework.

5. Primary schooling has been free since 2003, enabling 1.3 million poor children to benefit from primary education for the first time (UNESCO 2006a).

6. Monthly salaries of ECD teachers were found to be generally below basic minimum wage rates recommended by the Ministry of Labor and Manpower Development (survey cited in UNESCO 2006a).

References

Biersteker, L., and A. Dawes. 2007. "Early Childhood Development." In *The Human Resource Development Review, 2007: Education, Employment, and Skills in South Africa*. Cape Town: Human Sciences Research Council Press.

Bredekamp, S. 1987. *Developmentally Appropriate Practice in Early Childhood Programs Serving Children from Birth through Age 8*. Washington, DC: National Association for the Education of Young Children.

Kamunge, J. M. 1988. "Report of the Presidential Working Party on Education and Manpower Training for the Next Decade and Beyond." Nairobi: Government Printer.

Kenya, MOEST (Ministry of Education, Science, and Technology). 1988. *Sessional Paper No. 6 of 1988: Education and Manpower Development for the Next Decade and Beyond*. Nairobi: MOEST.

————. 2003. *Education Statistics*. Nairobi: MOEST.

————. 2005. *Sessional Paper No. 1 of 2005: A Policy Framework for Education, Training, and Research*. Nairobi: MOEST.

Lefoka, J. P., and L. M. Matsoso. 2001. "An Investigation into Resources for the Early Childhood Care and Development Unit." Maseru. Unpublished consultancy report.

Lefoka, J. P., and T. Swart. 1995. "An Evaluation of the Early Childhood Care and Development Unit of the Ministry of Education, Lesotho." Unpublished consultancy report.

Lesotho. 1993. *The Constitution of Lesotho*. Retrieved August 30, 2006, from http://www.lesotho.gov.ls/constitute/gconstitute.htm.

————. 1995. *Education Act No. 10 of 1995*. Retrieved August 30, 2006, from http://www.lesotho.gov.ls/bills/education_act.pdf.

Lesotho. Ministry of Education and Training. 2004. *Education Statistics Bulletin*. Maseru: Ministry of Education and Training.

————. 2005. *Education Statistics Bulletin, Volume 1*. Maseru: Ministry of Education and Training.

Myers, R. 1997. "Removing Roadblocks to Success: Transitions and Linkages between Home, Preschool, and Primary School." *Coordinators' Notebook* 21: 12–21.

Ngware, M. W. 2004. "Draft Report of the Quantitative Study of the ECD Project, Nairobi." Unpublished draft report.

Njoroge, M. 1994. "Early Childhood Care and Education Program in Kenya." Working paper at a workshop on the child readiness/school readiness indicators in Washington, DC. Nairobi: MOEST.

Nyamweya, D., and P. Mwaura. 1996. "Transition from Preschool to Primary School in Kenya." World Bank Early Childhood Development Studies, 6. Nairobi: African Medical and Research Foundation.

Nziramasanga, C. T. 1999. "Report of the Presidential Commission of Inquiry into Education and Training." Harare: Government Printer.

Sebatane, E. M., and S. T. Motlomelo. 2001. "Needs Assessment for the Ministry of Education Early Childhood Care and Development Training Program." Maseru: Ministry of Education. Unpublished consultancy report.

Short, A., and P. P. Pillay. 2002. "Meeting the Challenges of ECD Training in South Africa." Paper presented at the OMEP World Council and Conference, Durban.

South Africa. 1983. *White Paper on the Provision of Education in South Africa.* Pretoria: Government Printer.

———. 1995. *White Paper on Education and Training.* Retrieved August 29, 2006, from http://www.info.gov.za/whitepapers/1995/education1.htm.

———. 2001a. *Education White Paper 5 on Early Childhood Development.* Retrieved August 29, 2006, from http://www.info.gov.za/whitepapers/2001 /educ179.pdf.

———. 2001b. *Nationwide Audit of ECD Provisioning in South Africa.* Pretoria: Department of Education.

———. 2002. *Revised National Curriculum Statement.* Pretoria: Department of Education. Available at http://www.education.gov.za.

———. 2005. "Draft Norms and Standards for Grade R Funding." *Government Gazette* 484 (October 14): 28134.

Sylva, K., and I. S. Blatchford. 1996. "Bridging the Gap between Home and School: Improving Achievement in Primary Schools." A report of four case studies commissioned by UNESCO and Technical Consultation, Addis Ababa. November 1994. Paris: UNESCO.

UNESCO (United Nations Educational, Scientific, and Cultural Organization). 1990. *World Declaration on Education for All.* Retrieved August 29, 2006, from http://www.unesco.org/education/efa/ed_for_all/background/jomtien_ declaration.shtml.

———. 2000. *The Dakar Framework for Action. Education for All: Meeting Our Collective Commitments.* Adopted by the World Education Forum, Dakar, Senegal, April 26–28. Paris: UNESCO.

———. 2004. "Enrollment Gaps in Pre-Primary Education: The Impact of a Compulsory Attendance Policy." UNESCO Policy Brief on Early Childhood, 21. Retrieved August 30, 2006, from unesdoc.unesco.org/images/0013/ 001374/137410e.pdf.

————. 2006a. "Impact of Free Primary Education on Early Childhood Development in Kenya." Policy Brief on Early Childhood, 30. Retrieved September 1, 2006, from unesdoc.unesco.org/images/0014/001433/143320E.pdf.

————. 2006b. "Pre-Primary Education: The Valid Investment Option for EFA." UNESCO Policy Brief on Early Childhood, 31. Retrieved August 30, 2006, from unesdoc.unesco.org/images/0014/001439/143986E.pdf.

United Nations Committee on the Rights of the Child. 2006. "General Comment No. 7: Implementing Child Rights in Early Childhood." Geneva: United Nations.

Wildeman, R. A., and C. Nomdo. 2004. *Implementation of Universal Access to the Reception Year (Grade R): How Far Are We?* Cape Town: Institute for Democracy in South Africa (IDASA). Retrieved August 29, 2006, from http://www.idasa.org.za/gbOutputFiles.asp?WriteContent=Y&RID=1175.

Zimbabwe. 1973. *Nursery School Education Act 822, Section 3 (1).* Harare: Ministry of Education.

————. 1987. *Zimbabwe Education Act.* Harare: Government Printer.

————. 1999a. "Report on the Evaluation of the ECD Joint Training Initiative." Harare: Ministry of Education, Sport, and Culture.

————. 1999b. *Statutory Instrument No. 72.* Harare.

————. 2000. *Demand and Supply of ECEC Teachers in Zimbabwe.* Harare: Ministry of Higher Education and Technology, Department of Manpower Planning and Development.

Zvobgo R. J. 1996. *Transforming Education: The Zimbabwean Experience.* Harare: College Press.

CHAPTER 13

Inclusive Education: A Mauritian Response to the "Inherent Rights of the Child"

Gilberte Chung Kim Chung and Cyril Dalais

As part of the *Education for All* movement that followed the World Conference in Jomtien, Thailand, in April 1990, most countries, including Mauritius, embarked on programs aimed at meeting children's basic educational needs as set out in the United Nations *Convention on the Rights of the Child* (CRC; 1989, arts. 28 and 29). While some countries may boast of 100 percent school enrollment, many, especially in Africa, have not yet been able to provide full-time education to their school-aged population due to many social and economic factors. However, Mauritius—a country in the Indian Ocean with 1.2 million people, of which 350,000 are children—is one of only a few African countries that have achieved universal primary education as set out in the World Declaration on Education (UNESCO 1990). Mauritius is determined to achieve Goal 2 of the Millennium Development Goals (United Nations 2000) for quality education:

> Government is committed to carrying out fundamental reforms in education with a view to providing world class quality education to enable young Mauritians to be employable in new sectors of the economy, to have

more fulfilling jobs, and also to be competitive at the international level (Jugnauth 2005).

The *Pledge in Favor of the Child* (National Policy for Children, 2003–15) highlights the government's determination to make Mauritius a "republic fit for children":

In consideration of our love and care for the 350,000 Mauritian children aged between 0 and 18, we, the citizens of the Republic of Mauritius, recognize that every Mauritian child has inherent rights:

. . . To live, to be nourished, to grow healthy, to receive care and support from their parents.
. . . To learn and develop to his/her full potential, to be protected from abuse and exploitation, to be safe, to be informed and to be heard.

In our capacity of adults, we are the child rights' duty-bearers.

Thus, it is our ardent commitment and we will strive to the best of our ability for these rights to be fully realized by the year 2015.

We pledge for a republic fit for children where every child will be given the opportunity to grow to his/her potential and become a responsible adult citizen (Mauritius 2003a).

In Mauritius, the Education Act of 1957 (amended in 1991) states in general terms the right of education for all citizens. Free access to education started in 1977 in regular mainstream primary and secondary schools from standard 1 primary to higher school certificate (age 5–20). The national educational reform launched in 2002 and focusing on access, relevance, and achievement was further given a boost with an amendment to the Education Act, which rendered schooling compulsory up to age 16 as of January 2005. To remove the barriers that could hinder access to schools, as of 2006, the government of Mauritius provides free transportation to school for all students across the island.

Mauritius, like most countries, considers education a major undertaking that has helped its progress considerably since free education was introduced in the late 1970s. It also considers education a major factor in sustainable development. Education is partially subsidized at the preschool level and is free at public primary, secondary, and tertiary levels.

Education, though the responsibility of the state, also concerns parents and members of the community at large. Close partnership with all stakeholders is essential; this includes the private sector through schools—run by private individuals, laypersons, or missionaries—that have been mostly accessible to minority groups.

For the great majority of Mauritian children, access to mainstream education can be described as a success story. Until recently, however, one group of children did not have access to free education: children with disabilities—physical, sensorial, psychological, and social. This chapter provides a case study of how Mauritius has addressed the needs and rights of these children through an inclusive education process.

Inclusive Education: A Brief History

A review of the history of attention to children with special needs as it evolved in Europe illustrates the "special education" shifts in resource-rich countries over the past 200 years. Evans (1998) summarizes five phases. During phase 1 (1775–1875), it was acknowledged that some children needed special services and support. In response, schools and institutions were created, generally by religious and other charitable organizations, to care for these children. During phase 2 (1875–1945), society recognized that it had a responsibility for children with special needs. This recognition led to the creation of specialized services. In phase 3 (1945–70), services expanded rapidly, most often in segregated settings located outside of and away from the community.

The major breakthrough for persons with disabilities came in phase 4 (1970–90), which was characterized by individualization, normalization, integration, and mainstreaming. During this period, children with special needs began attending the same schools as other children. Initially they were put into separate classes within the same setting. While this approach was an improvement over the isolation of many institutional settings, mainstreaming frequently did not result in true integration for children with special needs.

Phase 5 began in the 1990s. Again, there was a major conceptual shift to inclusion: creating environments responsive to the differing developmental capacities, needs, and potential of all children. For children with special needs, inclusion means a shift in services from simply trying to fit the child into "normal" settings, with supplemental support for their disabilities or special needs, to promoting the child's overall development in an optimal setting.

The Experience in Mauritius

In Mauritius in 2004, out of a population of 350,000 children, an esti-mated 3,000 disabled children needed special assistance (Mauritius 2004). Historically and currently many *can'ts* and *don'ts* are in the way of children with special educational needs as they try to access mainstream educa-tion. Parents of children with disabilities are too often the main cause of their child's nonattendance in school because parents often believe that their disabled child won't fit in.

A United Nations Children's Fund (UNICEF)–sponsored survey (Mauritius 2004) identified other reasons that children with special needs do not have access to education; only half of the children with disabilities surveyed had access to educational facilities for reasons including the following:

- No school in the region can cater to their needs.
- Schools for special education have limited seating capacity.
- Parents are not informed of existing educational facilities.
- Parents and others do not think that educating a child with special needs is necessary.

Another major difficulty that parents of children with special needs have had to overcome is that of convincing teachers, educators, and school administrators who—though they believe in the child's basic rights to education—have many explanations why they cannot have disabled chil-dren in their classes, schools, playgrounds, or systems. Their explanations include the following:

- The school is not equipped to educate children with special needs.
- They do not have time to give the child the special attention he or she would require.
- The child will not fit in this school; he or she will disturb other children.
- Transportation is not available.
- The facilities do not have ramps or adapted toilets and other furniture.
- The teachers are not trained to do such specialized teaching.
- The pupil ratio is too high.
- The curriculum is not flexible enough.

More difficult to address is the general belief that children with special educational needs belong to a special category (that is, they are a minority and therefore have no great political impact). In addition, addressing their needs is expensive; therefore children with special needs will be considered only after the majority has access to basic education. Their turn will come next.

Without a clear government policy in favor of children with special needs, the vast majority of these children stay home; their rights, as set out in CRC, are not met.

Schools for Children with Special Education Needs

Without easy access to mainstream education, many parents of children who have special educational needs have taken action. Between 1946 and 1965 (when Mauritius was still a British colony) the British Government, by an Act of Parliament, created three specialized schools—for the blind, deaf, and "educationally subnormal" (renamed "mentally handicapped" in 2007)—run by nongovernmental organizations (NGOs) but entirely funded by the government. Since the 1970s, after the country's independence in 1968, parents have created NGOs to provide for their children's educational needs. Schools have been created for children with visual, hearing, and mental disabilities and for dyslexic children. These privately run special schools started as philanthropic projects. Volunteers would help care for the children. Parents would raise funds at local and international levels and they continue to do so, although it has become more difficult because international funds have dwindled due to the classification of Mauritius as a developing country. Government grants through social services were available toward caring and educational expenses, while funds for other operating costs (such as specialized supportive services and equipment) have been contributed by parents. Because many schools for special education have been set up by individuals and are run as private fee-paying schools, only families with financial means can afford to place their children there.

From Segregation to Inclusion: A Long Road

Several Scandinavian countries have led the way in inclusion, integrating their children with special educational needs in the overall educational process and opening their doors to all children, whatever their abilities or disabilities. Their approach is holistic; every child is educated as a whole person: socio-medico-psycho and pedagogical needs are met at the same institution (International Special Education Congress 2000; Savolainen, Kokkala, and Alasuutari 2000).

Unfortunately this holistic approach has not been the case in countries in Sub-Saharan Africa where parents have had to take the initiative and provide the best they could while waiting for governments to take over. To accelerate the process of inclusion and get governments to assume full responsibility, one can work through the following:

- mobilizing and empowering parents;
- documenting case studies;
- lobbying forcefully through prominent personalities—social leaders, respected community leaders, and politicians—genuinely committed to the cause;
- sensitizing the public through media, featuring real-life situations and success stories;
- informing policy dialogue to develop political will and commitment;
- elaborating a national policy and strategy paper addressing the rights of children with special needs; and,
- sustaining an educational program with implementation and close monitoring, evaluation, and research.

Moving from segregation to inclusion requires a well-informed policy dialogue at several levels that will lead to a national policy, strategies, and actions that are well defined with a time frame and with access to human, material, and financial resources. Informed policy dialogue does not suffice, however, but must bring about political will and political commitment, which are essential.

Figure 13.1 illustrates the path that influenced government policy in Mauritius.

Consultation and Partnership Building

The situation for children with special needs has changed in Mauritius since the 1990s. Information has been circulating through the community at large, and some of the issues related to children with special needs are being addressed at both national and international levels as more parents

- come to know and respect the child's right to education;
- are determined to see this right implemented by the authorities; and,
- work together to facilitate access to schools with facilities and specialized pedagogical approaches.

Figure 13.1. The Path from Exclusion to Inclusion for Special Education Needs (SEN) in Mauritius

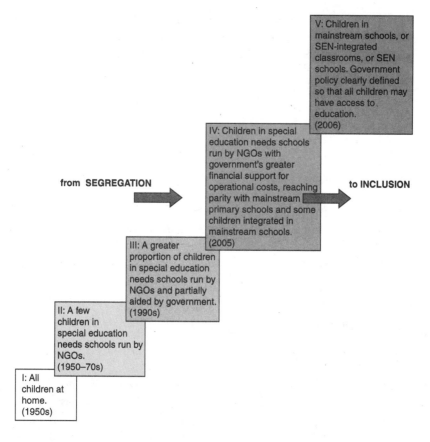

Source: Prepared by Gilberte Chung Kim Chung for this book.

In August 2004, following the adoption of the *National Policy for Children* (Mauritius 2003a) and the adoption in July 2004 of a National Plan of Action (Mauritius 2003b), parents and members of NGOs catering to children who had been excluded because of disabilities and poverty started to prepare a policy and strategy document (Mauritius 2006a) with the collaboration of representatives from the lead ministries and parastatal bodies involved with the survival, development, and protection of children.

Setting Priorities

Drawing from the *National Policy for Children*, the concerned group set out priorities with the publication of a plan of action and cost estimates for implementation for an initial two-year period. This plan was discussed with the local authorities and the principle of parity (that is, that all children should have access to free primary education) was accepted. The cost per child was calculated; children attending special schools were allocated a per capita grant equal to what a child in mainstream education receives.

In 2005, the budget for children with special needs more than quadrupled from MUR 4 million to MUR 17 million (US$1 = MUR 30). With government endorsement of the policy and strategy paper (Mauritius 2006b), the principle of inclusion of children with special educational needs was accepted. Additional resources will be allocated to develop special services to support children with special educational needs who will be mainstreamed, as well as their teachers and parents. More specialized services will be created for those children who will not be able to attend ordinary schools or specialized classes on the sites of normal schools because of their serious disabilities. Some children will still need home-based assistance because parents still have difficulties accessing daycare facilities for them.

While addressing the needs of children totally excluded from mainstream education, representatives from both governmental and nongovernmental organizations have also addressed the educational needs of approximately 15,000 children faced with considerable learning difficulties because they live in pockets of poverty. These children attend 30 schools within educational priority areas (*Zone d'Education Prioritaire*, or ZEP). A similar number of children in other schools are also failing their Certificate of Primary Education (CPE) every year; they, too, need remedial education within the mainstream. Several initiatives have been launched that will help to identify these children early during their preschool years and bring services to them.

A National Policy for Special Education Needs

Mauritius is tackling the problem of exclusion in the following ways.

1. *Creating a clear policy regarding all children's right to education*— School is compulsory for children 5–16 years old. A new policy gives children with special needs access to education through adapted and relevant pedagogical programs. Government acknowledges that children with special educational needs should be included as far as possible within the general education environment, which is commonly referred to as inclusive education. The fundamental guiding principles of the policy include:

- parity and equity regarding quality educational services;
- inclusion and integration of all children in the educational system; and,
- partnership with all relevant ministries, the private sector, and parents.

2. Setting up structured systems aimed at meeting everyone's needs— This process includes creating relevant programs of learning specific to each special need, from the children with intellectual disabilities to the gifted and talented children. It also includes close collaboration between ministries, private partners such as NGOs, and parents.

*3. Removing all barriers that hinder the child's access to school—*Access should be provided for children with special needs to school, whether in mainstream, integrated classrooms or units, or special education needs schools, as well as access to home-based programs. For example, access to mainstream schools can be enhanced by providing a supplementary food program to children with parents' consent and free transportation to all children from home to school.

*4. Formulating and implementing specific support programs to stop the failure at the end of the primary sector, and bringing in remedial programs—*The high rate of failure at the end of the primary cycle is mainly because children are taught in a "one-size-fits-all" approach: they are not screened at an early age for possible health problems or minor impairments, and promotion is automatic. Providing support services within the classroom and the school through the collaboration of all school personnel will help to address some of these issues. Actions include development and improvement of relevant pedagogical material for each specific disability or ability. Staff training at all levels is required in disabilities and special needs education in each specific domain; specific support services with a team of professionals should be provided in schools and at the regional level. The following two examples illustrate some current actions:

*A support program during the primary cycle: Zone d'Education Prioritaire (ZEP) in primary schools in deprived regions with a low pass rate of the CPE—*These schools now operate within a framework where parents, the school community, and the private sector collaborate in food and health programs. A team of liaison officers, social workers, and parent-mediators help in providing a stable social and emotional environment. By 2010–15, program evaluation will prove that these children have had better opportunities to reach their potential at the primary level and they stand a better chance of continuing their studies at the secondary level.

A remedial program after the primary cycle: Prevocational Education (PVE) at the secondary level—These prevocational schools provide a different curriculum aimed at giving pupils who have twice failed the CPE examinations an opportunity to reorient themselves in a preprofessional stream. After a transitory phase of out-station PVE classes, most PVE classes are now on the premises of mainstream schools; some problems exist regarding the acceptance of these "different" kids cohabiting with "bright" children. Some schools have been able to transform into "welcoming" schools; others have yet to transform their school culture. This effort is being maintained while upgrading the national educational system from early childhood to postsecondary to make it inclusive for all with a proper learning organizational and referral policy.

5. Implementing a new strategy for early screening, early intervention, remedial action, and evaluation—Prevention, early screening, diagnosis, and rehabilitation of children with special educational needs are important parts of the plan of action. The introduction of a *3 Earlies Initiative* helps achieve this priority. Parents, working with the child, become integral to the educational and rehabilitation process. The Preschool Trust Fund, with specialized outreach programs for teachers and parents through *Lacaz zanfans*, has access to more than 30,000 preschool-age children. These programs include the training of educators, facilitators, and special agents working in home settings and in 1,100 preschool units. If screening is systematic, many children who are at risk can be identified and rehabilitated.

6. Focusing on early childhood development—In the national reform of education launched in 2002, major efforts have been made to give the best start possible to all young children. Early childhood development has been a main component of the educational reform. Through the institution of the Preschool Trust Fund, the government has facilitated and regulated all preschools in Mauritius and has provided developmentally appropriate practices. The young child is thus at the center of education from birth to preschool, and then to primary school.

7. Instituting the "Bridging the Gap" initiative—Because the passage from preprimary (3–4 years old) to primary standard 1 (5 years old) is difficult for many children, "Bridging the Gap," an initiative to help children in this transition, was launched.

8. Ensuring intersectoral collaboration—Intersectoral collaboration is essential. Ministries that are actively collaborating with the Ministry of Education include Health and Quality of Life; Women's Rights, Child Development, and Family Welfare; and Youth and Sports. Regular meetings are held with the Ministry of Finance to explain the implementation of the *National Policy for Children* and the budgetary lines. The support of the Ombuds Office for Children was acquired. Representatives of NGOs joined forces and this partnership is being consolidated through the establishment and development of a Special Educational Needs Unit.

Developments

Transforming all our schools into inclusive schools for children with disabilities is not possible yet in our Mauritian context. Even though ranking at the Certificate of Primary Examinations was abolished in 2002 and there is less stress among students, teachers, and parents,

- teaching is still exam oriented;
- teachers have not been trained to teach children with disabilities;
- technical advice is lacking for the use and repair of specialized equipment;
- facilities are inadequate; and,
- ancillary or support teachers are not provided in the class.

Indeed, school communities in Mauritius are not ready for an immediate national implementation of totally inclusive schools. The process is incremental. Steps have been taken to establish pilot projects, using the NGOs' model of integration. Some NGOs already have integrated classrooms in the mainstream system following the UNICEF program started in the 1990s.

Three models are used:

- *Inclusion through individual integration*: Children with physical disabilities or mild intellectual or sensorial disabilities are individually integrated into a regular classroom with the additional input of a consultancy support service and ancillary staff or support teacher who will provide assistance to the classroom teacher and one-to-one interaction.

- *Integrated classrooms in mainstream schools*: More severely disabled children are provided access to education—in either mainstream public schools or schools run by NGOs for children—in a special education class (integrated classroom) operating full-time on the mainstream school premises.
- *Special education needs schools*: Children who cannot be integrated because of their specific special needs are provided access to education in special education needs schools or specialized schools. These specialized schools could be twinned with a local mainstream school for joint activities.

The Inclusive Reform Strategy

The shift from exclusion to inclusion or from segregation to integration cannot be made without planning and mobilization of resources—human, material, and financial. A prefabricated inclusion model does not exist; inclusive education needs to be developed and implemented after building consensus among all stakeholders and considering local conditions, contexts, cultures, and traditions. Parents' wishes have to be considered; some believe that their child with a disability can learn, grow, and develop with peers in a normal setting, while other parents prefer integrated classrooms and specialized schools. In Mauritius, all participants in this consultation believe that the priority is to provide education to each child with a disability according to one of the three models above and to make each model as integrated and inclusive as possible.

Inclusion is a process; the provision of educational services for children with special needs will take time. A proper plan of action within a set time frame is needed to achieve inclusive *Education for All*; the 2015 deadline of the World Education Forum in Dakar (UNESCO 2000) is the target date for Mauritius to provide education to as many as possible.

Planning, managing, and implementing such programs requires a good appraisal of the situation, needs, and resources. Experienced, trained staff who can draw from a strong database, develop the program, and set up evaluation processes is a precondition to inclusive education. Several levels of interventions must start simultaneously; these must be as comprehensive as possible and staggered in initial and transitional phases within a self-reinforcing frame. Figures 13.2 and 13.3 represent the planned phases.

Figure 13.2. Goals to Absorb More Children in the Educational Systems in Mauritius, 2004–08

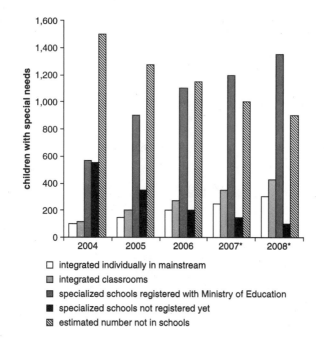

☐ integrated individually in mainstream
▨ integrated classrooms
■ specialized schools registered with Ministry of Education
■ specialized schools not registered yet
▧ estimated number not in schools

Source: Prepared by Gilberte Chung Kim Chung for this book.
*Projection.

Conclusion

In its determination to see every child at school, Mauritius is creating a society for all, where people will learn to live together and respect their differences and abilities. A measure of our degree of civilization will be in how our country takes care of our underprivileged and excluded people until the quality of life of each is improved as best as possible. It is not a question of assistance to the needy, but the provision of education as an acquired right to every human being. Education is about reaching one's potential; if all partners and stakeholders work together, there is no reason why we cannot succeed.

The government of Mauritius is committed to reaching parity. The Special Education Needs Unit will set up the regulatory framework with defined norms and standards so that by 2015, *access, equity,* and *quality* will be achieved regarding education for children with special needs.

Figure 13.3. Goals to Provide Educational Services for All Children with Disabilities in Mauritius by 2015

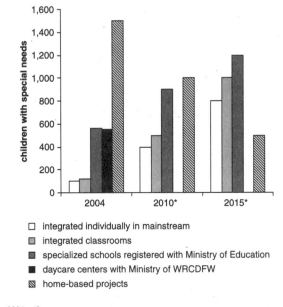

☐ integrated individually in mainstream
▣ integrated classrooms
■ specialized schools registered with Ministry of Education
■ daycare centers with Ministry of WRCDFW
▨ home-based projects

Source: Mauritius 2006a, 40.
*Projection.

No child is to be forgotten in this national educational reform. Through close collaboration of NGOs and the commitment of the Ministry of Education, children with disabilities will at last be able to say that they can go to school like all their peers.

The task is gigantic but in the 1970s parents stood up and founded their own schools. Today—at more than 20 private specialized schools run by NGOs and 3 special needs schools founded by an act of parliament and funded by government—about 1,250 children with special needs have access to schools. Others are in the mainstream and this number will increase. There is a will to create more educational facilities and there is hope that by 2015 positive actions will be taken.

Nonetheless, other fields of disabilities still have not been taken care of and no expertise is available to address the issues. Parents will continue to mobilize themselves. It is the government's role to facilitate endeavors to provide an education adapted to the needs of the children.

Mauritius, like many other underdeveloped or developing countries, has a long way to go to achieve quality and inclusive *Education for All.*

However, education wonderfully evolves and tries to improve, modernize, and enrich itself, opening itself to diversity and embracing all. The national reform of education is definitely democratizing our educational system, and children with special needs may start hoping that they will be able to go to school and have their needs addressed.

These positive changes are in line with the commitment of Mauritius to *Education for All* and the implementation of the Convention on the Rights of the Child, whereby state parties must "ensure that the disabled child has effective access to and receives education, training, health care services . . . in a manner conducive to the child's fullest possible social integration" (United Nations 1989, art. 23.3).

Mauritius is a step ahead of many other countries, and it must continue to forge its way courageously toward the goal of *Education for All* by 2015, including access as well as equity and quality.

This generation of children is looking to all of us adults as models, guardians, protectors, and leaders of their future. They are telling us: "Don't let us down."

References

Evans, J. L. 1998. "Inclusive ECCD: A Fair Start for All Children." *The Coordinators' Notebook* 22, 1–23.

International Special Education Congress. 2000. *Report of the International Special Education Congress "Including the Excluded."* University of Manchester, U.K.

Jugnauth, A. 2005. President's speech. Prime Minister's Office and Ministry of Finance. July 29.

Mauritius. 1957 (amended 1991). *Education Act.* Ministry of Education.

———. 2003a. *National Policy for Children: A Republic Fit for Children and Vision 2015 for the Mauritian Child.* Ministry of Women's Rights, Child Development, and Family Welfare.

———. 2003b. *National Policy for Children: Plan of Action.* Ministry of Women's Rights, Child Development, and Family Welfare.

———. 2004. *National Survey on Children with Disabilities.* Ministry of Social Security.

———. 2006a. "Special Education Needs and Inclusive Education in Mauritius." Policy and strategy document. Ministry of Education and Human Resources.

——— 2006b. "Special Education Needs and Inclusive Education in Mauritius: The Way Forward." Policy guidelines and orientation. Ministry of Education and Human Resources.

Savolainen, H., H. Kokkala, and H. Alasuutari, eds. 2000. *Meeting Special and Diverse Educational Needs: Making Inclusive Education a Reality*. Helsinki: Ministry for Foreign Affairs of Finland, Department for International Development Cooperation, and Niilo Mäki Institute.

United Nations. 1989. *Convention on the Rights of the Child*. New York: United Nations.

————. 2000. *United Nations Millennium Declaration*. Retrieved September 6, 2006, from http://www.un.org/millennium/declaration/ares552e.pdf.

UNESCO (United Nations Educational, Scientific, and Cultural Organization). 1990. *World Declaration on Education for All*. Retrieved October 24, 2006, from http://www.unesco.org/education/efa/ed_for_all/background/jomtien_declaration.shtml.

————. 2000. *The Dakar Framework for Action. Education for All: Meeting Our Collective Commitments*. Adopted by the World Education Forum, Dakar, Senegal, April 26–28. Paris: UNESCO.

CHAPTER 14

Parenting Challenges for the Changing African Family

Judith L. Evans, Chalizamudzi Elizabeth Matola, and Jolly P. T. Nyeko

Many families are in crisis in the Majority World and industrialized nations. These families are struggling as a result of political, social, and economic conditions that undermine their ability to provide appropriate supports to their children. Whereas in the past, societies could claim a relatively normalized parenting pattern—either an extended family model, a community/tribal model, a nuclear family, or some other stable pattern—now many societies report that their family norms are disrupted. This chapter explores some of the social, economic, and political forces that are having an impact on African family norms and practices, discusses the importance of families in supporting young children's development, and presents principles for working with parents in the rapidly changing African context.

The Changing African Family

Globalization is a major force that affects families worldwide. Structural Adjustment Programs (SAPs) have affected demographic patterns and behavior and family patterns, poverty is growing, and employment is becoming more precarious (Antoine 1995). Bigombe and Khadiagala

(2003) conclude that globalization has resulted in "double marginalization" across the continent: local incomes have had an absolute decline in relation to the global economy and socioeconomic disparities have widened in countries that have taken advantage of globalization. Globalization has (1) influenced migration patterns, (2) led to trends that threaten the family, and (3) affected the roles and choices of who parents young children (Amin 2002; Apter 2002; Cooper 2001; Martin and Widgren 1996; Preston-Whyte 1993).

Migration
The following section discusses the influence of globalization on migration patterns in Africa.

Rural to urban—People leave rural areas because of declining agricultural productivity, lack of employment opportunities, and lack of access to basic physical and social infrastructure. In much of Africa, rural to urban migration has been seen as essential to expand job opportunities, enhance social mobility, and increase income. However, the expectation of higher incomes and standards of living in urban areas is seldom realized. Urban poverty is widespread and growing (United Nations Environment Programme n.d.). Urbanization is on the rise in Africa. About one-third (34.6 percent) of Sub-Saharan Africans lived in urban areas in 1995, up from 11 percent in 1950. It is expected that one-half (50.7 percent) of Sub-Saharan Africa's population will be urban by 2025 (United Nations Population Division 2005). While about 40 percent of the population lived in urban areas in 2005, many of these people continue to support families in rural areas and, in many instances, rural families have become dependent on remittances from those living in urban areas. This dependence and the absence of those who have moved to urban areas have changed household dynamics.

Out-migration—In addition to migration from rural to urban areas, there is migration to other countries. Migration previously took place between countries in Africa (for example, people migrated from Lesotho, Malawi, Swaziland, and Zambia to economically stronger South Africa). In more recent years, the worsening of economic circumstances has forced the best educated Africans to seek economic opportunities in Europe, the Middle East, and even North America (Adepoju 2000). The crisis from the out-migration of professionals has drawn international attention. For example, health workers were the focus of the World Health

Organization's (WHO) Health Day in April 2006. Of particular concern was the out-migration of health professionals from Africa. It was noted that "more nurses from Malawi are in Manchester than in Malawi, and more Ethiopian doctors are in Chicago than Ethiopia" (Crush 2006). There was a plea for the European Commission to end recruitment of health workers from Sub-Saharan Africa and press for a global code of conduct on ethical recruitment.

These migration patterns have altered household roles, one of which is childrearing (Ferraro 1991; Leliveld 2001; Modo 2001). In a study of out-migration in Swaziland, Leliveld (2001, 1845) concludes that "the out-migration of Swazi men to South African mines has forced women to undertake the rearing of children alone; many households lack the stabilizing influence of a father and are thus incapable of providing the support network that is the foundation of family stability." He also notes that while the large numbers of single women in Swaziland have increased poverty levels, paradoxically, women have more control of household resources and are freer to channel more resources toward health than are women who live with men.

Migration as a result of wars and violence—Migration is not always motivated by economics. Political instability, violence, and wars have also contributed to the migration of refugees who may be displaced internally or forced to leave their country. About 10 million people have been the victims of forced migration. By 2005, African populations represented one-third of the world's refugees (UNHCR 2006).

Who migrates? The mobility of young males in search of opportunities in urban areas remains a constant feature of migration, but not all migrants are men; women also migrate. Crush (2006) reported on a study of South African women who migrate. The study concluded that women's reasons for migrating are more linked to their relationships to men and the extended family than are men's reasons for migrating. In practical terms, most emigration for women is undertaken in a family context rather than individually. These findings confirmed an earlier study by Meekers and Calves (1997), who determined that women migrate primarily to accompany their husbands. Single women and those who are heads of the household also have higher migration rates.

Trends

Globalization has led to trends that threaten the family, as discussed in the following section.

Shift in roles—In today's economy both the husband and wife have to generate income. However, the transition to wage-earning households has taken place without a corresponding shift in the power relations between the sexes, producing tensions that further destabilize the family. As noted by Lauras-Lecoh (1990), the solidarity between spouses is weakened by the separation that results from migration. Silberschmidt's (1999, 2001) work with the Kisii in Kenya describes changes in household structures as control over resources has shifted gradually away from men to women. These shifts have had an impact on the role of men in childrearing. (See chapter 8 for a specific description of men's role in the lives of children.) Out-migration has also diminished men's roles.

Smaller family size—Life in urban areas is characterized by less space, poor housing, and a dependence on a monetary economy, all of which have influenced family size. In addition, the value of children has changed; they are no longer seen as active contributors to a farm economy but as a drain on limited resources.

Early or no marriage—One of the consequences of the changing view of the value of children is that young men and women are getting married, or raising families without being officially married, at increasingly younger ages. Parents see early marriage as a way of more immediately realizing the economic value of a daughter's dowry. Parents who are struggling to raise many children may choose to have their adolescent daughters marry earlier than they would have in different circumstances (Bigombe and Khadiagala 2003).

The impact of HIV and AIDS—In Africa, the AIDS epidemic has had far-reaching effects on family (UNAIDS 2000; Whiteside 2002). According to the United Nations Children's Fund (UNICEF), by 2004 more than 1.9 million children had been orphaned by AIDS, resulting in an increase in child- and grandparent-headed households (UNICEF 2004). When parents are sick or have died, the older children in the family struggle to fulfill the parenting roles, even if they are still very young. Sometimes they drop out of school to care and provide for their brothers and sisters and even to care for their sick parents. Children are called on to take on these roles because of the weakening of the extended family system, which has been depleted of its economic and psychological resources. As a result, many children have been denied their right to grow up with their parents and to experience parental love and guidance

(Belsey 2003). (See chapter 5 for a more detailed description of the impact of HIV/AIDS on Africa and chapter 15 for a description of programs being developed to address the situation of young children.)

Who Parents?

In the traditional African context, a parent was anybody who performed the role of parents—anybody who had taken over that responsibility. This tradition helped to ensure that societal values and culture were respected, upheld, and enforced. The on-the-job training many parents formerly received from extended family members or from religious and cultural traditions is largely unavailable to contemporary parents (Evans et al. 2004). Yet some traditions remain.

Multigenerations—Bigombe and Khadiagala (2003) reported on a study of 300 three-generation households in two metropolitan areas of South Africa. The study revealed that about 9 in 10 African elders live in multigenerational households, and that the ethos of the African extended family appears to be intact even in the urban settings. The study noted that more than 80 percent of the top, middle, and bottom generations in the 300 families reported harmonious relations between generations.

Increasingly, grandmothers are becoming primary caregivers. This situation is evolving largely in response to the impact of AIDS on the parenting generation and the need for others to take on childrearing responsibilities. A study by Cattell (1997) in KwaZulu-Natal Province found that many of the grandmothers taking on this role have a positive attitude. They perceive themselves as important in building families, educating the next generation, and providing generational continuity.

Single parents—In many parts of Africa, single- and female-headed households have become dominant (Antoine and Nanitelamio 1991; Jones 1999; Wallman 1996). In some instances grandmothers are available to support daughters (and sometimes granddaughters) who are single parents, and, in fact, some grandmothers become the primary caregiver, as is often the case in Botswana, for example (Andrews et al. 2006).

Given the multiple disruptions to family life in Africa, there is a need to be concerned about the kind of parenting that young children receive, regardless of who, willingly or unwittingly, has a parenting role. The next section discusses the importance of the family in providing appropriate supports to children, particularly the youngest children.

A Focus on Families and Communities

International conventions and declarations reinforce the importance of families in supporting children's rights and well-being. The United Nations Convention on the Rights of the Child (CRC) defines the rights of children (rights holders) to appropriate supports as they grow up. In terms of children's rights, the family is responsible, but not solely, for guaranteeing these rights. In addition, the CRC stipulates that the family must be supported by the state: "States parties shall render appropriate assistance to parents and legal guardians in performance of their child-rearing responsibilities and shall ensure the development of institutions, facilities, and services for the care of children" (1989, art. 18.2). Furthermore, within the CRC, "parents" include mother and father: "States parties shall use their best efforts to ensure recognition of the principle that both parents have common responsibilities for the upbringing and development of the child . . . The best interests of the child will be their basic concern" (art. 18.1).

A further indication of international support for strengthening families is the fact that at the Malta World NGO Forum, 1994 was declared the International Year of the Family (IYF). Its theme was "promoting families for the well-being of individuals and societies" (UNESCO 1993). The intent of IYF 1994 was to raise awareness, interest, concern, support, and action on behalf of the family. In 2003, a commitment to family was reaffirmed in the *Proclamation of the Tenth Anniversary of the International Year of the Family*. The proclamation stated that the tenth anniversary "will be devoted to a reaffirmation of commitments made and the identification of further actions, including encouraging the incorporation of effective family policies and programs into national development strategies" (United Nations 2004).

In addition to an international imperative to support families as they support young children, programming experience reinforces the importance of working with parents and families to maximize child outcomes. In the late 1990s, the World Health Organization commissioned a review of programs seen as effective in improving the health, nutrition, and psychological development of children in disadvantaged circumstances. The review, *A Critical Link* (WHO 1999), led to the conclusions that the most effective programs

- focus on children who are in the "critical window" of life: improvements before birth and during the first 2 to 3 years of life have the greatest impact on the child's future growth and development;

- focus on children who are most at risk: the greatest improvements were seen in children who were impoverished and undernourished;
- combine several interventions: for example, programs to promote good nutrition, improve mother-child interactions, stimulate psychosocial development, and improve the child's health; and
- involve parents and other caregivers in improving the child's care.

The Importance of Care

The most important factor in a child's healthy development is to have at least one strong relationship (attachment) with a caring adult who values the well-being of the child. Lack of a consistent caregiver can create additional risks for children (Engle, Lhotská, and Armstrong 1997).

One of the keys to supporting the child's optimal development is to provide appropriate care. Care includes much more than keeping the child safe and free from harm. Care is an interactive process. The parent/ caregiver interaction with the child determines the quality of care received and the ways in which the child develops (Engle, Lhotská, and Armstrong 1997; WHO 1999). In the best of circumstances, a key characteristic of a good care provider is her or his ability to be responsive to the child's behavior. The ability to be responsive necessitates having time, as well as being physically and mentally healthy. When caregivers are under stress from too many responsibilities and insufficient resources, they may be unable to respond appropriately to children. So, while the ultimate goal of parenting programs is to enhance children's well-being, this cannot be achieved without considering the needs of parents, the family, and the community. The next section discusses principles that need to be applied when creating parenting programs.

Strengthening Care for the Youngest Children through Parenting Programs

The broad objective within parent programs is to create awareness of the importance of the caregivers' role in relation to supporting children's growth and development, and to strengthen or modify caregivers' attitudes, beliefs, and practices in relation to caring for a child. While all children need the care described previously, how the needs are manifested and provided will differ from culture to culture. Ultimately, parent programs should empower caregivers in ways that will improve their care of and interaction with young children and enrich the immediate environment within which children live.

It is important to keep in mind that any caring adult can provide parenting, whether or not they are a parent or even a family member. Thus programs for families—if they are to be effective as a strategy for supporting children—need to be available not only to the child's parents, if they are present, but also to anyone in the community who can or does have an impact on the child's life, including child minders, family members, care providers, educators, and community resource people. In Africa there is a tradition of children being raised by the extended family and the community. This tradition is an important place to start when creating parenting programs.

The creation and implementation of programs for parents, families, and communities with young children (from birth to age 3) is not well developed in Africa. Within the early childhood development (ECD) field worldwide there is limited experience in the development and evaluation of parenting programs (Dahinten and Willms 1999; Evans 2006). Yet, the available evaluations suggest that there are positive long-term outcomes for all those who participate in such programs—parents, children, and those who provide the service (Evans 2006; Kağitçibaşi et al. forthcoming; Myers and Hertenberg 1987; Nufio de Figueroa, Ramirez, and Urquía 2004). However, there is still much to be learned. From those projects that appear to be successful, it is possible to derive a set of principles to guide the development of parent programs:

Assume that the people who are caring for children are doing their best—It is important to begin with the assumption that all those who take on a parenting role seek to do the best they can to provide for their children, but many are operating within enormous constraints. For example, as a result of the AIDS pandemic, many grandparents have become the primary parent. Prior to taking on the parenting role, grannies were struggling to feed themselves. The burden of taking responsibility for their children's children adds an additional stress. And, even when they are able to feed the child, they frequently lack the resources and energy to do much more than that. They may not be able to provide appropriate guidance, counseling, and psychosocial support. Children under the care of other children or grandparents may well miss support for their development as compared with their counterparts in other forms of households.

Do no harm

We have systematically allowed people to feel incompetent and inadequate in raising their own children.

—Salole (n.d., 10)

It is important to ensure that parenting programs are supportive of families' existing culture, support systems, available care, and individual needs. This principle may sound like a cliché but, in many programs, parents are still asked to assimilate materials that are imported from other cultures and to take on practices that may cause more confusion and self-doubt than improvement in their abilities as parents (Evans 1994).

Base processes for working with parents within the economic, political, and cultural context—In designing programs to reach children and families, it is important to start with a specific and informed understanding of the political, economic, social, and cultural forces at work in a given setting. This principle may seem self-evident, yet too often program developers or funders select a program model that has worked successfully in some other place and set about trying to adapt it to local needs. Often the match between the model and the community is less than ideal. The assumptions about the community may turn out to be inaccurate and misleading. In addition, the process of program selection has most likely excluded the community, making community ownership difficult to achieve. Therefore, it is important to do a localized and participatory strengths and needs assessment that will lead to a better understanding of the supports available and the challenges faced by families who are most at risk within a given context.

In creating parenting programs in Uganda, Nyeko (2004) argues that it is important to recognize the long-term impact of the political instability and wars that have led to the loss of lives and property since independence in October 1962. She states that by 2002 in northern Uganda alone, 23,520 people had been killed by the insurgency perpetrated by rebel forces. The war has also resulted in the loss to the economy of about US$1.33 billion. These human and economic losses have a heavy and negative effect on the family institution and structure; they adversely affect and alter the norms and values of society that once guaranteed and ensured family stability.

In addition to the impact of civil war, Uganda is experiencing modernization and development. Many practices that were once unheard of or unacceptable are increasingly gaining popularity and acceptability and are now actually viewed as fashionable. Sexual activities that were not condoned in the past are being promoted under the guise of "human rights." More than 60 percent of young people between the ages of 15 and 24 are now sexually active. Uganda has one of the highest rates of teenage pregnancies in the world; a staggeringly high number of children are involved in prostitution and drug abuse, and a high number are street children.

The high cost of living has resulted in longer working hours for parents and guardians, hence there is less time to guide and mentor young children. Consequently, many children are left in the hands of caregivers who are neither trained in childrearing and care nor interested in the children's welfare and development. These children are exposed to abuse and various kinds of torture. Children are now mentored by television, newspapers, magazines, peers, and the Internet. Musicians and film actors receive more attention from children than most parents and are more likely to influence children than their own parents.

Nyeko is taking these trends into account in the parenting curriculum she is creating. The following principles (among others) are included in her curriculum:

• It is important to safeguard children from the effects of social disintegration.
• Spiritual strengthening enables children to have something to hold onto in the face of societal challenges and storms of life; it provides an anchor.

Identify specific childrearing practices that will affect child outcomes— While understanding the broad political, economic, and social context is the beginning, it is then important to identify and understand the value of traditional supports related to parenting. In Africa, and in Malawi in particular, parenting skills are traditionally transferred to children while they are still young. Children care for their siblings while their parents work in the field or go to other work outside the home. Children bathe their brothers and sisters and even cook for and feed them. Children also help with household chores and are sometimes sent to sell things to earn money for the family. In some countries these tasks may be regarded as child labor, yet in this case parents feel they are training their children to be reliable adults.

Within some cultural groups in Malawi, boys and girls as young as age 6 participate in initiation ceremonies where they are oriented on issues of parenting and what it means to be an adult. As they reach puberty, they are given more information to prepare them for parenthood. Women who are pregnant for the first time also undergo initiation ceremonies where they are taught how to care for the child as well as the husband. However, only the woman is trained in how to make her husband happy, care for young children, keep her house clean, and live in harmony with her community members. Men are not given such training. As a result there is a large gap between what women and men know concerning childrearing. In urban settings, and for some cultural groups, these initiation ceremonies do not take place. Thus, an increasing percentage of the population receives little or no orientation to the parenting role.

Even if people have gone through the traditional initiation process, appropriate child care is a universal problem in Malawi. Many parents do not understand, or have no knowledge of, what they are required to provide to support their child's growth and development. Take, for example, feeding a young child. Parents feel that if children are given enough food, that will be sufficient to make them grow and develop. And while mothers do their best to feed the child, they lack awareness of what constitutes nutritious food for a young child; junk food is quickly becoming more common in urban areas. In addition, it is common for young children to be fed only once a day, like adults. Women cook a meal for the family that is shared among everyone in the household, with men and boys being served first and women and young children eating last. The practice of cooking only one meal a day happens regardless of how much food is available in the home. Many mothers also lack skills in food preparation and preservation, meaning that during some parts of the year they have food and at other times there is nothing to eat. As a result, children in all parts of the country are malnourished.

Children also lack early learning and stimulation opportunities. Even where materials are available, parents do not play the mediation/facilitation role of fostering children's exploration and learning. Many children, especially those in poor rural and urban areas, are not bathed and their clothes are not washed, despite the availability of water. In some cases children in urban settings are not allowed to play or socialize with other children in the same neighborhood. Overall, many children grow up in poverty-stricken homes and environments. Young children therefore face many challenges that affect their ability to reach their full potential.

Given a grounding in some of the traditional beliefs and practices, the next step is to learn more about specific subpopulations where children are most at risk of delayed and debilitated development.

Identify those families who could benefit most from a parenting program—The literature suggests that children within low-income and single-parent families are more likely to benefit from a parenting program than children in middle-class families (Dahinten and Willms 1999; Evans 2006; WHO 1999). Therefore, within a given context, it is appropriate to understand more about low-income families and what they face before developing a specific program with them.

In Malawi, Matola (2004) identified a rural population of low-income, women-headed households that she felt could benefit from parenting support. She undertook a study to better understand the dynamics within these households to determine their strengths and needs. She then worked with the women to determine the kinds of capacity-building activities they wanted and required. In her study, Matola interviewed the women and observed their interactions with their children. In addition, she assessed the context within which they live in order to understand the supports (or lack thereof) for these women in their communities.

The study documented some of the many hardships single women face as they raise their children. One reality is that when mothers are engaged in economic activities outside the home, young children are left at home alone most of the day, which exposes them to various forms of abuse. In addition, the children lack much-needed love and guidance as well as support throughout the day.

Even when mothers are with their young children, they do little to support the child's development. The mothers lack knowledge about what young children require and how to provide that through appropriate care. The results are high rates of malnutrition and other nutrient-deficiency illnesses, as well as children who are ill-prepared for school and for life.

Many school-age children drop out because they lack the money for school fees and other supplies due to the low earning capacity of the mothers or the lack of resources in their homes and environments. Fathers are seldom present. Some children have never seen their fathers; in other cases, the father is unknown. The children miss their fathers, struggle with their identity, have feelings of abandonment and alienation, and, in many cases, lack self-confidence.

Looking at the context, Matola (2004) quickly identified the lack of community supports for these women as one of the major issues. She concluded that it was important to sensitize the community to the challenges these women face and to find ways for the community to support the women, rather than stigmatizing them. Matola also recognized the need to develop supports beyond the community. She concludes that laws concerning marriage, divorce, and maintenance of children need to be changed as a part of creating an enabling environment.

Based on information gathered, capacity-building activities were created. Matola (2004) reports that participants in the research made the following five recommendations:

1. Money-lending institutions should lend money to poor single mothers living in poverty in rural communities in order for the single mothers to be able to meet their needs as well as the needs of their children.
2. Single mothers should be informed about women's and children's rights as well as laws that relate to marriage registration, divorce procedures, and the maintenance of children.
3. Single mothers' clubs should be formed in the community for sharing information on child care.
4. Single mothers should be informed about strategies to keep their children in school.
5. Single mothers should be educated and trained in child care.

While the basic content of the training that was developed focused on the interaction between mother and child to improve the kind of care that children are currently receiving, the training also provided women with skills so that they could become economically independent and address the issues they had identified as important.

Create processes for working with parents that incorporate both traditional and scientifically validated childrearing practices into parental and community support programs—Curricula for parent education programs come from a variety of sources. Historically curricula have been packaged by professionals who have little or no knowledge of the cultures within which the materials will be used. Fortunately the practice of importing curricula is being questioned. There is increasing recognition that local practices are often as good as (and sometimes better than) what might be introduced from outside. To build on local strengths it is important to create an interactive process that shifts some of the power and control from the program developer to the local population (Ball and Pence 2006). Rather than imposing Western ideas about childrearing, programs for parents should be developed with parents through a dialogue that "respects different views and allows different voices to be heard—valuing diversity and with an openness to creating new knowledge and new ideas" (Arnold 1998, 1).

The challenge that project designers face is how to value diversity and be truly open to supporting existing knowledge in more than token ways while also introducing new child development practices and beliefs that have been shown to be effective. The project design process should:

- build confidence in local positive practices, while building trust that what is being offered from outside may also be of value;
- recognize, respect, and build on existing traditional strengths while acknowledging and responding to the need for people to access new information; and,
- share experiences and generate solutions while introducing ideas that may contradict current practices, beliefs, and realities (Evans 2006).

Many traditional practices within African cultures have great value. For example, the traditional responsiveness of African mothers to their infant's needs provides opportunities for care that are not found in Western cultures where the child and mother lead a much more separated and prescribed relationship. The typical Ugandan mother in a rural area will have her baby with her 24 hours a day. They will go to the garden together with the baby strapped on the mother's back. The responsive care she is able to provide enables the child to develop a sense of trust and confidence. The tradition of breastfeeding on demand is now recognized by many as far better than breastfeeding on a schedule. In addition, while debates continue in the West about the merit of cosleeping, in African cultures, where cosleeping is the tradition, there are seldom reports of infant crib death.

While some traditional practices need to be retained or strengthened, others need to be understood in terms of their complexity and impact on modern society. For example, Nyeko describes her own experience of being parented within a polygamous family:

> I grew up in a polygamous family with three stepmothers and 29 brothers and sisters. I was one of the younger children but fourth in my mother's household. My mother was not the most favored of the wives (though at one time she was!), therefore life was not the best for the children.

One practice that is no less complex has more severe consequences: in some cultures, such as in the Malawi village, chiefs have the responsibility for sexually initiating young girls in their passage to adulthood. This practice has contributed greatly to the spread of HIV.

The challenge for a parenting support program in the complexity of a polygamous household is how to build relationships within the family that support everyone's role and that ultimately provide children with the support they require for healthy growth and development.

It needs to be recognized that to change people's behavior, one must respect who they are and what they do before they will be open to learning something new. If a program starts with local understanding of what children need, builds upon traditional practices that are helpful, and introduces new knowledge in the context of dialogue, sharing, and brainstorming, these new practices are more likely to make sense and take hold than if people are simply given information.

It is helpful to remember that even when introducing scientifically validated information, choices about how to raise their children belong to parents and communities, except in cases where practices violate a child's human rights. However, even the definition of what constitutes human rights is still being debated.

Create community and national support for families—Most parent education programs aim to change the primary caregiver. The programs focus on educating the caregiver to better understand children's development process, to provide more appropriate care for the child, and to interact more effectively with the child. However, in many settings, it is not enough to change the beliefs and practices of caregivers (primarily mothers, but also including grandmothers and older siblings). There is a need to also address what is happening for those in the immediate family, within the community, and even within the wider culture in terms of their support for changes taking place for those caring for young children.

For example, there is a call to include men in parenting programs. (See chapter 8 for a discussion of the role of fathers in ECD.) To do so, more research is needed on men's traditional role in childrearing and what it would mean to change that role. In Nigeria, Hua (2004) was concerned about how to involve fathers in the care of their children. She undertook a study that examined the role that fathers play in early childhood care and development among the Tiv in Nigeria. Focus group discussions indicated that the fathers' current attitudes, beliefs, and practices in relation to child care are deeply rooted in their cultural settings. Also evident were the ways in which fathers' roles have intergenerational family support, with grandparents playing a major role in childrearing. The care of children was and still is a communal role. Of particular interest to Hua was the fact that if fathers' roles are to change, it is necessary to create a culture of men's involvement in childrearing. There is a need for a "male-friendly environment" for childrearing if men are to be more involved in supporting their children's development from an early age. In other words, Hua recognized it would not be sufficient to simply provide parenting training for fathers; the wider society has to change and be supportive of these new roles.

But frequently if there are changes in parenting beliefs and practices, even if they are accepted within a community and subculture, these changes run the risk of running afoul of the systems that exclude or marginalize certain children. Health services may be inaccessible or unaffordable; education and employment opportunities are closed to certain families or ethnic groups; social services keep families in cycles of dependency rather than gradually empowering them. It is important to know what supports or impediments exist within the legal and regulatory context (de Graaf, Prinsen, and Vergeer 2000; Matola 2004).

Therefore, for parenting support programs to make a difference, it is important to take a systemic view and create programs to strengthen all the systems that must eventually support and sustain families and even, if necessary, to change the economic and social systems that are destroying families and communities. Those systems are created as a result of national and local policy. As Matola (2004) discovered in her study, current policy in Malawi needs to be examined to see the ways in which the rights of women-headed households and their young children are addressed. (See chapter 9 for a discussion of ECD policy.)

Conclusion

In summary, current economic, political, and social trends have left many African families fragmented. In many African countries where the majority of children are at risk (as a result of biological inheritance and/or environmental conditions) there is an urgent need to provide supports to those who care for children. There is a need for communities and families (supported by the government through policies and services) to respond to changes in the kinds of support they provide for children who are entering an even more rapidly changing world.

Because the prevalence of single-parent families is becoming a major trend of African families, there is a need to develop policies and programs targeted at expanding the economic opportunities of single mothers. Most African countries do not have legislation that guarantees maternity leave for single working mothers, for example. Child care for single mothers is also necessary to reduce the social and economic burdens on these families. Those who parent need support in developing literacy, economic, and social skills that can sustain them as participating members of a culture and community. They also need opportunities to increase their knowledge and understanding of what it means to raise a healthy, well-developed child.

Bigombe and Khadiagala (2003) are quite optimistic about the ability of African family structures to evolve in response to changes in the availability of economic, educational, and health opportunities. They note that these changes will continue to reflect the tensions between traditional and modern values and structures, and that while the changes are complex, there is adaptability and flexibility within African social and cultural contexts and an ability to respond. Although there have been widespread accounts of families abandoning key traditional practices in favor of modern ones, the major trend remains the creation of systems of marriage and family organization that draw on both traditional and contemporary norms. As Lauras-Lecoh (1990) noted, a dominant feature of the African family is its ability to "make new things out of old" and to draw forth new solutions from the traditional resources of family institutions.

References

Adepoju, A. 2000. "Recent Trends in International Migration in Sub-Saharan Africa." *International Social Science Journal* 52 (2): 383–94.

Amin, S. 2002. "Africa: Living on the Fringe." *Monthly Review* 53 (10): 41–50.

Andrews, M., D. Galeforolwe, N. Ratsoma, and J. L. Evans. 2006. "Botswana National Integrated Early Childhood Development Baseline Study." Report prepared for UNICEF Botswana. Gaberone: UNICEF.

Antoine, P. 1995. "Population et urbanisation en Afrique." *La Chronique du CEPED*, 17: 1–4.

Antoine, P., and J. Nanitelamio. 1991. "More Single Women in African Cities: Pikine, Abidjan, and Brazzaville." *Population: An English Selection* 3: 149–69.

Apter, D. 2002. "Globalization and Its Discontents: An African Tragedy." *Dissent* 49 (2): 13–18.

Arnold, C. 1998. "Early Childhood: Building Our Understanding and Moving towards the Best of Both Worlds." Paper presented at "International Seminar, Ensuring a Strong Foundation: An Integrated Approach to Early Childhood Care and Development," Institute for Educational Development, in conjunction with Aga Khan University, Karachi, Pakistan. March 23–27.

Ball, J., and A. Pence. 2006. *Supporting Indigenous Children's Development: Community-University Partnerships*. Vancouver, BC: UBC Press.

Belsey, M. 2003. *AIDS and the Family: Policy Options for a Crisis in Family Capital*. Geneva: United Nations Department of Economic and Social Affairs, Division for Social Policy and Development.

Bigombe, B., and G. M. Khadiagala. 2003. *Major Trends Affecting Families in Sub-Saharan Africa*. Retrieved September 5, 2006, from http://www.un.org/esa/socdev/family/Publications/mtbigombe.pdf.

Cattell, M. G. 1997. "Zulu Grandmothers' Socialization of Granddaughters." *Southern African Journal of Gerontology* 6 (1): 14–16.

Cooper, F. 2001. "What Is the Concept of Globalization Good For? A Historical Perspective." *African Affairs* 100 (399): 189–213.

Crush, J., ed. 2006. *Gender and the Brain Drain from South Africa*. Southern African Migration Project, Migration Policy Series 23. Retrieved August 10, 2006, from http://www.queensu.ca/samp/sampresources/samppublications/policyseries/policy23.htm.

Dahinten, V. S., and J. D. Willms. 1999. *Parent Education Programs for Early Child Development: A Review of the Literature*. Unpublished document. Geneva: Aga Khan Foundation.

de Graaf, Y., B. Prinsen, and M. Vergeer. 2000. *The Netherlands: Experienced Mothers Are the Key. Parents and ECD Programmes*. Early Childhood Matters, 95. The Hague: Bernard van Leer Foundation.

Engle, P. L., L. Lhotská, and H. Armstrong. 1997. *The Care Initiative: Assessment, Analysis, and Action to Improve Care for Nutrition*. New York: UNICEF Nutrition Section.

Evans, J. L. 1994. "Childrearing Practices: Creating Programs Where Traditional and Modern Practices Meet." *Coordinators' Notebook, 15*. Washington, DC: Consultative Group on Early Childhood Care and Development.

———. 2006. *Parenting Programs: An Important Early Childhood Intervention Strategy*. Education for All Global Monitoring Report. Paris: UNESCO.

Evans, J. L., A. Ahmed, C. Day, S. Etse, R. Hua, B. Missani, C. Matola, and L. Nyesigomwe. 2004. "Capacity Building across Cultures and Contexts: Principles and Practices." *International Journal of Educational Policy, Research, and Practice* 5 (3): 105–22.

Ferraro, G. P. 1991. "Marriage and Conjugal Roles in Swaziland: Persistence and Change." *International Journal of Sociology of the Family* 21 (2): 89–128.

Hua, R. 2004. "Involving Fathers in Early Childhood Care and Development." Unpublished master's major project, University of Victoria, Victoria, British Columbia, Canada.

Jones, S. 1999. "Singlehood for Security: Towards a Review of the Relative Economic Status of Women and Children in Woman-Led Households." *Society in Transition* 30 (1): 13–27.

Kağitçibaşi, C., D. Sunar, S. Bekman, N. Baydar, and Z. Cemalcilar. Forthcoming. "Continuing Effects of Early Intervention in Adult Life: The Turkish Early Enrichment Project 22 Years Later." *Journal of Applied Developmental Psychology.*

Lauras-Lecoh, T. 1990. "Family Trends and Demographic Transition in Africa." *International Social Science Journal* 42 (4): 475–92.

Leliveld, A. 2001. "The Effects of Restrictive South African Migrant Labor Policy on the Survival of Rural Households in Southern Africa: A Case Study from Rural Swaziland." *World Development* 25 (1): 1839–49.

Martin, P., and J. Widgren. 1996. "International Migration: A Global Challenge." *Population Bulletin* 51 (1): 46–47.

Matola, C. E. 2004. "Assessment of Interaction and Stimulation in Single-Mother Low-Income Families." Unpublished bachelor's major project, University of Victoria, Victoria, British Columbia, Canada.

Meekers, D., and A. Calves. 1997. "'Main' Girlfriends, Girlfriends, Marriage, and Money: The Social Context of HIV Risk Behavior in Sub-Saharan Africa." *Health and Transition* 7 (1): 361–75.

Modo, I. V. O. 2001. "Migrant Culture and the Changing Face of Family Structure in Lesotho." *Journal of Comparative Family Studies* 32 (3): 89–128.

Myers, R. G., and R. Hertenberg. 1987. *The Eleven Who Survive: Toward a Re-examination of Early Childhood Development Program Options and Costs.* Washington, DC: Consultative Group on Early Childhood Care and Education.

Nufio de Figueroa, C., M. I. M. Ramirez, and J. B. M. Urquía. 2004. "The Future Will Be Better: A Tracer Study of CCF's Early Stimulation Programme in Honduras." Practice and Reflections Series 21, The Hague, Bernard van Leer Foundation.

Nyeko, J. 2004. "Parenting Made Easy: A Personal Experience of a Ugandan Parent." Unpublished paper.

Preston-Whyte, E. 1993. "Women Who Are Not Married: Fertility, 'Illegitimacy,' and the Nature of the Households and Domestic Groups among Single African Women in Durban." *South African Journal of Sociology* 24 (3): 63–71.

Salole, G. n.d. "Working Intuitively or According to Plan: A Case for Bricolage in Development Work." Unpublished manuscript.

Schafer, R. 1997. "Variations in Traditional Marriage and Family Forms: Responses to the Changing Pattern of Family-Based Social Security Systems in Sierra Leone and Kenya." *History of the Family* 27 (2): 197–209.

Silberschmidt, M. 1999. *Women Forget That Men Are the Masters: Gender Antagonism and Socioeconomic Change in Kisii District, Kenya*. Uppsala: Nordiska Afrikainstitutet.

———. 2001. "Disempowerment of Men in Rural and Urban East Africa: Implications for Male Identity and Sexual Behavior." *World Development* 29 (4): 657–71.

UNAIDS (Joint United Nations Programme on HIV/AIDS). 2000. *Report on the Global HIV/AIDS Epidemic*. New York: UNAIDS.

UNESCO (United Nations Educational, Scientific, and Cultural Organization). 1993. *Promoting Families for the Well-Being of Individuals and Societies*. Malta World NGO Forum Summary: Launching the International Year of the Family 1994. Mediterranean Conference Center, November 28–December 2. Paris: UNESCO.

UNHCR (United Nations High Commissioner for Refugees). 2006. *2005 Global Refugee Trends*. Geneva: UNHCR.

UNICEF (United Nations Children's Fund). 2004. *Parenting Education Toolkit*. New York: UNICEF.

United Nations. 1989. *Convention on the Rights of the Child*. Retrieved September 5, 2006, from http://www.unicef.org/crc/.

———. 2004. *Proclamation of the Tenth Anniversary of the International Year of the Family*. Retrieved September 5, 2006, from http://www.un.org/.

United Nations Environment Programme. n.d. *GEO: Global Environment Outlook 3—Past, Present, and Future Perspectives*. Retrieved September 6, 2006, from http://www.grida.no/geo/geo3/english/410.htm.

United Nations Population Division. 2005. *World Population Prospects: The 2004 Revision. Volume 3: Analytical Report*. Retrieved September 6, 2006, from http://www.un.org/esa/population/unpop.htm.

Wallman, S. 1996. *Kampala Women Getting By in the Age of AIDS*. London: James Currey.

WHO (World Health Organization). 1999. *A Critical Link: Interventions for Physical Growth and Psychological Development*. Geneva: WHO, Department of Child and Adolescent Health and Development.

Whiteside, A. 2002. "Poverty and HIV/AIDS in Africa." *Third World Quarterly* 233 (2): 313–32.

CHAPTER 15

ECD and HIV/AIDS: The Newest Programming and Policy Challenge

Patrice L. Engle and Erika Dunkelberg, with Shireen Issa

The numbers are clear: as many as 16 percent of the orphans[1] in Sub-Saharan Africa, or 7 million, are younger than 6 years old; 36 percent, or 16 million, are ages 6–11 (UNICEF, UNAIDS, and USAID 2004). More than half of all orphaned children in Sub-Saharan Africa are younger than 12. Yet, as chapter 5 in this volume illustrates, the youngest children are often invisible to program planners. That chapter illustrates in stark terms the impact of the HIV/AIDS pandemic on children, including the size of the problem and the impact on young children, such as risks of poorer health care, malnutrition, and lack of psychosocial support. This chapter examines programs and policies that have attempted to address the multiple needs of these young children and their families. The first section focuses on programming approaches and examples for young children; the second section describes policy options.

Programming for Young Children Affected by HIV/AIDS

The consensus is growing on what all children need, as well as on the best programmatic responses for children who are orphaned or vulnerable, but these responses are still reaching only a tiny percentage of those in need.

Community-driven interventions at the household level that aim to strengthen the ongoing capacities of affected families and communities appear to be the most cost-effective (Desmond and Gow 2002; Richter, Manegold, and Pather 2004; Subbarao and Coury 2003). Responses must occur on all levels, linking local actions with those at the national and global levels (Levine 2001) and should aim to make a difference over the long term (Williamson 2000, cited in Richter, Manegold, and Pather 2004). The 5 strategies and 12 principles endorsed by the UNAIDS Committee of Cosponsoring Organizations (2002) and additional principles added by Family Health International (2001) further guide the work with children affected by HIV/AIDS. Three principles relevant to all children are

- strengthening the protection and care of children affected by HIV/AIDS within their extended families and communities;
- enhancing the capacity of families and communities to respond to the psychosocial needs of children affected by HIV/AIDS and their caregivers; and
- linking care programs with other HIV/AIDS programs to provide a holistic and comprehensive support system to families and communities.

Much less consensus exists on how to make these responses developmentally appropriate for younger children (ages 0–8) who have been orphaned or made vulnerable by HIV/AIDS. None of these principles or strategies reflects the particular vulnerabilities of children under 8 or the unique challenges of programming interventions for this age group. Care for younger children is more time consuming and may require more knowledge and resources than care for older children. Care for younger children occurs primarily in the family and includes appropriate feeding, care during illness, attention to hygiene practices, emotional support, and stimulation and learning. The period from birth through entry to school represents a window both of opportunity and of risk for later development.

Any programming for younger children affected by HIV/AIDS must link with other HIV/AIDS programs to provide a holistic and comprehensive system of support to families and communities. Programming for younger children has three unique characteristics: (1) services must be *easily accessed* by caregivers who may be overloaded; (2) responses must *support the family*, improving their livelihood as well as their ability to provide care; and (3) programs must include *age-appropriate psychosocial support* to help children understand and deal with bereavement, changes, and loss.

Easily accessible services—The first years of a child's life are critical for survival, growth, and development. To ensure a good start in life, all children need immunizations, timely health care, growth monitoring and promotion, good hygiene and sanitation, and love and nurturance in the family. Quality basic services should be easily accessible to overstretched caregivers and be provided without discrimination at low or no cost.

Services for these children should include early learning and care programs that provide feeding, access to health care, opportunities for learning and play, and psychosocial support. The value of child care programs is being recognized; for example, the list of recommendations for faith-based organizations (FBOs; Olsen, Knight, and Foster 2006) now includes providing day care and other support services that ease the burden on caregivers. A study in Zambia (Haihambo et al. 2004) found that child care programs offered a respite to caregivers, supported children's learning and social-emotional development, gave the child a place to play and explore, and helped the child to be ready for school. The study found that children who remained in the family home and attended a day-care center did better in terms of health, nutrition, and child development than did those in institutional care. The day-care center provided stimulating group experiences and the children were able to interact with other children without stigmatization. The researchers also noted, however, that there were no quality controls on these child care centers, and quality varied enormously.

Family support—Any support for younger children must work through their caregivers, on whom so much of the well-being of young children depends. Caregivers may be old or young, overworked, living on a low income, and, in many cases, may feel isolated trying to cope with the circumstances. Supporting caregivers—both financially and emotionally—must be a component of any response for young children. In the Zambia study (Haihambo et al. 2004), children in extended family homes appeared to have their psychosocial needs (for love, attachment, consistency, normalcy, a sense of their own history and families, and integration within their communities) met to a greater extent than children in orphanages. However, their caregivers tended to be older and they reported illness, exhaustion, and constant worry over finances and the children's future.

Age-appropriate psychological support—Programs targeted to young children affected by HIV/AIDS and their caregivers should emphasize psychosocial support as well as nutrition, health, early stimulation, and play. For young children, the most important sources of support are a return to normalcy, opportunities to play, and a connection with at least one consistent caregiver who thinks that the child is special.

How to provide psychosocial support to younger children is still a huge challenge for many programs. In Uganda, Nyeko and Nalwadda (2005) reported that "the psychological state of children is a matter of concern but there is no clear understanding of the issue. This is an area of expertise that is particularly lacking" (11). Their review of 14 programs showed psychosocial support to be limited in most. In some programs, it was assumed that children under 8 were "too young to understand" (47). However, interviews with young children and caregivers in a Zambian study (Haihambo et al. 2004) showed that young children can talk about their circumstances and make judgments about what has happened to them. Young children in residential care reported, for example, "my mother does not want me any more"; "they put my father in a hole and then they brought me here"; "I cannot play with other children because my blood is bad" (HIV-positive child). However, many had aspirations (such as, "I want to be a doctor, to operate people [sic]") and expressed satisfaction with their current situation (for example, "they give me macaroni"). Young children are capable of expressing themselves, but adults may need to learn to listen to children. Adults should be able to recognize changes in young children's behavior, such as being withdrawn or aggressive, that changes are caused by loss, and recognize other symptoms such as guilt and anger (Nyeko and Nalwadda 2005). Adults need to be able to communicate in ways that young children can understand; they need to be able to give age-appropriate psychosocial support.

Stigma continues to be a challenge, as does physical and sexual abuse. A formative evaluation in KwaZulu-Natal (Kvalsvig and Taylor 2004) showed high rates of abuse of young children reported by all early childhood development (ECD) practitioners in their survey. Dealing with these situations with young children is particularly challenging. In South Africa, the Fatherhood Project (Human Sciences Research Council of South Africa n.d.) tries to reduce the amount of abuse by showing positive role models of men in caregiving situations.

Program Options

This section includes examples of programs that meet the unique needs of children 0–8 affected by HIV/AIDS. These programs reflect to varying degrees the three characteristics of a response to young children mentioned previously; common elements include the following:

Easily accessible services

- Access to services in health, nutrition, and social welfare
- Access to early learning environments for children—particularly preschools or day care—that meet children's needs for play, learning, being with other children, and food, as well as caregivers' needs for respite and time to work

Family support

- Psychosocial support to caregivers provided through home visiting or groups, including home-based care for ill adults
- Direct cash or material assistance to families or to livelihood creation
- Community ownership and management of the process; involvement of communities in caring for young children

Age-appropriate psychosocial support

- Opportunities for children to express themselves and have a voice in decisions

Numerous information sources were used to prepare the following list of programs. Some of the programs were presented at the Third International Conference on ECD in May 2005 in Ghana. Other programs were gleaned from presentations and through correspondence (including project literature and evaluation materials sent by the programs) in the months following the conference; still others were described on Web sites and in publications such as *From Faith to Action* (Olsen, Knight, and Foster 2006), *Christian Aid News*, and the Bernard van Leer Foundation reports. Programs were included if they existed in more than one location and served a relatively large number of young children. Where possible, funding sources and qualitative or quantitative evaluations are included in the following summaries.

Ghana: Manya Krobo Queen Mothers Association

The Manya Krobo Queen Mothers Association (MKQMA) was formed in 1998. By 2003, it consisted of 371 queen mothers across six districts of the Manya Krobo Traditional Area in the Eastern Region of Ghana where HIV prevalence is high (Tuakli-Ghartey 2003). As Tuakli-Ghartey (2003) notes, queen mothers and male chiefs or kings are regarded as community leaders in Ghana, with queen mothers responsible for community children whose parents die or are too ill to care for them. In the Manya Krobo District, each queen mother cares for up to six orphans in her home. Historically, the queen mother provided for orphans' basic education, medical care, food, clothing, and miscellaneous expenses, using monthly dues paid by members of the Queen Mothers Association. Recently, however, as a registered nongovernmental organization (NGO), the MKQMA has received support in the forms of leadership training, capacity building (training and material support), financial resources, food, and material support from various international NGOs, FBOs, the Ghana government, and individuals.

An evaluation of the Queen Mothers project (Tuakli-Ghartey 2003) suggests that although the model is innovative, it has problems. For example, no criteria exist for who can be a foster parent or how many children each can handle. Second, questions have been raised about the low level of spending for children and the quality of care. Finally, this program is not directed specifically to younger children, and the respondents in the evaluation did not identify any children below age 6; theoretically, however, it could address their unique needs.

Kenya: Kenya Orphans Rural Development Program (KORDP)

Established in 1996, KORDP focuses on children affected by AIDS and HIV/AIDS issues (KORDP n.d.). In addition to its programs in Kenya, which cater to almost 6,000 children affected by HIV/AIDS, KORDP works with sister organizations in the Democratic Republic of Congo, Rwanda, Tanzania, and Uganda through Orphans Development Program International. KORDP's programs serve communities in districts of Kenya chosen for the greatest need.

Funded primarily by the Bernard van Leer Foundation and American Jewish World Service, KORDP works by mobilizing communities to establish and participate in the operation of ECD centers catering to children between the ages of 3 and 6, 66 percent of whom are affected by HIV/AIDS. The program works through community-based committees that govern each ECD center. Each center serves 60–100 children aged 3–9 affected by HIV/AIDS, with a catchment area of one to two villages (KORDP n.d.). KORDP nurses regularly visit communities to monitor children's health. The program trains community members in child development, the needs of young children—especially those affected by or infected with HIV/AIDS—and general awareness about HIV/AIDS. KORDP also provides inputs, such as seeds, dairy goats, pigs, or chickens for enhanced food security and trains caregivers (who have more free time because of the ECD center) in income-generating activities related to these inputs.

KORDP confronts challenges including difficulties in meeting administrative costs because funders often provide support for project activities only; keeping the spirit of volunteerism alive in communities; and the need for training and ongoing support for community committees, ECD centers, and the communities themselves.

Kenya: Mwana Mwende Child Development Center

The Mwana Mwende Project started in 1997 in the Machakos District as a project of the Mwana Mwende Child Development Center, a local NGO. Its target group is children under 3 and teenage mothers. The project is primarily funded by the Bernard van Leer Foundation and the International Child Resource Center. The project has developed a parent support and education program that trains parents on child and youth development, community development, and participatory processes; it provides counseling to improve the care of young children, particularly those under 3 (Bernard van Leer Foundation 2006).

Kenya: Speak for the Child Project

Supported by USAID's Displaced Children and Orphans Fund and USAID/Kenya's LINKAGES project and designed and implemented by the Academy for Educational Development's (AED) Ready to Learn Center, Speak for the Child (SFC) was initiated in March 2001 in South Kabras, Western Kenya (Lusk et al. 2003). SFC supports families and communities in caring for young children under 5 affected by HIV/AIDS; the project has had a significant impact on young children and families (AED 2003).

SFC works in seven districts in Western Kenya. In 2005 in four districts 5,250 children were enrolled; mentors conduct weekly visits. In three other districts, about 3,800 children were on an extended support program, with paid preschool fees, regular deworming, bednet retreatment, and monitoring of weight and school attendance (D. Lusk, personal correspondence, December 11, 2005). SFC includes the following program activities:

- Regular home visits by trained mentors (village women) to support vulnerable households, particularly with respect to nutrition, health, and psychosocial and cognitive care. The mentors listen, encourage, and help the caregiver to problem-solve and to access resources and services.

- Preschool fees to send children in vulnerable families to local preschools;
- Immunizations and health cards;
- Capacity building of community committees working to increase human and financial resources; and
- Support groups for caregivers and mentors.

Monitoring children and families is ongoing by the mentors, who conduct community surveys to rapidly identify and target young children affected by HIV/AIDS. Once children are in the program, the mentors do baseline assessments and monitor child and caregiver outcomes, including immunizations, preschool attendance, home visits, attendance at support groups, and financial needs.

In the third quarter of 2005, SFC conducted annual assessments to evaluate the impact of the program on 1,437 children in the Bungoma and Vihiga districts (the project caters to 1,500 children in each district).[2] Compared with the baseline, immunization rates increased significantly in Bungoma and Vihiga. The frequency of children's illnesses decreased significantly from 92 percent to 9 percent in Bungoma and from 84 percent to 49 percent in Vihiga. Enrollment in preschool doubled in both Bungoma and Vihiga. With respect to caregiver behaviors that support learning, the assessments found that in Bungoma, the percentage of caregivers who told children stories or sang songs to them "at least sometimes" rose from 2 percent to 41 percent. The percentage of caregivers who "never" or "seldom" provided play materials for children dropped from 30 percent to 14 percent, while the percentage providing play materials "often" or "always" rose from 29 percent to 42 percent. In Vihiga, the percentage of caregivers "always" telling children stories and singing songs to them rose from 26 percent to 37 percent. The percentage of caregivers who "never" or "seldom" provided play materials dropped from 37 percent to 12 percent, while the percentage who provided them "sometimes" rose from 31 percent to 52 percent (D. Lusk, personal correspondence, December 11, 2005). Detailed analysis of improvement with respect to other indicators is contained in SFC's annual assessment and key results report (Lusk 2005).

According to Lusk (personal communication 2005), SFC served 9,050 children in 2005 at an average direct cost of less than $4 per month per child served, or $48 per year, which included the cost of immunizations, preschool, home visits, support groups, and SFC community committee meetings and community capacity building. When the cost of local management, including running the SFC committees, is included, the average monthly cost per child increases to $4.50 (Lusk 2005). Communities have begun to generate and contribute their own resources to sustain the project activities.

Some of the challenges SFC faced are highlighted in a project report (Lusk et al. 2003). To address these challenges, SFC simplified strategies for identifying the most vulnerable groups for services, limited the number and location of families that the home visitor had to cover, and expanded the age range from 0–4 years to 0–9 years.

Malawi: Integrated ECD Implementation

Malawi has a long history of integrated health, nutrition, and child development services that date back to 1966, when the first community-based child care center in Malawi was started. In the 1970s, the Association of Preschool Playgroups in Malawi took over the establishment and operation of preschool services in the country, supported by the government of Malawi in collaboration with the United Nations Children's Fund (UNICEF). Community-based child care was linked with Community-Integrated Management of Childhood Illnesses (C-IMCI); these two approaches were merged in 2002 to form the integrated early childhood development (IECD) approach. In 2003 Malawi launched the IECD policy, which included orphans and vulnerable children (OVC).

A key feature of IECD implementation in Malawi is the community-based child care center (CBCC) program. The program was initiated in 1989 in three study districts, inspired by findings of a government-commissioned rural child assessment conducted in 1988 (Chalamanda 2005). The assessment revealed that 1.4 million children under 5 were living in Malawi, and that 1.2 million of these lived in rural areas without preschools. While the CBCCs did not receive much community support in their early days, they saw a revival in the 1990s because of the growing numbers of orphaned children affected by HIV/AIDS.[3]

Today, CBCCs are viewed as a fundamental vehicle for providing social and emotional support to children affected by HIV/AIDS. In 2003, Malawi had 1,892 CBCCs, which were unevenly distributed by districts with a concentration in rural areas (Malawi 2003d) as well as 1,503 preschools countrywide concentrated in urban and semi-urban areas. These centers served 83,581 children in 2004/5, of which approximately 43 percent were registered as single or double orphans (UNICEF Malawi 2005). The CBCC program has a training manual and activity guidelines. However, the training does not treat issues of children affected by HIV/AIDS apart from issues affecting all children; doing so might have helped ECD providers respond more appropriately to these children. Many CBCCs are run by volunteers and are difficult to sustain without continued training and support.

South Africa: African Solutions to African Problems (ASAP)

African Solutions to African Problems (ASAP 2005) builds the capacity of community-based organizations (CBOs) to care for children affected by HIV/AIDS in South Africa. Through its partnerships for three years ending in 2005, ASAP cared for a total of 4,000 children affected by HIV/AIDS. ASAP's programs include the following examples:

- *Thandukaphila Drop-In Center* in Northern KwaZulu-Natal, which started in 1996, assists HIV/AIDS-infected and affected families, especially orphans. The center provides day care for 80 children under age 6 affected by HIV/AIDS, operates a drop-in center for 450 school children, and coordinates 30 home-based caregivers working with 200 HIV/AIDS and tuberculosis clients. The center serves 1,000 children affected by HIV/AIDS in 18 surrounding communities.
- *Etafeni Playgroup Project* in Nyanga Township, Capetown, coordinates outreach programs to support child-headed families, provide home-based care to families infected and affected by HIV/AIDS, educates mothers on early childhood development, and provides skills development in the community. The Etafeni group runs five ECD centers serving 300 children affected by HIV/AIDS.
- *Kakaretso Development and Training Trust* in Qwa Qwa operates 42 ECD centers serving more than 2,000 children affected by HIV/AIDS (infants, toddlers, and youth) as well as families and caregivers.

South Africa: Ikamva Labantu (American Jewish World Service)

The Ikamva Labantu Child and Family Centers and Family Enrichment Centers Project (supported by American Jewish World Service) aims to upgrade preschools to child and family centers that provide care for children in the context of their families (Partnering Communities in Development n.d.). In 2005, the project was being piloted in 50 schools that are beginning to operate as satellites to a newly established Family Enrichment Center. Every month 80 families with children in the preschools are supported. The Family Enrichment Center provides access to medicine, health, and capacity building for home-based caregivers and preschool managers. The Family Enrichment Center is staffed by a doctor, a nurse, a community services coordinator, and 10 "foot soldiers" who collaborate to conduct workshops, training, skills development, capacity building, and monitoring for the satellite centers. The foot soldiers are principals of day-care centers who have run their own centers for many years. They focus on the needs of families and children. An initial evaluation has shown that the foot soldiers benefit from the project and are becoming more and more effective in their fieldwork.

To evaluate the effectiveness of the training, an outside agency compared six centers with trained staff with six centers with untrained staff (Symba Social Investment Management n.d.). Four of the six centers with trained staff were as good or better than the centers with untrained staff, but the other two were very poor, suggesting the need for sensitization before initiating training.

South Africa: South Africa Hospice

In the South Africa Hospice program, an integrated community-based home care model provides support to families while a family member is dying and aims to ease the child's transition after the death of a parent. Interventions include day-care centers; training of caregivers in bereavement care; play, art, and music therapy; and developmental stimulation. The program eases the child's transition by beginning prior to the parent's death rather than afterward (Fox et al. 2002).

South Africa: Thandanani Children's Foundation

Thandanani Children's Foundation works in 11 communities in Pietermaritzburg and 3 communities in Richmond, South Africa. It supervises 130 volunteers who provide care and support to 1,600 children affected by HIV/AIDS and supports seven early learning centers (ELCs) in these communities. The organization trains and equips volunteers (community residents) to implement two systems of support for children affected by HIV/AIDS: (1) home-based support and (2) day care and early learning support for preschool children through community-based ELCs. Thandanani's primary strategies include assignment of community volunteers to support each household, support for those households identified as being in dire need of emergency assistance, provision of access to professional welfare services and counseling as well as access to recreational and therapeutic weekends, facilitation of the establishment of home-based food gardens and volunteer-driven income-generating projects, and support for community-based ELCs that provide care and support to preschool children affected by HIV/AIDS. Thandanani is supported by a variety of donors including the Catholic Agency for

Overseas Development (CAFOD), Christian AID, Development Cooperation Agency of the Catholic Children's Movement in Austria (DKA Austria), Stichting Kinderpostzegels Nederland (SKN in Netherlands), Starfish, Missio, Secours Catholique (in France), the Nelson Mandela Children's Fund, and the Wiphold Foundation.

Swaziland: Neighborhood Care Points (NCPs)

UNICEF in Swaziland has worked with the government to develop Neighborhood Care Points (UNICEF 2005). The NCP initiative is a vehicle for providing integrated services for children. It grew from the *Shoulder to Cry On* child protection initiative, which recognized that children, especially children affected by HIV/AIDS, have extremely limited access to basic food, education, health, and social services. NCP refers to a decentralized place or point in a given community where neighbors come together to provide care for neighborhood children. This place could be a house, church, community shed, or even under a tree. Communities are mobilized to provide a visible place for children to gather so that they are no longer invisible to the rest of the community. Community members help by identifying and supporting a resident volunteer to meet the needs of the children affected by HIV/AIDS. NCPs focus on preschool-aged children and on informal education, which frees older children to attend school. In areas that are affected by drought, food aid is critical for the initiation of NCPs. Communities also identify NCP sites. The NCPs are viewed as service points that may be developed and scaled upward to become part of a national strategy for addressing the needs and rights of children affected by HIV/AIDS.

In 2004 the NCP project provided care for more than 6,000 children in four regions through 198 NCPs and 862 volunteer caregivers trained in ECD (UNICEF 2005). By the end of 2005, 31,500 children received services in 415 NCPs, but NPCs still reach only 20 percent of the children in need. UNICEF supports the NCP project by providing cooking pots, recreational kits, and hygiene materials; the World Food Program provides food assistance. In some communities, NCPs collaborate with multisectoral Community-Integrated Management of Childhood Illnesses (C-IMCI) teams for outreach health services and training. Caregivers are trained in ECD, in providing psychosocial support, and in responding to child abuse. The ECD training sessions encourage communities to recognize their roles in addressing children's developmental needs.

In 2005 Swaziland's Ministry of Education provided support for all school-aged children affected by HIV/AIDS in the NCPs to attend school. Those who remain in the centers are younger children, and the program is becoming more oriented toward them. In addition to the standard problems of lack of long-term funding and lack of recompense for workers, the need is substantial for training and capacity building for the volunteer caregivers in ECD. The coverage of NCPs is still small compared to the number of communities that need and want the program.

Uganda: Action for Children's Community/Home-Based Integrated ECD Program: A Grandparents Action Support Project[4]

SBAction for Children (AFC), a Christian charity, was established in 1995 in Uganda. Twenty-two AFC staff members operate in five districts of Uganda covering the Central, North, West, and East Regions with the aim of providing rescue, protection, and advocacy for children, 90 percent of whom have been directly or indirectly affected by HIV/AIDS. AFC emphasizes collaboration with community leadership, especially local councils and community management committees.

The staff recognized that 80 percent of younger orphans were being cared for by grandparents (mainly grandmothers) who "most of the time complained that they are weak and frail and cannot do anything" (Nyeko and Nalwadda 2005, 45). With funding from the Bernard van Leer Foundation, they initiated the Grandparents Action Support (GAS) project both to improve the well-being of young children 0–8 affected by HIV/AIDS and to strengthen grandparents' capacity to care for vulnerable children. Grandparents have been mobilized to establish nine home-based ECD centers located within their villages where they send the children daily from 8:00 a.m. to noon for early learning, stimulation, nutrition, and health services (Nyeko and Nalwadda 2005). Grandparents are supported with training and counseling in good parenting practices and are provided information on ECD, hygiene and sanitation, food security, and community participation. Grandparents are further supported by action support groups with five grandparents per group. Monitoring and evaluation occurs through home visits, review meetings, and community meetings.

The program is implemented in nine zones at the parish level. Each zone selects leaders and one child counselor who implement the project. By 2005, 908 children under 8 (the majority were between ages 3 and 5) were enrolled. The oldest grandparent was 90 years old, while most grandparents were between 62 and 65 years old. A seven-month interim evaluation of the project showed that GAS had developed innovative strategies with the grandparents. Even in its early days, the project showed a multiplier effect, with nonproject families learning the strategies adopted by GAS families, then implementing them in their homes (Nyesigomwe 2005).

Some challenges that the project encounters include higher rates of common illnesses among the children in these households, distance from health facilities, very old caregivers and very young child-headed households, and lack of access to antiretroviral drugs for those who are HIV-positive.

Uganda: Uganda Orphans Rural Development Program

Operating in Uganda's Masindi, Mbale, and Tororo Districts, Uganda Orphans Rural Development Program (UORDP) focuses on providing care and support for HIV/AIDS orphans and their families and communities. Started in 2003, the program benefits 800 children affected by HIV/AIDS. Its five interconnected components are ECD, HIV/AIDS prevention, income-generating activities, health, and household food security. UORDP works with 10 groups comprising 12 to 15 caregivers per group. Each group manages an ECD center, works with community health workers to provide health and hygiene services to the children, is trained in organic farming and in small business skills, is provided with seeds and tools, and is supported with a loan or livestock (Nyeko and Nalwadda 2005).

Zambia: Kondwa Day-Care Center

Kondwa Day-Care Center was created in response to the exhaustion that home visit volunteers observed among the guardians of orphaned children: Some guardians did not have time to go to work or rest when caring for orphaned children; some were even having trouble providing enough food for the young children in their care. The day-care center was designed to give guardians a break and to allow children to socialize and enjoy nutritious meals. Children at ages 6 and 7, just prior to school entry, have opportunities for play and learning, nutritional support through home gardening, material support including preschool fees, and emotional support from spiritual guidance, memory boxes, and counseling (Christian Aid Society and UNICEF 2005).

Best Practices and Challenges

Despite the relative invisibility of young children, some of the programs just described were found to target younger children in age-appropriate ways. Most of the programs reviewed include access to services, some form of preschool attendance, and a community role. Most have either home visits or groups for caregivers to provide psychosocial support and information. Some programs involve cash grants or livelihood increases, but almost none give young children a voice or a role in decision making about their future. A few have evaluations, but these are mainly qualitative.

Best Practices

These programs promoted good practices that include some of the following common elements:

- Development of age-appropriate psychosocial responses
- Use of available community-level resources
- Coordinated approaches to service delivery via a network of established service agencies providing relevant services
- Services that combine the provision of resources and materials with education, training, counseling, and other support, as needed
- Emphasis on appropriate training for and routine monitoring of program staff, volunteers, and others involved in service delivery
- Promotion of family and community ownership through participatory planning and service delivery
- Recognition of the challenges posed by food insecurity and implementation of measures to address these issues through food supplies to very needy children affected by HIV/AIDS and through other means (including the enhancement of income-generating skills) for other families affected by HIV/AIDS
- Income-generating activities and skills enhancement as strategies for alleviating the economic stress on households (nuclear, extended, or foster families) affected by HIV/AIDS and facilitating the care and development of children affected by HIV/AIDS
- Both home- and center-based services that cater to the specific and general needs of vulnerable children
- Links to preschool opportunities, as appropriate, and reliance on preschools as places where care and education provided by families can be further enriched by trained teachers
- Recognition that intervening prior to a parent's death is likely to be more effective than afterward (Kvalsvig and Taylor 2004).

The operational guidelines for ECD and HIV/AIDS (UNAIDS, World Bank, and UNICEF 2003) are an excellent source of guidance for programming for young children affected by HIV/AIDS. These guidelines set out the elements that programs should include and discuss key issues, such as financing and assessment.

Richter, Foster, and Sherr (2006) stress the importance of investing in the strengthening of everyday systems of care, integrating services, and supporting all vulnerable children as follows:

Prioritize everyday systems of care (families, schools, and communities)—The most appropriate and sustainable sources of psychosocial well-being for young children come from caring relationships in the home, school, and community. Supportive families and communities nurture and sustain children's resilience. All efforts to enhance the psychosocial well-being of young children must ensure the support of these natural systems of care in everyday life. Children under stress are calmed and reassured when their familiar surroundings and everyday activities are restored.

Invest in long-term integrated services to promote psychosocial well-being—The psychosocial well-being of children and their primary caregivers is best supported by integrated services that address economic, material, social, emotional, and spiritual needs. Long-term investments in community development, health, education, and family support services are more sustainable and successful than short-term, crisis-driven interventions.

Realize the right of all children to access these integrated services—Rights are fulfilled through state provisions to which all caregivers and their children are entitled, including education, health, and social services. Universal access also addresses many of the most pressing needs of very vulnerable children. Services and programs must take into account the differing needs of younger and older children—girls and boys—and children living in a variety of settings.

Demand that more governments take the lead in guaranteeing the right to access services—Governments must lead and fund a coordinated effort that matches the generally vigorous responses to support vulnerable children, which have so far come from civil society. Systems to guarantee universal access to health and education must be strengthened. Social security underpins formal and informal community-based safety nets.

Earmark resources for applied research to expand the evidence base—We need to learn from experience and apply lessons learned from other fields, rather than treat HIV/AIDS as a special case in all respects. More evidence, including impact assessments, is crucial to guide and sustain appropriate and effective action (Richter, Foster, and Sherr 2006).

Challenges

Providing effective ECD services for children affected by HIV/AIDS presents a unique programming challenge, particularly in Sub-Saharan Africa because of the already large and growing population of such children. Issues that have provided the most challenges to these programs relate to cost, sustainability, capacity building, targeting, and going to scale.

Family- and community-level approaches face challenges of community and volunteer fatigue. Often families, communities, and even the most well-intentioned local-level groups have a limited understanding of and appreciation for the specific needs of these children. For example, the long-term sustainability of programs that rely heavily on volunteers, such as the Queen Mothers project, is of serious concern in communities experiencing volunteer fatigue.

Although an integrated approach to ECD is critical for success, policy and implementation mechanisms in most countries are dictated by vertical delivery structures that promote a silo-based approach to education, health, economic development, and emotional well-being. Some projects described previously, such as the Grandparents Action Support project, the Neighborhood Care Points project, and Malawi's government-supported IECD implementation, have achieved such integration, but most community-level projects focus on only one or two domains.

Listening to children's ideas can be one of the most important interventions that a program can encourage (Nyeko and Nalwadda 2005). In their formative evaluation of the role of ECD providers in KwaZulu-Natal in South Africa, Kvalsvig, and Taylor (2004, viii) found that "the most striking finding . . . is that children's feelings are seldom addressed": Despite the severity of the experiences they had been through, there was no evidence that children were receiving help. Haihambo et al. (2004) in Namibia recommend that children should have a role in decision making to the extent that their age and maturity allow, but this role did not seem to be a component of many of these programs. Many of the programs include services and family support, but fewer include adequate psychosocial support for families or the children themselves.

Whether and how to target orphans apart from all children affected by the HIV/AIDS crisis is unresolved. Some projects deliberately do not target orphans for fear that this would further alienate and stigmatize them. Without isolating orphans, however, it is important to recognize and cater to their specific needs, which may be otherwise overlooked in project activities. Local nomination of children is often used, but this may result in a demand for covering a larger number of children.

Poor quality of child care centers or day-care centers; the lack of training in issues related to HIV/AIDS, loss, bereavement, and support; and lack of quality control must be resolved in programming for young children. These centers cannot be just warehouses for children to wait for parents and caregivers to return, but must be centers for learning and development. Improved quality and training are not free.

One of the biggest challenges, however, is the issue of project sustainability and scale in the face of limited donor and community resources. Most of these examples are small in scale, reaching only a fraction of those children in need. Even if donor funding for program activities continues at its current level, few donors support large-scale activities or long-term administrative costs, without which sustaining qualified staff and other necessary resources is difficult (KORDP n.d.). The surest means for facilitating sustainability at all levels is to encourage government involvement and long-term commitment. Without national policies and plans that promote ECD programming for HIV/AIDS and include policies for children affected by HIV/AIDS, community-level projects will not achieve the scale of coverage that is required to effectively address the needs of this growing group of children. Within this context, the next section addresses the policy framework required to support a scaling up of ECD programming for HIV/AIDS.

The Policy Framework

As seen in the previous section, countries' experiences with ECD in the context of HIV/AIDS are limited to small-scale interventions led primarily by local communities. ECD programs in general are limited; the median gross enrollment ratio of children in preprimary programs in Sub-Saharan Africa is 12 percent, compared with 36 percent in all developing countries. National AIDS interventions are generally not designed to address affected young children's developmental needs. Education ministries focus principally on school-age children and provide school health education.[5] Health ministries focus on the medical aspects of prevention and treatment, but less on the mitigation of the effects on young children. Not surprisingly, young children are falling through the cracks of existing national HIV/AIDS interventions. To scale up ECD interventions in the context of HIV/AIDS, young children's unique needs must be reflected in key strategic national development policy documents. A favorable policy environment that acknowledges these needs provides the framework for such scaling up.

Key national planning documents, such as the Poverty Reduction Strategy Papers (PRSPs), national HIV/AIDS policies and strategic frameworks, and national OVC policies[6] need to reflect young children's specific needs as development priorities. The PRSPs are prepared by governments and describe a country's macroeconomic, structural, and social policies and programs to promote growth and reduce poverty. National HIV/AIDS strategic frameworks provide the framework as to where to invest, how to sequence investment, and what specific actions will have the greatest impact (World Bank 2004).

In particular, OVC policies provide the policy framework for mainstreaming ECD interventions in the context of HIV/AIDS. Efforts to mainstream the ECD response should not compete with the OVC agenda, but rather strengthen it. The ECD and OVC agendas pursue the same objective: the well-being of children infected or affected by HIV/AIDS. However, because the specific needs of young children affected by HIV/AIDS are often not recognized, many countries do not give attention to them in OVC policies and action plans. ECD practitioners and policy makers must advocate for OVC policies that include younger as well as school-age children. This recognition could begin with the reporting in the data collection process. The OVC Rapid Country Assessment, Analysis, and Action Planning process (RAAAP; POLICY Project 2005),[7] for example, could count orphans by age group and analyze the situation and age-appropriate interventions for the very young, such as those described earlier in the Program Options section.

In 2004 the World Bank and UNICEF, together with UNAIDS, provided an orientation in Dar es Salaam and small "seed funds" to five Sub-Saharan African countries (Ghana, Malawi, Rwanda, Tanzania, and Zambia) to support their efforts to scale up ECD interventions in the context of HIV/AIDS. The seed funds became available in 2005. The objective of these funds was to assist governments and civil societies, first, to bring together the HIV/AIDS and ECD communities and, second, to provide an initial platform for both civil society and government to develop action plans and policies to support the scale-up of these interventions for young children, as a component of programs for all children affected by HIV/AIDS.

The five countries have been striving to scale up their ECD response in the context of HIV/AIDS. With the exception of Ghana, a country with low levels of HIV/AIDS prevalence in the general population (with only pockets of infection in specific areas), these countries have high prevalence rates, limited ECD coverage, and active multicountry HIV/AIDS programs (MAPs).[8] The countries' efforts to combat HIV/AIDS have been built on different and complex scenarios; their efforts are works in progress. This section provides recommendations based on the lessons learned from these countries on how to scale up the response by positioning ECD in national development policies and how to access existing funding to support the implementation of ECD programs in the context of HIV/AIDS.

Ghana

Ghana, like Rwanda, has a favorable policy environment. Ghana's commitment to ECD is reflected in the ECD policy adopted in 2004. The Ghana National Commission on Children, now the Children's Department, led these efforts under the auspices of the Ministry of Women and Children's Affairs (MOWAC). As a matter of government policy, preschool is being made an integral part of the basic formal education system. The government, in its White Paper on the report of the Education Reform Review Committee, decided in 2004 to make two years of preschool education for 4- to 5-year-olds part of the free and compulsory universal basic education structure (UNICEF Ghana *Country Program Action Plan, 2006–2010*). Ghana also approved its national OVC guidelines that year (Ghana 2004). Furthermore, Ghana has strong HIV/AIDS policies. Ghana's National HIV/AIDS Strategic Framework II (Ghana AIDS Commission 2000), covering the period 2006–10, addresses the needs of vulnerable groups, including women and young children as well as OVCs. The program strategy includes addressing young children's needs through prevention of mother-to-child transmission (PMTCT) and mobilization of resources for children affected by HIV/AIDS. The MAP program has been particularly effective in supporting children affected by HIV/AIDS through the civil society organization (CSO) window (Amoa 2005). For example, the Ghana Queen Mothers program was supported by the Ghana AIDS Response Fund (GARFUND) Project. Yet, more programs could also be supported. A World Bank funding mechanism, the Multicountry HIV/AIDS Project (MAP) being implemented by the Ghana AIDS Commission, also has flexible funding windows for the national response through decentralized funding of NGOs/CBOs providing orphan care and support.

Table 15.1. Policy Environment in Ghana, Malawi, Rwanda, Tanzania, and Zambia

	PRSPs focus on ECD	PRSPs focus on AIDS/OVC	National AIDS strategic plan/ strategic frameworks	National ECD policy	National OVC policy	ECD AIDS action plan
Ghana	Yes, as a strategy to develop human resources	Yes, HIV/AIDS a priority including OVC	Yes, PMTCT and care & support for orphans; home-based care	Yes	Yes	Yes, prepared by cosultant but not implemented
Malawi	Yes	Yes, OVC including malnourished under 5-year-olds	Yes, PMTCT and reduce impact on children and orphans with child support groups	Yes	Yes, refers to CBCC	Yes, activities outlined at the central, regional, and local levels for each stakeholder
Rwanda	Yes, priority sector = education	Yes, seen as cross-cutting issue but no specifics on ECD/OVC	Yes, PMTCT	Being drafted	Yes, children infected/affected by AIDS but not specific to the needs of young children	Yes, under discussion
Tanzania	No	Yes, HIV as a cross-cutting issue	Yes, Goal 9 impact mitigation on orphans	No, but there is an ECD/EFA Plan 2003–2015	No, TACAIDS effort leading develop national OVC policy	Yes, drafted in consensus
Zambia	Yes, under education sector	Yes, improve quality of life of OVC support provided to CBOs/FBOs			Yes	Yes

Sources: Ghana (2005); Ghana AIDS Commission (2000); Malawi (2002); Rwanda (2002a); Tanzania (2003); Zambia (2002a, 2002b).

Note: CBCC = community-based child care center; CBO/FBO = community-based organization/faith-based organization; OVC = orphans and vulnerable children; PMTCT = prevention of mother-to-child transmission; PRSP = Poverty Reduction Strategy Paper; TACAIDS = Tanzania Commission for AIDS.

Malawi

Malawi has experience on ECD programming and has endorsed and adopted a national ECD policy (Malawi 2003c). The ECD policy establishes that children under 5 are eligible for ECD programs free of cost, including community-based child care centers or public and private preschool playgroup institutions. Broader policies, including the Malawi PRSP (Malawi 2002) and National AIDS Plan (Malawi 2003c), also incorporate ECD issues. The Malawi PRSP establishes that ECD is a priority for action under the education sector. The PRSP makes HIV/AIDS part of a multisectoral analysis and explicitly discusses the effects of HIV/AIDS as it applies to children affected by HIV/AIDS and their families. The National Strategic Framework (Malawi 2000) also refers to young children affected by HIV/AIDS. Malawi also has a national policy on OVC (Malawi 2003d). The plan is aligned with the national policy on ECD and incorporates ECD interventions as a strategy to mitigate the effects of HIV/AIDS on children. From a policy perspective, Malawi is one of only a few countries in Sub-Saharan Africa that have mainstreamed the issues of young children and orphans within its national policies. Seed funding provided by the World Bank to implement these policies is being managed by an NGO, the Association of Preschool Playgroups.

Rwanda

Rwanda's PRSP (Rwanda 2002b) recognizes the importance of ECD. The education sector's strategic plan incorporates ECD as one of the strategies to reach the *Education for All* (EFA) goals. Further, a national OVC policy was adopted in 2003 (Rwanda 2003). The ministry responsible to lead this initiative, the Ministry of Gender and Family Promotion, has yet to develop its capacity. There is no champion from the government to lead the response, and the NGO capacity on ECD is limited.

Tanzania

HIV/AIDS affects about 2 million children in Tanzania; about 4 percent of reported HIV/AIDS cases are children under 5. As in the other countries, the effects of HIV/AIDS are compounded by poverty. Unfortunately, the strong NGO and CSO presence has not been complemented by a strong government commitment or leadership. For example, ECD issues are not properly integrated in social development policies. ECD is not mainstreamed in the current PRSP (Tanzania 2000). The National HIV/AIDS Strategic Framework (Tanzania 2003) deals with young children's needs from a sectoral response. The civil society has made tremendous efforts to spearhead the ECD HIV/AIDS response. An ECD network of NGOs—the Tanzania ECD Network—has been actively undertaking different interventions for young children affected by HIV/AIDS. The Tanzania ECD Network developed recommendations for an ECD EFA action plan (Tanzania ECD Network 2003) that explicitly refers to the effects of the AIDS pandemic on young children's opportunities to thrive. The plan calls for concrete actions to support the care of young orphans by providing child care and community-based integrated ECD services. However, because these recommendations come from the non-governmental sector, funds are not attached.

Zambia

Zambia has been steadfast in its determination to move the ECD HIV/AIDS initiative forward. With the backing of the Ministry of Education, the country is building interest and support. Zambia's commitment to ECD is reflected in the education sector's plan to introduce preschool in basic schools in rural areas. The national HIV/AIDS policy (Zambia 2002a) gives priority to children affected by HIV/AIDS and the provision of community-based interventions. The ECD HIV/AIDS efforts are aligned with efforts for all children affected by HIV/AIDS and are woven together into the country's Fifth National Development Plan (Zambia 2006b). The National Child Policy (Zambia 2006a) establishes essential services that include ECD services for preschool children ages 0–6. Zambia has made significant progress in mainstreaming HIV/AIDS in its PRSP (Zambia 2002b). CSOs have been involved in the initiative, and the Ministry of Education is continuing a set of steps to support CSOs to access MAP and other available funds.

Summary

Ghana, Malawi, Rwanda, Tanzania, and Zambia are at different stages in the development and implementation of policies that support ECD interventions. Ghana, Malawi, Rwanda, and Zambia have included ECD as part of their strategies to reduce poverty and develop human resources. Most PRSPs treat HIV/AIDS as a cross-cutting priority area, but OVC issues are most often subsumed within the context of care and support for families living with HIV/AIDS (Bonnel, Temin, and Tempest 2004). In terms of the more specific national HIV/AIDS policies, most countries' HIV/AIDS strategic frameworks (organizing structures for the design and implementation of country responses to HIV and AIDS) include OVC issues. All of the countries except Tanzania have developed specific OVC policies; Ghana and Malawi also have a national ECD policy.

Having the right policies in place facilitates the process of mainstreaming the ECD and HIV/AIDS agenda. However, policies should be designed with budgets to support their implementation and action plans to identify roles and responsibilities for all involved agencies. Inclusion of ECD and HIV/AIDS issues in the policies does not guarantee their implementation if budgets and responsibilities are not straightforward. PRSPs are stronger on proposed policies for children affected by HIV/AIDS than on budget allocations or targets to be achieved. Even the countries with positive policies have experienced considerable hurdles in securing government funds to support the implementation of their policies. Budget commitments are vital to accelerate the response.

On the nongovernmental response, further efforts are needed by the ECD community to design ECD programs that address the needs of young children affected by HIV/AIDS and to secure funding available through international organizations. Local communities and CSOs now have the opportunity to access donor funding to support interventions for young children affected by HIV/AIDS. The Global Fund for HIV/AIDS, Tuberculosis, and Malaria committed $1.5 billion over two years. The United States' PEPFAR[9] initiative, launched in 2003, pledged $15 billion over five years to 12 African countries, with 10 percent earmarked for children affected by HIV/AIDS. The World Bank, through the multicountry HIV/AIDS programs (MAP) for Africa, has committed more than $1 billion since 2000 to support countries' battles against HIV/AIDS. In most cases, the largest portion of MAP funding is channeled through the local response window. In many countries this window supports interventions for children affected by HIV/AIDS. According to an interim review of MAP programs (World Bank 2004), the CSO window appears to be the best performing component of MAP operations, therefore offering the promise of expanding this major source of funding to CSOs. Community-based organizations (CBOs) working on ECD issues may not be aware of such funding or the mechanisms for accessing these funds. CBOs working on HIV/AIDS are not aware of the importance of adapting their OVC interventions to the developmental needs of the very young.

The seed funds provided by the World Bank and UNICEF are being used to support an array of activities, including sensitizing CSOs and governments about the importance of incorporating specific actions that target young children in their line ministry and organizational plans, designing ECD HIV/AIDS action plans, mapping activities of existing programs, and identifying mechanisms to help CBOs and FBOs to tap into existing funds. These efforts are the beginning. ECD organizations and line ministries still need to identify the venues set by National AIDS Commissions (NACs) and donors to submit proposals. For example, in Malawi, MAP funding has been pooled (together with funding from other sources such as PEPFAR and Global Funds for AIDS) and is managed by umbrella organizations. In Rwanda, the CSO component is implemented under two modalities: through umbrella NGOs that provide subgrants to smaller NGOs and through cross-cutting community development committees. The challenge for CSOs in these countries and others is to understand the procedures and mechanisms in their countries to access donor funds. Also, governments need to understand that partnering with NGOs is strategic for expanding programs for young children affected by HIV/AIDS.

Key steps that these countries could take include the following:

- CSOs need to address their National AIDS Commissions to learn about the availability of funds. CSOs need to learn about the funding sources and identify mechanisms to access the funds—from whom, how, when, and what could be supported. This process requires familiarization with the grant application, submission, review, and approval process.
- Simultaneously, civil society and respective ministries responsible for the needs of young children should sensitize the National AIDS Commission on the importance of responding to children's needs so that the NAC will be receptive to using existing resources for ECD activities and laying the groundwork for the next MAP programs.
- When line ministries already possess an approved policy or strategy and participate in the MAP financing of its program, they should identify the component of their ECD policy that deals with HIV/AIDS and have it included in their ministry submission to the NAC.

Conclusions

The case studies presented in the Program Options section and the experiences of the five Sub-Saharan African countries on ECD and HIV/AIDS interventions show that even though at least 7 million young children have been orphaned by HIV/AIDS and many more are affected by HIV/AIDS, society's response has been limited to a handful of small-scale interventions run mostly by NGOs. The quality and scale of these programs varies widely. Malawi is perhaps the most experienced country on ECD, yet the bulk of orphan needs and psychosocial needs still falls upon community providers, not the government. At the moment, the CBCC programs are small in number compared to children's needs.

Various programmatic responses were described in the Program Options section, and there is sufficient guidance to identify what needs to be done. This programmatic expertise should inform policy makers about interventions, tools, and evidence for effective interventions for young children affected by HIV/AIDS. Strong national institutions and policies can complement community initiatives but cannot substitute for national and local capacity and commitment for ECD.

In Sub-Saharan Africa, information is limited on how and when to include younger children in HIV/AIDS programming. Many opportunities could be used. For example, home-based care strategies for people living with HIV/AIDS could be expanded to integrate parenting education or counseling on childrearing practices. Similar interventions could be linked to the prevention of mother-to-child transmission (PMTCT). Also, as extended families become overstretched, child care settings become even more necessary to support care providers. Attention to young children's needs does not need to be translated into further vertical programs but should facilitate their inclusion into existing interventions, such as PMTCT care for PLWHA (people living with HIV/AIDS) or OVC issues.

Further work is needed in several areas, from mapping existing responses and evaluating their effectiveness, to building new efforts into existing programs and helping CSOs to access funds for their work through changes on both sides. Data on the coverage and impact of these interventions affect government capacity to design appropriate policies and programs. Much of the grassroots organizations' work goes undetected. Not all CSOs are formally registered and constituted, which makes it even more difficult to assess, for example, the areas of highest coverage of services or the quality of those services and to advocate with policy makers for effective intervention models.

Another critical need is research on indicators of child well-being (particularly for younger children) to evaluate the effectiveness of interventions. This research is an essential means of convincing governments to commit to ECD HIV/AIDS programming over the long term.

Progress has been made in recognizing the unique needs of the youngest children affected by HIV/AIDS and in beginning to understand what should be included in programs to meet their needs and ensure their rights. However, until parental deaths begin to decrease, a large number of such children will be neglected.

Notes

1. An orphan is defined by the Joint United Nations Programme on HIV/AIDS (UNAIDS) as a child under 18 years of age who has lost one or both parents.

2. The changes took place over a little less than one year. The children in Bungoma were enrolled in June 2004 and a baseline was taken at that time; the assessment took place in May/June 2005. The children in Vihiga were enrolled in late August 2004; the baseline was taken in September and the annual assessment was in August 2005 (D. Lusk, personal correspondence, December 11, 2005).

3. Later evaluations suggested that the lack of support was a result of the CBCC's top-down approach; "lack of capacity at community level; limited technical and financial support from government; lack of coordination, policy, and implementation framework; lack of teaching/learning/play materials at centers; dependence on volunteer service providers; and lack of trained service providers at community level" (Chalamanda 2005).

4. Information on AFC's programs, unless otherwise noted, has been obtained through reports compiled by AFC staff and information available on its Web site.

5. For example, see http://www.freshschools.org.

6. The definition of orphans and vulnerable children used by the international community refers to children 0–18 years old, hence covering the ECD age group.

7. Launched in 2003, the purpose is to undertake an analysis of the children affected, infected, and orphaned by AIDS as well as those vulnerable, and the response in each country; then, based on the analysis, to produce a national OVC plan of action to scale up and improve the response. A first round of RAAAPs was carried out in 16 countries in 2004. In most countries, the OVC action plans are a result of the RAAAP process.

8. The World Bank has supported MAPs since 2001.

9. President's Emergency Plan for AIDS Relief.

References

AED (Academy for Educational Development). 2003. *Speak for the Child: Improving Care of Orphans and Vulnerable Children Age 5 and Under.* Washington, DC: AED.

African Solutions to African Problems. 2005. Retrieved November 2, 2006, from http://www.africansolutions.org/about.html.

Amoa, S. 2005. "Overview of HIV/AIDS Situation in Ghana and Ghana's National Response." Presentation given at the World Bank Headquarters, Washington, DC.

Bernard van Leer Foundation. 2006. Mwana Mende Child Development Centre. Retrieved December 12, 2006, from http://www.bernardvanleer.org/partners/africa/kenya_-_mwana_mwende.

Bonnel, R., M. Temin, and F. Tempest. 2004. "Poverty Reduction Strategy Papers: Do They Matter for Children and Young People Made Vulnerable by HIV/AIDS?" Africa Region Working Paper Series 78. New York: UNICEF and World Bank.

Chalamanda, F. 2005. "Historical Background on IECD Implementation in Malawi." Unpublished.

Christian Aid Society and UNICEF. 2005. A Matter of Belonging: How Faith-Based Organizations Can Strengthen Families and Communities to Support Orphans and Vulnerable Children. New York: UNICEF.

Desmond, C., and J. Gow. 2002. "The Current and Future Impact of the HIV/AIDS Epidemic on South Africa's Children." In AIDS, Public Policy and Child Well-Being, ed. G. A. Cornia. New York: UNICEF.

Family Health International. 2001. Care for Orphans, Children Affected by HIV/AIDS, and Other Vulnerable Children: A Strategic Framework. Arlington, VA: Family Health International.

Fox, S., C. Fawcett, K. Kelly, and P. Nblaati. 2002. Integrated Community-Based Home Care (ICHC) in South Africa: A Review of the Model Implemented by the Hospice Association of South Africa. Pretoria: South Africa National Department of Health.

Ghana. 2002. Early Childhood Care and Development Policy. Accra: Ministry of Women and Children's Affairs.

———. 2004. National OVC Guidelines. Accra: Ministry of Women and Children's Affairs.

———. 2005. Growth and Poverty Reduction Strategy (GPRS II) 2006–2009. Retrieved October 25, 2006, from http://siteresources.worldbank.org/INTPRS1/Resources/ghanacostingofgprs_2(Nov-2005).pdf.

Ghana AIDS Commission. 2000. Ghana HIV/AIDS Strategic Framework 2001–2005. Accra, Ghana: Ghana AIDS Commission.

Global Monitoring Report Team. 2006. Education for All: Early Childhood Care and Education. EFA Global Monitoring Report 2007. Paris: UNESCO.

Haihambo, C., J. Hayden, B. Otaala, and R. Zimba. 2004. HIV/AIDS and the Young Child: An Assessment of Services Provided to Children Affected and Infected by HIV/AIDS in Windhoek, Namibia. Windhoek, Namibia: University of Namibia Press.

Human Sciences Research Council of South Africa. n.d. *The Fatherhood Project*. Retrieved October 26, 2006, from http://www.hsrc.ac.za/fatherhood/index.html.

KORDP (Kenya Orphans Rural Development Program). n.d. Retrieved October 27, 2006, from http://www.kordp.org/.

Kvalsvig, J. D., and M. Taylor. 2004. Report to REACH [Rapid and Effective Action for Combatting HIV-AIDS]: Study on Orphans and Vulnerable Children in KwaZulu-Natal. University of Natal-Natal, South Africa.

Levine, A. 2001. "Orphans and Other Vulnerable Children: What Role for Social Protection?" Paper presented at World Bank/World Vision Conference, Washington, DC, June 6–7.

Lusk, D. 2005. *Bungoma and Vihiga Annual Assessments: Key Results*. Washington, DC: AED.

Lusk, D., J. Mararu, C. O'Gara, and S. Dastur. 2003. *Community Care for Orphans and AIDS-Affected Children. Case Study: Kenya*. Washington, DC: AED.

Malawi. 2000. *National HIV/AIDS Strategic Framework 2000–2004*. Lilongwe: National AIDS Commission and Office of the President and Cabinet.

———. 2002. *Malawi Poverty Reduction Strategy Paper*. Retrieved November 3, 2006, from http://povlibrary.worldbank.org/files/Malawi_PRSP.pdf.

———. 2003a. *Gender Audit*. Lilongwe: Ministry of Gender and Community Services.

———. 2003b. *National HIV/AIDS Policy: A Call for Renewed Action*. Lilongwe: National AIDS Commission and Office of the President and Cabinet.

———. 2003c. *National Policy on Early Childhood Development*. Lilongwe: Ministry of Gender, Youth, and Community Services.

———. 2003d. *National Policy on Orphans and Other Vulnerable Children*. Lilongwe: Ministry of Gender, Children, and Community Services.

Nyeko, J., and R. Nalwadda. 2005. *Improving the Quality of Community-Based Psychosocial Support Services to HIV/AIDS-Affected Children Aged 0–8 Years in Uganda: An Evaluative Assessment of Models of Care*. Uganda: Uganda Action Research Program, Action for Children.

Nyesigomwe, L. 2005. "Strengthening the Capacity of Grandparents in Providing Care to Young Children Affected by HIV/AIDS." *Journal of Intergenerational Relationships* 4 (1): 55–63.

Olsen, K., Z. S. Knight, and G. Foster. 2006. *From Faith to Action: Strengthening Family and Community Care for Orphans and Vulnerable Children in Sub-Saharan Africa*. Retrieved October 26, 2006, from http://www.firelightfoundation.org/fta%20–%20Africa%20ready.pdf.

Partnering Communities in Development. n.d. Retrieved October 27, 2006, from http://www.ikamva.com/.

POLICY Project. 2005. *Executive Summary: OVC RAAAP Initiative Final Report.* Rapid Country Assessment, Analysis, and Action Planning (RAAAP) Initiative on behalf of orphans and other vulnerable children in Sub-Saharan Africa. Retrieved November 3, 2006, from http://www.policyproject.com/pubs/countryreports/AFR_OVC_RAAAP.pdf.

Richter, L., G. Foster, and L. Sherr, L. 2006. *Where the Heart Is: Meeting the Psychosocial Needs of Young Children in the Context of HIV/AIDS.* The Hague: Bernard van Leer Foundation.

Richter, L., J. Manegold, and R. Pather. 2004. *Family and Community Interventions for Children Affected by AIDS.* Pretoria: Human Sciences Research Council.

Rwanda. 2002a. *Draft HIV/AIDS and Education Policy and Strategic Planning Framework 2002–2006.* Kigali: Ministry of Education, Science, Technology, and Scientific Research (MINEDUC).

———. 2002b. *Poverty Reduction Strategy Paper.* Retrieved October 31, 2006, from http://povlibrary.worldbank.org/files/Rwanda_PRSP.pdf.

———. 2003. *National Policy for Orphans and Other Vulnerable Children.* Kigali: Ministry of Local Government, Information, and Social Affairs.

Subbarao, K., and D. Coury. 2003. *A Template on Orphans in Sub-Saharan Countries (Social Protection).* Washington, DC: World Bank.

Symba Social Investment Management. n.d. "An Evaluation of Ikamva Labantu's Early Child Development Training, Implemented by ABE Development Trust." P.O. Box 297, Sea Point 8060, South Africa.

Tanzania. 2000. *Poverty Reduction Strategy Paper.* Retrieved October 25, 2006, from http://povlibrary.worldbank.org/files/tanzaniaprsp.pdf.

———. 2003. *National Multisectoral Strategic Framework on HIV/AIDS 2003–2007.* Dar es Salaam: Tanzania Commission for HIV/AIDS and The Prime Minister's Office. Retrieved October 25, 2006, from http://www.tanzania.go.tz/pdf/tacaidsnmf.pdf.

Tanzania ECD Network. 2003. *Towards Tanzania's ECD EFA Action Plan 2003–2015.* Draft.

Tuakli-Ghartey, J. 2003. "A Rapid Assessment of the Orphan Foster Care Program of Manya Krobo Queen Mothers." Presented to the Ghana AIDS Commission, Accra, Ghana.

UNAIDS (Joint United Nations Programme on HIV/AIDS) Committee of Cosponsoring Organizations. 2002. *Principles to Guide Programming for Orphans and Other Children Affected by HIV/AIDS.* New York: UNICEF/UNAIDS.

UNAIDS, World Bank, and UNICEF. 2003. *Operational Guidelines for Supporting Early Child Development in Multisectoral HIV/AIDS Programs in Africa.* Washington, DC: World Bank.

UNICEF (United Nations Children's Fund). Ghana. 2005. *Country Program Action Plan, 2006–2010.*

———. Malawi. 2005. *Country Office Annual Report.* Lilongwe: UNICEF-Malawi.

———. Swaziland. 2005. *Swaziland's Neighborhood Care Points (NCPs) Initiative as a Vehicle for the Provision of Integrated Services for Children.* Mbabane, Swaziland: UNICEF-Swaziland.

UNICEF, UNAIDS, and USAID. 2004. *Children on the Brink 2004: A Joint Report of New Orphan Estimates and a Framework for Action.* Retrieved October 25, 2006, from http://www.unicef.org/publications/files/cob_layout6-013.pdf.

World Bank. 2004. *Interim Review of the Multicountry HIV/AIDS Program (MAP) for Africa.* Washington, DC: World Bank.

Zambia. 2002a. *National HIV/AIDS/STI/TB Policy 2002–2005.* Lusaka: National AIDS Council.

———. 2002b. *Zambia Poverty Reduction Strategy Paper 2002–2004.* Retrieved October 25, 2006, from http://povlibrary.worldbank.org/files/11240_Zambia_PRSP.pdf.

———. 2006a. *Draft National Child Policy.* Lusaka: Ministry of Youth Sport and Child Development.

———. 2006b. *Fifth National Development Plan 2006–2010.* Lusaka: Ministry of Finance and National Planning. Retrieved December 12, 2006, from http://www.cspr.org.zm/Reports&Updates/FNDP.pdf.

CHAPTER 16

Supporting Young Children in Conflict and Postconflict Situations: Child Protection and Psychosocial Well-Being in Angola

Michael Wessells and Carlinda Monteiro

War and its aftermath pose enormous challenges to the well-being of young children and their mothers. During and following armed conflict, young children face serious protection threats such as attack, separation from parents (Ressler, Boothby, and Steinbock 1988), sexual and gender-based violence, land mines, and displacement (Machel 2001). The world's 30 million displaced people, half of whom are under 18 years of age, include significant numbers of young children living in difficult conditions of overcrowding, poverty, and lack of basic necessities. Young children are also at risk of recruitment into armed groups, either through abduction or by being born into armed groups. Girls in southern Sudan who had been abducted by the Lord's Resistance Army (LRA) in northern Uganda are sexually violated by soldiers or by LRA leader Joseph Kony. Children born in what amounts to breeder camps in Sudan are reared from an early age to be the next generation of LRA soldiers (Wessells 2006). In Angola, children born into families that were part of the opposition group UNITA (the National Union for the Total Independence of

Angola) were reared to be soldiers or to provide sexual services for UNITA soldiers or other men (Stavrou 2005). Because nearly half of contemporary wars are protracted, lasting 10 or more years (Smith 2003), many children grow up in a situation in which war is a constant feature of their social reality.

Psychologically, young children are far from immune to traumatic experiences (Eth and Pynoos 1985; Pynoos, Steinbery, and Goenjian 1996; Terr 1991). Often they are affected by witnessing deaths or rapes, deaths of family members or friends, loss of their homes, and disruption of the daily routines that provide a sense of structure and continuity, among other things. Also, mothers, who suffer from a wide array of health and psychosocial risks in conflict environments, may be overwhelmed or depressed by their war experiences, making it difficult for them to provide care and protection for their young children (McKay and Mazurana 2004). During war—which destroys food supplies and the health infrastructure and worsens poverty—young children, who are the most vulnerable, are at increased risk of malnutrition and disease, including HIV/AIDS (Machel 2001). War's disruption of cultural patterns is itself a major stressor for people and is a source of infant malnutrition and mortality. For example, in Gorongosa, Mozambique, the war altered the cultural practice of *madzawde*, a tradition that spaced children's births by several years, enabling several years of breastfeeding and close maternal-infant relations, in addition to anchoring the living community to its spiritual roots and providing a sense of meaning. War-related disruption of madzawde damaged both the natural feeding schedule as well as mother-infant attachment and relations (Igreja 2003, 2004), increasing the risk of failure to thrive (Ward, Kessler, and Altman 1993).

Typically, the postconflict environment presents stresses and dangers as prevalent as those that occur during the fighting. In many southern African societies, presumably postconflict societies suffered from waves of banditry and crime (Minter 1994), as had occurred following the wars of the former Yugoslavia. Young mothers, including many who have no husbands, frequently struggle daily to feed their children or to pay for necessities such as health care. Distressed by poverty and rates of unemployment as high as 80 percent, families experience heightened stress, which may lead to higher rates of family violence. Children from abusive families are the most severely affected of all war-affected children (Garbarino and Kostelny 1996). After the war, babies and young children born outside of marriage or as a result of rape suffer severe stigmatization and isolation (Carpenter 2007). With the infrastructure and economy in ruins and lacking access to basic services, local people frequently challenge the term *postconflict*, asking, "Where's the 'post'?"

In light of these needs, a high priority for the early childhood development (ECD) field is to extend its concept and practice to war zones. Indeed, agreement is increasing on the importance of providing ECD supports to children in conflict and postconflict zones, though there is less agreement about how to do it. Extreme poverty, a paucity of government services, and logistical and security challenges militate against relatively costly interventions or Western interventions that may be culturally inappropriate or unsustainable in war-torn countries. Perhaps the greatest challenge, however, is scale. Although some young children are at greater risk than others, nearly all children in war zones have been affected by the war and have significant health, protection, and psychosocial needs.

This chapter aims to shed light on the question how to provide ECD support in emergency settings. Using the case of Angola, it describes numerous low-cost, community-based, sustainable supports for young children that are tailored to both the culture and the situation. After summarizing the war and situation for Angolan children, this chapter identifies practical tools that can be applied on the large scale that is needed.

The Angolan Wars and the Aftermath

War in Angola followed a pattern of internal fighting with outside influences and of massive civilian impact. Although the term *war* frequently evokes images of different nations fighting, more than 90 percent of contemporary wars are internally fought within state boundaries (Smith 2003). In contrast to the wars fought a century ago, in which most of the casualties were soldiers, nearly 90 percent of the casualties in contemporary wars are civilians (Garfield and Neugut 1997; Sivard 1996; UNICEF 1996). Armed groups cause high civilian casualty rates through terror tactics such as targeting civilians and destroying their crops and animals to control an area; widespread destruction of the health infrastructure; interruption of basic services; food insecurity; and masses of displaced people living in difficult conditions in which basic needs go unmet.

Cycles of Conflict

War in Angola is best described as a series of conflicts punctuated by brief interludes of relative quiet. Initially, war erupted in 1961 as Angolans fought for their liberation from Portuguese rule. Although independence was achieved in 1975, rival political groups—mainly the People's Liberation Movement of Angola (MPLA), which became the government, and UNITA—fought over control of the country. The civil war soon became a proxy war engaging the Cold War superpowers: the former Soviet Union backed the socialist MPLA; the United States and South Africa backed UNITA. In 1991, a brief ceasefire enabled national elections, but when UNITA lost, the country plunged back into fighting. During a particularly brutal period of fighting from 1992 to 1994, nearly 1,000 people died daily as the result of war (Lodico 1996). UNICEF (1995) estimated that during this period, approximately 320 out of 1,000 children died before reaching age 5. By this time, Angola had become one of the most extensively land-mined countries worldwide; it had 5 to 10 million land mines in a population of 11 million people.

The signing of the *Lusaka Protocol* in 1994 ushered in four years of relative peace. However, UNITA's political will for peace was weak, and fighting erupted again in 1998, continuing until 2002 when UNITA leader Jonas Savimbi was killed. As in previous phases of the war, this period exacted a heavy toll on children under 5 years old, who are considered the most dispensable and least prioritized during conflict. When households are attacked and adults flee, babies and young children are frequently left behind. On long marches through the bush, mothers are often forced to abandon the youngest children, whose sounds could invite enemy attention. Highly dependent on their mothers, many babies and young children die if their mothers die. Even if their mothers live, the combination of extreme danger and deprivation may cause infants to stop nursing. Also, in situations of starvation, parents often have to choose which child will survive; typically they choose an older, more "useful" child. Young children who have been abandoned, lost, or orphaned are often placed in orphanages, where they are likely to lose their identity and the possibility of family reunification. Even if young children remain under adult care, parents are typically so focused on survival that they do not give their children the attention, affection, and stimulation they might have enjoyed under more stable circumstances. Often, parents who have been with military groups lose their ability to make decisions, encouraging a sense of fatalism and lack of responsibility toward their children.

The Postwar Situation

When the war ended in April 2002 with the signing of the *Luena Ceasefire*, it left a complex humanitarian emergency in its wake. Nearly one-third of Angolans—3.5 million people—were internally displaced; half the displaced and wider population were under 12 years of age and lacked basic necessities and access to health care and education. At that time, Angola had the third-highest infant mortality rate (250 out of 1,000) in the world and high rates of maternal mortality (1 out of 50 died in childbirth).

After the war, there was little awareness of the situation of young children, and there were even fewer supports available to them. Most parents exhibited scant awareness of young children's distinctive needs and vulnerabilities. Overwhelmed by their war experiences and feeling helpless or confused about what to do in the postwar era, parents often communicated these emotions to children and were generally ill-equipped to support young children. Teenagers, who might have provided support, had few reference points for the appropriate care of young children. The war had disrupted both parenting skills and the transmission of child care skills to older children. Also, families were reluctant to look after young orphaned and separated children. Human capital was in short supply; there was a shortage of people knowledgeable about young children and how to support them. These factors, with resource scarcities and the absence of organized ECD activities as part of community traditions, made for a nearly complete lack of ECD supports for Angolan children. Although policy statements called for ECD supports, children under 5 years old were not prioritized in practice.

Tools to Support Young Children

Supports for young children in war zones are easier to call for than to construct. In addition to issues of logistics, security, and resource scarcity, thorny issues arise concerning concept as well as practice. Poorly conceptualized efforts frequently have limited, unsustainable impact, and some violate the humanitarian imperative of "do no harm." For this reason, it is useful to outline both the strategy and the tools that have proven effective in the work of Christian Children's Fund (CCF) in Angola.

Program Strategy

CCF's program efforts stand on four strategies, the first of which is the use of an ecological approach recognizing that to support young children, it is necessary to support their caregivers. Ecological approaches emphasize the importance of social influences at multiple levels—family, peer group, school, community, and society—on children's development

(Bronfenbrenner 1979; Dawes and Donald 2000). Young children's well-being is strongly linked with that of their mothers, who typically provide care and protection. Research has shown consistently that the single most important factor in enabling children's well-being is the care of a competent, emotionally available adult caregiver (Garbarino, Kostelny, and Barry 1998). In the Angolan and Sub-Saharan African contexts, this principle should be expanded to include sibling caregivers, because it is not uncommon for an older sister to care for children who have been weaned. Unfortunately, the accumulation of severe stresses in the conflict and postconflict situations overwhelms some mothers, causing depression, poor lactation, health problems, and difficulties providing care and protection. While other mothers exhibit relatively high levels of resilience, the impact of war and hardships may have degraded their parenting skills, made them less attentive to young children's needs, or encouraged a fatalistic attitude toward their children's health and well-being. In this context, it is useful to focus on supporting both mother and child and their relationship rather than focusing on young children alone.

The second strategy, community mobilization, is to use an empowerment model rather than a service model for emergency support. When well-intentioned agencies provide services for war-affected children and adults, they risk creating dependency and tacitly encourage local people to take a relatively passive role that is antithetical to recovery and sustainable development. Psychologically, a key to recovery is for people to regain a sense of personal and collective efficacy and the ability to influence their children's well-being. In fact, following an overwhelming experience, the reassertion of control—even in small ways—is a valuable source of psychosocial support. In collectivist societies such as Angola, in which people define their identity less in individual than in social terms and value the group good over the individual good (Triandis 2001), the reassertion of control is best achieved by facilitating collective planning and action. As people organize themselves and plan for their children's future, they engage in a process of collective healing that allows them to put the time of war behind them, reweave the shattered social fabric, form relationships offering support, and rekindle hope for the future. Encouraged to think about child protection, community groups can become local mechanisms for monitoring and reducing risks, and for preventing abuse and exploitation of young children. Even in the initial phase of emergencies, it is vital to begin building the foundation for development. Well-planned, participatory community action helps to rebuild civil society, provides a platform for sustainable development, and enables support for large numbers of children.

The third strategy is program integration. Both donor categories and field programs are often organized by sector, with little interaction across sectors. At best, the result is a nonholistic approach that misses important opportunities to build synergies. At worst, it wastes resources and overlooks the necessity for supporting the healthy development of the whole child. To address this problem, CCF Angola uses an integrative strategy of building psychosocial and protection supports for young children into multiple sectors of humanitarian assistance. This approach is highly congruent with the recently developed guidelines prepared by the Inter-Agency Standing Committee (IASC 2007) Task Force on Mental Health and Psychosocial Support in Emergency Settings.

The program integration strategy also cautions against the excessive targeting of particular people, a problem all too visible in many relief efforts. Exclusive focus on a particular group can create jealousies, marginalize those not receiving aid, and divide communities at the moment when they most need unity. In this respect, a program integration strategy makes the support of young children one element in a wider system of supports for all children.

The fourth strategy is to use a culturally grounded approach. Through extensive ethnographic research, CCF Angola has mapped local beliefs and practices, identifying resources such as healers, rituals, and other cultural practices that are then used to support children. Recognizing that not all cultural practices are positive, the CCF team takes a critical stance by avoiding romanticizing local culture and by respecting children's rights. In addition to reducing ethnocentric biases, this approach helps to avoid problems of imposing outsider views of childhood, what is good for children, and how to support children. When outsider views are privileged, as occurs in many situations, the results are the disempowerment of local people, the marginalization of local practices, and the conversion of humanitarian aid into a form of neocolonialism (Dawes and Cairns 1998; Wessells 1999). Also, the privileging of outsider approaches encourages local people to view their own culture as inferior, a view deeply entrenched as the result of hundreds of years of colonialism. If this view is degrading, it also cripples the belief in one's own culture and people that is fundamental to empowerment and sustainable development. At the same time, however, CCF Angola seeks to draw on the useful tools and concepts of Western science. Effective implementation of this strategy, then, is to blend local and Western approaches, with local people making decisions about which tools to use and how to achieve the best mix. Some of the main tools used are discussed in the following section.

Child-Centered Spaces

In emergency settings, it is vital to provide children with a safe place to play and learn and to integrate with others under the guidance of competent adults. During and following the war, children had few safe places to play, were often left on their own, were exposed to multiple risks, and had little structured activity. Also, school-aged children had poor access to education. Experience in many war zones indicates that emergency informal education is a vital source of protection (Nicolai and Tripplehorn 2003). Well-designed emergency education provides safety from hazards, teaches children how to avoid prominent risks in their environment, and builds intellectual and psychosocial competencies conducive to resilience. Also, teachers can be trained to recognize and refer or support at-risk children, increasing their psychosocial well-being.

CCF Angola uses a distinctive approach to emergency education by establishing community-owned child-centered spaces (CCSs). These provide informal education and give children a safe place to play, a predictable and supportive environment, the opportunity to build life skills such as basic literacy and cooperation, and activities such as drawing, singing, dancing, and storytelling that enable emotional expression and integration. Owing to the damage inflicted by war, the CCSs often are conducted in open spaces under the guidance of people selected by the community as trusted helpers of children. The volunteers who run the centers receive training in healthy child development, the impact of war on children of different ages, how to support children, and methods of nonviolent conflict resolution. Themes of peace and skills of nonviolent conflict resolution are much needed to break cycles of violence and establish values and behavior conducive to peace.

Although CCSs typically provide support for older children for several hours each day, they also designate particular hours for young children ages 3–6 and for mothers and their babies. Young children engage in activities designed to advance their sensorimotor and cognitive skills as appropriate for their age and individual competencies. The 3- to 6-year-olds also play games, learning to cooperate, take turns, and integrate with others their age. For mothers of infants, emphasis is placed on positive interactions with her baby, learning about the developing child's abilities and limits, and discussing practices of positive parenting. Sharing the appreciation of their children, the mothers tend to discuss the problems they face and offer support to each other. In this manner, psychosocial support is provided to mothers without psychological or psychiatric intervention, which is neither indicated in most cases nor available in rural areas. As a result, mothers become better situated to provide appropriate care and protection for their children.

Reflections on Past, Present, and Future

If supporting mothers is important, it is also vital to support the emotional well-being of all parents, grandparents, and other adults who serve as caregivers of young children. Many adults feel overwhelmed and hopeless or fatalistic, yet may be poorly positioned to see this, much less to do something about it. Feelings of being overwhelmed and hopeless arise, in part, from people's inability to unload their war experiences which, in Angola, have been described as one grief or loss piled on top of many others. War and postwar contexts seldom provide space in which people can take stock of how they have been affected and begin a process of recovery and transition supportive of their roles as parents and citizens in the current situation. Also, one of the worst effects of protracted war is that the abnormal comes to seem normal. Because war disrupts patterns of child care and community organization, it is useful to help adults recover some of the elements of past practice that could support children currently.

To address these issues, CCF Angola has found it useful to conduct community workshops for adults, offering space for reflection about the past, present, and future. The workshops use a highly participatory methodology featuring drama, discussions of traditional healing and practices, past norms of care for children, and the importance of Angolan culture. Because most participants are illiterate, the workshops use visual aids and metaphors in place of abstract written materials. For example, to illustrate the devastating effects of war, the facilitator gave each participant a large sheet of paper and asked each person to spend two minutes tearing it up, which most participants did with considerable enthusiasm. The participants were then asked to spend 15 or 20 minutes putting the paper back together, an activity that evoked much frustration. Following this activity, the participants discussed how easy it is to destroy something having unity and integrity and how difficult it is to rebuild it following extensive destruction. They also reflected upon how the war had destroyed or disrupted patterns of marriage and parenting, living in stable communities, practicing rituals honoring the ancestors who are believed to protect the living, norms of handling conflict nonviolently, and traditional social processes wherein community members engaged in collective planning and action. In this reflective space, people also discussed how the war had affected them and their families, with many reporting that this workshop had been the first time they had discussed the war, achieved a sense of solidarity in their suffering, and begun the process of coming to terms with their traumatic experiences and losses.

Equally important was the discussion of the present and the future. Having discussed the past, participants identified how the war had changed practices for the worse and how those changes continued into the present. This evoked discussion of possible ways of reawakening valuable past practices and transforming or ending undesirable current ones. The facilitator helped to guide the discussion toward children, asking which current care practices regarding young children were negative and what improvements were possible. As they generated ideas for improvement, parents moved from a fatalistic view toward a more empowered stance. Also, the collective discussion of their future created a sense of hope and collective empowerment to move themselves, their families, and their villages beyond the war and its negative residues. The resulting sense of hope and collective empowerment is as important for rebuilding the community systems necessary to support family well-being as it is for improving family life and the well-being of young children.

Training in Child Care and Protection

Skills in parenting and child care were necessary adjuncts to the changes in awareness produced by the workshops described above. For this reason, CCF trainers and trained community volunteers conducted participatory workshops on issues such as feeding infants, providing stimulation, and managing undesired behavior. Because the use of harsh corporal punishment was prevalent, CCF staff developed reflective methodologies designed to create receptivity to alternate, nonviolent means of behavior management. In one exercise, the trainer asked a group of mothers to close their eyes and think back to when they were young and were being punished by their parents. Asked how they felt, the participants described being afraid, feeling very upset or ashamed, and feeling hurt. In a space of quiet reflection that followed, at least one mother typically had an "Aha!" experience in which she realized that this was how she was making her children feel at present. Wanting to change this potentially harmful child care practice, the group then discussed alternate means of discipline.

As part of this integration approach, half-day training sessions were also conducted with local staff of humanitarian agencies working in camps for displaced people. For example, staff of therapeutic feeding centers learned how to provide stimulation and interaction that aided children's recovery. Staff involved in food distribution learned how to organize constructive activities for children while mothers waited to receive food. To reduce the burdens of long waits at health clinics, staff of the clinics also learned how to organize activities for children, including activities that engaged mothers. These training sessions, although only a small step, evoked considerable enthusiasm from the trainees, who said that the children's activities they provided had increased the impact of their services.

In villages, sensitization sessions were also conducted for the general public about special risks to children, including young children. Through dialogue and role plays, people learned how to reduce risks such as poor hygiene, lack of latrines, and psychosocial risks associated with marginalization. In some communities, youth groups organized discussions of issues such as HIV/AIDS that affect both parents and young children. The mobilization of youth groups as trainers or sensitizers fits with CCF's global approach of helping communities form or mobilize local mechanisms for raising awareness of threats and for monitoring, action, and prevention. Typically, this awareness raising is achieved through children mapping the risks in their villages and presenting the results through role plays, which often evoke much excitement among villagers. Out of the excitement come discussions facilitated by CCF staff about how the village could organize itself to address the threats. This process leads to the formation of Child Well-Being Committees consisting of children as well as adults and serving as catalysts for community action. Through these means, young children's needs become more visible in situations that typically promote children's invisibility. As rural villagers acquire new awareness of the situation of young children and develop skills to support them, they experience feelings of increased empowerment and hope because of the good they can do for children, who are the ones who will continue their families and traditions.

Policy Advocacy

To institutionalize practices supportive of young children on a wide scale, it is essential to educate and conduct advocacy work with policy leaders. At both provincial and national levels, CCF staff work in collaboration with child protection coordination groups, advocating for improved practices concerning separated children. In particular, CCF advocates against institutionalization as the first means of supporting separated or unaccompanied young children, because institutions are too poorly resourced, overcrowded, and ill equipped to provide appropriate care for young children. Although institutionalization may be necessary as a temporary arrangement, the emphasis should be on family tracing and reintegration or appropriate foster care arrangements (Tolfree 2003).

CCF Angola also advocates for the establishment of ECD supports for children nationwide. The idea of institutionalizing ECD supports nationally, however, is difficult to sell to a government with very low capacity, scant presence in many rural areas, and that faces the manifold needs associated with the new era of resettlement and transition to peace. For these reasons, it is vital for international NGOs, donors, other African governments, and intergovernmental agencies to build the capacities of the Angolan government, leverage the funding needed, and pressure for additional supports.

As this chapter shows, it is possible to conduct useful ECD interventions even in war and transitional settings. Now the question is whether we will muster the political will to take the urgently needed steps to support the protection and well-being of young children even in the world's most destitute and largely forgotten corridors of war.

References

Bronfenbrenner, U. 1979. *The Ecology of Human Development.* Cambridge, MA: Harvard University Press.

Carpenter, C. 2007. *Born of War: Protecting Children of Sexual Violence Survivors in Conflict Zones.* Bloomfield, CT: Kumarian.

Dawes, A., and E. Cairns. 1998. "The Machel Study: Dilemmas of Cultural Sensitivity and Universal Rights of Children." *Peace and Conflict: Journal of Peace Psychology* 4 (4): 335–48.

Dawes, A., and D. Donald. 2000. "Improving Children's Chances." In *Addressing Childhood Adversity,* ed. D. Donald, A. Dawes, and J. Louw, 1–25. Cape Town: David Philip.

Eth, S., and R. Pynoos. 1985. "Developmental Perspective on Psychic Trauma in Childhood." In *Trauma and Its Wake,* ed. C. Figley, 36–52. New York: Plenum.

Garbarino, J., and K. Kostelny. 1996. "The Effects of Political Violence on Palestinian Children's Behavioral Problems." *Child Development* 67: 33–45.

Garbarino, J., K. Kostelny, and F. Barry. 1998. "Neighborhood-Based Programs." In *Violence against Children in the Family and the Community*, ed. P. Trickett and C. Schellenbach, 287–314. Washington, DC: American Psychological Association.

Garfield, R. M., and A. I. Neugut. 1997. "The Human Consequences of War." In *War and Public Health*, ed. B. S. Levy and V. W. Sidel, 27–38. New York: Oxford.

IASC (Inter-Agency Standing Committee). 2007. "IASC Guidelines on Mental Health and Psychosocial Support in Emergency Settings." Final version. Retrieved August 12, 2007, from http://www.humanitarianinfo.org/iasc/content/products.

Igreja, V. 2003. "The Effects of Traumatic Experiences on the Infant-Mother Relationship in the Former War Zones of Central Mozambique." *Infant Mental Health Journal* 24 (5): 469–94.

———. 2004. "Cultural Disruption and the Care of Infants in Postwar Mozambique." In *Children and Youth on the Front Line*, ed. J. Boyden and J. de Berry, 23–41. New York: Berghahn.

Lodico, Y. C. 1996. "A Peace That Fell Apart: The United Nations and the War in Angola." In *UN Peacekeeping, American Politics, and the Uncivil Wars of the 1990s*, ed. W. J. Durch, 103–33. New York: St. Martin's Press.

Machel, G. 2001. *The Impact of War on Children*. Cape Town: David Philip.

McKay, S., and D. Mazurana. 2004. *Where Are the Girls?* Montreal: International Centre for Human Rights and Democratic Development.

Minter, W. 1994. *Apartheid's Contras: An Inquiry into the Roots of War in Angola and Mozambique*. London: Zed Books.

Nicolai, S., and C. Tripplehorn. 2003. *The Role of Education in Protecting Children in Conflict*. London: Humanitarian Practice Network.

Pynoos, R., A. Steinbery, and A. Goenjian. 1996. "Traumatic Stress in Childhood and Adolescence." In *Traumatic Stress*, ed. B. van der Kolk, A. McFarlane, and L. Weisaeth, 331–58. New York: Guilford.

Ressler, E., N. Boothby, and D. Steinbock. 1988. *Unaccompanied Children: Care and Protection in Wars, Natural Disasters, and Refugee Movements*. New York: Oxford University Press.

Sivard, R. L. 1996. *World Military and Social Expenditures 1996*. Washington, DC: World Priorities.

Smith, D. 2003. *The Atlas of War and Peace*. London: Earthscan.

Stavrou, V. 2005. *Breaking the Silence*. Luanda, Angola: Christian Children's Fund.

Terr, L. 1991. "Childhood Traumas." *American Journal of Psychiatry* 148: 10–20.

Tolfree, D. 2003. *Community-Based Care for Separated Children*. Stockholm: Save the Children Sweden.

Triandis, H. 2001. "Individualism and Collectivism: Past, Present, and Future." In *The Handbook of Culture and Psychology*, ed. D. Matsumoto, 35–50. New York: Oxford University Press.

UNICEF (United Nations Children's Fund). 1995. *The State of Angola's Children.* Luanda, Angola: UNICEF.

———. 1996. *State of the World's Children.* New York: UNICEF.

Ward, M., D. Kessler, and S. Altman. 1993. "Infant-Mother Attachment in Children with Failure to Thrive." *Infant Mental Health Journal* 14: 208–20.

Wessells, M. G. 1999. "Culture, Power, and Community: Intercultural Approaches to Psychosocial Assistance and Healing." In *Honoring Differences: Cultural Issues in the Treatment of Trauma and Loss*, ed. K. Nader, N. Dubrow, and B. Stamm, 267–82. New York: Taylor and Francis.

———. 2006. *Child Soldiers: From Violence to Protection.* Cambridge, MA: Harvard University Press.

CHAPTER 17

Strategic Communication in Early Childhood Development Programs: The Case of Uganda

Cecilia Cabañero-Verzosa and Nawsheen Elaheebocus

The case has been made. A large body of research supports the economic, political, and scientific arguments favoring investment in early childhood development (ECD). Investment in ECD has a high rate of return, benefiting children's physical, emotional, social, and intellectual development; increasing their performance at the primary level; and reducing dropout rates. Policy makers, donor agencies, and government officials recognize the critical importance and benefits of ECD as manifested in two international initiatives, *Education for All* (EFA) and the Millennium Development Goals (MDGs). Both public and private funding for ECD, albeit inadequate, has increased significantly. The World Bank has increased its investment in ECD programs from approximately US$126 million in 1990 to $1.5 billion in 2005.[1] Similarly, independent research organizations and think tanks such as the Ford Foundation, Rand Corporation, Aga Khan Foundation, and PNC Financial Services group[2] are increasingly investing in ECD research and program implementation.

Despite the recognition of the importance of these programs and the increases in investments, the situation for ECD remains dire in much of the world—especially in Africa. The World Bank has increased its cumulative lending for ECD in Africa from $8 million (between 1990 and 1996) to $125 million (between 1997 and 2005), but much more will be needed for ECD programs to have any significant impact (Garcia 2001). Africa still has the world's highest infant mortality rates (92 per 1,000 live births), one-third of all African children who survive to the age of 6 are stunted, and 95 percent of Africa's 5- to 6-year-olds have no access to preschools (World Bank 2002). So the questions are raised: Why are ECD interventions not having the intended impact, and, with current levels of investments, what can be done to improve the situation?

This chapter argues that strategic communication enhances the effectiveness of development programs. It demonstrates that communication activities applied strategically and coherently to development objectives help to bring about better results. Drawing primarily from Uganda's experience in the Nutrition and Early Childhood Development Project (NECDP), this chapter makes the case for the value of strategic communication in ECD programs, demonstrates the use of strategic communication activities in bringing about behavior change, and illustrates how the use of well-targeted strategic communication tools and techniques contributes to the successful implementation of ECD programs.

The Need for Strategic Communication in ECD Programs

An analysis of World Bank project documents[3] reveals that ECD projects often falter during implementation due, primarily, to five recurrent factors: (1) a lack of ownership of ECD programs and an inadequate understanding of the benefits of ECD at the subnational and regional levels of government; (2) ineffective coordination among key stakeholders and insufficient capacity in implementing agencies; (3) delays in procurement and disbursement of funds and an unreliable flow of resources from national to district levels; (4) sociocultural factors impeding behavior change at the grassroots level; and (5) complex implementation arrangements due to the cross-sectoral, integrated ECD approach. A failure to anticipate and address these factors during project design might delay project implementation and thwart program effectiveness.

Strategic communication is a powerful tool that can seal the gaps between policy discourse, project objectives, and effective implementation. This multilevel tool can secure stakeholder support through persuasive, well-targeted messages and serves as the bridge that translates support for a development objective into action. A strategic communication plan crafted at the beginning of the project cycle and integrated into the project design can help to identify political, social, and cultural risks that could affect program sustainability, with recommendations on how to mitigate those risks. Moving beyond the traditional one-way communication approach to disseminating information, strategic communication aims at engaging stakeholders in a two-way dialogue to ensure that project objectives are aligned with the needs and demands of project beneficiaries. As such, strategic communication can fuel a significant change in behavior or perception, or both, among key stakeholders by identifying and addressing conflicts and building consensus among stakeholders whose support is needed to achieve project goals. A wide range of communication activities can be used to support ECD programs, depending on the sociopolitical and cultural climate in which the program operates.

Key Concepts of Strategic Communication

Following are some key concepts that ECD policy makers and practitioners should keep in mind when designing, planning, and implementing ECD projects.

Aim for behavior change as the ultimate goal—The success of strategic communication programs can be measured through changes in attitude, behavior, and practices of specific stakeholder groups that are critical to the achievement of project objectives. Behavior change is a long-term process that requires a clear understanding of people's actions and beliefs, barriers impeding a change in behavior, the knowledge required to influence their behavior, and the ways that such information can be communicated effectively. This process involves a careful sequencing of communication activities based on five key stages of change that individuals undergo when presented with a new idea:

- becoming aware of a problem;
- understanding, acquiring new knowledge, and learning new skills;
- becoming motivated to do something about the problem;
- adopting the desired behavior; and
- sustaining the practice of the new behavior.

Literature on attitude research identifies various ways to design behavior change interventions such as the use of power and authority;

negotiations to identify and share interests and agree on how resources can be shared; incentives, both monetary and nonmonetary; and persuasion. Strategic communication focuses on the use of persuasion in crafting messages that resonate with audiences. Communication practitioners recognize the role that incentives play in creating an enabling environment that will encourage people to consider adopting new attitudes and behaviors, as well as the value of credible third-party spokespersons who wield power and authority and can advocate on a development issue. Thus, a well-designed communication strategy will attempt to use various modes of social influence relevant to a given audience and context.

Use a client-centered approach—World Bank project documents demonstrate that ECD project teams tend to rely on ad hoc information dissemination activities such as national conferences, educational campaigns, road shows, and radio talk shows to raise awareness on the importance and benefits of ECD. While this approach might be informative, it is highly organization driven, and it fails to take into account the client's perspective and their reasons for not adopting recommended ECD behaviors and practices. Strategic communication promotes the adoption of a client-centered approach that focuses on the needs of beneficiaries. This approach involves understanding the client's attitudes, beliefs, and practices as well as the cultural, structural, and social barriers and perceived costs of adopting new behaviors and providing clients with tools and techniques to overcome those barriers.

For example, assuming that parents' failure to practice ECD-appropriate behaviors is due to a lack of awareness on their part can be misleading. Parents may be well aware of the right behavior, but socioeconomic or cultural factors may impede their ability to practice it. Understanding the client's perspective and the underlying reasons for their behavior by unmasking the barriers to change is fundamental in bringing about a change in behavior. If the project objective is to change the attitudes of parents toward sending children to preschool, for example, identifying parent's misconceptions about preschool, locating the possible structural, cultural, or economic barriers that may be preventing them from doing so, and finding ways to address those barriers might be a more effective approach than disseminating information about the benefits of preschool. Similarly, while talk shows might be a successful channel for communicating the devastating effects of malnutrition on children's development and learning, parents might not understand how their particular feeding practices might contribute to malnutrition, and they may be unaware of alternative feeding practices. It is the responsibility of policy makers and practitioners to create the appropriate policy frameworks, institutional structures, and incentives to facilitate the behavior change process.

Client-centered communication activities integrated in the project design can help to increase the probability that stakeholders will be able to undertake appropriate ECD actions. This implies that project teams seek first to understand the audience's perspectives as they shape the ECD project intervention. Focusing on the clients and developing a clear understanding of their needs through formative research helps to define the issues, identify the desired behavior change, segment audiences, frame the right messages, and select an effective mix of communication channels. Only the client has the choice and the power to decide what to do with the messages heard. If communicated well, the take-away messages should steer them in the direction of positive change and sustain behaviors consistent with the project's expected development outcome. Moreover, the client-centered focus of the project provides several avenues for strengthening the capacity-building efforts necessary to sustain long-term behavior change. These avenues include the education of parents and caregivers in feeding and child care practices, the training of teachers and child care workers as counselors and communicators, and, equally important, the engagement of policy makers and parliamentarians as advocates and agents of change.

Communicate with key decision makers—ECD practitioners need to anticipate the potential risks and barriers to successful implementation of the ECD program by identifying and addressing the needs of influential stakeholders who could potentially derail the program. Often, ECD practitioners successfully communicate with downstream audiences (parents, child caregivers, and teachers) to convey the benefits of ECD interventions, but neglect to communicate with upstream audiences (donors, government officials, policy makers, and legislators). There is a practical necessity to get the "buy-in" of those at the highest level, who make it possible for the project to move forward. Policy makers, government officials, and local leaders need to understand the rationale behind ECD reforms in a way that makes sense to the national and local priorities and that is politically palatable. The technical language that is often used in ECD programs is rarely persuasive. While ECD program goals may be clear to project teams, these goals need to be interpreted for various audiences, both upstream and downstream.

The use of strategic communication techniques to build support for an ECD program was exemplified in the Uganda Nutrition and Early Childhood Development Project (NECDP), implemented between 1999 and 2005.

Case Example: Uganda Nutrition and Early Childhood Development Project

The NECDP aimed to improve the health and nutritional status and the cognitive and psychosocial development of preschool children. The project covered about 8,000 communities in 20 of Uganda's 39 districts. These communities were selected based on their levels of malnutrition, infant mortality, and primary school enrollment rates. The NECDP sought to (1) halve the prevalence of malnutrition among preschool children in the project areas by the end of the project; (2) increase school readiness of preschool children; (3) raise enrollment in primary schools and reduce dropout and repetition rates; (4) improve psychosocial and cognitive development; and (5) double the proportion of mothers practicing appropriate child care.

A strategic communication approach, going beyond the mere dissemination of information, was instrumental in identifying barriers to successful project implementation. To gain in-depth understanding of the perceptions of key stakeholders, the communication strategy was guided by intensive communication research. This communication strategy aimed to promote behavior change among parents and caregivers as well as policy makers and community leaders.

Communication Research

The project team undertook a three-part research process consisting of (1) qualitative research on complementary feeding practices in northern Uganda to supplement existing information available on the rest of the country; (2) local knowledge and treatment of worms in Uganda; and (3) communication research to uncover perceptions, beliefs, and practices relevant to ECD in Uganda. Research findings revealed that cultural practices and beliefs about childrearing were not consistent with the recommended notions of parenting advocated by the project (Neema et al. 2002). For example, parents' notion of a "good" child was one who was obedient, polite, and respectful, did not ask for food all the time but liked to eat, and did not cry. The "bad" child was described as one who cried unnecessarily, wanted to be held frequently, fought with other children, was disrespectful, disobedient, ill-mannered, and destructive. Ugandan parents did not fully appreciate playful and affectionate interaction between parents and young children. Their concept of an appropriate parent-child relationship was one that consisted mostly of parents providing for their child's basic needs and disciplining the child. The project recommended a child-centered pedagogy that encouraged children to be active and inquisitive to stimulate their psychosocial and cognitive development and that increased parent-child interactions to foster emotional development.

In addition, the study exposed some clear misconceptions about children's health and nutrition that, unless rectified, could have potentially hindered the achievement of the project's objectives. For example, some parents believed that deworming medication was too strong for children and might kill them, and that certain foods were taboo. The latter belief often caused parents to prohibit much-needed nutritious food during illness.

Communication research was instrumental in formulating and undertaking communication activities to help parents recognize the benefits of the child-centered pedagogy and appropriate health and nutrition practices by exposing them to new information and by crafting persuasive messages that acknowledged parents' current beliefs and demonstrated the benefits of the desired behavior.

Formative research also identified and helped to address an important political and institutional barrier. While the government of Uganda was committed to investing in young children—as demonstrated by the establishment of a 10-year investment plan for children's health and nutrition, water and sanitation, basic education, and child protection—parliamentary support for the project was not readily apparent. Mass media articles were critical of the project and reported on the contentious discussions in the parliament. As such, the project faced two key challenges: (1) to educate and motivate parents and caregivers to adopt positive behavior change in the care, feeding, and learning of children; and (2) to build coalitions of support for the project and to develop national champions for nutrition and child development programs.

Behavior Change

A strategic feature of the communication plan was its synchronized approach, which linked project objectives with corresponding communication activities at each major stage of behavior change. The field team, composed of partners from the various project stakeholders, organized a communication planning and message development workshop to reach agreement on the important elements of the communication strategy. A structured decision-making template (see annex 17.1) served as a road map to help define the five communication management decisions that needed to be addressed in formulating an effective communication strategy. Using the formative research results, the project team arrived at the following key management decisions in communication planning:

1. **Behavior.** To help attain expected project outcomes, communication activities focused on addressing misconceptions and barriers to changing behavior in (1) complementary feeding practices; (2) personal hygiene, sanitation, and deworming practices; and (3) ECD practices and positive parental interaction (PPI).

2. **Audience.** To effectively promote and influence behavior change, audiences were segmented to prioritize action and to tailor messages accordingly. Parents and caregivers of children ages 0–6 were identified as the *primary audience* whose behavior needed to change in order to achieve the project's objectives. These parents and caregivers either lacked knowledge on proper child care and feeding practices or they had the knowledge but lacked the necessary skills. The primary audience was further divided into five groups: (1) pregnant women and mothers who had newly delivered; (2) mothers and caregivers of children under 6 months; (3) mothers and caregivers of children aged 6 months to 2 years; (4) mothers and caregivers of children aged 2–6 years; and (5) fathers and male adult family members of children ages 0–6 years.

   The *secondary audience*—defined as those people who influence the behavior of a primary target audience—consisted of grandparents, siblings, community elders, health workers, teachers, religious leaders, and community child care workers.

   The *tertiary audience* included those people in positions of authority or influence over a large group of people—those who were involved in formulating policy and providing financial resources, services, and products that facilitate the adoption of new behaviors. This group consisted of political leaders, including parliament members, ministers, heads of government agencies, district level officials, local authorities, and village councils.

3. **Take-away message.** To frame meaningful and persuasive messages that could influence the adoption of new child care behaviors, the take-away messages focused on the specific client's needs, targeted

their beliefs or opinions, and answered the question, "What does this have to do with me?" One message does not fit all. Care was taken to develop messages that were realistic, memorable, concise, and culturally sensitive (see box 17.1). Formative research served as a navigational tool that guided the message content.

4. **Channels of communication.** To successfully reach specific target audiences, channels of communication were selected based on availability, accessibility, affordability, and credibility. Specific local conditions and audience characteristics determined which channels could best support target behaviors and public outreach activities. The medium is as important as the message. The project team used a mix of channels that provided adequate reach and frequency needed to target specific audiences, effectively combining the mass media, print, community-based channels, and interpersonal communication, as shown in annex 17.2.

5. **Monitoring and evaluation.** To track implementation progress and assess the effectiveness of communication activities, a local research organization was hired to implement a monitoring and evaluation

---

Box 17.1

Cultural, Social, and Religious Context

The project's messages had to take into account Uganda's cultural diversity, as reflected in diets, attitudes, and beliefs. For example, in some parts of the country, grain-based diets are prevalent, while in others, plantain, milk, and meat are more common staples. In some of these cultures, traditional chiefs are influential figures who can convince people to change their behavior.

The target populations included Christians of different denominations, as well as Muslims. Among these groups, religious leaders have significant influence on behavior. In many households where a man is present, he is the "head" of the home and is commonly served food first and offered the best and most generous portion. At the same time, a large proportion of Ugandan households are headed by single women, who must balance the need to earn income with the demands of child care. In these cases, an older sibling—usually the eldest daughter—or another relative carries a lot of responsibility for child care, feeding, and play.

Source: Verzosa 2005.

plan. Six waves of research were carried out over two years to track changes in knowledge, attitudes, and practices in randomly selected project areas. For each wave, 480 interviews of primary caregivers of children 0–6 years of age were conducted from a random sample from three subcounties within each of the four districts. Measurable success indicators to assess effectiveness of the communication program focused on the target audience and addressed the following questions: Is the target audience being exposed to the messages as intended? Can the target audience recall any of the messages? Did the target audience correctly understand the meaning of the messages? Is the target audience motivated to modify current behavior after exposure to the messages? Has the target audience changed behavior?

The template with the five communication management decisions helped the communication team to navigate the road to behavior change. Measuring results against clear benchmarks helped to determine the impact of communication activities on increasing knowledge, developing positive attitudes, and promoting the adoption of new behavior. These results allowed project teams to refine and adapt communication strategies that supported sustained practice of desired behavior. As households and communities grow increasingly aware of the benefits of good child care practices and respond positively to messages promoting positive behavior, the project team will continue to monitor progress made along the behavior change continuum.

Downstream Behavior Change: Promoting Better Child Care Practices

The NECDP communication component focused on increasing parents' knowledge and supporting positive attitudes, beliefs, and practices regarding specific parent behaviors, including weaning (defined as breastfeeding up to 18 months and introduction of complementary foods at 6 months old and not earlier); deworming children initially, then every six months when there is reinfection; and early childhood development focusing on positive parental interaction and greater involvement of fathers in the care of children under 6 years old.

Reversing the pattern of practices that were detrimental to children's health and well-being involved convincing parents and primary caregivers to alter long-held beliefs and to adopt appropriate behavior. Changing this behavior required more than just handing out leaflets and information materials.

With clear outcome objectives of improved child health and nutrition, the communication strategy set out key process objectives to support behavior change interventions; it included the following communication activities:

- Launch of a multimedia communication plan that emphasized proper weaning practices, deworming, and ECD-related behaviors. Communication activities helped parents and other caregivers to understand the relationship between stunting and specific behaviors such as feeding during illness or ensuring that children eat adequate amounts of food. The plan included modeling the new behavior, providing information on parent and caregiver success in adopting the new behavior, imparting skills, and giving instructions to clear up misconceptions about specific child feeding practices.
- Training of health workers and daycare and preschool teachers on the communication campaign objectives and their role in making the project a success. To make them effective communicators, teachers and health workers were also trained to improve their interpersonal and communication skills, which are essential to nutrition counseling and promoting the adoption of good child care practices.
- Implementation of monitoring and evaluation activities to ensure that materials developed were disseminated through cost-effective communication channels and that these messages reached the target audience. Radio was identified as a popular communication channel, reaching more than 90 percent of Ugandans, while only 34 percent of Ugandans read newspapers and 17 percent watch television.
- A national advocacy effort aimed at parliamentarians, officers of the Ministries of Health and Education, district officials, and community leaders.

Upstream Behavior Change: Building Networks of Champions and Advocates of ECD among Key Policy Makers

Advocacy efforts among policy makers and parliamentarians help to create coalitions of support and a favorable policy environment that promotes programs essential to the growth and development of young children. In the Uganda project, advocacy was mounted through upstream communication aimed at changing the mindsets of policy makers and parliamentarians, as well as the media—increasing awareness and improving understanding at the national level of the serious problem of stunting and child malnutrition.

To gain support within the parliament, a parliamentary advocacy group was established. During a communication strategy brainstorming session with the then Minister of Finance, parliamentarians were identified as key allies. The minister then approached several parliamentarians whom he believed would be project advocates among their colleagues.

A study/observation tour was organized to familiarize parliamentarians with successful ECD programs in Kenya. They also participated in regular field visits to keep them abreast of project developments. As key communicators and influencers of change, media specialists were also sensitized and trained through information seminars and a six-week distance learning course on strategic communication.

The advocacy committee helped to raise awareness of the issue of stunting and its implications both for children's development and the long-term development of the country. To keep parliamentarians informed about the project status, the project provided them with audiotapes that captured in radio program format the latest information on activities and emerging issues. This format was chosen to accommodate their busy schedules; they could listen to the tapes while driving. The members of the advocacy committee were also given media skills training to help in their advocacy efforts. The three-month run-up to the parliamentary vote on the project was very contentious, and it appeared that the project might not be passed, but the project's efforts to build alliances through the project advocacy committee were invaluable in securing parliamentary approval.

Evaluating Communication Impact

Findings from the evaluation studies suggested that messages heard through different communication channels with varying reach and frequency influenced changes in attitudes and behavior in households. The evaluation of communication activities involved six waves of research over two years to track changes in knowledge, attitudes, and practices in randomly selected project areas. For each wave, 480 interviews of primary caregivers of children 0–6 years of age were conducted from the random sample of three subcounties within each of the four districts.

Evidence from the longitudinal evaluation study confirms project impacts of (1) improved health and nutritional status, (2) improved knowledge and practices in child care, (3) increased effective demand for health and nutrition services, (4) increased demand for schooling, and (5) enhanced local and social capacity.

1. **Improved health and nutritional status.** Malnutrition among young children 0–36 months was reduced by 30 percent in the project area, from 24.4 percent to 17.1 percent. Among severely malnourished children, wasting was reduced 50 percent. A comparison between areas benefiting from NECDP interventions and nonproject areas after 18 months of project implementation shows encouraging trends in

   - increased exclusive breastfeeding of infants until they reached 6 months of age (14 percent versus 1 percent);
   - improved supplementary feeding practices, for example, children fed with more legumes (66 percent versus 33 percent);
   - higher immunization rates (73 percent versus 58 percent);
   - improved intake of vitamin A (13.6 percent increase in project areas versus a significant decline of 17 percent in nonproject areas); and,
   - increased deworming among children under 72 months of age (38 percent versus 8 percent).

   Community-based communication activities complemented and reinforced the media-driven messages. These included nutrition counseling, group meetings, home visits, and training of community health workers and teachers.

2. **Improved knowledge and practices in child care, health, and nutrition.** Key messages linked positive behavior to desirable benefits, for example "a healthy child is a happy child," "children learn through play," "a healthy child is the pride of every family," and, "you can save money by ensuring your family's good nutrition and health." Respondents in project sites had significantly improved knowledge and positive attitudes toward schooling, parent-child interactions, and the parental role as compared with those in nonproject sites.

3. **Increased effective demand for health and nutrition services.** Communication activities helped to stimulate the demand for improved health outcomes by educating households and communities about the benefits of adopting better health and child care practices. In particular, Child Fairs, existing service delivery channels for integrated health and nutrition, were successful in increasing demand for deworming medicine and vitamin A supplements. About 60 percent of those given deworming medicine received it through the Child Fairs. An evaluation of the communications activities conducted by Steadman Research Services (2003) noted that Child Fairs contributed to increased intake of vitamin A and, where provided, deworming medicine, and sustained

immunization rates. A longitudinal evaluation report revealed that Child Fairs proved to be cost-effective for service delivery, costing $1.00–$1.33 per child (Alderman et al. 2003). The communication strategy also included entertainment and education to deliver persuasive messages through songs, skits, dramas, and demonstrations.

4. **Increased demand for schooling.** Campaign messages on the benefits of parental positive interaction and related ECD practices appear to have had reinforcing effects on increasing demand for early schooling. The longitudinal study confirmed a positive impact on enrollment both relative to the control group and relative to the initial enrollment in the project communities, particularly for preschool-age children. Findings further suggest that by age 12.5, the average child in the project area will have higher school attainment than children in non-project areas.

5. **Enhanced local and social capacity.** Tapping the potential of radio as the most popular source of information, radio programs were aired to inform and encourage community participation in nutrition-related income-generating activities. Nongovernmental organizations (NGOs) worked closely with those who wanted to apply for community grant schemes. Local skills were developed in planning and implementing microprojects, and social capital was built through community associations that fostered mutual cooperation for mutual benefit. Many communities contributed more than the mandatory 25 percent of the total project cost.

Conclusion

Strategic communication can be a potent tool for enhancing effectiveness of ECD interventions. Experience in the use of communication activities in development projects across sectors has shown that a client-centered, research-driven, and participation-based communication strategy elaborated and integrated during project design provides a clear understanding of the perceptions and positions of key stakeholders and addresses perceived fears and barriers to change. Communication research that provides both qualitative and quantitative information and encourages stakeholder participation helps project teams to understand the importance of ECD interventions, not from the technocrat's point of view but, more importantly, from the audience's perspective. An understanding of audience perceptions and beliefs will help teams to frame messages that resonate with the needs of these audiences, to select communication channels that are both popular and effective, and to identify indicators to track changes in knowledge, attitudes, and behaviors.

A project team has two key responsibilities to its clients and audiences. First, the team needs to recognize that the audience is paramount as the team develops ECD interventions. The work of the team begins with searching for a deep appreciation of the audience's perspective on ECD issues, stock knowledge, and set of beliefs that drive their current ECD-relevant practices. Second, the team needs to address the sociocultural and institutional barriers that hinder the audience's ability to practice new ECD behaviors. Because strategic communication aims for behavioral outcomes, it is no longer sufficient to judge communication effectiveness in terms of persuasive messages delivered through effective channels of communication. Rather, the task of identifying barriers to the practice of new behaviors becomes integrated into the task of communicating the benefits of adopting new practices. When audiences learn the benefits of ECD practices and make a voluntary decision to adopt new practices, the project team's task is half-achieved. It is only when audiences are able to put into practice what they have learned about ECD that teams can consider their work truly successful.

Annex Table 17A.1. Five Communication Management Decisions Template

Management objective: _____

		Message			
Audience	Behavior	Take-away message	Supporting data	Channels	Evaluation

Source: Verzosa 2002.

Annex Table 17A.2. Five Communication Management Decisions Applied in NECDP

Early Childhood Development

Objectives

- Acknowledge the "voice" of the child: refers to giving children an opportunity to be heard in a family; engage in two-way conversation
- Provide a safe environment for play: refers to the idea of giving a child a favorable environment for play at home and in the community
- Improved understanding of the parents' role—"how": refers to assessing the role of parents in childrearing and describes how parents can fill that role
- Improved understanding of the parents' role—"when": refers to finding opportunities for parents to interact with their children
- Improved understanding of the benefits of positive parental interaction (PPI)

Audience	Behavior	Take-away message	Communication channels	Evaluation of communication activities
Parents of children 0–6 years of age	Parents should talk to and listen to their children. Parents should refrain from being too controlling and should not see themselves as the sole authority. Parents should change the attitude that children are "seen and not heard."	Our family will be happier and achieve more if we all discuss things together, including our children. I believe, parent-child discussions produce the following benefits: • increase of self-esteem and self-worth in the child, • increase of child's confidence, • full development of child's talents and prospects, • promotion of communication skills, • improvement of family unity, and • reduction of potential for conflict in the family.	Interpersonal communication (home visits) Child's Fair Radio Print Theatre Video	Baseline study Formative communication research

(continued)

Annex Table 17A.2. Five Communication Management Decisions Applied in NECDP *(continued)*

Audience	Behavior	Take-away message	Communication channels	Evaluation of communication activities
Parents of children 0–6 years of age	Parents should create a more stimulating environment for their children to grow up in by: playing together, encouraging questions and answers, storytelling, singing, telling riddles and proverbs, and providing local toys.	I will interact more with my children because it will help them to grow better and become brighter. I believe interaction has the following benefits • confident children, • polite and bright children, • responsible children, • more productive children, • children who grow well, • children who learn to work hard, • independent decision makers, • increased self-esteem, and • increased self-acceptance.	Interpersonal communication (home visits) Child's Fair Group media (meetings) Print Institutional media (religious organizations and schools)	Baseline study Formative communication research

Parents and caregivers	Parents should improve their understanding and appreciation of the importance of play in a child's development.	I will encourage my children's play and participate myself whenever possible because I believe play has the following benefits for my child: • improvement in physical growth and strength, • improvement in social skills, • relaxation/reduction of stress, and • stimulation of intellect and improved mental development. All the above will improve my child's development and make him or her a more successful adult.	Interpersonal communication (home visits) Child's Fair Group media (meetings) Institutional media (religious organizations and schools)	Baseline study Formative communication research

Source: Verzosa 2005.

Notes

1. Since 1990, the World Bank has financed 74 ECD projects in about 47 countries. Of these projects, 15 have been freestanding operations and 59 have been human development projects with an ECD component (World Bank 2006).
2. In September 2003, PNC Financial Services Group, Inc. launched "PNC Grow Up Great," a 10-year, $100 million program to improve school readiness for children from birth to age 5 (Karoly, Kilburn, and Cannon 2005).
3. An illustrative sample of World Bank ECD project documents (Project Appraisal Documents, Implementation Completion Reports, and Operational Evaluation Department Reports) was selected and reviewed to provide examples of projects implemented in Africa (Uganda, Eritrea); stand-alone ECD projects (Eritrea, Kenya, Indonesia, the Arab Republic of Egypt); and a case of implementing the integrated approach to ECD (Jordan). See the World Bank references at the end of this chapter for detailed project information.

References

Alderman, H., P. Engle, P. Britto, and A. Siddiqi. 2003. "Longitudinal Evaluation of Uganda Nutrition and Early Childhood Development Project (NECDP)." Draft report. World Bank, Washington, DC.

Garcia, M. 2001. "Early Child Development—Increasing World Bank Investment in Africa." In *A Directory of Early Child Development Projects in Africa Supported by the World Bank*, 1–8. Washington, DC: World Bank.

Karoly, L. A., M. R. Kilburn, and J. S. Cannon. 2005. *Early Childhood Interventions: Proven Results/Future Promise*. Retrieved September 9, 2006, from http://www.rand.org/pubs/monographs/2005/RAND_MG341.pdf.

Neema, S., D. Adams, R. Kibombo, and C. Baume. 2002. *Formative Communications Research on Early Childhood Development*. Uganda Nutrition and Early Childhood Development Project. Kampala, Uganda: Ministry of Health.

Steadman Research Services. 2003. "Evaluation of Communication Activities: Uganda Nutrition and Early Childhood Development Project, Wave 6." Unpublished report, Kampala, Uganda.

Verzosa, C. C. 2002. "Determinants of Behavioral Intention in Developing Country Organizations." Unpublished doctoral dissertation, Department of Communication, University of Maryland, College Park.

———. 2005. "Counting on Communication: The Uganda Nutrition and Early Childhood Development Project." World Bank Working Paper 59. World Bank, Washington, DC.

World Bank. 1997. "Project Appraisal Document: Republic of Uganda Nutrition and Early Childhood Development Project." Human Development I, Africa Region. Report 17182-UG. World Bank, Washington, DC.

———. 1998. "Project Appraisal Document: Republic of Indonesia Early Child Development Project." Human Development Sector Department (EASHD), Report 18151. World Bank, Washington, DC.

———. 2000. "Project Appraisal Document: Government of Eritrea Integrated Early Childhood Development Project." Human Development Trust Fund Administration, Africa, Report 20373. World Bank, Washington, DC.

———. 2002. Opening Doors: Education and the World Bank. Retrieved September 9, 2006, from www1.worldbank.org/education/pdf/OpenDoors. pdf.

———. 2003. "Project Appraisal Document: Hashemite Kingdom of Jordan Education Reform for Knowledge Economy I Program." Human Development (MNSHD) Report 25309. World Bank, Washington, DC.

———. 2004. "Implementation Completion Report: Republic of Kenya Early Child Development Project." World Bank, Washington, DC.

———. 2005. "Project Appraisal Document: Arab Republic of Egypt Early Childhood Enhancement Project." World Bank, Washington, DC.

———. 2006. ECD Projects. Retrieved September 9, 2006, from http://web. worldbank.org/.

Evaluations and Research

CHAPTER 18

The Synergy of Nutrition and ECD Interventions in Sub-Saharan Africa

Harold Alderman and Patrice L. Engle

In addition to enhancing well-being, childhood nutrition is valued as a means to fulfill human potential. Even skirting the difficulty of estimating the economic value of reduced mortality because of improved nutrition, investing in nutrition can be shown to have economic returns as great or greater than those commonly found in a diverse set of interventions covering education, water and sanitation, trade reform, and private sector deregulation (Behrman, Alderman, and Hoddinott 2004). While a portion of these economic returns comes from reduced costs of health care needed for a well-nourished population, the majority comes from increased productivity over a lifetime. Such calculations take the focus of nutrition beyond child survival, adding the critical roles of child development, school retention, and achievement, as well as subsequent productivity (Myers 1992).

Thus, programs to improve the nutrition of children complement the programs for early childhood development (ECD) covered in this volume. This synergy occurs in two ways: through the interaction of nutrition and cognitive development, and through the interaction of programs aimed at improving both nutrition and ECD approaches. Regarding the first, malnutrition impairs a child's cognitive abilities, often irreversibly. Even when special educational programs can mitigate the consequences of early nutritional deprivation on cognitive development, these programs are more costly than prevention and they compete for funds needed for broader educational objectives. Regarding the second synergy, many of the most promising interventions in nutrition are similar to programs that provide direct cognitive stimulation to children or provide caregivers with the knowledge of how to further child development. Many of these programs improve nutrition and caregiving at the same time by improving family caring practices that result in a parent being more attentive to the child, feeding the child more appropriately, and providing more stimulation. Nutrition interventions may also improve the child's ability to solicit attention, therefore increasing the amount of caregiving that the child receives (Pollitt et al. 1993). Thus, the potential exists for synergy as well as for economies of scope.

This chapter briefly assesses the evidence on both forms of interaction between nutrition and other aspects of ECD. In the first form—the interaction of nutrition and cognitive development—extensive literature exists, mostly from outside Africa, which can be reviewed here only briefly. Because this interaction is largely driven by biological processes, the global literature is likely to be fully relevant for Africa. In the second form, however—the programmatic interaction of nutrition and cognitive stimulation—we will hone in on examples from Sub-Saharan Africa.

Synergy of Nutrition and Cognitive Development and School Readiness

Nutrition can affect cognitive development through two broad means. First, malnourished children may interact less with caregivers or service providers than do other children. The malnourished child may be less likely to seek stimulation from the environment and from caregivers; caregivers may invest less in the child, providing less of their time or being disinclined to enroll the child in school or preschool programs. The second pathway from malnutrition to cognitive development is through the capacity to learn. This improved capacity may be a direct consequence of nutritional status on the development of the brain or a consequence of exploratory behaviors associated with nutritional status. Also, a hungry child may be less likely to pay attention in school or preschool and thus learn less even if he or she has no long-term impairment of intellectual ability.

Though intuitively plausible, it is often difficult to ascertain or quantify the causal pathway between nutrition and learning or of cognitive functions. Many of the observable factors that affect nutrition, such as family assets and parental education, are also factors that affect learning. Similarly, unobservable attitudes about investment in children and in intrafamily equity influence decisions for health, nutrition, and schooling in a complex manner. Thus, while many studies document associations between nutrition and schooling (see Pollitt 1990 and Behrman 1996 for reviews), far fewer studies accurately portray the causal impact of child nutrition and cognitive development. However, in recent years, a substantial number of studies indicate the short- and long-term impacts of malnutrition on cognitive development (Glewwe 2005).

The preponderance of evidence supports the view that "severe malnutrition in early childhood leads to deficits in cognitive development if the children return to poor environments" (Grantham-McGregor, Fernald, and Sethuraman 1999a, 66). Mild to moderate malnutrition has also been associated with deficits in cognitive development (Pollitt 1990). This impairment may begin in utero; recent evidence that assesses the impact of low birthweight over a wide range of weights indicates that the relationship between birthweight and cognitive function carries into the range of normal weights, even in developed countries (Richards, Hardy, and Wadsworth 2001; Matte et al. 2001). Even if, as Richards, Hardy, and Wadsworth (2001) observe, this association between birthweight and cognitive ability partially attenuates over time—they followed a cohort for 43 years—the significant difference in function at age 8 explains subsequent educational attainment. Similar patterns linking growth faltering in young children to cognitive development have been regularly reported, generally using associations but occasionally with direct observations in experimental settings. Malnourished children score poorer on tests of cognitive function, have poorer psychomotor development and fine motor skills, have lower activity levels, interact less frequently in their environments, and fail to acquire skills at normal rates (Grantham-McGregor et al. 1997; Grantham-McGregor, Fernald, and Sethuraman 1999a). The causal nature of such a relationship is indicated by a randomized distribution of supplements during pregnancy and early childhood in Guatemala. Not only were treated children observed to have improved cognitive development in preschool years (Martorell 1997), the cohort has been followed into adult years with higher schooling and wages noted for the treatment group (Maluccio et al. 2005).

Nutritional impairment does not only affect intellectual development; studies of famines in China and the Netherlands indicate that children born in these periods are at elevated risk of psychological disorders such as schizophrenia (St. Clair et al. 2005).

Similar evidence documents the link between intellectual development and micronutrients. For example, a meta-analysis indicates that the intelligence quotients (IQs) of individuals with an iodine deficiency were, on average, 13.5 points lower than those of comparison groups. Moreover, interventions have shown that providing iodine to pregnant women can reduce this gap (Grantham-McGregor, Fernald, and Sethuraman 1999b). Less evidence exists, however, that iodine provided to children can reverse this prenatal cognitive development gap for the treated generation. In the case of iron deficiencies, anemia is regularly associated with impaired cognitive development. However, while iron supplementation trials for school-age children consistently indicate improved cognition, this result is less regularly observed with interventions for iron-deficient younger children. Nor are vitamin A and zinc—important to reduce mortality and to foster growth, respectively—generally found to influence cognitive performance directly.

Studies, many from developed countries (see, for example, the literature reviewed in Behrman, Alderman, and Hoddinott 2004), trace such improved cognitive development to future earnings or other long-term economic outcomes. These impacts are both direct—on average, the higher a person's IQ, the higher the earnings, controlling for years of schooling—and indirect, stemming from the fact that higher cognitive development encourages more and earlier schooling. In the absence of detailed studies on nutrition and participation in preschool programs that control for household characteristics, it is necessary to extrapolate from studies of grade-school participation. Those studies in this field that distinguish the distinct contributory role of nutrition from associations do show a measurable impact of malnutrition on school enrollment. For example, Glewwe, Jacoby, and King (2001) track children from birth through primary school and find that better-nourished children start school earlier and repeat fewer grades, controlling for family characteristics. Alderman, Hoddinott, and Kinsey (2006) show that increased stunting of children younger than age 2 in Zimbabwe has a causal impact on years of schooling completed 15 years after the nutritional shock.

A few studies have attempted to investigate the link between hunger and classroom performance, using experimental design. Available results, however, are not conclusive regarding long-term consequences, perhaps, in part, because controlled studies are hampered by difficulties in running experiments for an appreciable duration as well as the difficulty of encouraging parents to conform to the protocols of research design and the inability to use a placebo. Moreover, as Grantham-McGregor et al. (1997) show, although feeding children may improve attention, its impact on learning depends on the classroom organization. These observations are likely to hold for preschool programs as well, although the role of feeding programs and classroom structure has not been studied in a comparable manner for younger children.

The Programmatic Synergy of Community Nutrition and ECD Approaches

A common heuristic model of the production of nutrition is based on three pillars: the role of nutrients, either through food or supplementation; the role of health and sanitation services; and the role of child care. As such, working with caregivers is a plausible intervention complementing those administered as part of health services or to promote food access. These programs to improve child care most strongly overlap with programs to promote cognitive development directly (Engle, Menon, and Haddad 1999).

The Case for Approaching Nutrition as an Issue of Caregiver Training

To a fair degree, the emphasis on caregiving completes the circle from nutrition to learning through cognitive development discussed earlier because it takes knowledge about caring practices back to nutrition. However, this effect is not the same as the effect of education on nutrition. In part, this distinction recognizes that education makes a recognizable contribution stemming from any increases in earnings that it facilitates. At least four other pathways establish a direct link between education of the caregivers and their children (Glewwe 1999). Schooling (1) may transmit information about health and nutrition directly; (2) teaches numeracy and literacy, thereby assisting caregivers in acquiring information, for example, through newspapers; (3) exposes individuals to new environments, thereby making them receptive to modern medical treatment; and (4) imparts self-confidence. As shown in other studies, schooling may also enhance women's role in intrahousehold decision making and in their interactions with health care professionals (Smith et al. 2001).

The first of these pathways proved to be the strongest in Glewwe's (1999) study. However, information about health and nutrition may also be transmitted outside of the classroom, which provides the impetus for interventions aimed at changing knowledge and practices. Other inferential evidence from Africa supports this view. For example, Bhargava and Fox-Kean (2003) show that maternal scores on cognitive tests had a stronger relation to diet and diet quality in Kenya than did parental education. Using observations on more than 25,000 children in Ethiopia, Christiaensen and Alderman (2004) estimate the impact of improving the percentage of women in a community that can recognize malnutrition. They find that increased information so that all women can correctly diagnose growth faltering will have approximately the same impact on malnutrition as universal female primary education, although the effects are independent and additive.

Many interventions that promote better nutrition through improved caregiving also provide cognitive stimulation. For example, reduced breastfeeding—an effect of low birthweight as well as a common cause of childhood malnutrition—is also a well-documented influence on cognitive development, even in developed countries (Grantham-McGregor, Fernald, and Sethuraman 1999a).

Community growth promotion is one widely advocated approach to promoting exclusive breastfeeding up to the age of 6 months, as well as other aspects of child care, such as proper supplemental feeding at the time of weaning and the use of oral rehydration when a child has diarrhea. Often the emphasis in such programs is on child weighing. However, an emphasis on weight and charts is actually a limited and relatively ineffective interpretation of growth promotion (Ruel 1995). Growth promotion can provide an opportunity to impart knowledge face to face, hence the stress on community mobilization in many programs. Although many growth promotion programs also facilitate the provision of inoculations, vitamin supplements, and deworming medicine (and occasionally also provide supplementary feeding), their role in promoting behavioral change has most in common with ECD programs, particularly those designed as family support rather than center- or home-based programs (Kagitcibasi 1997).

Evaluation of Growth Promotion Programs in Africa

Globally the record of growth promotion is mixed, in part because the concept covers a broad and somewhat diverse set of activities (Ruel 1995). Despite endorsements of growth promotion in various fora (see, for example, Allen and Gillespie 2001) and in numerous case studies (Alderman, Hoogeveen, and Rossi 2006), few studies are in peer-reviewed publications and none known to these authors use either randomized design or statistical matching to construct a counterfactual. That is, most studies are not able to ascertain plausibly what the state of nutrition would be in the treated community in the absence of the intervention.

This chapter summarizes the results of two recent studies in Madagascar and Uganda that address this gap.

SEECALINE, Madagascar—The first study looks at a community growth promotion program in Madagascar, *Surveillance et Education des Ecoles et des Communautés en matiére d'Alimentation et de Nutrition Elargie*, or SEECALINE (Galasso and Yau 2005). This project is a large-scale intervention being phased in since 1999 from an earlier pilot program. By mid-2005, it covered more than 3,500 sites. Although at various times the project has distributed supplementary food in response to political unrest or cyclones, emergency food distribution is a minor component of its services. Rather, SEECALINE focuses primarily on mobilizing awareness of child care and hygiene through education sessions and demonstrations organized by trained community nutrition workers that enable mothers to take care of their children rather than depend on external assistance. The project's activities also include micronutrient supplementation and administration of deworming medicines. Non-governmental organizations (NGOs) are contracted to initiate community organization and coordinate activities.

The Madagascar case study is not based on a randomized design, nor does it have directly comparable data on control groups. To assess a counterfactual and thus attribute impacts, the authors compare the malnutrition rates of children in project sites as a function of participation duration. That is, the study concentrates on the differential impacts of longer exposure to the project, as opposed to assessing project participation compared with no participation. Importantly, they identify the length of exposure to the project as a function of observable community characteristics, using a technique called nonparametric propensity score matching that matches individuals in the treatment to a weighted group of individuals in the control who are closest in a set of observed characteristics.

The analysis found that the returns to exposure to the project are positive; communities with an additional two years of exposure to the project have malnutrition rates 7–9 percentage points lower than communities with less time in treatment. The impact is larger in the poorest communities.

Moreover, for communities with only an additional year of exposure, the impact is confined to the cohort of children younger than age 1. Improvements for children 12–36 months old are only observed for the longer period of additional exposure.

NECDP, Uganda—A second study, the Uganda Nutrition and Early Childhood Development Project (NECDP), provided an opportunity to assess the impact of child growth promotion in a large-scale setting using a combination of a randomized design and a difference-in-differences comparison. The specific objectives of the project, initiated in 1998 with support from a World Bank credit, were to

- create awareness in families and communities of children's rights and needs;
- build on the knowledge and skills of families and communities so as to provide proper health care, appropriate child nutrition, ECD, and protection; and
- increase the skills and capacity of families and communities to mobilize resources and manage their own income-generating activities, thereby enhancing their ability to care for children.

In particular, the project aimed to

- help communities organize services for children younger than age 6 through growth monitoring and the promotion and establishment of early child care and education (ECE) facilities;
- strengthen the capacity of families and communities through sensitization, education and skills training on ECD, nutrition, and training for savings and income generation; and
- provide support on food security projects or ECD programs run by communities through community grants and incentives.

Project activities were divided into three broad categories: community-based interventions, parish-level activities, and support to national and district programs. The first category included training for caregivers on relevant child care needs and training for resource mobilization and child growth promotion, including nutrition counseling. This growth promotion was provided by two volunteers per community, who were provided a bicycle as well as training. Also, communities under the project had access to a grant of $1,500 ($1,250 from the credit). This grant could be used to establish food security projects or ECE interventions. The community determined the specific intervention to be funded from this grant through a process of participatory community planning. Finally, the project included provisions for a larger innovations grant for which communities could apply. Approximately 20 percent of the communities selected ECE interventions, with widely different percentages by district or NGO organizers.

For reasons of financial constraints, 25 districts were originally selected for the project over the initial five-year period. The selection was based on infant and under-5 mortality rates and the prevalence of malnutrition (severe and moderate stunting). The number of districts increased to 34, both in the process of obtaining parliamentary approval and due to redistricting during the implementation. Within each selected district, the district government selected subcounties based on relative poverty.

The sampling approach for the household survey was influenced by the costs and logistics of revising households and the need to design survey instruments, including tests of cognitive development, in the local languages. For these reasons this aspect of the analysis was concentrated on a single region, with the understanding that other aspects of the evaluation would be conducted more broadly. Because one aspect of the overall evaluation was to assess the additional impact of regular provision of albendazole (an anthelmintic to deworm children) the eastern region was selected for this study, based on the results of a study by the Vector Control Unit of the Ministry of Health, which indicated the highest rates of worm loads in Uganda (Kabatereine et al. 2001; Alderman et al. 2006).

The sample used cluster-based sampling with three strata. Fifty parishes were randomly selected from the parishes in the project site and randomly assigned to either group A—which received all ECD services as well as the experimental delivery of albendazole at child health days—or group B—which received all the core ECD services. A control group was also selected. In particular, one subcounty that was not in the project but adjacent to it was selected for each subcounty in the project. All parishes in these subcounties were then listed and 25 parishes were randomly selected. Two villages from each parish selected were then chosen, again using a list of all the villages in the parish. This step reduced the number of villages where a household listing would be required. A census of households was then conducted in each sample village and households containing at least one child between age 0 and 6 were selected randomly.

The Institute of Public Health (IPH) of Makerere University administered a baseline questionnaire to 2,250 households (750 in each stratum) between January and March 2000. Each household with a child under 5 was revisited in the same season in 2003. Only a few households were not available for the resurvey. As is generally the case in rural communities, refusals were negligible. The use of global positioning systems (GPS) facilitated locating the households in the resurvey. Households in the sampled parishes that had fostered children who were orphaned or otherwise had changed households since the baseline were also included in the 2003 sample. If an original household no longer had a child under 5, and thus was not able to contribute information relevant to the ECD evaluation, it was dropped from the survey after the roster was filled in and a replacement household with a suitable child was selected.

Many communities did not begin child growth promotion until late 2001, and some community grants were not allocated until 2002. Thus, while the original evaluation plan envisioned at least two years between the provision of initial community services and the resurvey, the actual duration of the project at the time of the second round was shorter than planned.

The main result on the impact of the set of project interventions is based on a difference-in-differences estimate of impact. Denoting nutritional status in the treatment (project communities) and the control group as NT and NC respectively and the second and initial visits as t and 0, this result is expressed as

$$EDD(b) = [E(NTt) - E(NCt)] - [E(NT0) - E(NC0)].$$

This approach accommodates any differences between the communities at the time the project was initiated, using a pretest-posttest control design. Because the analysis also includes covariates such as parental assets, education, access to sanitation, as well as the age and sex of the child, the difference-in-differences comparison actually addresses any initial differences in unobservable characteristics that have a linear impact on the outcome.

There was no statistical difference between the weight-for-age of children under 5 in project sites at the time of the baseline survey and the nutritional status in the same age cohort in the control group. Three years later there still was no significant difference in the nutritional status of the 0–5 age cohorts taken as a group. However, those children younger than age 1 in the project sites were 0.4 standard deviations heavier than children in the corresponding age bracket in the control sites, a difference that is statistically significant at the 0.01 level. The magnitude of this difference is unaffected if the analysis is performed on a sample restricted to those households that were included in both rounds, in effect constructing a difference in differences that compares younger siblings with their older siblings in the treatment population with a similar comparison in the control group.

What might explain this particular pattern? The higher impact of the project on the youngest cohort is consistent with the results from Madagascar, but in this case they may be explained by the late introduction of the project services. In particular, the relatively recent introduction of community-based growth promotion would imply that older children would have passed through the most vulnerable ages prior to the availability of this service. To see whether this interpretation is plausible, it is necessary to look at health-seeking behaviors. In particular, the project sites adhered more closely to the guidelines on exclusive breastfeeding than did the control group. For example, there was a significant difference across groups in the date that fluids other than breast milk were introduced in the resurvey period. In this population, the most common pattern is too-early introduction of foods or liquids. The major effect of the nutrition education was a delay in the introduction of complementary foods closer to the recommendation of 6 months old. Although interpretation of this date is ambiguous—both early and late introduction could be harmful—additional analysis shows that the probability that fluids are introduced before 6 months old declined in the second round where the project was introduced. Similarly, the introduction date of solid foods was somewhat later in the treatment communities. Finally, between the two rounds, the project communities had a significant decline in the probability of early cessation of breastfeeding, defined as stopping before the age of 6 months, which was not noted in the control group.

The project also encouraged diet diversification. Two-thirds of the caregivers in the intervention group reported giving the children one or more forms of legumes (beans, nuts, soya) in the week preceding the resurvey, compared with one-third of the children in the control group. The number of times legumes were consumed in the week was 20 percent higher for the treatment communities. Milk was also consumed one-third more frequently in the treatment communities, as were fruits and vegetables. However, there was no significant difference in the frequency of consumption of meat, chicken, or eggs. The project also encouraged more frequent feeding of young children. However, there was no significant difference in frequency of meals across groups.

These child-feeding practices can affect the growth of very young children and thus contribute to the difference in weights of children as young as a few months, as observed in this data set. In addition, other behaviors that affect health but not necessarily the growth of young children may have been influenced by the project. In particular, because the community mobilizers organized child health days, children in the project sites avoided a general negative trend in vitamin A supplementation in the period between the two surveys. Because a subset of the treatment group received albendazole on the child health days, this group also differed from the baseline as well as from the control group. However, children younger than age 1 were not given albendazole. Thus, while it is not possible to completely distinguish which of these changes account for any changes in nutrition status, because these behaviors are known to contribute to health, they can be considered promising indicators of the means by which the project influenced nutrition.

Also, modest but consistent improvements in early stimulation in the home, as evidenced in responses to a set of questions on caregiver interaction and attitudes, were noted. For example, intervention fathers were more likely to give physical care to children than control fathers in the posttest but not the pretest. At the posttest, intervention group parents were more likely to report spending time in learning activities (counting, naming objects, drawing, and so on), taking the child out of the village (increasing exposure), having a special place for the child to play, and sending the child to the ECD center, where there had been no difference initially. At the posttest, intervention parents were much more likely to value early learning for later schooling and to see a role for fathers in this activity, which was not evident at the pretest.

A few changes in measured cognitive skills of children ages 3.5 through 5.9 were seen at the posttest, primarily in numeracy skills. However, the differences were relatively modest, particularly compared with the larger impact on parenting attitudes and behaviors. These behaviors and attitudes were assessed for children 2–4, and therefore were more likely to have been affected by the intervention (effects are often stronger in younger children). Another reason why few improvements in skills were noted is that the communication messages were more consistently administered than the ECD intervention of a child care center, which relatively few communities asked for and of which relatively few were functional at the time of the evaluation. To the degree that the changes in attitudes of caregivers presage future improvements in measured abilities of children, these changes in attitudes can lead to other project outcomes. There may be economies of scope—that is, cost savings from linking service provision—on the delivery of these services.

Conclusion

Nutrition projects have the potential to complement ECD programs both by ensuring that a child has avoided physical impairment and also by mobilizing communities to deliver messages to caregivers that enhance their ability to nurture a child, both through feeding practices and stimulation. There is ample global evidence that successful nutrition programs, as well as participation in a learning environment, can add to a child's capacity to learn. Moreover, the evaluations of recent community-based growth promotion programs in Sub-Saharan Africa discussed here indicate that this approach is capable of influencing behaviors—as well as changing attitudes—and, thus, achieving measurable improvements in nutritional status. Many programs in other African countries as well as other regions combine similar interventions through parenting that include both improved nutrition and development (such as, Jordan's "Better Parenting Initiative," Cuba's *Educa tu Hijo,* Albania's "Gardens for Children," The Gambia's "Baby Friendly Community Initiative," and Senegal's positive deviance project combining iron supplementation and stimulation). Programs that facilitate these improvements in nutritional status can also be vehicles for enhancing cognitive as well as social and emotional development. Although such additional improvements— over those directly attributable to improved nutrition—are possible, without knowing the capacity of community-based programs to add services and to provide these services in a sustainable manner, it will be necessary to closely monitor the scaling up of such child services. This monitoring is doubly important because ECD projects tend to be very context specific. Moreover, while the interaction of ECD and nutrition programs has been studied in a few programs (Watanabe et al. 2005), the manner by which one intervention can heighten—or undermine— another is still fairly unexplored. For this reason, such studies are likely to be particularly informative.

Note

The authors would like to thank Claudia Rokx and Emanuela Galasso for helpful comments on an earlier draft.

References

Alderman, H., J. Hoddinott, and B. Kinsey. 2006. "Long-Term Consequences of Early Childhood Malnutrition." *Oxford Economic Papers* 58 (3): 450–74.

Alderman, H., H. Hoogeveen, and M. Rossi. 2006. "Reducing Child Malnutrition in Tanzania: Combined Effects of Income Growth and Program Interventions." *Economics and Human Biology* 4 (1): 1–23.

Alderman, H., J. Konde-Lule, I. Sebuliba, D. Bundy, and A. Hall. 2006. "Increased Weight Gain in Preschool Children Due to Mass Albendazole Treatment Given during Child Health Days in Uganda: A Cluster Randomized Controlled Trial." *British Medical Journal* 333 (7559): 122–26.

Allen, L., and S. Gillespie. 2001. "What Works? A Review of the Efficacy and Effectiveness of Nutrition Interventions." Asian Development Bank, Nutrition and Development Series 5, Manila.

Behrman, J. R. 1996. "Impact of Health and Nutrition on Education." *World Bank Research Observer* 11 (1): 23–37.

Behrman, J., H. Alderman, and J. Hoddinott. 2004. "Hunger and Malnutrition." Paper prepared for "Copenhagen Challenge." In *Global Crises, Global Solutions*, ed. B. Lomborg. Cambridge, UK: Cambridge University Press.

Bhargava, A., and M. Fox-Kean. 2003. "The Effects of Maternal Education versus Cognitive Test Scores on Child Nutrition in Kenya." *Economics of Human Biology* 1 (3): 309–19.

Christiaensen, L., and H. Alderman. 2004. "Child Malnutrition in Ethiopia: Can Maternal Knowledge Augment the Role of Income?" *Economic Development and Cultural Change* 52 (2): 287–312.

Engle, P., P. Menon, and L. Haddad. 1999. "Care and Nutrition: Concepts and Measurement." *World Development* 27 (8): 1309–37.

Galasso, E., and J. Yau. 2005. "Improving Nutritional Status through Behavioral Change: Lessons from the SEECALINE Program in Madagascar." Development Research Group, World Bank.

Glewwe, P. 1999. "Why Does Mother's Schooling Raise Child Health in Developing Countries? Evidence from Morocco." *Journal of Human Resources* 34 (1): 124–59.

———. 2005. "The Impact of Child Health and Nutrition on Education in Developing Countries: Theory, Econometric Issues, and Recent Empirical Evidence." *Food and Nutrition Bulletin* 26 (suppl.): S235–50.

Glewwe, P., H. Jacoby, and E. King. 2001. "Early Childhood Nutrition and Academic Achievement: A Longitudinal Analysis." *Journal of Public Economics* 81 (3): 345–68.

Grantham-McGregor, S., L. Fernald, and K. Sethuraman. 1999a. "Effects of Health and Nutrition on Cognitive and Behavioral Development in Children in the First Three Years of Life. Part 1. Low Birthweight, Breastfeeding, and Protein-Energy Malnutrition." *Food and Nutrition Bulletin* 20 (1): 53–75.

————. 1999b. "Effects of Health and Nutrition on Cognitive and Behavioral Development in Children in the First Three Years of Life. Part 2. Infection and Micronutrient Deficiencies: Iodine, Iron, and Zinc." *Food and Nutrition Bulletin* 20 (1): 76–99.

Grantham-McGregor, S., C. Walker, S. Chang, and C. Powell. 1997. "Effects of Early Childhood Supplementation with and without Stimulation on Later Development in Stunted Jamaican Children." *American Journal of Clinical Nutrition* 66: 247–53.

Kabatereine, N. B., E. Tukahebwa, S. Brooker, H. Alderman, and A, Hall. 2001. "Epidemiology of Intestinal Helminth Infestations among School Children in Southern Uganda." *East African Medical Journal* 78 (6): 283–86.

Kagitcibasi, C. 1997. "Parent Education and Child Development." In *Early Child Development: Investing in the Future*, ed. M. E. Young. Amsterdam: Elsevier.

Maluccio, J. A., J. Hoddinott, J. R. Behrman, A. Quisumbing, R. Martorell, and A. D. Stein. 2005. *The Impact of an Experimental Nutritional Intervention on Education into Adulthood in Rural Guatemala.* Washington, DC: International Food Policy Research Institute (IFPRI).

Martorell, R. 1997. "Undernutrition during Pregnancy and Early Childhood and Its Consequences for Cognitive and Behavioral Development." In *Early Child Development: Investing in the Future*, ed. M. E. Young. Amsterdam: Elsevier.

Matte, T. D., M. A. Bresnahan, M. D. Begg, and E. S. Susser. 2001. "Influence of Variation in Birthweight within Normal Range and within Sibships on IQ at Age 7 Years: Cohort Study." *British Medical Journal* 323: 310–14.

Myers, R. 1992. *The Twelve Who Survive: Strengthening Programs of Early Childhood Care in Developing Countries.* London: Routledge.

Pollitt, E. 1990. *Malnutrition and Infection in the Classroom.* Paris: UNESCO.

Pollitt, E., K. S. Gorman, P. Engle, and R. Martorell. 1993. "Early Supplementary Feeding and Cognition: Effects over Two Decades." *Monographs of the Society for Research in Child Development* 58 (7): v–99.

Richards, M., R. Hardy, and M. Wadsworth. 2001. "Birthweight and Cognitive Function in the British 1946 Birth Cohort: Longitudinal Population-Based Study." *British Medical Journal* 322: 199–203.

Ruel, M. 1995. "Growth Monitoring as an Educational Tool, an Integration Strategy, and a Source of Information: A Review of Experience. In *Enhancing Child Growth and Nutrition in Developing Countries: Priorities for Action*, ed. P. Pinstrup-Andersen, D. Pelletier, and H. Alderman. Ithaca, NY: Cornell University Press.

Smith, L. C., U. Ramakrishnan, A. Ndiaye, L. Haddad, and R. Martorell. 2001. "The Importance of Women's Status for Child Nutrition in Developing

Countries." Draft research report, International Food Policy Research Institute (IFPRI), Washington, DC.

St. Clair, D. M., M. Xu, P. Wang, Y. Yu, Y. Fang, Z. Feng, X. Zheng, et al. 2005. "Rates of Adult Schizophrenia Following Prenatal Exposure to the Chinese Famine of 1959–61." *Journal of the American Medical Association* 294 (5): 557–62.

Watanabe, K., R. Flores, J. Fujiwara, and L. Tran. 2005. "Early Childhood Development Interventions and Cognitive Development of Young Children in Rural Vietnam." *Journal of Nutrition* 135 (8): 1918–25.

CHAPTER 19

The Impact of ECD Programs on Maternal Employment and Older Children's School Attendance in Kenya

Michael M. Lokshin, Elena Glinskaya, and Marito Garcia

After Kenya gained independence in 1963, the welfare of poor households with young children emerged as a critical concern for the newly self-reliant nation. To meet child care needs, government and civil society organizations formed early childhood development (ECD) centers, which provided day care and education to preschoolers. The number of ECD centers grew rapidly. In the early 1960s, only a small proportion of children were enrolled in ECD centers. By the mid-1990s, however, 20,000 ECD centers provided day care and primary school preparation for more than 1 million 3- to 7-year-old children (about 20 percent of the population in this age group). The change in the choice of child care options

This chapter draws heavily on work published by the authors in the *Journal of African Economies* (Lokshin, Glinskaya, and Garcia 2004), which gives greater detail on the theory, methods, and results. The authors are grateful to Uwe Deichmann for his help and recommendations with global positioning system data analysis, and to Andrew Dabalen and Bènèdicte de la Brière for many stimulating discussions.

reflected the changing composition of the labor force. Women spent more time working outside the home, poor landless households migrated to urban areas, and a growing share of women worked in industry. Despite the increasing number of ECD centers and their multiple benefits, the government education budget since 2000 has reflected a heavily skewed preference for university education on a per capita basis, leaving only a small share of funds for preschool education (UNESCO 2005). As a result, the rates decreased for both the growth of primary education enrollment and transition to secondary education. A review of the education sector identifies policy initiatives that the Kenyan government can implement to reverse the negative trends in access, equity, and quality of education in the country (World Bank 1997). But taking such policies to a national level requires better information about the costs and benefits of ECD programs and their effects on household behavior (van der Gaag and Tan 1998). Understanding these issues can help governments to design more effective policies for households with small children.

The availability and cost of child care play an important role in the decisions that households make about allocating labor and choosing between informal home care and ECD. A mother's decision to join the labor force is based on her expected earnings compared with the costs of available day care. Insufficient child care options could be a barrier for women with children to join the labor force (for example, Kimmel 1998). The custodial role of ECD centers frees female household members for other activities and allows mothers to enter the labor market. The additional income newly employed mothers bring home can be significant and may lift some households out of poverty. In the longer term, the increased work experience may also lead to increased job skills and higher earnings for household members. Better employment options, in turn, may decrease the reliance of low-income families on government subsidies and increase their self-sufficiency.

Research in developing countries also indicates that females other than the mother, especially young daughters, provide free child care, releasing mothers for paid work (for example, Deutsch 1998). For example, Psacharopoulos and Arriagada (1989) find that in Brazilian households, the presence of younger siblings has a negative effect on school attendance of older children. In El Salvador, girls missed more school than boys because they stayed home to help with chores (Bittencourt and DiCicco 1979). Deolalikar (1998) finds significant differences in girls' (but not boys') school enrollment in households with children under 3 in Kenya. He reports a particularly strong effect for girls attending secondary school. The presence of a child 3 or younger reduces the probability that a girl aged 14–17 would be enrolled in secondary school by 41 percent, conditional on other determinants of enrollment. The corresponding effect for boys is only 5 percent. These studies indicate that when child care centers are unavailable or too costly, older siblings are more likely to provide child care.

The Kenya Household and ECD Centers Surveys

The data for this research come from two sources. The first is the 1994 Kenya Welfare Monitoring Survey (WMS II; World Bank 1994), which provides information on 10,860 households (59,200 individuals). For our analysis we use a sample of 6,624 households with children between ages 3 and 7. The survey includes questions on household incomes, expenditures, employment and wages, education, health, and child outcomes. The questionnaires also yield data on the arrangements and expenditures for child care. A drawback of the data for this analysis is the unavailability of the urban-rural indicator. The most recent estimates show that 26 percent of the total population lived in urban areas in 1992 (World Bank 1997).

The second data source used in this chapter is the Kenya Early Childhood Development Centers Survey (KECDCS) that the Kenyan Ministry of Education carried out in 1995. The survey covers more than 800 child care facilities in 17 urban centers and rural districts (including pastoral areas). KECDCS is based on a stratified random sample that includes ECD centers of all types of sponsorship (Mukui and Mwaniki 1995). The survey collected information on each ECD center's location, child enrollment, operating expenditures, financial status, and facilities. It also collected data on the characteristics and salaries of teaching and nonteaching staff, the extent of turnover, and child feeding practices.

Using a gazetteer maintained by the U.S. National Imagery and Mapping Agency (National Geospatial-Intelligence Agency, n.d.), we determined the geographic coordinates of the towns for the ECD centers in the survey and found some of the households that lacked location information in WMS II. With the geographic information for both data sets, we matched households in WMS II with ECD centers in KECDCS.

Female Labor Supply and the ECD System in Kenya

Kenya has a predominantly rural, low-income economy. About 80 percent of the Kenyan labor force is employed in agriculture, and half of these workers are involved in subsistence farming (noncash agriculture). According to WMS II, nearly all women with small children (ages 3–7) work outside the home. Rural women who work "for cash" find employment as casual laborers on tea, coffee, sisal, and sugar plantations, as tenders of cash crops or food crops of their wealthier neighbors, and as workers in various rural enterprises. Urban low-skilled women earn cash as domestic servants, petty traders, or small-scale retail traders. Women with more skills tend to be employed in garment making, sales, clerical work, teaching, and health services. Some of these jobs make it possible for women to bring children to work. But most mothers who work as paid laborers or formal-sector workers cannot take care of their children at the same time.

To define who is working or employed, we categorize all individuals who reported wages or salary earnings as "working in cash occupations." Employment rates for males are significantly higher than rates for females across all age groups. About 70 percent of men aged 26–35 work, compared with only 33 percent of mothers in the same age group. The rate of paid employment declines with age among both men and women: 54 percent of all men and 25 percent of all women older than 46 years work outside the home.

A household's decision about its labor supply is influenced by their productivity at home and in the labor market. Small children require care, and a mother's productivity at home is, in many cases, higher than her potential return from outside work. For all age groups the percentage of working mothers declines with the number of small children in the household. The employment rate is lower for young mothers (aged 18–25) than for older mothers. The most economically active women are 26- to 35-year-old mothers. Among them the employment rate reaches 46 percent for women with one child, which is comparable to or higher than the employment rates of women with no children. In households with four or more children, only about 25 percent of mothers work for wages.

Other household members may participate in household production as child care providers. The data indicate that the more elderly members there are in a household, the less likely the household is to send pre-school-age children to an ECD program.

The ECD System in Kenya

The first privately run preschools in Kenya appeared in the 1940s, catering exclusively to the European and Asian communities. Later, day care centers became established on coffee, tea, and sugar plantations and in urban centers. During the struggle for independence in the 1950s, ECD centers were started in the emergency villages in Central Province. The number of preschools grew rapidly after independence in 1963. In 1986, about 700,000 children were enrolled in 12,100 ECD centers; in 1991 these numbers had risen to about 900,000 children in 17,600 ECD centers. By 2004, approximately 27,000 ECD centers provided care and early education to more than 1.2 million children. In the mid-1990s about 60 percent of ECD centers in Kenya functioned as community-operated programs. Religious organizations, nongovernmental organizations (NGOs), private individuals and companies, and local authorities established and ran the other centers.

An organized curriculum for Kenya ECD centers was not established until the mid-1980s. By then, the Ministry of Education had assumed responsibility for training preschool teachers, supervising and inspecting preschool programs, developing a locality-specific curriculum, and conducting research on and evaluation of ECD programs. In 1984 the National Center for Early Childhood Education (NACECE), established at the Kenya Institute of Education with the assistance of the Bernard van Leer Foundation, became responsible for curriculum development and the training of trainers. In 1985, District Centers for Early Childhood Education (DICECE) began to supervise ECD activities and train teachers at the district level (World Bank 1997). All but the local government-run centers rely heavily on fees for paying their day-to-day operating expenses. The majority of ECD funds are spent on teachers' salaries.

The prices charged by ECD programs vary considerably. Fees are not set nationally, but rather by village or urban parent-teacher associations. These associations manage more than 75 percent of the ECD centers in Kenya (Myers 1992). Fees vary depending on the quality of preschools. Centers that employ more educated teachers, have smaller classes, provide food, and offer other means to enhance learning charge higher fees (Glinskaya and Garcia 1999). Land, buildings, furniture, and teaching and play materials are donated by churches, local authorities, and parents.

Explaining the Effect of Availability of Child Care on Household Behavior

Our theoretical framework for modeling the effect of availability of ECD centers on household behavior is based on the assumption that a household makes choices about their consumption of child care, children's schooling, market goods, and leisure. A household's decisions about the quality of child care and education for its children and about the amount of time each household member should work are motivated by the desire to achieve the highest level of household welfare. We assume that two forms of child care are available to households in Kenya: free child care that can be provided by the mother, other adult household members, or older siblings, and paid child care provided by ECD centers. We can define four household demand equations corresponding to (1) a mother's labor force participation decisions, (2) use of child care facilities by young children, (3) school participation of older children in the household, and (4) labor participation decisions of other household members. In the data we observe the binary indicators (demand index functions) that correspond to the latent demand variables. We define these variables as follows:

- *Mother's work status*: A household in which a mother of preschool-age children reported receiving cash earnings is defined as a household with a mother who works outside the home. More than half of all households with small children have working mothers.
- *Use of child care facilities*: A household having at least one preschool-age child attending an ECD center is classified as a household that uses paid child care facilities. About 18 percent of households use child care facilities as a form of day care for their children.
- *School participation*: The indicator dummy variable is equal to 1 for households in which all children of school age are at school; otherwise, this dummy variable is equal to 0. About one-quarter of Kenyan households have at least one school-age child not in school.
- *Work status of the other household members*: A household is classified as having "other working household members" if at least one adult reported working for cash. According to this definition, 75 percent of households are classified as households with "other working members."

Explanatory variables in our model include the mother's age and her level of education, household size and demographic composition, household nonwage income, the number of children of different ages, as well as the average level of wages in the district. Several key variables of interest are discussed here:

- *Price per unit of child care quality (Pq)*: We identify the effect of child care prices on household behavior through district-level differences in these prices in two ways. In our first approach—estimating care prices from the household expenditures on child care—we assume that the price per unit of child care quality is uniform within a district and therefore use the average district-specific household expenditure as a proxy for the child care price. We calculate the average household expenditures on child care for 43 districts in Kenya with an average of 150 households in each district. In our second approach—calculating the price of care based on the information on centers' fees—we estimate the quality-adjusted price of outside-home care using the hedonic regression approach. KECDCS collected extensive information about the characteristics of the child care provided and the fees charged by ECD centers. These data are used to estimate a model of fees for ECD facilities as a function of a facility's characteristics.

- *Mother's offered wage and wages of other household members*: The wage rates available to each household member in the household have been imputed using a Mincer's type earning function regression with a control for selectivity. Monthly earnings have been calculated as a ratio of the reported earnings and the number of months the respondent worked for those earnings.

Using these definitions of the dependent and independent variables, the model of household behavior is estimated by the method of the Semi-Parametric Full Information Maximum Likelihood (SPFIML). The method allows us to estimate the system of simultaneous binary equations without specifying an exact functional form of the joint distribution of the error terms and instead by approximating this distribution nonparametrically.

Table 19.1 presents the estimated coefficients for the model that uses the average local household expenditure on child care as a proxy for the price of child care. The estimations show that the rising price of care has a negative effect on maternal employment. Moreover, the higher the potential wage rates of the mother, the more likely it is that she will participate in the labor force. Younger mothers, single mothers, and mothers from households where the education of the head is higher are more likely to work outside the home.

As expected, a high price for child care decreases the probability that the household will use outside-home care. Households in which the mother has a higher wage rate are significantly more likely to use paid care. Households with children aged 0–2 are less likely to use ECD centers. One explanation could be the economy of scale based on the number of children, which increases the productivity of other household members at home. In other words, once someone is taking care of one

Table 19.1. Maternal Employment and ECD Use: Simultaneous Estimation of the Equations for the System of Household Demand

	Mother's work status		Children in ECD centers		Children at school		Other household members' work	
	Coeff.	Std. err.	Coeff.	Std. err.	Coeff.	Std. err.	Coeff.	Std. err.
Log of mother's wage	7.637**	3.344	4.936**	1.655	3.118	5.411	-0.096	3.199
Log of other's wage	0.403	0.281	0.193	0.194	0.221	0.335	8.006***	1.304
Cost of child care	-0.886*	0.536	-3.229***	0.401	-1.721**	0.613	0.065	0.472
Characteristics of the household								
Household size	-0.955	5.119	7.824**	3.657	9.805	8.025	5.754	4.905
Number of children age 0–2	-0.079	1.004	-1.623**	0.700	-2.294**	1.389	1.527*	0.939
Number children age 3–5	1.137	1.004	-0.567	0.674	-1.075	1.343	1.008	0.907
Number of children age 6–7	-0.036	1.000	3.242***	0.691	-0.662	1.377	-1.544*	0.935
Number of children age 8–12	-0.223	0.895	-1.700**	0.632	-3.812**	1.365	-0.538	0.860
Number of children age 13–16	0.075	0.904	-1.659**	0.654	-4.197***	1.296	-0.207	0.865
Share of adult males	-0.172	0.774	-1.557**	0.569	-0.404	1.218	1.054	0.726
Share of adult females	-0.007	0.713	-1.436**	0.511	-0.441	1.185	1.274*	0.687
Share of elderly	-0.829	1.107	-1.100	0.829	0.015	1.734	1.781*	0.994
Share of children					Reference category			
Single mother household	0.696***	0.234	0.070	0.168	-0.230	0.262	-1.628***	0.220
Single mother and other	0.507**	0.284	0.116	0.200	-0.339	0.338	-1.708***	0.256
Nuclear family household					Reference category			
Nuclear family and other	0.167	0.151	0.200**	0.097	-0.082	0.165	0.479***	0.150
Other types of households	0.187	0.187	0.016	0.134	-0.113	0.205	0.394**	0.166
Nonwage household non-agricultural income	0.065	2.205	1.262	1.811	10.288*	6.604	8.905**	4.711

Nonwage household agricultural income	2.750	3.724	2.179	2.155	6.739*	3.256	-0.046	3.010
Age of household head	-3.187*	2.044	-2.053	1.399	-0.607	2.234	1.680	1.710
Age of household head squared*100	2.350	2.011	0.906	1.461	0.042	2.159	-3.333**	1.747
Gender of household head	-0.845***	0.224	0.015	0.131	-0.441**	0.214	-0.022	0.160
Education of household head	6.277***	1.378	2.452***	0.814	12.254***	1.772	1.571	1.324
Characteristics of the mother								
Age	1.404***	0.377	2.937	2.148	3.260	4.476	1.867	2.760
Age squared*100	-1.564***	0.459	-2.144	2.719	-0.795	5.409	-0.684	3.470
No formal education				*Reference category*				
Preschool education	0.493	0.391	0.539**	0.277	1.820**	0.605	-0.003	0.340
Standard 1–8 education	0.090	0.157	0.120	0.092	1.106***	0.297	0.248	0.159
Primary education certificate	0.372**	0.179	0.197**	0.102	1.515***	0.328	0.495***	0.177
Junior secondary education	0.469*	0.268	0.018	0.145	1.474**	0.506	0.570**	0.262
Secondary education certificate	0.039	0.356	-0.014	0.196	0.624	0.612	0.436	0.375
Trade test certificate	-0.447	0.628	-0.386	0.373	0.356	1.004	0.010	0.607
Other postsecondary education	0.710	0.548	-0.231	0.311	1.151	0.904	0.609	0.620
University and above	-0.747	0.925	-1.275**	0.565	1.068	1.725	-0.318	0.869
Mean salary in the district	-3.061***	1.010	5.470***	0.598	8.411***	1.487	-0.256	0.633
Constant	0.104	1.854	-6.137***	1.033	-10.744***	3.200	0.832	1.863
N [Log likelihood]	6,645 [-11,327.74]							

Source: Lokshin, Glinskaya, Garcia 2004.
Note: Average per locality household expenditure on child care is used as a proxy for cost of child care.
*Significant at the 10 percent level. **Significant at the 5 percent level. ***Significant at the 1 percent level.

child, he or she can take care of two, whereas if a household puts both children in a child care center it would have to pay double the price. Households with children aged 6–7 are more likely to use ECD centers. An important finding is that the presence of older children (8 years and older) has a significant negative effect on paid care use. This finding may support the hypothesis that older children act as substitutes for the mother in home production and particularly in child care.

The probability that school-age children attend school is negatively and significantly related to the price of day care. Higher wage rates for mothers have a positive, although statistically insignificant, effect on the likelihood of children attending school. The presence of school-age siblings decreases the probability that children are at school. Higher levels of education of the household head and the mother have a positive effect on children's school attendance.

The estimation of the model in which we approximate costs of child care using center fees to determine quality-adjusted prices in the locality is shown in a longer version of this chapter (Lokshin, Glinskaya, and Garcia 2004). Aside from some differences in the magnitudes of the effects, the behavior of the main variables of interest in the quality-adjusted method confirms the predictions of the average household expenditure method. Mothers with higher potential wages are more likely to work outside the home. The effect of wages on maternal employment is significant. Higher costs of child care prevent mothers from working outside the home, decrease the probability that school-age children attend school, and decrease the probability that small children attend preschool.

Simulations

To examine the effects of the estimates just summarized, we simulate how households would respond to changes in the specific parameters used in the model (see table 19.2).[1] A 10 percent increase in the mother's potential wage rate would encourage mothers to work outside the home. The proportion of households with working mothers would increase from 53.1 percent to 62.3 percent, which corresponds to an elasticity of mother's labor supply with respect to the market wage of 1.48. This elasticity measures the responsiveness of mothers switching to paid work. According to WMS II, all prime-aged women participated in work activities, and only those who worked for a wage were classified as participating in the labor market. Such high labor supply elasticity is not unusual for Africa. Dabalen (2000) reports that the elasticity of women's labor supply with respect to the market wage in South Africa is close to unity.

A 10 percent increase in wages also has a strong effect on children's enrollment in paid child care facilities. The proportion of households using preschool facilities would rise by 7.7 percent, indicating that households treat child care as a "normal good" and increase child care consumption

Table 19.2. Simulation of the Effects of Various Policies and Changes in Demographic Characteristics on Household Behavior (SPFIML[a] Estimation)

	Simulated probability			
	Mother's work status	Children in ECD centers	Children at school	Other household members' work
Policy options				
Mother's wage rate				
Baseline	53.1*	17.2*	64.3	75.5
Baseline + 10%	62.3*	24.9*	67.3	76.4
Elasticity	*1.48*	*3.09*	*0.45*	*0.12*
Cost of child care				
Baseline	52.9	17.8	63.5	75.5
Fully subsidized	63.2	78.7	77.5	74.9
Elasticity	*−0.35*	*3.01*	*0.36*	*0.01*
Other household members' wage				
Baseline	52.9	17.7	63.8*	70.5*
Baseline + 10%	53.3	17.9	64.1*	80.4*
Elasticity	*0.08*	*0.11*	*0.05*	*1.23*
Household nonwage income				
Baseline	52.9	17.7	63.8*	75.6*
Baseline + 10%	53.0	17.7	63.9*	75.6*
Elasticity	*0.02*	*0.00*	*0.02*	*0.00*
Household demographics				
Household type				
Single mother	65.3*	19.3	60.9	46.6*
All other	51.3*	17.4	64.3	77.6*
Education of household head				
Baseline	53.1*	17.4*	67.1*	75.9
Baseline + 1 year	54.3*	17.9*	68.9*	76.2
Elasticity	*0.22*	*0.28*	*0.26*	*0.04*
Household size				
Baseline	53.0	17.9	62.1	75.6
Baseline + 1 member	52.4	19.5	63.5	75.6
Elasticity	*−0.11*	*0.82*	*0.22*	*0.00*

Source: Lokshin, Glinskaya, Garcia 2004.
Note: a. Semi-Parametric Full Information Maximum Likelihood.
*The corresponding estimated coefficient is significant with at least 90 percent probability.

with a higher income. School participation is also positively correlated with mothers' wages. A 10 percent increase in wages would result in about a 3 percent increase in the proportion of households that send all of their school-age children to school. Changes in the wages of women with children have a rather small effect on the labor supply of other household members.

The simulated effect of a policy that would fully subsidize the cost of child care is consistent with the predictions of the theory. Free child care would quadruple the use of ECD facilities by Kenyan households with preschool-age children.[2] This high elasticity suggests that households in Kenya are quite sensitive to the costs of care and that policies that affect child care costs can have a pronounced impact on household behavior and, consequently, on poverty alleviation and children's education. Maternal rates of labor force participation would rise and the percentage of households with children at school would increase. The effect of a change in child care cost on other household members' labor supply is small.

If household members other than the mother have access to higher wages, their level of labor force participation increases substantially. A 10 percent increase in their wage rate would increase the proportion of households with working adults other than the mother by 9.9 percent. This wage increase positively affects the use of child care facilities as well, although the effect is small compared with that obtained from changes in mothers' wages or costs of care. The percentage of households in which all the school-age children attend school would also increase.

Our simulations indicate that an increase in household nonwage income does not significantly affect the level of mothers' employment and the participation of children in ECD programs. The income effect on school enrollment is nontrivial with an implied elasticity of 0.02. This estimate is on the lower bound of elasticities compiled by Behrman and Knowles (1999) in their survey of 42 studies in 21 countries. They found a median elasticity of 0.07 for nonwage income's effect on schooling. The effect of nonwage income on household behavior could, however, depend on intrahousehold resource allocation.

Single mothers are more likely to work outside the home than are married women with children. According to the model, about 65 percent of single mothers participate in the labor force compared with 51.3 percent of married mothers. Households headed by a single mother are more likely to use ECD facilities but less likely to enroll children in school. We also found that the educational level attained by the household head positively influences mothers' labor force participation, the use of child care facilities outside the home, and children's school attendance. Additionally, in larger households mothers are less likely to work for pay than those in smaller ones, are more likely to use child care facilities, and the school-age children have a higher level of school enrollment.

Gender Differences in Children's School Enrollment

Our model also allows us to analyze gender differences in household demand for education. The heterogeneity in a household's approach to investment in schooling for girls and boys may mask the results presented above. To test how various parameters affect the schooling of children of different sexes, we re-estimate our model of household demand separately for girls and boys. For these estimations we create two new binary variables equal to 1 if all school-age girls (boys) in the household are in school and equal to 0 otherwise. We estimate the school enrollment equation simultaneously with three other demand equations on the sample of households with small children. Table 19.3 shows the simulated probabilities of school enrollment.

The differences are striking in the effects of increased maternal wages and costs of child care on the school enrollment of boys and girls. While a 10 percent increase in mothers' wages reduces girls' enrollment by 8.8 percent (elasticity of –1.5), it actually raises boys' attendance by 11 percent (elasticity of 1.27). These results may be driven by different interactions of income and substitution effects in household decisions about girls' and boys' schooling. Higher wages for the mother would increase household income and induce the household to demand more schooling for its children (income effect). At the same time, higher wages would make the time the mother spends at home more expensive, and the household may decide to substitute other households members for the mother in some home production activities (substitution effect). For boys the income effect clearly dominates the substitution effect: Higher wages of the mother increase boys' school enrollment. For girls the situation is the opposite: In response to an increase in mothers' wages, households would replace mothers with adolescent girls in home production activities, so girls' school enrollment would drop.

The effect of an increase in the cost of care confirms this hypothesis. A 10 percent increase in child care costs reduces girls' school attendance rate by 3.3 percent but increases boys' attendance, albeit insignificantly. Higher costs of care would lower the household demand for paid care. To care for its small children, the household may either reduce the labor

Table 19.3. Simulation of the Effects of Various Policies on School Attendance (SPFIML[a] Estimation)

Increase by 10%	Simulated probability of a household having all of its children in school		All children in school
	Girls 8–16 years old	Boys 8–16 years old	
Mother's wage rate			
Baseline	67.3*	75.5*	64.3
Baseline + 10%	58.5*	86.5*	67.3
Elasticity	*−1.50*	*1.27*	*0.45*
Cost of child care			
Baseline	68.1*	70.2	63.5*
Baseline + 10%	64.8*	70.3	61.3*
Elasticity	*−0.51*	*0.01*	*−0.36*
Other household members' wage			
Baseline	68.7	70.3	63.8
Baseline + 10%	70.0	70.7	64.1
Elasticity	*0.19*	*0.06*	*0.05*

Source: Lokshin, Glinskaya, Garcia 2004.
Note: a. Semi-Parametric Full Information Maximum Likelihood.
*The corresponding estimated coefficient is significant with at least 90% probability.

supply of the mother outside the home or use other household members as child care providers. As the simulation shows, the household decides to sacrifice girls' schooling and instead use them in home activities to allow the mother to work for wages. No such effect occurs for school-age boys. Changes in child care costs and changes in maternal wage rates have the same effect on total school enrollment rates: enrollment for girls declines and enrollment for boys slightly increases.

Conclusions

Our research shows that economic incentives have a powerful effect on the work decisions of women with children in Kenya. The level of wages available to them and the costs of child care affect women's labor force participation. Child care costs affect which child care arrangements households choose. High costs of ECD programs discourage households from using outside arrangements for their preschoolers and increase the number of households that rely on home-provided care. High child care costs also have a negative effect on the level of maternal employment. Households with single mothers rely more often on paid child care, and such households would be the most affected by changes in child care costs.

Both the cost of care and the level of wages available to the mother affect older children's school enrollment. However, these factors have different effects on boys' and girls' schooling. Higher prices for child care have no significant effect on boys' schooling but significantly decrease the probability that girls will attend school. While an increase in mothers' wages raises the school participation of boys, it decreases the school participation of girls.

Government subsidies for child care may increase the number of mothers who work outside the home, thus increasing the incomes of poor households and lifting some families out of poverty. Subsidies would also have a positive effect on the school participation of older girls in the household.

The results of this study clearly indicate that in addition to increasing the future productivity of children, low-cost ECD programs are likely to have more immediate benefits, that is, the twin effects of releasing mothers' time for paid work and of allowing older girls to participate in school. Thus, well-targeted ECD programs may be seen as optimal economic investments that affect both the current and future welfare of households with small children.

Notes

1. In a given simulation, a certain value of the variable of interest is assigned to all the households in the sample (for that reason, the proportion of the households in the "baseline" category used in tables 19.2 and 19.3 is not equal in the different simulations). The simulated probabilities are generated for each household by integrating over the estimated heterogeneity distribution and averaging the probabilities across the sample. Next, the value of the variable of interest is changed, and the new set of probabilities is generated. The effect of the changes in the particular parameter is calculated as the difference in these simulated probabilities.

2. While the authors are not aware of any studies that calculated comparable elasticities in Kenya, or in any other African country, the results from Uganda's National Commitment to Basic Education project (World Bank 2000) indicate that when free schooling was introduced in Uganda in 1997, primary school enrollment immediately doubled from 2.6 to 5.2 million children and reached 6.5 million in 1999. This result corresponds to elasticities comparable to those in this chapter.

References

Behrman, J. R., and J. C. Knowles. 1999. "Household Income and Child Schooling in Vietnam." *World Bank Economic Review* 13 (2): 211–56.

Bittencourt, S., and E. DiCicco. 1979. *Child Care Needs of Low-Income Women: Urban Brazil*. Washington, DC: Overseas Education Fund and League of Women Voters.

Dabalen, A. 2000. "Essays on Labor Markets in Two African Economies." Unpublished doctoral dissertation, University of California at Berkeley.

Deolalikar, A. 1998. *Primary and Secondary Education in Kenya*. Sector Review. Washington, DC: World Bank.

Deutsch, R. 1998. *Does Child Care Pay? Labor Force Participation and Earning Effects of Access to Child Care in the Favelas of Rio de Janeiro*. Washington, DC: Inter-American Development Bank.

Glinskaya, E., and M. Garcia. 1999. *Early Childhood Development Centers in Kenya*. Washington, DC: World Bank.

Kimmel, J. 1998. "Child Care Costs as a Barrier to Employment for Single and Married Mothers." *Review of Economics and Statistics* 80 (2): 287–99.

Lokshin, M., E. Glinskaya, and M. Garcia. 2004. "The Effect of Early Childhood Development Programs on Women's Labor Force Participation and Older Children's Schooling in Kenya." *Journal of African Economies* 13 (2): 240–76.

Mukui, J., and J. Mwaniki. 1995. "National Survey of Early Childhood Development Centers." Report prepared for the World Bank and Ministry of Education, Nairobi, Kenya.

Myers, R. 1992. "Towards an Analysis of the Cost and Effectiveness of Community-Based Early Childhood Education in Kenya: The Kilifi District." Report prepared for Aga Khan Foundation.

National Geospatial-Intelligence Agency. n.d. Retrieved November 25, 2006, from http://www.nga.mil.

Psacharopoulos, G., and A. Arriagada. 1989. "Determinants of Early Age Human Capital Formation: Evidence from Brazil." *Economic Development and Cultural Change* 37 (1): 683–708.

UNESCO (United Nations Educational, Scientific, and Cultural Organization). 2005. *Early Childhood Care and Education in Kenya: Policy Review Report*. Early Childhood and Family Policy Series, 11. UNESCO Education Sector, Division of Basic Education, Early Childhood and Inclusive Education Section. New York: UNESCO.

van der Gaag, J., and J.-P. Tan. 1998. *The Benefits of Early Child Development Programs: An Economic Analysis*. Washington, DC: World Bank.

World Bank. 1994. *Kenya Welfare Monitoring Survey II*. Retrieved November 6, 2006, from http://www.worldbank.org/.

————. 1997. "Staff Appraisal Report. Republic of Kenya Early Childhood Development Project." Washington, DC: World Bank.

————. 2000. *Can Africa Claim the 21st Century?* Washington, DC: World Bank.

CHAPTER 20

Madrasa Early Childhood Development Program: Making a Difference

Peter Mwaura and Bishara T. Mohamed

The Madrasa[1] Early Childhood Development Program is a regional initiative in East Africa that began in the 1980s. From its beginning in the Coast Province of Kenya in 1986, the program has resulted in the establishment of quality, affordable, culturally appropriate, and sustainable preschools among the socioeconomically disadvantaged Muslim communities in East Africa. It expanded to Zanzibar's two islands, Pemba and Unguja in 1990 and to Uganda in 1993. Although the program is similar in the three countries, each country works within is own context to meet the specific needs of its main partner, the communities.

The overall goal of the Madrasa Early Childhood Development Program is to improve the well-being of young children from marginalized communities through ensuring a supportive religious, cultural, and learning environment in their early years. More specifically, the community-based Madrasa Early Childhood Development Program aims to provide Muslim children in underprivileged communities with access to high quality, culturally relevant, and affordable early childhood programs that will ground them in Islam and increase their readiness for, access to, and success in later schooling.

The responsibility for the development and management of the Madrasa preschools lies with the communities who own and operate the schools. The process of creating and implementing Madrasa preschools is focused on building the capacity of community members, including teachers, members of school management committees (SMCs), parents and others, to provide quality services and create responsive and supportive educational institutions that are technically, financially, and organizationally sustainable.

Background

Prior to the establishment of the Madrasa Early Childhood Development Program, Muslim children in East Africa were a disadvantaged lot. They lacked access to quality, culturally appropriate, mainstream education from the preschool to the university level and were caught in a vicious cycle: lacking appropriate early childhood opportunities, many children did not enter into high-performing schools, they performed badly in primary school, attended poor secondary schools (if they attended at all), and had reduced opportunity for additional schooling, resulting in limited employment opportunities.

Those children who attended secular preschools went to Christian-sponsored schools in the morning and the traditional Quranic schools later in the day, leaving little time for leisure and play. In addition, exposure to two different curricula—one based on Christianity and the other based on Islam—became a source of cognitive, social, and spiritual dissonance.

The educational disadvantage of the Coast Province Muslims in Kenya has an historical root. According to Brown and Sumura's (1999) evaluation report, Christian missionaries introduced Western education in East Africa in the late 19th century. Apart from providing people with reading and writing skills, their motive was to convert people to Christianity. By the time Christian missionaries came to the region, Islam was already well established in the coastal areas of East Africa, mainly through the activities of traders from the Middle East. Missionary attempts at converting people through education came into conflict with the established Quranic schools. Western education therefore was not readily embraced; the majority of Muslim communities—not only in East Africa but in other parts of the world—were concerned (and still are) about how to get access to Western education without compromising values and identity.

That Muslims were educationally disadvantaged was acknowledged in the *Kenya Education Commission Report* of 1965 (commonly referred to as the Ominde report). The report said in part,

> We found that the major religions, notably Christianity and Islam, regarded the very educational process as one-sided and incomplete, unless informed with the spirit, values, and the standards of religion . . . Whereas education that has spread elsewhere in Kenya under Christian auspices has assumed a secular form, Islamic education is wholly centered in Islam as a religion and a social and cultural system . . . The need for secular education was clearly recognized, as was also the danger that a neglect of it would increasingly place Muslims at a disadvantage in meeting the demands of a modern world. What was wrong with secular education was that it was not good enough (Kenya 1965, 34–36).

The educational disadvantage of Muslim students was a growing concern. By the early 1980s some members of the Muslim communities came together to address the problem. They clearly realized that Muslim children needed to have access to secular education and that they needed to be prepared to do well in school, which meant they had to have quality early childhood experiences. Leaders in the Muslim communities had the will to create such a program, but the community did not have adequate resources—financial, or in terms of knowledge and skills—to do so. Some members of the Muslim community therefore approached His Highness the Aga Khan, through the Aga Khan Foundation (AKF) East Africa, to assist in the establishment of quality preschools in under-resourced Muslim communities that ensured that the teachings of Islam as well as services (health, community development, and parent involvement) were integral to the curriculum. This action led to the creation of the Madrasa Early Childhood Development Program.

Focus group discussions among local Islamic communities and the original donor (AKF) assessed the Islamic communities' needs and resources. These discussions resulted in a partnership among the local and national Islamic leadership and international donors to create an early childhood education program that acknowledged, recognized, and celebrated culturally relevant education, traditions, and resources while providing Muslim children with experiences that supported their development. A national committee was created, and a highly respected Muslim educator, Bi Swafiya Said, was hired as program director.

Goals

The goal of the Madrasa Early Childhood Development Program was to create an effective, community-based, low-cost approach to early childhood education that would promote educational excellence in Muslim children from low socioeconomic backgrounds. From the beginning, the cost of establishing and equipping the community early childhood development (ECD) centers was kept at a minimum to make the preschools affordable to poor communities.

Also from the beginning, communities have had to make a commitment to program implementation. Community resources and labor are used to construct the schools and build furniture and cupboards for the classrooms. To further support cost-effectiveness, the play, teaching, and learning equipment and aids are made from locally available materials.

Curriculum

A core belief of the Madrasa Early Childhood Development Program is that the role of the preschool is to facilitate the development of healthy personality, skills, and abilities that enable Muslim children to fit creatively in the dynamic world of work while retaining their moral, spiritual, and cultural identity. The child-centered curriculum that was created, while originally an adaptation of a Western curriculum, was modified to be more culturally appropriate, incorporating Islamic teaching and practices, as well as providing children with learning skills and preparing them to succeed in secular primary schools.

Islam is a way of life; therefore the Madrasa Early Childhood Development Program is designed to enhance the full development of the child within the traditional, cultural, and religious values of the family and the community. For example, in an Islamic context, childhood extends from the period in the womb until a child reaches puberty. Adulthood in Islam can therefore begin at an age as young as 9 years for girls and about 11 years for boys. In Islam it is clearly indicated that early childhood ends at the age 7, when children are introduced to and prepared for day-to-day religious activities and the development of life skills. For example, fasting and the five prayers are taught to children at the age of 7, and it becomes compulsory for children to fast and pray during the holy month of Ramadan after they reach puberty. Children younger than 7 are given many opportunities for play and are encouraged to use play materials. During early childhood, there is no gender segregation for children's activities.

These values, beliefs, and traditions were incorporated into the Islamic Preschool Curriculum (Early Childhood Education Project Committee 1990). It has been revised several times, and is again under revision.

Management and Governance

The Madrasa Early Childhood Development Program operates under Madrasa Resource Centers (MRCs) in Kenya, Uganda, and Zanzibar. The three MRCs are coordinated by a regional office, and each MRC is managed by a project director and governed by a Madrasa national board. The Madrasa program is supervised by a regional committee that is responsible for policy, academics, research, and community endowment. While members of the national boards are drawn from volunteers in each country, members of the national committee are national, regional, and international volunteers.

Operational Activities

The operational activities involve, among others, sensitizing, educating, mobilizing, motivating, and empowering the communities on ECD issues; training and mentoring preschool teachers; monitoring and evaluating the progress of program implementation; disseminating information to a wide variety of stakeholders, including donors, government, and communities; conducting research on important issues related to ECD and the impact of the preschools; and ensuring that the preschools are technically, financially, and organizationally sustainable.

Program Sequence

Communities pass through five phases as they establish and run their preschools: contact, contract, implementation, graduation/certification, and postgraduation.

Contact

The activity cycle starts with the MRC's community development officers meeting with community leaders. Over time, focus group discussions are held to identify and prioritize community needs for their children. Discussions provide an opportunity to create awareness of the importance of early stimulation, children's needs and rights, how young children grow and develop, roles of parents and the community in the growth and development of young children, and the benefits of educating young children.

Having accepted that education, and particularly preschool education, is critical in solving some of the problems in the community, more specific discussions are begun on how the community can establish a quality preschool. MRC staff also work with communities and community leaders to understand the resources available and the expectations of different community members if the community decides to start a preschool. Through the discussions, the roles and responsibilities of the community and the MRC are clarified and agreed upon.

Beginning at the contact stage, the communities are made to understand that they own the program. The process activates community commitment and willingness to establish a quality preschool. Beyond the short-term goals of sensitization and mobilization to create a preschool, the process awakens the community's consciousness to existing community problems; they become aware of their responsibility and ability to make a difference for their children, which both leads to the development of indigenous capacity through new knowledge, skills, and practices and encourages greater self-reliance.

Contract

It usually takes up to a year to establish whether communities have an interest in and are willing and ready to commit themselves to the requirements of the program. When communities decide to commit themselves to the project, a partnership agreement is signed with the MRC to formalize the process of working together to establish a Madrasa preschool. The contract clarifies the terms and conditions of interaction—including benefits and penalties—all of which are aimed at setting up a quality preschool.

The MRC agrees to provide an incentive grant of up to US$1,000 to improve the learning environment; provide two years of training for school management committee (SMC) members, teachers, and parents; work with the community to periodically evaluate the quality of the preschool; promote capacity building of community members in school management; and provide ongoing mentoring and support, even beyond graduation as a certified Madrasa preschool.

The community agrees to provide a school building (renovated or newly built) with a toilet and a playground; appoint or elect the SMC (at least 2 members must be women out of a minimum of 7 and a maximum of 11 members); and identify women to be trained as teachers. The newly appointed or elected SMC then starts the process of school registration and opens a bank account.

Implementation

The implementation phase involves, among other tasks, constructing or rehabilitating classrooms and other crucial structures necessary to create a quality teaching and learning environment; training and mentoring teachers; and training and supporting the SMCs.

Once implementation is underway, communities and MRC staff together evaluate schools every six months. At the end of each evaluation, they hold joint meetings to agree on the progress made and to set up objectives to improve the performance of the school before the next evaluation. This process is very important in making communities understand elements of quality preschool education, and it puts the onus on communities to ensure they manage quality preschools. After two to three years of intensive training, support, monitoring, and evaluation, the preschool program graduates.

Graduation and Certification

As noted, the MRC and SMCs work together to evaluate the extent to which the schools have satisfactorily met the criteria for community involvement, a quality teaching and learning environment, and responsible management as set out in the contract. Madrasa preschools that meet quality standards are then certified and graduated. Teachers and school managers are also certified. Parents are acknowledged for their participation and given a certificate of appreciation for their involvement. Once graduated, schools usually become members of the Madrasa Graduated School Association (GA), which is managed by its membership.

Postgraduation

The MRC gives ongoing support to the teachers and the communities of the graduated schools by mentoring and providing in-service courses for the teachers and further training for SMCs and GA members.

Table 20.1 presents data on the scope of the three East African MRCs in 2005. The program has graduated 153 preschools and nearly 20,000 preschool children; it has trained more than 6,000 teachers and SMC members through long, medium, and short courses.

Research within the MRC Program

The monitoring and evaluation system created in the MRC program is geared toward ensuring that the schools provide sustainable high-quality teaching and learning environments and practices as well as effective

Table 20.1. Primary Beneficiaries of the Madrasa Resource Center Program as of 2005

	Kenya	Uganda	Zanzibar	Total
Preschools contracted	66	50	74	**190**
Schools graduated	51	38	64	**153**
Children graduated	4,795	3,963	11,064	**19,822**
Children enrolled in MRC preschool in 2005	3,035	2,331	4,743	**10,109**
Girls enrolled in MRC preschool in 2005 (percent)	47.6	49.2	50.4	**49.1**
MRC teachers trained in two-year course	479	189	593	**1,261**
Other teachers trained in one-year course	2	26	258	**286**
Other teachers trained in short course	918	1,469	229	**2,616**
School management committee members trained and in training	797	271	849	**1,917**

Source: Mwaura 2006.

management and financial systems to ensure the maximum positive outcomes for children, now and in the future.

Research has played a key role throughout the history of the MRCs. In preparation for the program, several studies were conducted to better understand the reasons why Muslim children were not gaining access to primary school and not doing well when they attended. Poor preparation was one of the key issues. The Madrasa preschool program was developed based on the results of these studies.

Four years into the program, AKF commissioned a tracer study (Wamahiu 1995) to assess the impact of the intervention on the later school success of children who were part of the program in 1987 and 1988. The impact of the MRC could be seen. The study found, among other promising results, that MRC graduates were consistently ranked among the top pupils in standard 1, and they generally fell in the upper 20 percent in the subsequent classes up to standard 4.

In 1999 a longitudinal study was set up to conduct more systematic research of the MRC environment. The study sampled eight MRC schools from among those schools that had graduated by 1999 in each of the three countries and compared them with non-MRC preschools. Using an adapted version of the Early Childhood Environment Rating Scale (ECERS) the study found that MRC preschools have a better quality teaching and learning environment than normative preschools in each country (Mwaura 2004).

In early 2000, a more extensive study was undertaken to assess the impact of the Madrasa program on the teaching and learning environment and on the cognitive development of children from Madrasa and non-Madrasa preschools.[2] The study asked four questions:

- Does a preschool experience make a difference in the cognitive development of children?
- Does the type of preschool provision make a difference in the cognitive development of children?
- What is the quality of the teaching and learning environment provided for preschool children?
- Does the quality of the teaching and learning environment influence the cognitive development of preschool children?

The study sample included 17 preschools in Kenya (9 MRC and 8 non-MRC preschools), 18 preschools in Uganda (13 MRC and 5 non-MRC), and 18 preschools in Zanzibar (10 MRC and 8 non-MRC).

Quantitative and qualitative methods were used to answer questions. For each school, demographic data were collected and the teaching, learning, and play environments were assessed in terms of indoor space, furnishings, learning materials, outdoor space, and equipment. Teaching methods were observed and the school financial and management records were reviewed. Schools were assessed in terms of their accessibility and the sufficiency and appropriateness of equipment and materials. School management was also examined.

One-to-one interviews were conducted with teachers on selected areas of interest, for example, their training. Some members of the SMCs were also interviewed. Focus group discussions were held with parents, SMCs, and teachers. They addressed topics related to perceived successes to date, an assessment of the challenges ahead, and their vision for the future.

At least two persons were involved during the assessment in each school—the lead researcher and one MRC staff member, who would either be the director, the lead trainer, or the monitoring, evaluation, and research liaison officer.

The results indicated that compared with other normative preschool programs in East Africa, including the government District Centers for Early Childhood Education (DICECE) in Kenya, Madrasa preschool children enjoy a better learning environment. The Madrasa preschools were found to be better on all of the environmental dimensions assessed using the revised edition of the Early Childhood Environment Rating Scale (ECERS-R) by Harms and Clifford (1998) and the curriculum-related

extension (ECERS-E) by Sylva et al. (1999). In this chapter the revised
and the extended ECERS are referred to as ECERS-RE. The MRC
preschools were significantly better on 73 percent of the dimensions,
compared with normative preschools. The highest rating for the MRC
preschools was teacher-child interaction (mean = 5.1), followed by literacy (mean = 4.6), early mathematics (mean = 4.4), and language and
reasoning (mean = 3.9). Learning activities and science were rated the
lowest, below the minimum acceptable standard.

Madrasa preschools were found to have a total mean score higher
than the non-Madrasa preschools. The mean total ECERS-RE scores for
the MRC preschools was found to be 4.1 (SD = 0.78, range = 1.77–5.3)
while that of non-MRC preschools was 3.025 (SD = 0.87 and range =
1.48–5.6; see figure 20.1).

The study sampled 464 children (221 boys and 243 girls): 157 and 174
children were from non-Madrasa and Madrasa preschools respectively
and 133 children were from homes. The sample included all three countries, Kenya (144), Uganda (99), and Zanzibar (221). The children were

**Figure 20.1. Learning Environment Scores in MRC and Non-MRC Preschools in
Kenya, Uganda, and Zanzibar**

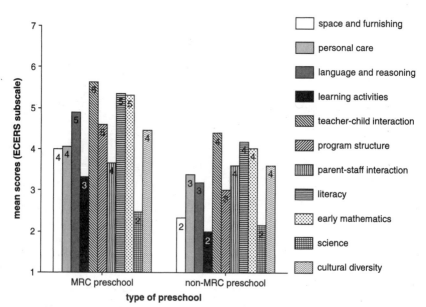

Source: Mwaura 2006.
Note: ECERS = Early Childhood Environment Rating Scale.

tested at three points: pretest, posttest 1, and posttest 2. A standardized assessment was conducted, adapted from the British Ability Scales (Elliott, Murray, and Pearson 1978) and the African Child Test. The sample was controlled for age, gender, cohort, country, parental education, and number of siblings in a family. Repeated ANOVA[3] measures and t-tests were used in the data analysis.

Figure 20.2 presents the rate of change in mean test scores on cognitive measures between the pretest, posttest 1, and posttest 2, by whether children had a preschool experience. Clearly those children who had a preschool experience performed better than those who remained at home during the preschool years.

Overall, the MRC preschools provide the greatest value added in terms of children's intellectual development. Children from MRC preschools did significantly better than either those who did not attend preschool or those who attended other preschools in East Africa. MRC preschool children had a margin of 42 percent higher value-added mean scores against the home children. Also MRC preschool children later perform better in school, as compared with other children either from home or from other

Figure 20.2. Rate of Change in Cognitive Measures of Children in Preschool and Those at Home

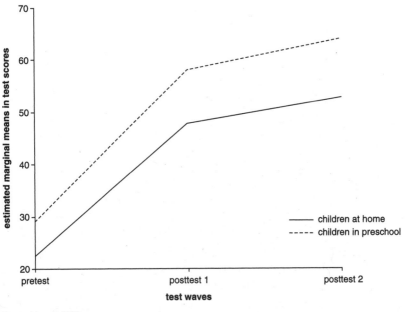

Source: Mwaura 2006.

normative preschools. Children from the MRC preschool programs were more likely to be ranked in the upper half of their class on examinations, compared with children from home (with no preschool experience) or those from other preschools. Their superior performance is notable; from the time of their primary school admission interviews, MRC children perform much better than other children, according to teachers.

The difference between preschool children's intellectual performance and the performance of those who do not attend preschool was evident as early as 60 days after the preschool year began. During preschool, girls were relatively but not significantly better than boys in intellectual performance. However, once in primary school, significantly more girls were in the upper half of examination score distribution than boys in all the first four grades. While more data collection and analysis are required on the percentage of children who remain in school across the preschool and home children, the initial analysis indicates a higher rate of remaining in school for those who had a preschool experience than for those who did not attend preschool.

Mwaura (2004) drew the following conclusions from the impact study:

- Preschool experience has a significant and positive influence on the cognitive development of children.
- The gains in cognitive development are larger for preschool children than for children who stay home.
- The gains in cognitive development are larger for Madrasa preschool children than for non-Madrasa preschool children.
- The quality of the environment is a significant predictor of cognitive development.
- The quality is higher in Madrasa preschools than in non-Madrasa preschools.
- MRC children enjoy a comparatively better indoor and outdoor play and learning environment, particularly in the areas of language, human interaction, mathematics, and literacy.
- The psychosocial climate as indicated by the teacher-child interaction is better in MRC than in non-MRC preschools.
- MRC graduates have a comparative advantage in psychosocial and cognitive performance and enter into primary school comparatively more ready to learn.
- Gains are greater in cognitive development among Madrasa preschool children between entry into preschool (posttest 1) and first year than in the subsequent year (between posttest 1 and posttest 2).

Impact of the Program on the Community

Although the program has not carried out a study to show the impact of the MRC program on teachers and SMCs, observations from MRC teacher trainers and community development officers indicate a positive outcome. Members of SMCs, about 40 percent of whom are women, are working in many other community programs, thus contributing to the development of their communities. The preschool teachers, who are either primary school graduates or those who dropped out before completing secondary school, are now gainfully employed professionals. They are valued and respected in the community and they take leadership in various community activities. They act as role models for young girls in the community (Morgan and Muigai 2000).

To complement the quantitative impact studies, Mwaura (2002) also carried out a qualitative study of effectiveness. He identified the following features of the Madrasa preschool program that are fundamental to making the program effective:

- *The starting point is readiness.* Readiness is characterized by the community's ability to identify not only their problems but also their strengths and weaknesses and their belief in the long-term benefits that would accrue as a result of the intervention.
- *People make a difference.* MRC staff identified the local mosque committee as the key to entering communities. The spiritual respect that is given to the members of the mosque committee facilitates a smooth entry to the community, but not without some resistance. A key in overcoming the resistance was the person who initiated the process, in this case a highly respected woman known to the communities.
- *Working with the context leads to the development and implementation of appropriate strategies and activities.* The MRC operational framework is based on the social conditions, strengths, values, and expressed needs of the community. This framework resulted in the creation of a preschool education system that is economically, socially, and culturally sensible, accessible, and appropriate.
- *Management and governance structures at all levels support operations from the regional office to the communities.* Each structure has a specific responsibility that complements and is interlinked with the other, and all are accountable to make the program a success. This structure is linked to the national and regional bodies, which ensure quality through policies, guidance, and resources.

- *A quality control system ensures quality provision.* Quality in MRC operations includes community sensitization, mobilization, and empowerment by the community development officers; the training and mentoring operations by the trainers; and the monitoring and evaluation unit headed by a monitoring, evaluation, and research liaison officer. This system allows adequate support and supervision for those implementing the program.
- *A simple but comprehensive system of monitoring and evaluation, reflection, and feedback is fundamental.* The MRC places strong emphasis on reflective practices through integrated and participatory monitoring and evaluation. Based on the belief that each staff person contributes to the program, the system involves all stakeholders in the assessment exercise, which is organized as a capacity-building and development activity.
- *Intrinsic and extrinsic motivation, at the individual and community levels, is defined and actualized by the program.* The MRC has endeavored to instill the spirit of unity, hard work, and volunteerism. It operates under the human and spiritual philosophy of service to Allah and community, which forms the mystique behind individual and community participation in the program. The program has created a sense of mutual complementarity, responsibility, and accountability.
- *The community and MRC preschool partnership, which is established and sealed by a signed contract, is another feature of program effectiveness.* The contract gives a common vision, objectives, and direction to the working partners who are monitored and evaluated, and it culminates in the graduation of Madrasa preschools, signifying the success of the partnership and the accomplishment of the contract.
- *A donor program partnership, based on mutual respect—rather than just funds—is critical.* A relationship characterized by guidance and facilitation, rather than supervision, has been built between the funding agent and the program from the beginning. The Aga Khan Foundation, while retaining its donor status, gives crucial guidance to the program as well as freedom for the implementers to decide on their activities.
- *Challenges are part of the dynamics of an effective program.* Effectiveness does not necessarily mean challenge-free development. What is important is the way the challenges are perceived by staff and the community. It works when challenges are perceived as options.
- *The strength of a program lies in the people who are involved, beginning with the recruitment process and supporting continued investment in the development of individuals over time.* Investment in people is at the core of the

MRC. In an evaluation of the MRC, Waithaka (1999, 16) reported that, "The three MRCs are well staffed with appropriate caliber of staff that are generally enthusiastic about their work and are sufficiently knowledgeable about the target communities' educational, social, economic, cultural, and political situation. They appear to have the right attitudes toward, and are empathetic with, the target communities."

- *Processes in a program evolve over time.* In MRC the processes of mobilizing communities, training teachers, and monitoring and evaluating preschools have all developed over time; they are constantly under review. It is important to allow room for trying, sharing, and evaluating innovative ideas.
- *Integration has both content and contextual dimensions.* The content integration at MRC combines secular, religious, and cultural education and it also integrates education, food, health, moral, and psychosocial services. Contextual integration includes all stakeholders, not just in relation to what they bring to the program but also in how they benefit directly or indirectly from the program.
- *Focus on the outcomes.* Policy, operational, and managerial effectiveness are assessed by the results in the human product. Defining the primary beneficiary as the child, the program process must be linked to a positive impact on children's growth and development. The program must also be seen to have a sustainable impact on the participating community, particularly their awareness of local needs, the availability of community resources, and their ability to tackle many of their own challenges.

Conclusion

The Madrasa Early Childhood Development Program was initiated from the needs of poor Muslim communities and developed using existing structures and resources complemented with child development principles. The growth and development of the program, which has been a process based on reflective practices, has evolved into a learning system where lessons learned are translated into practice that takes the program forward. The program demonstrates many effective features; the impact study carried out between 2000 and 2004 has shown that Madrasa preschools have a comparatively good teaching and learning environment, and that children from these preschools tend to perform comparatively well cognitively.

The success of the Madrasa preschool program is also exemplified by the facts that (1) non-Muslim children are now joining the program; (2) many of the communities in all three countries are planning to start primary schools that offer an integrated primary curriculum; (3) some of the teachers are being "poached" to teach in private preschools; (4) several Madrasa-trained teachers have started their own preprimary schools that use an active learning approach; (5) the program started with a strategy of reaching out to communities, which has shifted to a situation where communities now reach out to the MRC for the services; (6) the program is now a major player in the development and implementation of national policy systems; (7) the program has been consulted by the government as well as nongovernmental agencies working on community mobilization, providing training for ECD, developing policy, creating teaching and learning materials, developing curriculum, and creating ongoing monitoring and evaluation systems and documentation related to early childhood education; and (8) the program is now visible beyond East Africa; Mozambique and some West African countries have sought assistance in establishing a similar program in those countries.

In conclusion, the Madrasa Early Childhood Development Program in East Africa has, in a sure, systematic, and committed way, demonstrated that children learning in a quality preschool can benefit at preschool and beyond. Paraprofessionals can be adequately equipped to deliver quality interventions in low-income settings; and poor communities can be empowered to invest time and resources in school provision and maintenance. The program has shown that even very poor communities have strengths that can be mobilized for the welfare of the whole community. Preschools can be sustained over time without ongoing donor supports, and preschool models can be designed to address the specific cultural and religious needs of a group and be appropriately adapted for populations with diverse cultural and religious backgrounds. Well-developed preschool programs with well-planned operational strategies can affect early childhood policy and delivery systems at national and local levels to improve the appropriateness, quality, and integration of programs and services for young children.

Notes

1. See Mwaura (2006).
2. In the impact study, Mwaura (2004) was supported by Prof. Kathy Sylva and Dr. Lars-Erik Malmberg of Oxford University.
3. Analysis of variance (ANOVA) is a collection of statistical models and their associated procedures in which the observed variance is partitioned into components due to different explanatory variables.

References

Brown, G. J., and S. Sumura. 1999. *The East Africa Madrasa Programme: The Madrasa Resource Centers and Their Community-Based Preschool Programme*. Geneva: Aga Khan Foundation.

Early Childhood Education Project Committee. 1990. *The Islamic Preschool Curriculum*. Mombasa: Madrasa Preschool Resource Center.

Elliott, C. D., J. D. Murray, and L. S. Pearson. 1978. *The British Ability Scales*. London: NFER-Nelson Publishing Co., Ltd.

Harms, T., and R. Clifford. 1998. *Early Childhood Rating Scale*. New York: Teachers College Press.

Kenya. 1965. *Kenya Education Commission Report*. Nairobi: Government Printers.

Morgan, P., and S. Muigai. 2000. *Canadian International Development Agency Program Evaluation: The Work of the Aga Khan Foundation in the Education Sector in East Africa*. Ottawa: Canadian International Development Agency.

Mwaura, P. 2002. "The Foundation of Madrasa Resource Center Programme Effectiveness." Paper presented at the "Effectiveness Initiative Workshop," Ahmedabad, India.

————. 2004. "Preschool Play and Learning Environment: A Study of the Quality of Pedagogical Ecology and Its Relationship to the Cognitive Development of Preschool Children in East Africa." PhD thesis. Kenyatta University, Kenya.

————. 2006. "Madrasa Resource Center Early Childhood Development Programme: Making a Difference." Draft paper.

Sylva, K., I. Siraj-Blatchford, B. Taggart, and P. Coleman. 1999. *The Early Childhood Environment Rating Scale Extension (ECERS-E): Four Curricular Subscales* (draft). London: Institute of Education.

Waithaka, D. 1999. *Organizational Development Assessment Report*. Mombasa: Madrasa Resource Center.

Wamahiu, S. P. 1995. *The Impact of the Integrated Madrasa Nursery Intervention Programme on Later School Success of Muslim Children in Mombasa: The Tracer Study Continued*. Nairobi: Aga Khan Foundation.

CHAPTER 21

Linking Policy Discourse to Everyday Life in Kenya: Impacts of Neoliberal Policies on Early Education and Childrearing

Elizabeth Swadener, Patrick Wachira,
Margaret Kabiru, and Anne Njenga

While Kenya did not follow a socialist path to postindependence nation building, as did several African nations (for example, Mozambique and Tanzania), its early postcolonial policies did reflect principles of universal access to education, health care, and other services often associated with the "welfare state." For example, for many (if not all) Kenyans, basic education, primary health care, and associated goods and services were free and relatively available for several years after their nation gained independence from the British in 1963. Like many Sub-Saharan African and Latin American nations, Kenya accrued large-scale debts to several multinational development banks, most notably the World Bank and the International Monetary Fund (IMF). Debt restructuring conditions and pressures from external donors have led to cost-cutting "austerity measures" that have undermined what remains of a "welfare state" in Kenya and directly affected the majority of families raising children (Gakuru and Koech 1995; Swadener, Kabiru, and Njenga 2000; Swadener and

Wachira 2003; Weisner, Bradley, and Kilbride 1997). Additionally, pressures of corporate globalization and free-market-based trade liberalization, combined with urbanization and associated family dislocation, rising unemployment, government corruption and economic mismanagement, and a worsening national infrastructure, have adversely affected Kenyan families. These patterns reflect larger patterns of neoliberal policy, as summarized by Tikly (2001, 165):

> The fragility of the African state in the context of international relations and the postcolonial status quo has ensured that many African states are more susceptible to global forces than are wealthier nations. This susceptibility provided the conditions of much of the imposition from the early 1980s of a new neoliberal orthodoxy in the political economy that has disrupted indigenous postcolonial hegemonic projects and accumulation strategies . . . this orthodoxy has severe implications for all areas of social welfare, including education, and has served to exacerbate social stratification.

In using a postcolonial lens to analyze impacts of structural adjustment programs (now termed "poverty reduction strategies") and other neoliberal policies on children and families in Kenya, we draw from Tikly (2001) who asserts that a central concern of using postcolonial critique is to "re-narrativize" (Hall 1996, cited in Tikly 2001, 152) the globalization story in a way that "places historically marginalized parts of the world at the center, rather than at the periphery of, in this case, education and globalization debates." Tikly further asserts that,

> Such a postcolonial critique is also centrally concerned with continuing impact on education systems of European colonialism and with issues of race, culture, and language, as well as other forms of social stratification, including class and gender in postcolonial contexts. A postcolonial critique draws attention to the transnational aspects of globalization and of social inequalities and seeks to highlight forms of resistance to Western hegemony (Tikly 2001).

A number of contexts for this chapter cannot be discussed in depth, but deserve mention. These include social and cultural contexts; background on Kenya's precolonial, colonial, and postcolonial history; and an understanding of frameworks for educational and social policy in Africa. We are aware of a large body of literature that constructs the African political and economic climate as in crisis. As Parpart and Staudt (1989, 1) put it more than a decade ago, "development first preoccupied Africanist literature, but crisis is now the dominant theme." It could be argued that the dominant theme in the new millennium is economic globalization and its impacts on Africa. We find fault with both dependency theory and statist perspectives for not sufficiently understanding the local contradictions and complexities of family life in Kenya or any other Sub-Saharan African nation. Thus, in our analysis of the impacts of neoliberal policies, we recognize the agency, resistance, and creativity that children and families in difficult circumstances in Kenya and other Sub-Saharan African nations experience in daily life. We also acknowledge the complexity and contradictions of locally enacted practices of popular culture in contemporary African contexts as we frame a postcolonial critique of neoliberal policies in Kenya.

In contrast to tenets of the welfare state, neoliberal policies emphasize free trade, deregulation, privatization, and decentralization of government programs and replace the idea of the public good or universal rights of citizens with individual responsibility and governmental accountability. The related discourse of blame, or "pathologizing of poverty" (Polakow 1993; Swadener and Lubeck 1995) in the United States and elsewhere (Polakow, Halskov, and Jorgensen 2001; Sibley 1995) has added to a recurrent deficit discourse that constructs those in poverty as having only themselves to blame. The radical restructuring and devolution of welfare policy and cutbacks in entitlement programs in the United States is well documented (for example, Cannella 2003; Ehrenreich 2001; Gordon 1994; Mink 1998; Polakow 1993; Schram 2000). The U.S. discourse has changed to reflect such "postwelfare" policies, including some states renaming social workers "self-sufficiency coaches" and some state social service agencies adopting the slogan "zero tolerance for unemployment." All such changes evidence a shift from entitlements to employment (though rarely providing a living wage or benefits), and away from education and work-related training to immediate job or volunteer placement.

Additionally, and much in evidence in African contexts including Kenya, cutting public expenditures for social services and national infrastructure (including roads, water, energy, and environmental protections) while deunionizing and reducing workers' rights and wages, are hallmarks of neoliberalism. In Kenya and across Africa, user fees and privatization of former state-run free services and resources are frequently part of the Structural Adjustment Programs (SAPs) and Poverty Reduction Strategy (PRS) initiatives. These economic reforms initiated at the behest of the World Bank and the IMF are based on a greater recognition of the role of the private sector, thus lay great emphasis on government divestiture from service delivery in many sectors. Particularly troubling has been the privatization of water whereby the government is seeking to move away from direct provision of water services and cede that authority to private water providers. This policy, provided under the *Water Act 2000* that sets out the legal framework for implementing the policy, would disadvantage the poor. Downsizing the civil service has also contributed to unemployment, which reached more than 60 percent in 2003.

For theoretical framings of our discussion of child and family policy and the "welfare state" in Kenya, we draw from postcolonial theories (Bhabha 1994; Dimitriadis and McCarthy 2001; Gandhi 1998; Mignolo 2000; p'Bitek 1986; Spivak 1999; wa Thiong'o 1993; Willinsky 1998) and theories of "postsocialist" conditions, including work by Fraser (1989, 1997), Gordon (1990, 1994), Polakow (1993), and Polakow, Halskov, and Jorgensen (2001). An understanding of Kenyan governing patterns and education policies is particularly informed by hybridity theory (for example, Bhabha 1994; McCarthy 1998; Spivak 1999), which deconstructs cross-migratory patterns, relationships between colonizers and colonized, and hybrid forms of information, policy, and shifting, mutually influenced practices. We also briefly raise possibilities for "decolonizing research methodologies" (Mutua and Swadener 2004; Smith 1999) in the context of collaborative research. Throughout this chapter, we reflect on the notion of governing the child, framed by Rose (1999), who asserted that "childhood is the most intensively governed sector of personal existence," and that "the child—as an idea and a target—has become inextricably connected to the aspirations of authorities" (p. 123). Similarly, we have appreciated the work of Hultqvist and Dahlberg (2001) on governing the child "in the new millennium," and we agree that there is "need for a continual critical scrutiny of the past, not for the sake of the past but for the sake of the present." As these authors further state, "today's discourses on the child reassemble past discourses in new patterns and inscribe different assumptions about the child" (p. 6).

This framing has led to several questions that we continue to reflect upon as they pertain to African contexts, particularly Kenya. How might the village raising its children differ from, and in, postmodern governmentalities, including the regulation of the child and family? How have increasingly globalized Western influences and related hybridity issues in postcolonial Kenya influenced social policy and governing patterns as they pertain to children and families?

Education Postindependence: From Harambee to the National Alliance Rainbow Coalition

Kenya attained independence in 1963. At the time, there was a need for an education system to replace the underdeveloped and racially segregated system that Kenya inherited from the colonial era. To meet the social, economic, and political goals of the newly independent country; foster a sense of nationhood and national unity; promote social equality and respect; and restore the cultural heritage of Kenyan people (Eshiwani 1990), a highly centralized education system was established in which government exercised control through financing and regulation. The government, however, continued to welcome the participation of the missions and other volunteer organizations in the provision of education.

Shortly after independence, however, it became increasingly evident that the government lacked sufficient resources to meet the population's demand for greater access to education. Thus, the Harambee schools were established, building on a grassroots spirit of education and child care from the Mau Mau independence struggle. These schools were community self-help projects in the spirit of Harambee, meaning "to pull together" for development. Grassroots communities, self-help groups, and the general population (*wananchi*) pooled their financial and material resources by constructing a building, donating a cow, or providing other materials for a local school or preschool.

Education policy in Kenya, as in most African nations, took various forms in its early, postindependence days. Cutting across political ideologies at the time of independence and shortly after, most emerging African nations had phenomenal growth in education and gave funding priority to education while always within resource-limited governments and governing strategies. Since independence, education in Kenya accounts for the largest portion of the government's expenditure: approximately 33 percent of the national budget is spent on education (Kathuri 2006), compared with 15 percent after independence in 1963 (Nieuwenhuis 1996), although less than 1 percent of the national budget goes to early childhood education and development. Significant progress was made in providing universal education to Kenyans, with the national enrollment rate in primary education reaching 95 percent in 1991, compared with 50 percent at independence. The high enrollment in primary education can be largely attributed to the combined efforts of the government, parents, local communities (Harambee movement), and nongovernmental organizations (NGOs). Postcolonial education in East Africa has been critiqued as reflecting the myth of modernization through schooling and Western education (Ferguson 1999; Vavrus 2002). As Vavrus (2002, 1) reflects, "the belief in a linear progression from underdevelopment to development by building more schools and increasing literacy rates has undergirded both socialist and liberal development policies since independence."

Primary schools did not historically charge fees, although cost-sharing measures related to structural adjustment programs have included fees for enrollment, testing, uniforms, books, building funds or Harambee fundraisers, and other incidental costs. The government meets the operational costs of running public schools through the Ministry of Education, Science, and Technology (MOEST). The government, through the Kenya Teachers Service Commission (TSC), is also charged with training teachers and paying salaries. Government spending on the development of school facilities, including teachers' housing, is minimal, and the responsibility is left largely to the Parent-Teacher Associations (PTAs), school committees, and the local community through Harambee or self-help schemes.

Presidential elections in Kenya in December 2002 ushered in a new government after 39 years of Kenya African National Union (KANU) party rule. Since that time, a number of policy issues affecting children and families have changed. In particular, the new government moved rapidly to fulfill its preelection promise of providing free and compulsory primary education to all public school students, starting with the new school year in 2003. The policy to provide free and compulsory education (also referred to as universal primary education) was in line with the campaign pledge of the new ruling party, the National Alliance Rainbow Coalition (NARC), and with the *Children's Act* (Kenya 2001), passed in 2002. The latter calls for free and compulsory education, conforming to the international charters that Kenya has ratified, including the *Declaration on Education for All* (EFA) at the World Education Conference in Jomtien, Thailand, in 1990 and the 2000 World Education Forum in Dakar, Senegal.

Free primary education was predicted to benefit more than 3 million children eligible for school who had been out of school due to numerous levies charged as part of mandated cost sharing. Primary school enrollment stood at 85 percent in 2002, down from 95 percent in 1990 (Rugene and Njeru 2003). Prior to the reintroduction of free primary education in early 2003, 6.2 million children were enrolled in Kenyan public primary schools (Siringi 2003) and, with the new policy, more than 1.5 million additional children have enrolled. Early childhood education enrollment stands at 35 percent of all eligible children and is anticipated to increase, although one initial impact of free primary education was the funding cuts to other programs, including early childhood/preprimary education. While free primary education was a welcome change, it happened rapidly and without the necessary infrastructure or a capacity-building plan for absorbing the large number of students who entered or reentered school. For example, there are insufficient classrooms, school furniture, or teachers for the influx of more than 1 million new learners. The additional resources availed by the government and its development partners to fund the free primary education provided for textbooks, stationery, science kits, and other instructional materials to the primary schools. Nontuition fees (including uniforms, food, some textbook fees, and other costs) are still in place, presenting barriers to many families—particularly those in the slums and those hit by HIV/AIDS, including the guardians of the nearly 1 million AIDS orphans in Kenya. Note that of the estimated 2.3 million orphans in Kenya, 46 percent are considered by UNICEF to have been orphaned as a result of HIV/AIDS (UNICEF 2006).

Early Childhood Care and Education in Kenya

In 1971 the government (with the assistance of the Bernard van Leer Foundation from the Netherlands) established the Preschool Education Project, based at the Kenya Institute of Education (KIE). Prior to that time, early childhood education (preprimary education for children ages 3–6) was the responsibility of local communities, NGOs, churches, and other volunteer organizations. By 1980, the Ministry of Education (MOE) took over full responsibility from the Ministry of Culture and Social Services and created preschool sections at MOE headquarters and the inspectorate. In 1984, the National Center for Early Childhood Education (NACECE) was established, in part for training preschool teachers, developing and disseminating appropriate curricula, and coordinating with external partners and other government agencies (Swadener, Kabiru, and Njenga 2000). Preschool teachers are not hired through the Kenyan government, although their training is facilitated by NACECE and the DICECE (District Centers for Early Childhood Education). Most rural preschools, for example, function on a Harambee basis, with a local community hiring the teacher, constructing the building, and providing other needed resources (such as a feeding program). This situation reflects a frequent (international) division between preschool and primary education, in which preschool programs and teachers' employment are private and locally governed.

Thus, the regulation and monitoring of preschools in Kenya (through national guidelines, district and local school inspectors, and DICECE trainers) reflects an interesting mix of indigenous and universal, mainly Western, assumptions about child development, "quality," and advocated "best practices." An emphasis on building national identity in a culturally diverse society and joining the international community reflects growing globalization—even as it is reflected in governing the youngest citizens and their preschool teachers and programs. Assumptions about universal "best practices" in early childhood education also permeate Kenyan early childhood guidelines and training, although most are balanced with traditional childrearing information (for example, the values of using traditional weaning foods, mother tongue stories, and intergenerational care). The Kenyan *Guidelines for Preschool Education* (Kenya Institute of Education 2000) were based on earlier United Nations Children's Fund (UNICEF) documents (Kabiru, personal communication), again demonstrating the hybridity of policy development and the influence of global donors. The guidelines tend to reflect the discourse of many other nations' early childhood planning documents, underscoring the shared discursive framing of the governing of childhood that has been part of national/international or local/global discourses.

Gender Issues: Economic and Social Marginalization

Women in precolonial Kenya occupied relatively prominent positions of power that were highly revered in the community's economic, political, and religious life (Chege and Sifuna 2006). Women had substantial rights to control the production and ownership of what was produced (Kiluva-Ndunda 2001). Much of their traditional authority and autonomy has been lost in colonial and postcolonial Kenya. In the colonial period, women were systematically and deliberately sidelined in the provision of education and in all sectors of social and economic development (Chege and Sifuna 2006). Colonialism introduced urbanization and intensified class and gender differences that existed in precapitalist societies (Robertson and Berger 1986). In postcolonial Kenya the gender segregation in the workforce has persisted, which can be traced to policies with roots in the colonial period, in which career training institutionalized a gender-segregated workforce (Chege and Sifuna 2006; Kiluva-Ndunda 2001).

By imposing a tax on each household, the colonial administration introduced a monetary economy that forced many Kenyan men to leave their homes, thus abandoning their traditional roles as farmers and household heads to work for wages on the settlers' farms. This absence placed considerable burdens on the women who were left behind to perform not only their traditional chores but also the work of the absent men. The new domestic roles for women yielded a new family economy that positioned women, in practical terms, as the de facto household heads (Chege and Sifuna 2006). In contemporary Kenya, women continue to bear the main responsibility for the welfare of Kenyan families, and one-third of Kenyan households are headed by a female (Adams and Mburugu 1994; Kilbride and Kilbride 1990), typically a single mother. Paid labor continues to be gender-segregated in postcolonial Kenya; women are frequently dominated and exploited. Males, for example, accounted for 79.1 percent of total formal employment, and women accounted for only 20.9 percent in 1989 (Kiluva-Ndunda 2001). Women also earn significantly less than males in all occupations. Girls and women are often oppressed in other ways, especially those dependent on their husbands, who yield more power economically and socially in Kenyan society. Women cannot inherit property; wife beating, rape, wife inheritance, and forced circumcision are all aspects of life among several of the ethnic groups in Kenya (Kilbride, Suda, and Njeru 2000; Ombuor 2001). Kilbride, Suda, and Njeru (2000) observed that having a baby before marriage may expose a girl to punishment by her parents or relatives and expulsion from school.

Against this backdrop of economic and social disadvantages for women, the *Children's Act* (Kenya 2001) considers children born out of wedlock the responsibility of the mother alone. There is no legal responsibility on the part of the father to support and maintain his illegitimate child unless he wishes to accept that responsibility and applies for such responsibility in court (Amisi 2001). Some child advocates have argued that the *Children's Act* should have incorporated the substance of the 1959 *Affiliation Act*, which became an Act of Parliament at independence. This legislation enabled the mother of a child born out of wedlock to seek a maintenance court order against the father in a range of circumstances, but it was repealed in 1969. In 2002, a children's rights group was helping a mother and her 2-year-old child to challenge a section of the *Children's Act* in High Court, saying that the new law discriminates against children born out of wedlock (Koome 2002). As Martha Koome, chair of the International Federation of Women Lawyers in Kenya, stated,

> It is very disheartening to know that child maintenance issues may have been more advanced in 1959, when the *Affiliation Ordinance* came into force, than today, when we have a *Convention on the Rights of the Child* and *The African Charter on the Rights and Welfare of the Child* (Koome 2002).

Widespread rural to urban migration caused by poverty and the devaluing of Kenyan agriculture has also contributed to the number of single-parent families, a phenomenon often described as dislocation (Kilbride and Kilbride 1990). Many female-headed households live in the sprawling slums of Kenya's major cities, particularly Nairobi, or remain in the rural areas with the father leaving to find work in a town or city. Austerity measures and a worsening economy have greatly affected mothers, as they often have little education due to a number of factors, including past discriminatory education policies that prevented equal participation in formal education, high dropout rates (due to exorbitant fees, parents would rather educate boys when where there is not enough money to educate both), high pregnancy rates, sociocultural perceptions about the role of women in the society (such as women should be dependent on men), cultural expectations and values (such as fear that a highly educated girl might have difficulties finding a husband or being a "good wife"), and a school curriculum that is not responsive to girls.

Children in Debt: Impacts of Structural Adjustment

Similar to other African countries, reductions by the Kenya government on spending for subsidized food, health care, and school-related expenses have meant that the cost of these basic necessities has been passed on to families, leaving them with fewer resources to devote to the education of their children. As a mother in Kisumu Municipality (near Lake Victoria) put it, "books, uniforms, building fund, admission fees are all required, and if you don't have them, children are sent home!" A father in rural Embu District (near Mt. Kenya) commented, "Life is very demanding—it is just living hand-to-mouth . . . we are supporting the (education) system rather than benefiting from the system and there is no going back!" (Swadener, Kabiru, and Njenga 2000, 176, 247).

Two widespread results have been an increase in school dropouts and a decrease in school enrollment, because families cannot afford fees and more children engage in income-generating activities to contribute to their family income or simply for their own survival. Ironically, this trend is corroborated by a World Bank (2001, 25) report, which states that "poverty-related deprivation contributes to low education attainment in Africa. Poor children spend more time than other children contributing directly or indirectly to the household income. As a result, they are less likely to spend out-of-school hours on school work . . . and more likely to be tired and ill-prepared for learning." Studies in a number of countries in Africa indicate that school enrollments declined in countries that adopted SAPs. Reimers and Tiburcio (1993, as cited in Brock-Utne 2000, 23) state,

> It is clear that the adjustment programs supported and promoted by the World Bank and IMF during the 1980s have not worked for many countries . . . International financial institutions are supposed to be part of the solution, not part of the problem, and their record has to be assessed by the number of success stories they can claim, not by whether they can or cannot be blamed for the failure.

Studies by UNICEF and other research teams have also documented the negative impacts of SAPs on children and other vulnerable groups in Africa (Bradshaw et al 1993; Kilbride and Kilbride 1997; Kilbride, Suda, and Njeru 2000). James Grant, former executive director of UNICEF, described structural adjustment as having a "human face," often that of a child (Grant 1993) and the authors have documented ways in which such macroeconomic policies and related local dynamics are directly linked to the quality of life experienced by families and the opportunities afforded their children (Swadener, Kabiru, and Njenga 2000). In fact, UNICEF used the phrase "children in debt" for several years to convey the strong correlation between Third World debt, SAPs, and children's increased risk. UNICEF estimated that if just one of every five dollars Africa pays for debt servicing instead went to primary education, there would be a place for every child in primary school (UNICEF 1996, 3).

At the level of family existence and economics, the impact of global recession and the related debt crisis is unevenly, though increasingly, documented (Bradshaw et al. 1993). Associated policies have included greater community cost sharing, higher prices to consumers, increased unemployment (Hancock 1989), and dislocation (Kilbride and Kilbride 1990, 1997). Walton and Ragin (1990, 877), in discussing impacts of over-urbanization, note that "the urban poor and the working class are affected by a combination of subsidy cuts, real wage reductions, and price increases stemming from devaluations and the elimination of public services."

The relationship between SAPs and related policies and an increase in child mortality and malnutrition rates in some parts of Kenya has also been noted by Gakuru and Koech (1995). This, combined with the sharp increase in female-headed households—many living in urban slums in extreme poverty far away from family supports—underscores the threat to a so-called welfare state in this and other Sub-Saharan African nations. However, lest we portray Kenyan families as passive victims of global economic policies, we would agree with Weisner, Bradley, and Kilbride (1997, cited in Swadener, Kabiru, and Njenga 2000, 265) that,

> African families face serious crises today. They are under economic, demographic, and political pressures of all kinds; yet, families are not mere hapless victims of global change. They are proactive, resilient agents and creators of change.

Global Policies/Local Lives: Impacts of Sociopolitical Change on Childrearing

In a national study documenting impacts of rapid social, economic, and cultural change on childrearing practices and early childhood education, the authors, with NACECE and DICECE collaborators, interviewed more than 460 parents, grandparents, preschool teachers, children, and community leaders in Kenya. Data were collected in eight districts and a cross-section of locations, including rural, urban, plantation, and traditional/pastoral settings (Swadener, Kabiru, and Njenga 1997, 2000). Although the study did not set out to document impacts of neoliberal, postsocialist policies, including structural adjustment measures, many of the narratives reflected such themes. Across these varied settings, parents and others concerned with the care and early education of young children described services that had been previously available to families that either had a cost share (such as a range of school-related costs) or were unavailable (such as basic medications or feeding programs in preschools). In other words, families were increasingly governed by policies stipulated by donors, including austerity measures and payment for services, most of which had previously been free.

Although at least primary education in Kenya is now "free," in most cases, poor families and, increasingly, middle-class families in Kenya cannot afford a public education. This issue was cited by families as one of the greatest economic hardships they faced—particularly when they were forced to decide which children they would educate, if any. Because preschool programs are still primarily private and community based, many parents also discussed their desire for more government or NGO assistance to make preschool more affordable and to reinstate health and nutrition services previously available.

The two following summaries, drawn from contrasting parts of Kenya, provide a glimpse into this manifestation of "children and the state," particularly in terms of impacts of neoliberal policies on childrearing and early education.

Increasing poverty

Unemployment is almost complete—some don't own land; [they] look for casual labor, squat on relatives' land, and are living a hand-to-mouth life most of the time.

Mother in Embu District

Responses to questions about social and structural changes affecting child-rearing and concerning the major problems facing families in Kenya were typically similar, often overlapping, with a discussion of changes leading directly into a list of social and economic problems. The most common themes were the overarching issue of increasing poverty and an array of related economic problems. First among these, in terms of the frequency with which financial problems were mentioned, was the cost of living; second was the rapidly rising cost of educating children in Kenya. The cost of living had several dimensions, including the loss of purchasing power for basic necessities for families or, as one Maasai mother put it, "the higher cost of everything." As the Kenyan press frequently laments, the gap between the day-to-day realities of the majority of citizens (*wananchi*) living in poverty and the distanced and donor-dependent economic policies of its government is widening (Swadener, Kabiru, and Njenga 2000, 266).

Housing constraints and safety

I have stayed in this slum since 1982 and sell charcoal. My parents died when I was young and I never went to school. I have five children and am a single mother. On a typical day I am just trying to get enough money for food and caring for my youngest children. I get some help from my children and often take them with me when I am selling charcoal. Before, people here were all living in cartons, then in 1984 they all burned. Now we are in tin houses. We only got a dispensary recently, and there is only one pay toilet for many families. My children and I are often hungry.

Single mother in Mukuru, Nairobi

Housing was another aspect of the high cost of living. Rents had become much higher and, as families grew, their living conditions were more crowded. A number of problems were associated with housing issues, ranging from discipline difficulties to the increase in the number of street children (as older out-of-school boys, for example, were often subtly encouraged to leave their mother's home, at least to find food or work on the street during the day). There were fewer open spaces, playgrounds, and other recreational settings for children, particularly in urban areas. Those interviewed in rural areas also described more squatters, some of whom were living on relatives' land and others just starting a small *shamba* (farm) on another's property. Some of these squatters were reported to be a source of "compound kids," the rural equivalent to "street kids" in urban areas. Such children were idle during the day, going home to get food and occasionally doing casual labor, and were seen as a bad influence on their age-mates.

Access to housing was also a growing problem in urban areas; rapid expansion of slums, estates growing through the addition of illegal extensions to existing housing units, and crowding were frequently mentioned by the parents interviewed in both Nairobi and Kisumu. Such uncontrolled growth frequently meant that few services were available (such as water, sewers or latrines, trash removal, or rubbish burning pits), making environmental hygiene a major problem. This, in turn, led to outbreaks of disease, including dysentery, which was particularly problematic in one of the Nairobi slums sampled in the study. Even when people were able to arrange temporary or semi-permanent housing in such slum settings, the possibility existed of entire neighborhoods being bulldozed by the city council or burning down in mysterious fires (Amisi 2001), rendering hundreds homeless in a single night.

Final Reflections

We agree with Scheper-Hughes and Sargent (1998, 1) that,

> the cultural politics of childhood speaks on the one hand to the public nature of childhood and the inability of isolated families or households to shelter infants and small children within the privacy of the home or to protect them from the outrageous slings and arrows of the world's political and economic fortunes. On the other hand, the cultural policies of childhood speak to the political, ideological, and social uses of childhood.

Such intersections of childhood with larger social, economic, and ideological discourses are at the heart of governing children and families and are in constant flux in Kenya, as elsewhere in the world. As James and Prout (1990, 1) state, "any complacency about children and their place in society is misplaced, for the very concept of childhood has become problematic during the last decade." Similarly, Stephens (1995, 8) argues that "[a] focus on childhood—and on other domains previously differentiated from the realm of political economics is thus important, insofar as it breaks the frame of dominant models of transformation in the world system." Stephens also argues that child and family researchers should rethink their studies "in the light of social and historical macroperspectives" (1995). We advocate a constant mixing of analysis of such macroperspectives with research focusing on the rapidly changing local perspectives of children, parents, and caregivers in order to better understand the complex dynamics of governing children and families in Kenya or other southern hemisphere settings.

While analyzing the many ways in which the state, multinational banks, and other bodies govern children and families in Kenya, we have been struck many times by the persistent patterns of colonialism and the contradictory spaces of postcolonial life that subtly resist colonial power relations. To quote Dimitriadis and McCarthy (2001, 117), "our period of intense globalization and the rise of multinational capital has played a large part in ushering in the multicultural age—an age in which the empire has struck back . . ." We strongly support calls from a growing number of indigenous scholars (such as Gandhi 1998; San Juan 1999; Smith 1999; Spivak 1999; wa Thiong'o 1993) for decolonizing research and moving beyond Western, imperialist models and analysis. We recognize the struggles and attempts to deal with the [im]possibilities inherent in carrying out decolonizing work, and we agree that the work of such scholars stands at the center of the "beginning of the presencing" (Bhabha 1994) of a disharmonious, restive, unharnessable knowledge that is produced at the site of postcolonial resistance. Such authors serve as transgressive authorizing agents whose positions at once marginalize and singularize the totalizing meta-texts of colonial/Western knowledge (Mutua and Swadener 2004).

We are also concerned about "overdetermined discourses" that construct the Third World and contribute to false binary categories of difference, often defined by Western scholars (Mohanty 1991). While we have not wanted to overemphasize the economic margins, we recognize that gross social inequities contribute directly to marginality and difficult circumstances for growing numbers of children and families in Kenya. Thus, in emphasizing the daily experiences of Kenyan families whose lives have been deeply affected by neoliberal global policies and growing assumptions of normative and universal discourses of development and early education, we have attempted to take the position of allies, or "allied others" (Rogers and Swadener 1999). Though policy analysis is critical, we agree with Schram (2000, 182) that a more radical response is also required:

> In the end, these considerations remind us that social justice is still contingent on all families being able to access basic social welfare entitlements. All families should be able to practice a "politics of survival." Parents should have nutritional assistance, housing, schooling, and the like. Parents should be able to have access to the basic services needed to raise their children . . . [and] they need not only to be effective parents but also productive citizens. Whether these universal entitlements should be guaranteed all at once under some comprehensive family policy or whether they should be built up one after another was decided a long time ago. The time for incrementalism to get radical and radicalism to get incremental is long overdue.

We believe, with Dimitriadis and McCarthy (2001, 119), that "a strategy of alliance might allow us to produce new antidiscriminatory pedagogies that will respond to this fraught and exceedingly fragile moment of globalized, postcolonial life." Such alliances should foreground the voices of children and families and should challenge the pervasive assumptions of late capitalism with indigenous and hybrid sensibilities and solutions.

These alliances at the local level can create more inclusive spaces for the formulation and enactment of policy by increasing the possibility that those at the margins are heard, so that policy and decision making are not left to the privileged few. Emerging indigenous governance structures should be supported, including policies that resist neoliberalism's emphasis on self-sufficiency. As this chapter documents, and as Tikly (2001) asserts, Structural Adjustment Programs have undermined the state and civil society, pointing to the need for policy change. We agree with Ngugi wa Thiong'o (1993) that there is a need to move the center toward correcting the economic and political structural imbalance between the West and Third World nations and to actively resist the social and structural imbalances between the few who control the resources and the silent majority who live in poverty (Cantalupo 1995; wa Thiong'o 1993). We join members of growing grassroots movements in advocating that governing patterns of children and families in Kenya be decolonized and democratized.

References

Adams, B., and E. Mburugu. 1994. *Women, Work, and Child Care*. Paper presented at the "Second Early Childhood Collaboration Training Seminar," Nairobi. June.

Amisi, O. 2001. "A Tale of Hard Work, Courage, and Generosity." *Daily Nation,* September 12. Retrieved November 12, 2006, from http://www.nationaudio. com/News/DailyNation/12092001/index.html.

Bhabha, H. K. 1994. *The Location of Culture.* London: Routledge.

Bradshaw, Y. W., R. Noonan, L. Gash, and C. B. Sershen. 1993. "Borrowing against the Future: Children and Third World Indebtedness." *Social Forces* 71 (3): 629–56.

Brock-Utne, B. 2000. *Whose Education for All? The Recolonization of the African Mind.* New York: Falmer Press.

Cannella, G. S. 2003. "Child Welfare in the United States: The Construction of Gendered, Oppositional Discourse(s)." In *Governing Children, Families, and Education: Restructuring the Welfare State,* ed. M. N. Bloch, K. Holmlund, I. Moqvist, and T. Popkewitz, 173–94. New York: Palgrave Macmillan.

Cantalupo, C. 1995. *The World of Ngugi wa Thiong'o.* Trenton, NJ: Africa World Press.

Chege, F., and D. N. Sifuna. 2006. *Girls' and Women's Education in Kenya: Gender Perspectives and Trends.* UNESCO report. Retrieved November 12, 2006, from http://www.education.nairobi-unesco.org/.

Dimitriadis, G., and C. McCarthy. 2001. *Reading and Teaching the Postcolonial: From Baldwin to Basquiat and Beyond.* New York: Teachers College Press.

Ehrenreich, B. 2001. *Nickel and Dimed: On (Not) Getting By in America.* New York: Holt.

Eshiwani, G. S. 1990. *Implementing Educational Policies in Kenya.* Washington, DC: World Bank.

———. 1993. *Education in Kenya since Independence.* Nairobi: East African Educational Publishers.

Ferguson, J. 1999. *Expectations of Modernity: Myths and Meanings of Urban Life on the Zambian Copperbelt.* Berkeley: California University Press.

Fraser, N. 1989. *Unruly Practices: Power Discourse and Gender in Contemporary Social Theory.* Minneapolis: University of Minnesota Press.

———. 1997. *Justice Interruptus: Critical Reflections on the "Postsocialist" Condition.* New York: Routledge.

Gakuru, O. N., and B. G. Koech. 1995. *The Experiences of Young Children: A Contextualized Case Study of Early Childhood Care and Education in Kenya.* Nairobi: Kenya Institute of Education and NACECE.

Gandhi, L. 1998. *Postcolonial Theory: A Critical Introduction.* New York: Columbia University Press.

Gordon, L., ed. 1990. *Women, the State, and Welfare.* Madison: University of Wisconsin Press.

———. 1994. *Pitied but Not Entitled: Single Mothers and the History of Welfare.* New York: Free Press.

Grant, J. 1993. *The State of the World's Children*. New York: UNICEF.

Hall, S. 1996. "When Was Postcolonial? Thinking at the Limit." In *The Postcolonial Question: Common Skies, Divided Horizons*, ed. I. Chamber and L. Curtis, 242–60. London: Routledge.

Hancock, G. 1989. *Lords of Poverty*. London: Macmillan.

Hultqvist, K., and G. Dahlberg, eds. 2001. *Governing the Child in the New Millennium*. London: Routledge/Falmer.

James, A., and A. Prout, eds. 1990. *Constructing and Reconstructing Childhood*. Basingstoke, UK: Falmer Press.

Kathuri, B. 2006. "Kenya: WB to Loan Kenya Sh5.6b for Learning." *East African Standard*, November 9. Retrieved November 12, 2006, from http://www.eastandard.net/hm_news/news.php?articleid=1143960881.

Kenya. 2001. *Children's Act*. Kenya Gazette Supplement No. 95 (Act No. 8). Nairobi: Government Printer.

Kenya Institute of Education. 2000. *Guidelines for Preschool Education*. Nairobi: KIE/NACECE.

Kilbride, P., and J. Kilbride. 1990. *Changing Family Life in East Africa: Women and Children at Risk*. University Park, PA: Pennsylvania State University Press.

———. 1997. "Stigma, Role Overload, and Delocalization among Contemporary Kenyan Women. In *African Families and the Crisis of Social Change*, ed. T. Weisner, C. Bradley, and P. Kilbride, 208–23. Westport, CT: Bergin and Garvey.

Kilbride, P., C. Suda, and E. Njeru. 2000. *Street Children in Kenya: Voices of Children in Search of a Childhood*. Westport, CT: Bergin and Garvey.

Kiluva-Ndunda, M. 2001. *Women's Agency and Educational Policy: The Experiences of the Women of Kilome*. Albany, NY: State University of New York Press.

Koome, M. 2002. "Spare a Thought for the 'Fatherless' Child." *Daily Nation*, August 20. Retrieved November 10, 2006, from http://www.nationaudio.com/.

McCarthy, C. 1998. *The Uses of Culture: Education and the Limits of Ethnic Affiliation*. New York: Routledge.

Mignolo, W. D. 2000. *Local Histories/Global Designs: Colonialist, Subaltern Knowledges, and Border Thinking*. Princeton: Princeton University Press.

Mink, G. 1998. *Welfare's End*. Ithaca: Cornell University Press.

Mohanty, C. 1991. "Under Western Eyes: Feminist Scholarship and Colonial Discourses." In *Third World Women and the Politics of Feminism*, ed. C. Mohanty, A. Russo, and L. Torres, 51–80. Indianapolis, IN: Indiana University Press.

Mutua, N. K., and B. B. Swadener, eds. 2004. *Decolonizing Research in Cross-Cultural Contexts: Critical Personal Narratives*. Albany, NY: State University of New York Press.

Nieuwenhuis, F. J. 1996. *The Development of Education System in Postcolonial Africa: A Study of a Selected Number of African Countries.* Pretoria: Human Sciences Research Council.

Ombuor, J. 2001. "Rape and Terror Rule over the Land." *Daily Nation,* September 12, 4.

Parpart, J. L., and K. A. Staudt, eds. 1989. *Women and the State in Africa.* Boulder, CO: Lynne Reiner.

p'Bitek, O. 1986. *Artist the Ruler: Essays on Art, Culture, and Values.* Nairobi: Heinemann Kenya.

Polakow, V. 1993. *Lives on the Edge: Single Mothers and Their Children in the Other America.* Chicago: University of Chicago Press.

Polakow, V., T. Halskov, and P. S. Jorgensen. 2001. *Diminished Rights: Danish Lone Mother Families in International Context.* Bristol, UK: The Policy Press.

Robertson, C., and I. Berger. 1986. *Women and Class in Africa.* New York: Holmes and Meier.

Rogers, L. J., and B. B. Swadener. 1999. "Reflections on the Future Work of Anthropology and Education: Reframing the 'Field.'" *Anthropology and Education Quarterly* 30 (4): 436–40.

Rose, N. 1999. *Governing the Soul: The Shaping of the Private Self,* 2nd ed. London: Free Association Books.

Rugene, N., and M. Njeru. 2003. "Free Primary School Starts Next Week." *Daily Nation,* January 4. Retrieved November 12, 2006, from http://www.nationaudio.com/News/DailyNation/04012003/News/News013.html.

San Juan, E., Jr. 1999. *Beyond Postcolonial Theory.* New York: St. Martin's Press.

Scheper-Hughes, N., and C. Sargent, eds. 1998. *Small Wars: The Cultural Politics of Childhood.* Berkeley, CA: University of California Press.

Schram, S. 2000. *After Welfare: The Culture of Postindustrial Social Policy.* New York: New York University Press.

Sibley, D. 1995. *Geographies of Exclusion: Society and Difference in the West.* London: Routledge.

Siringi, S. 2003. "Schools Act on Intake." *Daily Nation,* January 10. Retrieved November 12, 2006, from http://www.nationaudio.com/.

Smith, L. T. 1999. *Decolonizing Methodologies: Research and Indigenous Peoples.* London: Zed Books.

Spivak, G. C. 1999. *A Critique of Postcolonial Reason: Toward a History of the Vanishing Present.* Cambridge: Harvard University Press.

Stephens, S., ed. 1995. *Children and the Politics of Culture.* Princeton, NJ: Princeton University Press.

Swadener, B. B., M. Kabiru, and A. Njenga. 1997. "Does the Village Still Raise the Child? A Collaborative Study of Changing Childrearing in Kenya." *Early Education and Development* 8 (3): 285–306.

———. 2000. *Does the Village Still Raise the Child?: A Collaborative Study of Changing Childrearing and Early Education in Kenya*. Albany, NY: State University of New York Press.

Swadener, B. B., and S. Lubeck. 1995. *Children and Families "At Promise": Deconstructing the Discourse of Risk*. Albany: State University of New York Press.

Swadener, B. B., and N. K. Mutua. 2001. "Mapping Terrains of 'Homelessness' in Postcolonial Kenya." In *Homelessness in International Context*, ed. V. Polakow and C. Guillian, 263–87. Westport, CT: Greenwood Press.

Swadener, B. B., and P. Wachira. 2003. "Governing Children and Families in Kenya: Losing Ground in Neoliberal Times." In *Governing Children, Families, and Education: Restructuring the Welfare State*, ed. M. N. Bloch, K. Holmlund, I. Moqvist, and T. Popkewitz, 231–57. New York: Palgrave Macmillan.

Tikly, L. 2001. "Globalization and Education in the Postcolonial World: Towards a Conceptual Framework. *Comparative Education* 37 (2): 151–71.

UNICEF (United Nations Children's Fund). 1996. *The Progress of Nations*. New York: UNICEF.

———. 2006. *Africa's Orphaned and Vulnerable Generations: Children Affected by AIDS*. New York: UNICEF.

Vavrus, F. 2002. "Postcoloniality and English: Exploring Language Policy and the Politics of Development in Tanzania." *TESOL Quarterly* 36 (3): 373–97.

Walton, J., and C. Ragin. 1990. "Global and National Sources of Political Protest: Third World Responses to the Debt Crisis." *American Sociological Review* 55: 876–90.

wa Thiong'o, N. 1993. *Moving the Center: The Struggle for Cultural Freedoms*. Nairobi: East African Educational Publishers.

Weisner, T. S., C. Bradley, and P. K. Kilbride, eds. 1997. *African Families and the Crisis of Social Change*. Westport, CT: Bergin and Garvey.

Willinsky, J. 1998. *Learning to Divide the World: Education at Empire's End*. Minneapolis: University of Minnesota Press.

World Bank. 2001. *A Chance to Learn: Knowledge and Finance for Education in Sub-Saharan Africa*. Washington, DC: World Bank.

CHAPTER 22

Community-Based Approaches That Work in Eastern and Southern Africa

Jane E. Lucas, Jessica Jitta, Gareth Jones, and Katarzyna Wilczynska-Ketende

The family is the first-line care system for a young child. Assisting families must therefore be a high priority in any strategy to reduce infant and child mortality and improve the growth and development of young children.

Children who are impoverished and are poorly nourished are in the greatest danger of dying. Malnutrition is the underlying cause of 52.5 percent of all deaths of young children under 5 years (Caulfield, de Onis, Blössner, and Black 2004). Malnutrition weakens children, increasing their vulnerability to other common childhood illnesses, including pneumonia, diarrhea, malaria, and measles. In Sub-Saharan Africa 4.5 million children under 5 die each year, 29 percent of children under 5 are moderately or severely malnourished, and 9 percent have severe wasting. In some Sub-Saharan African countries, as many as 40 percent of children are moderately or severely underweight (UNICEF 2004). Many more suffer the consequences of moderately or severely stunted growth, which results from poor nutrition before birth and through early childhood.

They are often burdened by the cognitive and other developmental delays associated with stunting (Martorell 1997). The burden of frequent illness and lethargy additionally restricts the opportunities for an impoverished child to explore and learn.

The strategy of Integrated Management of Childhood Illness (IMCI) brings together well-tested health, nutrition, and child development interventions to prevent common childhood illnesses and provide lifesaving care and better nutrition for both sick and healthy children. The effectiveness of IMCI in protecting children by delivering better services through the health system has been documented in a large multicountry study (el Arifeen et al. 2004; Armstrong Schellenberg et al. 2004).

Yet, in Africa, many sick children die at home, often without having been seen by a health worker. In Malawi, for example, a survey found that 60 percent of childhood deaths occurred at home, and half of these deaths were children who had not been taken to a health facility (Balyeku, Matinga, and Bello 2004).

Extending the coverage of IMCI and other lifesaving initiatives to children who are difficult to reach by health and other services can prevent many childhood deaths. Home- and community-based interventions, with wide coverage, could prevent three-fifths of preventable childhood deaths (Jones et al. 2003). Interventions can also strengthen communities to organize safer environments for families, provide child care for their children, and encourage the fuller development of children and their families. The evidence and experience are sufficient to accelerate the scaling up of effective household and community interventions. There is no need to wait.

A Review of Household and Community Interventions

In 2005, United Nations Children's Fund (UNICEF) completed a review of interventions implemented in 18 countries in the Eastern and Southern Africa Region (ESAR) to improve family care practices and strengthen community efforts to organize more healthy conditions for children (Lucas et al. 2005).[1] These interventions were implemented through the household and community component of the IMCI strategy. Eighteen ESAR countries (see table 22.1) are actively implementing the household and community component, despite a lagging start behind the rollout of the other two IMCI components (improving health worker performance and health system supports).

The review focused on four countries—Malawi, South Africa, Tanzania, and Uganda—whose different experiences could contribute

Table 22.1. 18 Countries in the UNICEF/ESAR Implementing the IMCI Household and Community Component in at Least Three Districts

Botswana	Mozambique
Burundi	Namibia
Comoros	Rwanda
Eritrea	South Africa*
Ethiopia	Swaziland
Kenya	Tanzania*
Lesotho	Uganda*
Madagascar	Zambia
Malawi*	Zimbabwe

Source: Lucas et al. 2005.
Note: Thirteen countries in order of global ranking of under-5 deaths (high to low) are Ethiopia, Tanzania, Angola, Mozambique, Uganda, Kenya, Somalia, Malawi, Madagascar, Zambia, South Africa, Rwanda, and Zimbabwe. These 13 countries account for more than 95 percent of childhood deaths in ESAR.
ESAR = Eastern and Southern Africa Region; IMCI = Integrated Management of Childhood Illnesses.
*Focus countries in the review.

to an assessment of future directions in a regional strategy for children. In each country, a combination of interventions included home visits by community health workers or peer volunteers; mother support groups; immunizations, bednets, cooking demonstrations, and other outreach activities during village health days; and the establishment of community-based child care centers. Theater groups, village assemblies, and flyers provided wider community education. Activities to develop the capacity of communities to assess health risks, identify problems, and take action helped to engage wide community participation in creating the conditions for a healthier environment for families.

The comprehensive strategy supported child growth and development; disease prevention; home care for a sick child; care seeking for a sick child and compliance with the advice of a health worker; and the creation of a more supportive and enabling family and community environment for child health and development. Box 22.1 lists the IMCI key family and community practices promoted in the four focus countries.

The review documented the household and community interventions implemented in the four ESAR focus countries and answered two important questions about their effectiveness:

- Can the interventions implemented through the IMCI household and community component improve specific family care practices that affect child survival and development?

Box 22.1

Key Family and Community Practices to Promote Child Survival, Growth, and Development (Complete List of 17 Core and 2 Additional ESAR Practices)

Child growth and development

- Breastfeed infants exclusively for the first six months, taking into account policy and recommendations on HIV and infant feeding.
- From 6 months of age, feed children freshly prepared energy- and nutrient-rich complementary foods, while continuing to breastfeed up to two years or longer.
- Ensure that children receive adequate amounts of micronutrients (vitamin A and iron, in particular) either in their diet or through supplementation.
- Promote mental and social development by responding to child needs for care and through talking, playing, and providing a stimulating environment.

Disease prevention

- Dispose of feces, including children's feces, safely, and wash hands after defecation, before preparing meals, and before feeding children.
- Take children as scheduled to complete a full course of immunizations (Bacillus Calmette-Guérin [BCG]; diphtheria, pertussis, tetanus [DPT]; oral polio vaccine [OPV]; and measles) before their first birthday.
- Protect children in malaria-endemic areas by ensuring that they sleep under insecticide-treated bednets (ITNs).
- Provide appropriate care for HIV/AIDS-affected people, especially orphans, and take action to prevent further HIV infections.

Home care for a sick child

- Continue to feed and offer more fluids, including breast milk, to children when they are sick.
- Give sick children appropriate home treatment for illness.
- Protect children from injury and accident, and provide treatment when necessary.

Care seeking and compliance

- Recognize when sick children need treatment outside the home and seek care from appropriate providers.
- Follow health workers' advice about treatment, follow-up, and referral.

- Ensure that every pregnant woman has antenatal care. This includes her having at least four antenatal visits with an appropriate health care provider and receiving the recommended doses of the tetanus toxoid vaccine. Ensure that she seeks care at the time of delivery.

A supportive and enabling environment

- Prevent child abuse and neglect and take action when it does occur.
- Provide care to orphans and vulnerable children.
- Ensure that men, especially fathers, actively participate in the provision of child care and are involved in reproductive health.
- Ensure that every pregnant and lactating woman gets time to rest by reducing her workload.
- Register every child as soon as possible after birth.

- Are the interventions effective in addressing multiple family practices that together are likely to be effective as an integrated strategy to prevent childhood deaths and support healthy child development?

The review included an examination of the literature documenting the impact of family practices on child survival and development; a desk review of country and program documents, including a synthesis of the results of available surveys on family practices; key informant interviews; and site visits to view activities in each of the four focus countries.

The review also applied a model, first presented in the *Lancet* (Jones et al. 2003), to estimate the number of deaths of children under 5 that could be avoided with wide coverage of household and community interventions (referred to here as the Lancet model). Of particular interest in the review were estimates of childhood deaths that could be prevented in ESAR. (The ESAR estimates presented in this chapter are based on mortality data from 13 countries contributing 95 percent of regional under-5 deaths; see table 22.1 note.)

The Lancet model estimates potential childhood deaths from common causes (for example, diarrhea, pneumonia, measles, malaria, HIV/AIDS, and neonatal conditions) that could be averted by household-, community-, and health system–based interventions. The interventions identified in the model are not programmatic activities but rather are improved practices that have been identified in the scientific literature to have the greatest, most proximal impact on improving children's survival and health. The practices include, for example, infant feeding, the use of insecticide-treated bednets and other materials, the use of clean drinking water and safe sanitation and hygiene practices, and home treatment with oral rehydration therapy (ORT). Other interventions also represent a link between a life-saving service delivered by the health system, including immunization or treatment with antimalarials or antibiotics, and a household practice, representing a caregiver response to access the service. The following section reports the results of surveys on changes in family practices. It includes estimates from the application of the Lancet statistical model to ESAR data[2] on causes of childhood deaths to demonstrate the potential impact that improvements in key family practices could have in the region.

Survey Evidence on Changes in Key Family Care Practices

During the early stage of implementing the household and community interventions, the direct impact on child health and development is difficult to identify. Cumulative research, however, has linked improvements in specific key family practices to reductions in child mortality and improved psychosocial development in children. Documented improvements in these key family practices strongly suggest a related impact on child survival and development.

The review examined baseline and follow-up surveys on key family practices and on related environmental conditions, such as the availability of clean water and improved sanitation facilities. The surveys were conducted in four countries:

- Malawi, in sites within five project districts
- South Africa, in UThukela District
- Tanzania, in Mkuranga District
- Uganda, in Kasese District, Ntungamo District, and the Nutrition and Early Childhood Development Project.

While country programs used a core of common survey questions, some sites collected information on a wider range of specific practices than others. Examples of results that were more comparable across sites are reported below.

Household surveys found improvements in knowledge, attitudes, and family practices that are likely to have a significant impact on reducing childhood deaths, as well as promoting healthy psychosocial development.

In each of the survey sites, multiple care practices improved, suggesting that integrating interventions may have a greater impact on family practices, and thus on child survival and development, than the contributions of any single behavior change. Following are examples of changes seen in family practices affecting child growth and development, disease prevention, home care for sick children, and care seeking.

Growth Promotion and Development

Community-based interventions in the implementing sites increased awareness about breastfeeding, complementary feeding, and micronutrients to improve a child's development.

Breastfeeding—Exclusive breastfeeding is a complex behavior and is often contrary to community practices. As a result, it can be difficult to initiate and maintain exclusive breastfeeding of infants up to the recommended age of 6 months. Even with the recommendation to exclusively breastfeed up to 6 months, the World Health Organization (WHO) estimates that only 35 percent of infants aged 0–4 months are exclusively breastfed (WHO 2001). In Sub-Saharan Africa, the average exclusive breastfeeding rate is 28 percent (UNICEF 2004).

The benefits of breastfeeding have been well established. Breast milk provides all the essential nutrients for the infant less than 6 months of age. Breast milk passes the immunities of the mother to her infant; giving milk through the breast avoids the infant's potential exposure to contaminants, including unsafe water and unclean utensils.

A WHO meta-analysis of three observational studies found that, compared with nonbreastfed infants under 2 months of age, breastfed infants were 6 times less likely to die. Breastfed infants 2–3 months old were 4.1 times less likely to die and breastfed infants 4–5 months old were 2.5 times less likely to die (WHO Collaborative Study Team 2000). Breastfeeding reduces the risk of childhood deaths from multiple causes, but it has been demonstrated to have the greatest impact on diarrhea- and pneumonia-related mortality. An application of the Lancet model for estimating preventable deaths proposed that improved breastfeeding practices alone could prevent 233,000 (13 percent) of the 1.85 million deaths of children in Eastern and Southern Africa each year.

Breastfeeding also affects a child's psychosocial development. Fatty acids in breast milk contribute to brain and visual development in infants (Uauy and De Andraca 1995). A meta-analysis of 20 studies found that, compared with fed babies, breastfed infants scored 3 points higher for cognitive development. This difference was first seen at age 6 months and was found to persist until age 15 years (Anderson, Johnstone, and Remley 1999). The positive relationship that develops between mother and infant through breastfeeding also supports improved motor and cognitive development, as well as physical health.

Given the demonstrated importance of breastfeeding for the child's survival and development, the review looked at exclusive breastfeeding rates and the early initiation of breastfeeding where surveys of these practices had been conducted. Before intervention, exclusive breastfeeding rates at the implementing sites were at different levels (see figure 22.1), with the lowest at 0 percent in UThukela District in South Africa. After the sites continued the interventions for about three years, follow-up surveys identified improvements in exclusive breastfeeding rates from 14 to 43 percentage points across the sites, except in Ntungamo District (Uganda), which showed no improvement.

Figure 22.1. Children Exclusively Breastfed up to Age 6 Months in Five ESAR Programs, before and after Intervention

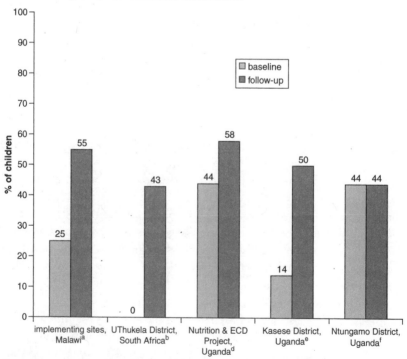

Source: Figure prepared by authors; see endnote 2 for survey sources for a.–f.
Note: ESAR = UNICEF's Eastern and Southern Africa Region.

Most implementing sites in South Africa and Uganda promoted breastfeeding through the counseling of mothers of young infants during home visits by community health workers (CHWs), other outreach workers, and peer counselors, as well as through community education activities. In Malawi, breastfeeding messages were delivered more typically through community education (mass media or drama events) and village assemblies, rather than through home visits.

The World Health Organization (WHO) and UNICEF (1990) recommend that newborns be put on the breast within the first hour after birth. The early milk, colostrum, helps to protect the young infants against illness. The early initiation of breastfeeding also contributes to the mother's ability to breastfeed effectively, her motivation to continue breastfeeding, and the development of a strong emotional bond between the mother and her infant.

Early initiation of breastfeeding increased in sites in three of the implementing programs for which there are data (see figure 22.2). Large improvements were achieved in UThukela (25 percentage points) and Ntungamo (31 percentage points). Failure to see greater gains in Malawi, where communitywide interventions were more common than home visits, could reflect poor targeting of interventions to pregnant mothers

Figure 22.2. Children Breastfed within One Hour of Delivery in Three ESAR Programs, before and after Intervention

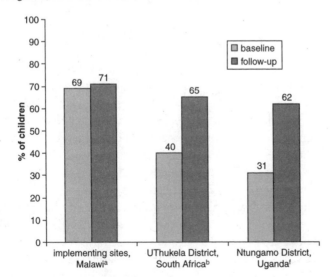

Source: Figure prepared by authors; see endnote 2 for survey sources for a.–f.
Note: ESAR = UNICEF's Eastern and Southern Africa Region.

as well as to persons who assist with home deliveries. However, the rate of early initiation of breastfeeding in Malawi is already higher than in the other sites (69 percent before the intervention and 71 percent after).

Complementary feeding—When young children reach about 6 months of age, breast milk alone can no longer meet their energy and growth requirements. The WHO and UNICEF (1990) guidelines on infant feeding recommend introducing complementary foods starting at 6 months of age, including adequate amounts of energy- and nutrient-rich foods and, for children not at risk of HIV transmission through breast milk, continuing breastfeeding for up to age 2 or longer.

Improving complementary feeding is critical to reducing malnutrition and stunting in young children. It is also necessary for preventing the deaths of almost 60 percent of children who die as a result of the underlying contribution of poor nutrition. Based on the Lancet model for estimating avoidable deaths, improving complementary feeding practices alone could prevent 126,000 (7 percent) of the 1.85 million annual deaths of children under 5 living in 13 countries in Eastern and Southern Africa (see table 22.1 note).

The review found a variety of activities to improve complementary feeding in the four focus countries. Community workers counseled mothers during home visits, information was spread throughout the community during village assemblies, and child health days provided an opportunity for cooking and feeding demonstrations. Community health workers, in cooperation with agriculture and community development workers, promoted backyard gardens.

Follow-up surveys gathered information on different aspects of feeding, depending on the change in practices that country programs were trying to achieve. In Malawi, the only country that provided information on the timing of the introduction of complementary foods, 55 percent of children received complementary foods by age 6 months in the implementing sites. In UThukela District, in South Africa, caregiver knowledge of the importance of the timely introduction of complementary feeding increased from 8 percent to 24 percent.

During the three years of implementing community-based interventions to improve food security in the Nutrition and Early Childhood Development (ECD) Project in Uganda, households reporting that they ate at least two major meals a day more than doubled from 23 percent to 50 percent in project areas. In the nonproject areas, the increase was less dramatic (31 percent to 41 percent).

Giving food to a breastfed baby—mixed feeding—younger than 6 months contributes to mortality. Continuing breastfeeding while introducing complementary foods in infants aged 6–11 months is associated with reduced mortality. However, mixed feeding appears to increase the risk of mother-to-child transmission of HIV through breast milk (Coutsoudis et al. 1999). The messages, especially in communities with a high prevalence of HIV, can be complicated, and continuing breastfeeding will not be recommended for all mothers. Consequently, in the Uganda Nutrition and ECD Project, for example, continuing to breastfeed infants up to and beyond 18 months decreased from 65 percent to 58 percent. Other surveys in Uganda examining the continuation of breastfeeding also found mixed results: an increase from 70 percent to 77 percent in the rates of children still breastfed at age 12–23 months in Ntungamo District and little change in the rates at about 33 percent for children still breastfed at age 20–23 months in Kasese District.

Micronutrients—Complementary foods often provide inadequate concentrations of essential micronutrients, and illness can further deplete micronutrient stores in the body. Providing adequate vitamin A, iron, and zinc—either through diet or supplementation—supports the healthy growth and development of young children, especially in areas challenged by frequent and severe childhood illness. The Lancet model estimates that ensuring adequate amounts of vitamin A as a preventive measure alone could prevent the deaths of an estimated 58,000 young children in Eastern and Southern Africa each year, and could prevent many disabilities caused by vitamin A deficiencies.

Vitamin A supplementation provides a good example of the importance of community-based interventions in reaching children who, for various reasons, do not routinely benefit from clinic services. Many countries recommend providing vitamin A supplements as a routine measure for young children. Even so, before implementation of the community-based interventions, rates were low—below 50 percent—in some areas (figure 22.3).

In South Africa, the UThukela project, starting at a low of 1 percent, was able to increase vitamin A supplementation to 62 percent. In this case, supplements provided through the health system were promoted through community-based interventions. Even where supplementation programs had been more effective, the proportion of children receiving vitamin A supplementation improved through community efforts, for example, increasing from 83 percent to 99 percent coverage in Mkuranga District (Tanzania).

Figure 22.3. Children Supplemented with Vitamin A in Six ESAR Programs, before and after Intervention

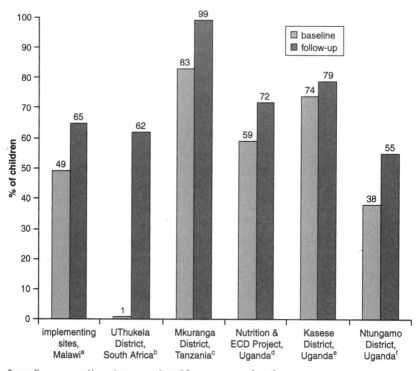

Source: Figure prepared by authors; see endnote 2 for survey sources for a.–f.
Note: ESAR = UNICEF's Eastern and Southern Africa Region.

Disease Prevention

In addition to providing a child with good nutrition, the most important practices that can prevent childhood illness are (1) personal and environmental hygiene, (2) immunization against childhood diseases, and (3) the use of insecticide-treated bednets to prevent malaria. Interventions reviewed in Eastern and Southern Africa included community-based activities to improve home practices to prevent illness and to help families take advantage of immunization and other support available through the health system.

Personal and environmental hygiene—Poor personal hygiene—affected by poor access to adequate sanitation facilities and clean water—contributes to diarrheal deaths. In Eastern and Southern Africa, more than 375,000 child deaths each year are related to diarrhea. Poor hygiene also contributes to disabilities from worm infestation and to skin and eye infections.

Improved handwashing and safe disposal of fecal material can greatly reduce the number of childhood deaths and disabilities. In a review of several studies, Esrey et al. (1991) found that safer disposal of feces alone was associated with reducing diarrhea-related child mortality by 20 percent to 80 percent.

The community-based interventions in the sites reviewed by UNICEF (Lucas et al. 2005) used different indicators to assess improved family practices and sanitation. Based on their indicators, the reported practice of washing hands after using the toilet improved from 45 percent to 78 percent in Mkuranga District (Tanzania) and from 20 percent to 45 percent in Ntungamo District (Uganda). In these districts, drama groups that were organized in collaboration with a university drama and music program promoted key hygiene practices. The groups learned key messages and then used song, dance, and roleplay to educate others. Messages were also delivered on village health days and in village assemblies.

Noticeable improvements were reported also in the practice of disposing children's feces appropriately, increasing from 50 percent to 83 percent in Malawi, from 76 percent to 91 percent in Kasese District (Uganda), and from 37 percent to 41 percent in Ntungamo District (Uganda).

While important, these recommended practices can be difficult to influence. Poor access to clean water and adequate sanitation facilities contributes directly to 90 percent of childhood diarrhea (WHO 1997). These conditions are common for much of the population in countries in Eastern and Southern Africa. Change in behavior requires easy access to water and latrines or toilets, as well as the motivation to use and maintain the facilities.

The implementing sites included in the review are poverty stricken, and improvements in hygiene practices often required integrated programs to provide latrines, safe water, and soap. Sites in at least four of the programs reviewed had an effective relationship between interventions to improve water and sanitation facilities and interventions to promote improved hygiene practices (table 22.2). Households gained access to safe water or more adequate sanitation facilities, or both, in implementing sites in Malawi, Tanzania, and Uganda. Based on the Lancet model, an estimated 51,000 deaths of young children in Eastern and Southern Africa could be prevented by improving hygiene practices supported by clean water and sanitation facilities.

Table 22.2. Access to Sanitation Facilities, Clean Water Sources, and Handwashing Facilities in Five ESAR Programs, before and after Interventions
(percent)

	Implementation sites, Malawi[a]		Mkuranga District, Tanzania[c]		Nutrition & ECD Project, Uganda[d]		Kasese District, Uganda[e]		Ntungamo District, Uganda[f]	
	Baseline	Follow-up	Baseline	Follow-up	Baseline	Follow-up	Baseline	Follow-up	Baseline	Follow-up
Households with drinking water from a safe water system/point	66	72	40	85	47	61	50	53	—	47
Households with pit latrines or flush toilet	—	—	40	90	88	88	87	91	—	77
Households with designated handwashing facilities with soap present	—	20	63	82	—	—	2	67	<1	16

Source: Table prepared by authors; see endnote 2 for corresponding references (a.–f.) for survey sources for all tables and figures in this chapter.

Note: ESAR = UNICEF's Eastern and Southern Africa Region; — = not available.

Immunization—Immunizations prevent an estimated 3 million child deaths globally each year; with wider coverage, they could prevent another 3 million deaths globally (World Bank 2001). In Eastern and Southern Africa, even as the measles cases decline in many areas, an application of the Lancet model estimates that immunizing all children just for measles, for example, could prevent the deaths of 25,000 children.

Immunization coverage depends on the availability of health services, as well as the efforts of families to seek vaccinations for their children. To receive a complete course of the most recommended vaccines (BCG, DPT, OPV, and measles) requires five contacts with a health worker before the child's first birthday and immunization services that are accessible and safe. Interventions focused on improving use of immunization services are likely to be insufficient without also strengthening clinic-based and health outreach services in isolated communities.

Consequently, immunization coverage in the sites providing survey information appeared to be affected by the strength of immunization services (figure 22.4). Where coverage of measles immunizations was high, as in Malawi and Tanzania, health services were able to respond to community demand for vaccines.

Reaching the last 20 percent of children not yet immunized has been difficult in all areas of the world. In Malawi and in Mkuranga District in Tanzania, this barrier has been broken: coverage is now near or above 90 percent for all vaccines. For this achievement, communities were mobilized to use immunization services by educating families in difficult-to-reach households about how, when, and where to receive vaccinations and by motivating them to take their children. At the same time, use was supported by improving the response of the health system to deliver immunization services, which included providing more access, lowering the cost, cutting waiting times, improving the safety of vaccines and their delivery, and missing fewer opportunities. In contrast, a generally reported deterioration of health services in Uganda during this period was reflected in a parallel deterioration in immunization coverage.

Insecticide-treated bednets—Every year, malaria contributes to the deaths of almost 300,000 children under 5 in Eastern and Southern Africa. In some areas of Tanzania, for example, malaria accounts each year for up to one-third of the deaths of young children (Tanzania and USAID 2006).

One of the main strategies to prevent malaria is the use of insecticide-treated bednets. Studies have found that sleeping under an insecticide-treated net can reduce child mortality by 17 percent (Lengler 2001).

Figure 22.4. Children Age 12–23 Months Immunized for Measles in Five ESAR Programs, before and after Intervention

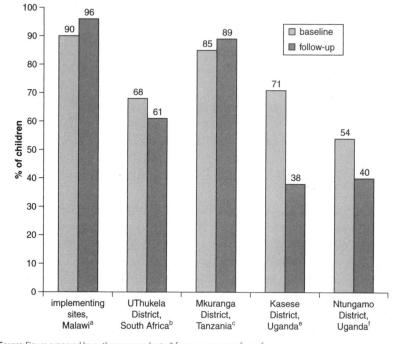

Source: Figure prepared by authors; see endnote 2 for survey sources for a.–f.
Note: ESAR = UNICEF's Eastern and Southern Africa Region.

In a rural area of Tanzania, social marketing and buying schemes stimulated an increase in the use of bednets by 50 percent, which was related to a subsequent decrease in the deaths of children under 5 by 25 percent (Schellenberg et al. 2001). Yet, without wide coverage of interventions to expand the use of bednets, in Tanzania only 21 percent of young children sleep under a bednet and only 2 percent under an insecticide-treated net. In Uganda, only 7 percent of young children sleep under a net, and none under an insecticide-treated net. In Malawi, 8 percent sleep under a net, and 3 percent under a treated net (UNICEF 2004).

The extent to which malaria can be reduced in young children depends largely on the effectiveness of community-based interventions to distribute insecticide-treated bednets, to make bednets affordable and accessible, and to help families use them correctly. Although information from the sites implementing community-based interventions is limited, there is evidence from sites in three programs in the UNICEF review (Lucas et al.

2005) that their efforts contributed to the wider use of bednets, although coverage remains low in Tanzania and Uganda (see figure 22.5).

Projects attempted to improve the knowledge of families about the effectiveness of insecticide-treated bednets in reducing malaria and supported strategies for increasing the availability, accessibility, and affordability of bednets. In Malawi, extension workers were particularly successful in increasing the use of bednets by children under 5 to 93 percent. Bednets were promoted during national and village health days. Workers trained community members on how to use and re-treat bednets and on the importance of their use for young children. They reinforced messages during the training of workers in community child care centers and helped communities include ways to buy nets when they set up revolving drug funds. Village committees ensured that the prevention of malaria featured prominently in village health plans.

The availability and affordability of nets and insecticide treatment packs continues to be a challenge, however, even where efforts have been intensive. In Malawi, a survey found that 77 percent of families in households without bednets said it was because they could not afford to buy them (Malawi 2004).

Figure 22.5. Children Age 0–59 Months Who Slept under a Bednet the Night Previous to Study in Three ESAR Programs, before and after Intervention

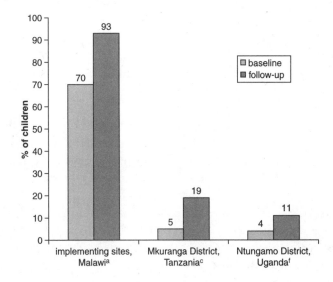

Source: Figure prepared by authors; see endnote 2 for survey sources for a.–f.
Note: ESAR = UNICEF's Eastern and Southern Africa Region.

Home Care for the Sick Child

Families provide critical home care for their sick children in three main ways: (1) they continue to feed and offer more fluids, (2) they give appropriate home treatment for specific infections, and (3) they take their children, when needed, for medical care.

Lost fluids from diarrhea, vomiting, and fever during illness must be replaced by more fluids, more frequently. Children also need to be actively fed during illness to prevent malnutrition and micronutrient deficiencies. Given that anorexia and lethargy are common during illness, caregivers need skills to encourage children to drink and eat, as well as knowledge about the content of what, how much, and how frequently to offer fluids and food. After the episode of illness, the child needs to be encouraged to eat more to catch up on any growth lost during illness.

Continue to feed and offer more fluids—Oral rehydration therapy (ORT) includes offering more fluids to sick children and continuing to offer food during illness to limit the poor effects on nutrition. Based on the Lancet model for estimating preventable deaths, giving ORT to prevent or treat dehydration while continuing feeding could prevent the deaths of 259,000 children in Eastern and Southern Africa each year.

The survey found mixed results from sites in five programs giving ORT to children with diarrhea (see table 22.3). Several explanations are possible for the reduced intake of fluids and foods when children are sick. Children might refuse to eat and drink, or caregivers might withhold food and fluids, thinking that they might contribute to the amount and duration of watery diarrhea. Surveys conducted in the Ntungamo District of Uganda after the initiation of community-based interventions found greater improvements in giving ORT to children with fever or an acute respiratory infection (see figure 22.6).

The prevalence of withholding food, breast milk, and fluids is high, ranging from 16 percent to 65 percent in developing countries (Hill, Kirkwood, and Edmond 2004). In Malawi, for example, "bad milk" from an illness of the mother is believed to cause a child's illness. Many mothers do not believe in increasing breastfeeding during diarrhea, even though studies have shown that children usually do not refuse breast milk when sick (Huffman and Combest 1990). Although some progress has been made, preventing deaths caused by dehydration appears to be a difficult task because practices are affected by cultural beliefs and lack of knowledge.

Table 22.3. Caregivers Giving Food and Fluids (ORT) during Diarrhea in Five ESAR Sites
(percent)

	Implementing sites, Malawi[a]		UThukela District, South Africa[b]		Mkuranga District, Tanzania[c]		Kasese District, Uganda[e]		Ntungamo District, Uganda[f]	
	Baseline	Follow-up	Baseline	Follow-up	Baseline	Follow-up	Baseline	Follow-up	Baseline	Follow-up
Children under 5 with diarrhea given ORT at home (ORS or HAF)	36 ORS	38 ORS	—	—	43	87	—	89	17	43
Children 0–23 months with diarrhea breastfed same or more	63	53	—	—	27	—	—	59	56	36
Children 6–59 months with diarrhea offered same or more fluids	39	76	31	26	31	—	59	61	51	58
Children 6–59 months with diarrhea given same or more solid or mashed food	8	47	33	44	—	—	34	57	51	37

Source: Table prepared by authors; see endnote 2 for survey sources for a.–f.

Note: ESAR = UNICEF's Eastern and Southern Africa Region; HAF = home available fluid; ORS = oral rehydration salts; ORT = oral rehydration therapy. — = not available.

Figure 22.6. Caregivers Giving Food and Fluids (ORT) to Children during Fever and Acute Respiratory Infection (ARI) in Ntungamo District, Uganda, before and after Intervention

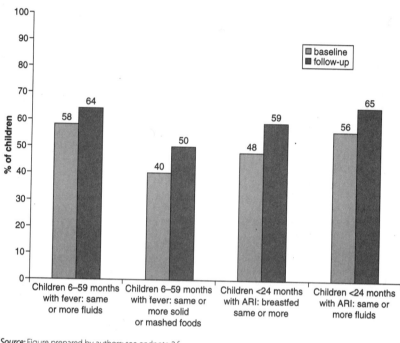

Source: Figure prepared by authors; see endnote 2.f.
Note: ORT = oral rehydration therapy.

Home treatment of infections—Prompt and correct treatment of non-severe malaria, pneumonia, and other infections in the home can reduce the severity of illness and save the lives of sick young children. Appropriate home treatment involves recognizing the illness early, using appropriate drugs promptly and correctly, avoiding ineffective or harmful treatments, and taking the child promptly to a health facility if the condition does not improve. Based on the Lancet model, gains in the treatment of malaria alone could prevent as many as 152,000 deaths of young children each year in Eastern and Southern Africa. When treatment with antimalarial drugs is extended from the clinic into the community and household, it is more accessible and can be given without delay.

Only a few examples were found where home treatment of infections was documented in the IMCI review both before and after interventions. Evidence shows, however, that home treatment improved in two programs. In Malawi, the proportion of children age 6–59 months treated at home for fever increased from 72 percent to 78 percent, and use of sulphadoxine-pyrimethamine (SP) for treating fever (malaria) increased from 18 percent to 27 percent. For children age 0–23 months with cough and difficult breathing (pneumonia), the proportion of children receiving an antibiotic at home was 30 percent in implementing sites, compared with only 14 percent in control sites. In Kasese District (Uganda), the proportion of children with fever treated at home increased from 14 percent to 26 percent. Although there is no baseline comparison, the follow-up survey found that 10 percent of children with fever were being treated with SP and 43 percent of children with pneumonia received antibiotic treatment at home.

In Malawi, the child's mother was the person who most typically administered drugs at home, and the main sources were drug shops or stalls. Another 16 percent of children who received treatment at home were given their drugs by a health facility. The community worker was mentioned as a source for only 3 percent of children. Counseling caregivers was an important intervention to improve home-based treatment in implementing sites in Malawi and in Kasese District (Uganda). In Kasese, home treatment of fever for young children increased from 14 percent to 26 percent, although the district was not one of the pilot sites for testing community-based distribution of antimalarial drugs.

Care seeking—Untreated illness, or delayed treatment, is a major cause of childhood mortality. When a child is too sick to be treated by the family at home, the family needs to recognize the severity of the child's condition, act quickly to seek care, and use lifesaving medical services. Health workers who can provide quality care need to respond effectively, with adequate supplies and equipment, to save the lives of severely ill children.

When illness is prolonged, the signs of illness change over the course of the illness; parents receive new information and constraining conditions shift. Consequently, parents make new decisions about seeking care over the duration of the child's illness. An indicator of poor care seeking, however, is that many children still die at home without medical care. Hill, Kirkwood, and Edmond (2004) cite eight studies that found that 7 percent to 72 percent of children who died had not been taken to a health facility. In the communities implementing the community component in Malawi, 7 percent of households with children under 5 reported at least one child death in the 12 months preceding the postintervention survey. Sixty percent of deaths occurred at home, and half of these deaths were children who had not been taken to a health facility (Balyeku, Matinga, and Bello 2004).

The aim of community-based interventions to improve care seeking is to help persons who care for a sick child at home to be able to respond quickly and appropriately to signs of severe illness. Most surveys obtained information on the caregiver's knowledge of danger signs, the precondition for recognizing that a child is seriously ill, and for then taking the child for care outside the home.

Although the surveys asked different questions, all the programs documented improvement—sometimes as much as four-fold—in the caregivers' knowledge of danger signs requiring the family to take the child immediately to a health facility. For example, in UThukela District (South Africa), the proportion of caregivers who could list at least two general danger signs increased from 28 percent to 63 percent. In Ntungamo District (Uganda), identification of blood in the stool as a danger sign improved from 18 percent to 79 percent. In the Malawi sites, identification of vomiting everything increased from 19 percent to 37 percent and, in Kasese District (Uganda), from 13 percent to 32 percent. Mothers identified that a child not able to drink or breastfeed is a danger sign in Malawi, 15 percent pre- and 48 percent postintervention, and, in Kasese District, 12 percent pre- and 33 percent postintervention. The proportion of caregivers who identified convulsions as a danger sign increased from 20 percent to 70 percent in Ntungamo District. The proportion of caregivers who identified weakness as a danger sign increased in Malawi sites from 41 percent to 67 percent and, in Ntungamo District (Uganda) from 49 percent to 79 percent. More complicated signs of dehydration, such as sunken eyes, are difficult to teach, but efforts in Ntungamo District achieved remarkable improvements from 30 percent before to 75 percent after interventions.

In general, community-based interventions need to support facility-based counseling of caregivers on danger signs for childhood illness because recognizing the severity of illness is a precondition for families to take urgent action. Even when families recognize danger signs, however, they may have other reasons for not seeking medical care for their sick child. Delays to care seeking in Malawi, for example, are considered to be affected by local beliefs. Before the project, 43 percent of caregivers believed that some of the conditions should not be treated in health facilities but, rather, should be treated by a traditional healer. Unfortunately, such conditions are among the most life-threatening, including malaria or fever (28 percent of childhood deaths), diarrhea

(24 percent), pneumonia (17 percent), and convulsions (9 percent). Although the proportion of caregivers identified as having these beliefs declined to 34 percent after the intervention, beliefs likely continued to influence decisions about which signs indicate that a sick child needs to be seen by a health worker (Balyeku, Matinga, and Bello 2004).

Unfortunately, the surveys have little information on how caregivers responded when recognizing the signs and severity of the child's illness. In Malawi and in Ntungamo District (Uganda), however, caregivers were asked what they would do if a child had cough and difficult breathing. In Malawi, before the intervention, 31 percent of caregivers reported that they would take the child for treatment. After the intervention, this response increased to 71 percent. In Ntungamo District (Uganda), 33 percent of caregivers before and 57 percent of caregivers after the intervention said that they would seek treatment for a child with cough and difficult breathing. These results suggest that the interventions helped families not only to identify a danger sign, but also to recognize that certain signs, such as difficult breathing, require immediate medical attention.

What families think about available health services can also contribute to delays in seeking care. In Malawi, for example, families who delayed seeking medical attention for their sick children perceived greater barriers in clinic care after community-based interventions attempted to improve care seeking (see table 22.4). When families were asked how the quality of services should be improved, caregivers mentioned that they would like to see improvements in drug supplies (74 percent), atmosphere— that is, more friendly and respectful and with minimal waiting time (61 percent), general cleanliness (18 percent)—and proper and easy-to-follow instructions (17 percent).

As these results indicate, community-based efforts to encourage families to seek care for their sick children will be undermined if clinic services, and

Table 22.4. Caregiver Reasons for Delaying Care Seeking for Sick Children in Malawi Implementing Sites
(*percent*)

Stated reason	Implementing sites, Malawi	
	Baseline	*Follow-up*
Lack of drugs	22	50
Long distance	14	36
Unsatisfactory quality of care	13	33
Financial costs	8	31

Source: Table prepared by authors; see endnote 2.a. for survey source.

access to them, do not also improve. For this reason, it is recommended that community-based interventions in the IMCI strategy be implemented with parallel improvements in the training of health workers, supervision, communication with clients, and drug supplies.

Coordinating a Package of Interventions for Greater Efficiency and Effectiveness

As presented previously, baseline and follow-up surveys in the five programs in the Eastern and Southern Africa Region found improvements in many of the individual key family practices promoted by the household and community component of the IMCI strategy. The strategy is comprehensive and is focused on the major causes of childhood deaths and poor development in developing countries rather than on a selective one or two causes. IMCI is also an integrated strategy because an individual child is likely to be vulnerable to several life-threatening conditions (Victora et al. 2004). In impoverished settings, saving a child from one condition does not prevent death from other causes. Thus, the IMCI strategy combines management and prevention interventions for multiple conditions for each individual child, at each contact of the child and his or her family with a community-based intervention, as well as with the health system.

Efficiency should increase by coordinating interventions. Currently, for example, vitamin A supplements are distributed with immunizations, reducing logistical requirements and other costs. Interventions to promote a set of key family practices also have cost benefits over programmatic efforts to target individual behaviors. There is a cost benefit of helping a mother to breastfeed and, at the same time, improving her personal hygiene; educating her on the use of insecticide-treated bednets, timely complementary feeding, and ORT use; and helping her to recognize when her infant needs to be treated at the health clinic. All these interventions are delivered through community interventions in the IMCI strategy.

Coordinating interventions within a package also makes them more effective and robust. Packages are useful, for example, in reducing missed opportunities. While weighing children, community workers can also check to make sure that the child is immunized or recognize when a sick child needs referral to a health clinic.

Combining interventions can also result in larger reductions of deaths. The Lancet model demonstrates that several interventions, primarily those related to improved nutrition (breastfeeding, complementary feeding, and micronutrients), prevent deaths of children under 5 across multiple causes. Breastfeeding and improved complementary feeding reduces deaths caused primarily by diarrhea and pneumonia as well as deaths caused by measles and malaria. The micronutrients vitamin A and zinc can also prevent some deaths due to multiple causes. Such interventions against multiple causes of death are particularly effective in a package of community-based interventions.

Despite the absence of evaluations of the impact on child mortality and development, wide-scale improvements in specific key family practices are likely to have reduced childhood deaths and improved the growth and development of many young children in the sites surveyed. The survey evidence also suggests that, by integrating several interventions in each of the communities, improvements were effected in multiple practices, each adding greater protection for children.

Table 22.5 summarizes the changes across the implementing sites reporting family practices. This summary includes those practices determined by the Lancet model likely to have the greatest impact on preventing childhood deaths. Care-seeking knowledge has also been included, as it affects the outcome of many childhood conditions. The table also provides an estimate of the potential number of deaths of children in Eastern and Southern Africa that could be prevented with wide coverage of each of these practices, based on the Lancet model.

Even though data sets are not complete, the surveys indicate that at least eight practices likely to save the most lives appear to have been improved in the Malawi implementing sites. In Kasese District, six key practices improved; in UThukela, Mkuranga, and Ntungamo Districts, each improved five key practices. The Nutrition and ECD Project achieved improvements in three of the four key practices surveyed.

It is not clear why some practices could be changed across sites and others not. As the discussion indicated, differences in interventions or the quality of their delivery could make a difference. In some cases, difficulties in measuring changes may have occurred. Nevertheless, there is evidence that each of these care practices, known to be key to reducing child mortality, was improved in the majority of sites where practices were measured. Even practices that are relatively difficult to improve—such as breastfeeding and complementary feeding, which usually require multiple contacts with families—were improved. Less improvement, however, was seen in the community practices, including immunizations, that required support from the health system to meet the increased demand for services from the community.

Table 22.5. Changes in Reported Practices That Are Likely to Have the Greatest Impact on Preventing Childhood Deaths

Practice	Estimated deaths preventable by full coverage of a single intervention across ESAR Percent*	Number*	Implementing sites, Malawi	UThukela District, South Africa	Mkuranga District, Tanzania	Nutrition & ECD Project, Uganda	Kasese District, Uganda	Ntungamo District, Uganda
Prevention								
Breastfeeding	13	223,000	↗	↗	—	↗	↗	✗
Insecticide-treated bednets and other materials	12	220,000	↗	n.a. (Not a malaria area)	↗	—	↗	↗
Complementary feeding	7	126,000	↗	↗	—	↗	↗	↗
Vitamin A	3	58,000	✗	↗	↗	↑	✗↗	↗
Water, sanitation, hygiene	3	51,000	↗	—	↗	↗	✗↗	↗
Measles vaccine	1	25,000	↗	↗	↗	—	↗	↗
Treatment								
Oral rehydration therapy	14	259,000	↗	↗	↗	—	↗	✗
Antimalarials	8	152,000	↗	—	—	—	↗	—
Care-seeking knowledge								
Knowledge of danger signs	—	—	↗	↗	—	—	↗	↗

Source: Summary of authors (confirmed by expert committee) based on data presented in this chapter.
Note: ↗ Improvement, ↑ little or no change, ↘ deterioration, ✗ mixed results, — no data, n.a. not applicable. ESAR = UNICEF's Eastern and Southern Africa Region. * Rounded to nearest percentage or thousand.

Conclusion

The evidence gathered here demonstrates that the household and community component of the IMCI strategy improves knowledge, attitudes, and the family and community practices that affect child survival, health, and development.

The review found that 18 countries in the Eastern and Southern Africa Region are actively implementing the IMCI household and community component. These countries use a variety of methods to improve family care practices and build the capacity of communities to improve the conditions that affect the health of their children.

Even in the absence of evaluations of impact, substantial research shows that wide-scale improvements in these specific behaviors are likely to reduce childhood deaths and improve the healthy growth and development of many young children in the sites surveyed. The evidence also suggests that, by integrating several interventions in each of the communities, improvements can be effected in multiple practices, each adding greater protection to children.

What remains is wide-scale implementation of known interventions. Based on the Lancet model for estimating preventable deaths, implementing wide coverage of a set of available interventions to strengthen family care practices could prevent more than 7 million deaths of children under 5 by 2015 in the Eastern and Southern Africa Region. This would succeed in meeting the Millennium Development Goal of reducing under-5 mortality by two-thirds in the region. There is no need to wait for new evidence or new technologies to accelerate efforts to achieve this goal.

Notes

1. This chapter reports some of the findings of the UNICEF review of the household and community interventions (Lucas et al. 2005). See the original report, available from UNICEF, for a more detailed description of program activities, a review of the literature on family practices, a model for estimating preventable deaths, survey results, and recommendations for a way forward. The Department for International Development (DFID) of the United Kingdom supported the review under the project *Strengthening UNICEF Human Rights Based Programming* (Sub Project 5).

2. The reference letters in figures 22.1–22.6 and tables 22.2–22.5 refer to the following survey sources. Sources are cited fully in Lucas et al. (2005).

(a) Malawi implementation sites

Baseline: Household baseline survey on key community child care practices in selected districts of Malawi, December 2000, supplemented by the DHS survey, 2000; baseline survey on early childhood care and development (ECCD), 2003.

Follow-up: Balyeku, Matinga, and Bello (2004).

(b) South Africa: UThukela District Child Survival Project

Baseline and follow-up: World Vision South Africa, final evaluation report, May 2004.

(c) Tanzania: Mkuranga District Child Survival Project

Baseline: AMREF baseline survey, January 2003.

Follow-up: Village health day and monthly household data from community-owned resource persons (CORPs), 2004.

(d) Uganda: Nutrition and Early Childhood Development Project (NECDP)

Baseline: UNICEF State of the World's Children (1998); Ministry of Health NECDP, baseline survey, November 2000.

Follow-up: Re-survey for NECDP final report, August 2003; Alderman et al., draft report, November 2003.

(e) Uganda: Kasese District

Baseline: Kasese District baseline study, 2001.

Follow-up: Family care practices in Uganda, 2003.

(f) Uganda: Ntungamo District

Baselines: Ntungamo District health service report, 1999; baseline survey report, February 2000; DHS survey, May 2000; Africare/UNICEF/Government of Uganda, baseline survey study report, 2001.

Follow-up: Mid-term evaluation KPC study, September 2001; Ministry of Health family care practices in Uganda, 2003.

References

Alderman, H., P. Britto, P. Engle, and A. Siddiqi. 2003. "Evaluation of Uganda Nutrition and Early Child Development Project." Draft report. World Bank, Washington, DC.

Anderson, J. W., B. M. Johnstone, and D. T. Remley. 1999. "Breastfeeding and Cognitive Development: A Meta-Analysis." *American Journal of Clinical Nutrition* 70: 525–35.

Armstrong Schellenberg, J. R., T. Adam, H. Mshinda, H. Masanja, G. Kabadi, O. Mukasa., T. John, S. Charles, R. Nathan, and K. Wilczynska. 2004. "Effectiveness and Cost of Facility-Based Integrated Management of Childhood Illness (IMCI) in Tanzania." *The Lancet* 364: 1583–94.

Balyeku, A., P. Matinga, and G. Bello. 2004. "Follow-Up Survey Report: Family Care Practices that Promote Child Health, Nutrition, and Development." Malawi Country Report. Government of Malawi and UNICEF, Lilongwe.

Caulfield, L. E., M. de Onis, M. Blössner, and R. E. Black. 2004. "Undernutrition as an Underlying Cause of Child Deaths Associated with Diarrhea, Pneumonia, Malaria, and Measles." *American Journal of Clinical Nutrition* 80: 193–98.

Coutsoudis, A., K. Pillay, E. Spooner, L. Kuhn, and H. M. Coovadia. 1999. "Influence of Infant-Feeding Patterns on Early Mother-to-Child Transmission of HIV-1 in Durban, South Africa: A Prospective Cohort Study. South African Vitamin A Study Group." *The Lancet* 354: 288–93.

el Arifeen, S. E., L. S. Blum, D. M. E. Hoque, E. K. Chowdhury, R. Khan, R. E. Black, C. Victoria, and J. Bryce. 2004. "Integrated Management of Childhood Illness (IMCI) in Bangladesh: Early Findings from a Cluster-Randomised Study." *The Lancet* 364: 1595–602.

Esrey, S. A., J. B. Potash, L. Roberts, and C. Shiff. 1991. "Effects of Improved Water Supply and Sanitation on Ascariasis, Diarrhoea, Dracunculiasis, Hookworm Infection, Schistomsomiasis, and Trachoma." *Bulletin of the World Health Organization* 69: 609–21.

Hill, Z., B. Kirkwood, and K. Edmond. 2004. *Family and Community Practices that Promote Child Survival, Growth, and Development: A Review of the Evidence.* Geneva: World Health Organization.

Huffman, S. L., and C. Combest. 1990. "Role of Breastfeeding in the Prevention and Treatment of Diarrhoea." *Journal of Diarrhoeal Disease Research* 8: 68–81.

Jones, G., R. W. Steketee, R. E. Black, Z. A. Bhutta, S. S. Morris, and the Bellagio Child Study Group. 2003. "How Many Deaths Can We Prevent This Year?" *The Lancet* 362: 65–71.

Lengler, C. 2001. *Insecticide-Treated Bednets and Curtains for Preventing Malaria.* Oxford: The Cochrane Library.

Lucas, J. E., J. Jitta, G. Jones, and K. Wilczynska-Ketende. 2005. *Implementing the Household and Community Component of IMCI in the Eastern and Southern Africa Region (ESAR).* New York and Nairobi: UNICEF.

Martorell, R. 1997. "Undernutrition during Pregnancy and Early Childhood: Consequences for Cognitive and Behavioral Development." In *Early Child Development: Investing in Our Children's Future,* ed. M. E. Young, 39–83. Amsterdam: Elsevier.

Malawi. Ministry of Health. 2004. "Follow-up Report on Family Care Practices that Promote Child Health, Nutrition, and Development." November.

Schellenberg, J. R., S. Abdulla, R. Nathan, O. Mukasa, T. J. Marchant, N. Kikumbih, A. Mushi, H. Mponda, H. Minja, and H. Mshinda. 2001. "Effect of

Large-Scale Social Marketing of Insecticide-Treated Nets on Child Survival in Rural Tanzania." *The Lancet* 357: 1241–47.

Tanzania and USAID (U.S. Agency for International Development). 2006. *Tanzania FY06 Country Action Plan.* Dar es Salaam: Government of the Republic of Tanzania and USAID.

Uauy, R., and I. De Andraca. 1995. "Human Milk and Breastfeeding for Optimal Mental Development." *Journal of Nutrition* 125 (Supplement 8): S1178–280.

UNICEF (United Nations Children's Fund). 2004. *The State of the World's Children 2005.* New York: UNICEF.

Victora, C. G., K. Hanson, J. Bryce, and J. P. Vaughan. 2004. "Achieving Universal Coverage with Health Interventions." *The Lancet* 364: 1541–48.

WHO (World Health Organization). 1997. *Health and Environment in Sustainable Development: Five Years after the Earth Summit.* Geneva: WHO.

———. 2001. *The WHO Global Data Bank on Breastfeeding and Complementary Feeding.* Retrieved August 28, 2006, from http://www.who.int/nutrition/databases/infantfeeding/en/index.html.

———. Collaborative Study Team. 2000. "Effect of Breastfeeding on Infant and Child Mortality Due to Infectious Diseases in Less Developed Countries: A Pooled Analysis." *The Lancet* 355: 1104.

WHO and UNICEF. 1990. *The Innocenti Declaration on the Protection, Promotion, and Support of Breastfeeding.* Florence: Innocenti Center.

World Bank. 2001. *Immunization at a Glance.* Washington, DC: World Bank.

Challenges and Ways Forward

CHAPTER 23

Can Early Childhood Programs Be Financially Sustainable in Africa?

Adriana Jaramillo and Alain Mingat

Research in Africa and other parts of the world suggests that preschool has positive impacts on primary school learning outcomes (see chapter 3). However, this in itself is not enough to justify that preschool activities be publicly funded. In a world of scarce resources, governments must consider financial sustainability—the cost and resourcing dimensions of early childhood services—in determining policy on their provision. This chapter[1] examines the financial sustainability of preschool programs by comparing the costs of preschool with primary school and of formal preschools with community-based early childhood programs, and then discusses ways that governments could allocate resources to preschool activities.

Considering Costs

For financial sustainability, three complementary aspects of cost play a role: (1) priorities and competition among alternative claims on government budgets and donor contributions, (2) cost-efficiency and the relation between spending and expected benefits, and (3) the differing costs of various delivery modes. Under the common label of preschool, for example, activities may differ in focus, implementation mode, and content. In addition, costs for similar program components may vary across countries.

Priorities and Competition among Alternative Claims

The indicative framework of the *Education for All* Fast-Track Initiative (FTI)[2] suggests that 50 percent of recurrent government spending on education be allocated to the primary cycle. If this proportion is accepted as a benchmark, the implication is that the other 50 percent of the education budget must cover all other levels (preschool, lower and upper secondary general, technical education, and higher education). While convincing arguments can be made for allocating more resources to preschool, other segments of the system can make similarly compelling claims. One could suggest that external funding be used to complement domestic public allocations for preschool, but the same argument holds for other sector needs. External funds are also scarce and, because the donor community has given priority to the goal of universal primary education, primary schooling is likely to absorb a significant proportion of donor financing. How, then, can adequate, financially sustainable funding be found for preschool?

A key question relating to financial sustainability is, "Are the benefits of preschool greater than the costs?" The answer requires an estimation of both costs and benefits, which suggests that careful studies be undertaken to obtain the relevant data and conduct the analysis. Jaramillo and Tietjen (2001) conducted such a study in Cape Verde and Guinea. While a detailed cost-benefit analysis of preschool programs in Africa is beyond the scope of this chapter, it is possible to compare formal preschools and nonformal community-based early childhood programs. First, however, it is useful to compare the costs of preschool and primary schools.

The Cost-Efficiency of Preschool in Relation to Primary School

Table 23.1 presents data on the unit costs of public preschool and primary education in four countries (Benin, Cameroon, Côte d'Ivoire, and Niger).

Within this small sample, it shows that publicly funded preschool can be relatively costly. There is some variation within this group of countries, but in all of them, preschool is more costly per pupil than primary education. On average, the unit cost of preschool is 0.236 times the per capita gross domestic product (GDP). This cost exceeds the cost of primary education, which, in this sample, is 0.139 times the per capita GDP. Thus, in this sample, preschool is 70 percent more costly. The authors are reluctant to use these figures as estimates for Sub-Saharan Africa however,

Table 23.1. Selected Data on the Cost of Public Preschool and Primary School in Four Countries

	Per capita GDP (CFAF 000)	Unit cost						Pupil-teacher ratio			
		CFAF		Per capita GDP		Preschool / Primary (a)		Preschool	Primary	Preschool/ Primary (b)	Ratio a / b
		Preschool	Primary	Preschool	Primary						
Benin, 1998	227	33,200	27,600	0.146	0.121	1.20		28	53	1.89	0.635
Cameroon, 1998	363	50,000	26,000	0.138	0.072	1.92		23	56	2.43	0.790
Côte d'Ivoire, 2000	464	107,300	49,055	0.217	0.106	2.05		23	43	1.87	1.098
Niger, 1998	105	63,779	36,972	0.608	0.352	1.73		20	39	1.95	0.885
Average 4 countries	—	—	—	**0.236**	**0.139**	**1.70**		**23.5**	**47.8**	**2.03**	**0.838**
Sub-Saharan Africa	—	—	—	0.170	0.129	1.37		27.2	44.6	1.64	0.838

Source: Bruns, Mingat, and Rakotomalala (2003).

Note: — = not available.

because these countries are unlikely to be representative of the region as a whole. Other sources (Bruns, Mingat, and Rakotomalala 2003) show that the unit cost of primary education in low-income Sub-Saharan African countries represents, on average, 12.9 percent of per capita GDP, while it is estimated at 13.9 percent in our sample of four countries.

Table 23.1 also shows the pupil-teacher ratio (PTR) in both primary education and preschool for our sample and for the region as a whole (Bruns, Mingat, and Rakotomalala 2003). In our sample, PTR is 23.5 in preschool and 47.8 in primary education, while the corresponding figures for the region are 27.2 and 44.6. These data suggest that even if our sample deviates from the average figures for the region, the overall pattern looks relatively the same. In our sample of four countries, the ratio of unit costs in preschool and primary education (1.7) is lower than that of PTR (2.0), which implies that teaching staff are paid less in preschool, on average, than in primary education (or that nonsalary inputs are less abundant in preschool than at the primary level). If it is mostly the salary argument that holds, the data imply that, on average, teacher salaries in preschool would represent about 81 percent that in primary education.

To estimate the ratio of unit cost in preschool and in primary education for the Sub-Saharan African region, we use this latter figure (0.81) and recalibrate the ratio found in our sample of four countries according to the ratio of the PTR in preschool and primary education in the sample and in the region. This calculation leads to a ratio of 1.37 between unit cost in preschool and primary schooling, which in turn implies that the average unit cost in preschool could represent about 0.17 unit of per capita GDP. (This figure results from weighing the percentage of preschool teachers with the figures known for primary teachers.) It is likely that, as within the sample, substantial variation exists from one country to another, depending both on the level of remuneration of personnel and the way the services are organized (for example, PTR varies between 15 and 47).

On the benefits side of preschool, it is possible to distinguish between benefits that arise during preschool itself and those that arise subsequently. During preschool, evidence shows that women whose children attend preschool are freed for productive activity, and that girls whose younger siblings have access to preschool may be more likely to be enrolled in primary education. For example, regarding the benefits associated with the reduction of opportunity cost of women and girls' time that could be associated with preschool, Lokshin, Glinskaya, and Garcia (2000) showed that, in Kenya, early childhood development (ECD) programs that target poor households boost the enrollment in primary school of older girls and increase the number of mothers who work, thus augmenting the family's income.

In terms of long-term benefits, one can expect that children who have benefited from preschool are better prepared for primary school (see chapter 3). Consequently they are less likely to repeat grades and drop out before completing primary school. Concerning the impact of preschool on improving the pattern of student flow in primary education, there are several elements for the analysis. From the estimates presented in table 23.2, we have the sense that a 50-percent coverage in preschool (which represents about a cost of two years of study for half of the relevant school-age population, that is the equivalent of one year at the preschool level) could imply a decrease of 6.2 percentage points in the repetition rate (from 20.4 to 14.2 percent) in primary education and a gain of 15.9 percentage points in the retention rate (from 65.3 to 81.2 percent). These improvements in student flow can be consolidated in a gain of 20 percent in the efficiency of resource use in primary education (the ratio of the number of student years effectively used to the number of student years required to produce the same number of outputs without either repetition or dropout). Twenty percent of a six-year cycle amounts to a gain equivalent to 1.2 years. Given that the unit cost of preschool is estimated on average to amount to 1.37 times that of primary education, we can conclude that the cost of preschool could be offset for up to 87 percent by the expected benefits incurred in the course of primary education.

If we want to be optimistic, without even looking at the benefits part of the equation, it can be concluded that most of the public spending in preschool could be recouped through efficiency gains in primary education.

Table 23.2. Simulation of the Survival Rate to Grade 5 and Repetition Rate According to Preschool Coverage in 24 Sub-Saharan African Countries

Preschool GER (%)	0	10	20	30	40	50	60
Repetition rate (%)							
All African countries	20.4	19.2	17.9	16.7	15.5	14.2	13.0
Francophone countries	22.7	21.5	20.3	19.0	17.8	16.6	15.3
Anglophone countries	15.3	14.0	12.8	11.6	10.4	9.1	7.9
Survival rate to grade 5 (%)							
Total effect	65.3	68.5	71.6	74.8	78.0	81.2	84.3
Indirect effect	65.3	67.4	69.5	71.6	73.7	75.8	77.8
Direct effect	65.3	66.4	67.5	68.5	69.6	70.7	71.8

Source: Authors' calculations.
Note: GER = gross enrollment ratio.

Other benefits (in particular in the course of preschool) need not be very important to allow for spending in preschool to achieve an acceptable balance between costs and benefits.

Being pragmatic and concrete, we may want to stress that these calculations are based both on average figures and on a delivery mode of preschool services that may not be the most efficient. Cleary, there is great variation in the possible ways to implement preschool activities—in terms of focus, content, and intensity of inputs per child. Therefore it is not totally convincing to base the assessment on a mix of delivery modes, some of which are inefficient.

If we could identify the most efficient ways of implementing a preschool system, the supposition is that this mode would provide the best possible combination of costs and benefits. The results stated suggest that the search for efficiency in preschool needs to continue. Careful analysis needs to continue because the justification for public investment in preschool probably rests on the capacity of a government to implement preschool activities that are more efficient than those currently provided.

The Respective Costs of Formal Preschool and Community-Based[3] Early Childhood Programs

Arguments cited earlier here and in other chapters in this book support the development of ECD activities in African countries, provided that they are organized efficiently. As noted, ECD activities can be implemented in various ways. The range of options is relatively wide and varies on several dimensions—content, institutional setting and financing, unit cost, and input mix. Even within one mode—public preschools—provision can be organized differently, resulting in quite different levels of unit cost. For example, within the Sub-Saharan Africa region, pupil-teacher ratio varies between 1 to 15 and 1 to 47. (Other things being equal, the cost per pupil is more than three times higher in the first than in the second case.) Within the sample of the four countries analyzed in table 23.1, the preschool unit cost (expressed as a proportion of per capita GDP) is four times greater in Niger (0.608) than in Benin or Cameroon (0.146 and 0.138, respectively).

Obviously, the magnitude of variability is much greater if we compare the costs of formal preschools (characterized by purpose-built structures, official employees with preservice training, adequate equipment and supplies) and truly community-based preschools (characterized by make shift structures, local teachers or caregivers with in-service training, less equipment and supplies). The cost per pupil in community-based activities is likely to be lower than that observed in a formal setting. The level of public spending per pupil is generally much smaller in community-based ECD programs than in public preschools. In the Sub-Saharan African context, we have data on both formal and community-based programs in Cape Verde, Guinea, Guinea-Bissau, and Senegal (see table 23.3).

Even though these cost estimates can be taken only for reasonable orders of magnitude, the data presented in table 23.3 clearly show that community-based programs are less costly in terms of public resources than formal public preschool programs (here between 1.78 and 5.37 times less costly) with an average figure of 4.2 percent of GDP.

The data also suggest that if there is wide variation in per-pupil spending in the public preschool system (as noted earlier in the Benin, Cameroon, Côte d'Ivoire, and Niger sample—table 23.1), it seems to be much less the case for community-based programs. (Across the four countries—Cape Verde, Guinea, Guinea-Bissau, and Senegal—costs are concentrated between 3.5 and 5.7 percent of GDP of the country.) This cost is obviously good news for the potential public finance sustainability of ECD investments in the context of the stringent constraints that countries face for achieving the various Dakar goals for *Education for All* (EFA).

However, it is not enough that community-based programs are less expensive to justify that they should be expanded. The benefits also need to be considered. The data on the benefits of community-based ECD programs are even scarcer than studies on the benefits of publicly funded preschools. If we focus on the impact of community-based programs on the frequency of repetition and dropout in the course of primary education, the only study we know is one by Jaramillo and Tietjen (2001) on Cape Verde and Guinea. In that study, outcomes were measured in terms of cognitive (language, basic concepts, and readiness for reading) and physical development at the outset of preschool, comparing public and community-based programs. The results show

Table 23.3. Per-Child Public Spending in Public and Community-Based Preschool Programs in Four Countries (Per Capita GDP Units)

	Public preschool (a)	Community-based preschool (b)	Ratio a / b
Cape Verde	0.066	0.037	1.78
Guinea	0.073	0.037	1.97
Guinea-Bissau	0.117	0.035	3.34
Senegal	0.306	0.057	5.37
Average	0.141	0.042	3.39

Source: Prepared by the authors with data collected through World Bank-funded projects. Data for Cape Verde from Jaramillo and Tietjen (2001).

that, despite the relatively substantial difference in per-pupil public spending, there is little difference, on average, in outcomes. If anything, the community-based programs tend to outperform the publicly funded preschools. However, variance in the quality of both formal and community-based programs is substantial.

A cost analysis within the health sector by Soucat et al. (2003) has implications for the costing of early childhood programs. The authors analyzed how to improve outcomes on health programs and identified what they call the bottlenecks for health service delivery and the new performance frontier. The authors argue that while a basic package of health services can make the difference in health outcomes, implementation bottlenecks, rather than the package, need to be costed. According to their findings, a new approach to budgeting will need to focus on strategies to overcome the bottlenecks to coverage with packages of known and predictable impact. Of key relevance for the work on ECD are the family and community-based service delivery packages.

Countries such as Guinea, Mali, and Tanzania have defined minimum or essential packages of care they want to provide. Some attempts have been made to cost and align funding for the packages, as in Burkina Faso and Zambia. Nevertheless, this approach has often failed to take into account the policy and operational constraints to its implementation. The coverage of the basic package, especially among the poor, is often well below what had been hoped. A likely explanation is that, in the real world, a basic package is not delivered as a set of separate disease-specific activities the way it is often costed. Instead, it is a part of a system in which service delivery modes determine the inputs and operational strategies more than diseases affect cost. To improve the coverage of the basic package, a country needs to address various systemwide bottlenecks, particularly in terms of human resources, physical accessibility, supplies, and logistics, as well as technical and organizational capacity. As a consequence, budgets are not—and should not be—organized by diseases. Practically, although the nature of the services still matters, a set of systemwide bottlenecks in service delivery rather than the basic package needs to be identified and costed.

Policy Implications

The policy implications of these findings are twofold and relatively straightforward: First, because community-based ECD programs and community- and family-based care for health service delivery are clearly less costly in terms of public finance than traditional formal approaches, while producing outcomes that appear to be at least equivalent or even better (as was the case for household and community-based interventions for modifying health indicators), there is a clear message that in times of stringent constraints on public resources, community-based integrated health, nutrition, and early education programs are to be preferred.

Second, if community-based programs are characterized by unit costs of about 5 percent of per capita GDP, while generating potentially similar levels of outcomes for children, these programs may not only be better than formal or traditional programs, they are also justified in terms of the allocation of public resources because the cost-benefit ratio of community-based ECD activities, instead of being 0.9 (1.2/1.4) in the case of formal preschool, stands at 3.1 (1.2 · 12.9/5). Even though this figure is to be taken only for its order of magnitude, it provides a reasonable level of confidence that extending ECD activities in a well-designed community-based model is to be considered as a serious option. Soucat et al. (2003) argue that 15 years of experience with the Minimum Package of Activities in countries such as Guinea or Mali have demonstrated that actions taken at the household level (such as exclusive breastfeeding and proper feeding practices, home care for common illness including diarrhea and acute respiratory infection, safe sexual behavior, use of bed nets, and so on) have a significant impact on outcomes such as under-5 mortality and nutritional development of children.

Creating an ECD Policy

This section of the chapter discusses three factors that contribute to developing a government's policy in terms of how it contributes to early childhood programming and includes a simulation model that can be used to calculate the level of resources needed. These determining factors are (1) the amount of public resources that could be mobilized to provide the services, (2) the coverage desired for the 0–3 population, and (3) the coverage desired for the 4–6 population. Each of these factors of policy formulation has important implications, which are described next.

Availability and Allocation of Public Resources to Early Childhood Programs

One element that could facilitate the definition of an ECD policy is the calculation of what could be, by the year 2015, the budgetary envelope to support early childhood activities. Given the integrated approach of ECD activities, the budget can be attached to both education and health, with the assumption that the budgets of these two sectors could contribute to the financing of the ECD activities.

Education—In most Sub-Saharan African countries resources for investment in early childhood activities are limited, representing less than 2 percent of the public resources mobilized for the education sector.[4] From an education viewpoint, the indicative framework of the Fast-Track Initiative suggests that the first six years of basic education (primary schooling) should be allocated 50 percent of the domestic public resources mobilized for the sector (representing 20 percent of total public revenues). This allocation leaves 50 percent for all other education-related activities. As noted, the competition for budgetary resources is likely to be very high, given the legitimate claims of different segments of the sector.

Clearly a balanced view is needed given the systemic nature of educational activities. For example, it is obvious that improving the proportion of the population achieving a complete cycle of primary schooling will generate pressure on secondary education and it will be necessary to provide some response to that demand. Yet, it has been shown that ECD and preschool activities provide a favorable basis for investments in primary education and life.[5]

The benefits of ECD have been demonstrated to surpass their costs. For example, van der Gaag and Tan (1998) calculated that in Bolivia, the cost-benefit ratio of the *Proyecto Integral de Desarrollo Infantil* program was between 2.38 and 3.06; Evans, Myers, and Ilfeld (2000) reported that in Brazil the cost of producing a first-grade graduate was less for *Programa de Apoio a Pequenos Empreendimentos* children and the savings exceeded the per-child cost of the program; and Meyers (2000) found that the Shishu Kaksha Centers in Nepal generated $4 million in savings to the government because of reduced primary school repetition. However, we do not have a measure by which to suggest that ECD activities should receive a given percentage of public resources as a general policy. In addition, the robustness of the education sector is different from one country to another. Therefore decisions will have to be made on a country-by-country basis. This said, it appears that in most Sub-Saharan African countries, ECD activities are not likely to be able to claim more than 5 to 7 percent of the education budget. This low percentage does not mean that countries are limited to these percentages. They can choose to express a stronger, or weaker, priority for these activities. Choices can be made along several dimensions. Table 23.4 provides the simulation model we developed to help calculate the funding needs. The cell for public resources devoted to ECD activities is shaded gray, denoting that the numerical value of the proportion is a matter of choice and can be changed based on the targets defined by the needs and available resources.

Health—Considering the expenditure framework for health, we know that on average, public spending for health is about half that of public spending for education, but private spending is larger in health than in education. Public spending in education in low-income Sub-Saharan African countries is, on average, between 3 and 4 percent of GDP. If ECD is to get between 5 and 7 percent of that envelope, it implies that public spending for ECD would amount to 0.15 to 0.25 percent of a country's GDP. If public spending for health amounts to 1.5 to 2.0 percent of GDP, a similar proportion devoted to ECD would suggest about 0.3 percent of GDP. This figure is at best a first approximation, suggesting an order of magnitude for ECD investment. In any case, individual countries will have to make a choice about the amount of resources they intend to allocate to ECD from the health sector budget. In the proposed simulation model, this choice is expressed as the proportion of GDP that could be progressively allocated to ECD activities out of the national health budget by 2015. Table 23.4 presents the target figures (as a percentage of GDP from the health budget for ECD).

Table 23.4. Policy Box: Elements That Contribute to Defining an ECD Policy

ECD policy elements	Target 2015
Public recurrent resources for ECD	
As % of public spending on education	6
From health as % of GDP	0.1
Age 0–3	
Coverage (%)	20
Coverage in the partly subsidized system (%)	75
Coverage in the fully subsidized system (%)	25
Age 4–5	
Coverage (%)	30
Enrollments in the community-based system (%)	70
Enrollments in the formal preschool system	30
Enrollments in the formal preschool system in privately financed schools (%)	35
Enrollments in the formal preschool system in publicly financed schools (%)	65

Source: Authors' calculations.
Note: Shaded cells indicate public resources devoted to ECD activities; the numerical value of the proportion is a matter of choice and can be changed based on the targets defined by the needs and available resources.

Coverage for the 0–3 Population

The second element in the definition of the ECD policy concerns the coverage envisaged for the 0–3 population. During the early years the limited range of child behavior is more easily supported in home settings; the main inputs from interventions include parental education related to health, nutrition, and psychosocial development and health and nutrition interventions. The unit costs proposed are consistent with those proposed in the Household and Community Package proposed in the Marginal Budgeting for Bottleneck for health results. The policies are expressed along two complementary lines:

- What proportion (from 0 to 100 percent) of the 0–3 population in the country is progressively and until 2015 going to benefit from ECD activities? And, if coverage is only partial, what targets (such as regions, population groups) are to be prioritized? This targeting, albeit important, does not concern the costing side of the policy.
- What proportion of the activities offered are to be delivered as fully financed by the state and how much is expected to come from community-financed activities, with only partial support from the state?

Coverage for the 4–6 Population

Children between ages 4 and 6 are more physically mobile, ready to form relationships with adults outside the family, and have sufficient language and cognitive development to engage in active interactions outside the home. This maturity favors center- or community-based programs. The provision policies for this age group are expressed similarly for the 0–3 age group, with the additional provision that a choice has to be made on the role and scope of the public sector as providers of formal preschool services.

Unit Costs of the Policies

As a part of determining coverage for the two age groups and defining the government's overall strategy, the costs of various options need to be factored into the ECD policy framework. The following section describes in more detail how the intended services will be delivered and the corresponding unit costs. Table 23.5 provides the unit cost estimates for partly and fully subsidized systems for the 0–3 population.

The partly and fully subsidized systems are alike in that the activities considered, overall, assist families to enrich the child's environment and provide parental education related to health, nutrition, and psychosocial

Table 23.5. Unit Cost Policy Box for Fully and Partly Subsidized Systems for the 0–3 Population

			Cost elements (US$) according to pcGDP (US$)	
			150	600
Fully subsidized				
Elements of recurrent costs				
Community level				
1 community leader per	80	Children		
Remuneration of				
community leader	2.5	Community	375	1,500
Training of community leader	0.35	pcGDP	53	210
Consumables	6	US$ per child		
Adviser level				
1 adviser for	40	Community leaders		
Remuneration	3.5	pcGDP	525	2,100
Consumables	2	pcGDP	300	1,200
Training of advisers	0.3	pcGDP	45	180
General services				
Administrators (basic)	5	Administrators		
1 supervisor per	20	Advisers		
Remuneration				
(admin./supervisor)	5	pcGDP	750	3,000
Consumables	300	pcGDP	45,000	180,000
Per child recurrent spending				
	0.0531	pcGDP	**12.1**	**30.3**
	6	US$		
		Primary EFA unit cost	19.7	78.8
Capital costs				
Community center				
construction	8,000	US$		
Partly subsidized				
Elements of recurrent costs				
Community level				
1 community leader per	80	Children		
Public subsidy per				
community leader	0.5	pcGDP	75	300
Top up per community leader		Community		
Training of community leader	0.35	pcGDP	53	210
Consumables	6	US$		
Adviser level				
1 adviser for	40	Community leaders		
Remuneration	3.5	pcGDP	525	2,100
Consumables	2	pcGDP	300	1,200
Training of advisers	0.3	pcGDP	45	180

(continued)

Table 23.5. Unit Cost Policy Box for Fully and Partly Subsidized Systems for the 0–3 Population (*continued*)

			Cost elements (US$) according to pcGDP (US$)	
			150	600
General services				
Administrators (basic)	5	Administrators		
1 supervisor per	20	Advisers		
Remuneration				
(admin./supervisor)	5	pcGDP	750	3,000
Consumables	300	pcGDP	45,000	180,000
Per child recurrent				
spending	**0.0218**	pcGDP	**9.3**	**19.1**
	6	US$		
		Primary EFA unit cost	19.7	78.8
Capital costs				
Community center				
construction	2,000	US$		

Source: Authors' calculations.

Note: Shaded cells represent the amount of the subsidy (also expressed in per capita GDP terms) provided by the state to help the community recruit and maintain an individual with adequate knowledge and skills to fulfill the task. **EFA** = *Education for All* Fast-Track Initiative; pcGDP = per capita gross domestic product.

development, and also provide services such as deworming, supplemental nutrition, vaccination, growth monitoring, and prevention of common childhood diseases.

This assistance is commonly provided by an individual, usually a community leader, specifically trained and located in the same community or nearby area so as to remain in regular contact with the families. This community leader's remuneration is fully or partly borne by the state. In a partly subsidized system the community leader could possibly be totally financed by the community. In both partly or fully subsidized options, the unit costs include annual training of the community leader and ongoing advice and support by a qualified adviser or supervisor from the district or regional level throughout the year. Similarly, unit costs include administrative costs of supervisors at the central level.

Table 23.5 provides a method to begin to estimate costs based on parameters that can be changed according to the situation. (This method is consistent with the estimates developed by Soucat et al. [2003]). For example, beginning at the community level, it is possible to estimate the unit cost by first identifying the average number of children for which a community leader is supposed to be in charge. Let's say that the community leader is in charge of an average of 80 children aged 0–3.

This assumption comes from the premise that one community leader can serve up to 20 families on a regular basis. Once the number of children to be served by a community leader is determined, the next decision is the remuneration for the community leader. In the fully subsidized option, the remuneration of the community leader is from the state; the level of yearly salary chosen is expressed in per capita GDP units. In the partly subsidized system, the shaded cell represents the amount of the subsidy (also expressed in per capita GDP terms) provided by the state to help the community recruit and maintain an individual with adequate knowledge and skills to fulfill the task. (The figure is 0 if no subsidy is provided to help the community finance the community leader.)

At the community level, two yearly costs are then considered: training and consumables. Consumables in this case include food, nutritional supplements, training materials, classroom materials, and so on. The cost of training is expressed in per capita GDP units and represents the cost per community leader. The cost of consumables is expressed in dollar terms because many of the goods concerned are bought on the international market and correspond to the amount per child for one year.

Estimating the costs for the adviser or supervisor follows a relatively similar pattern of (1) determining the number of community leaders per adviser; (2) their level of remuneration (paid by the state); (3) the cost of consumables to allow him or her to effectively assist the community leaders to be advised on a regular basis; and (4) a provision for his or her training every year. Finally, the recurrent unit cost depends also on the overhead incurred to run the program, that is, the cost of administrators and supervisors (depending on their number and their payment) and the amount of the goods and services they need to perform their tasks.

Based on these elements, the recurrent unit cost for both systems is calculated as a mix of a per capita GDP term and a dollar term. To complete the costing, a cell is provided to indicate the construction cost of a community center. This assumption is based on the need that in addition to home visits, the community leader needs to organize parent education sessions, conduct vaccination campaigns, and distribute drugs and nutritional supplements on a regular basis. The construction of such a center can be fully or partially subsidized by the community. These costs are expressed in dollar terms and can be used to help calculate the capital requirements for the 0–3 age group. (The example on table 23.6 uses the unit cost of building a classroom from table 23.5.) Finally, to provide an example of the unit cost in a given country, the dollar amounts are

Table 23.6. Unit Cost Policy Box for Fully and Partly Subsidized Systems for the 4–5 Population

			Cost elements (US$) according to pcGDP (US$)	
Fully subsidized (formal)				
Elements of recurrent cost				
1 teacher for	30	Children		
Remuneration of teacher	2.5	pcGDP	375	1,500
Materials and support	40	% of salary bill	210	840
Recurrent spending per child enrolled	**0.163**	**pcGDP**	**18**	**70**
		Primary EFA unit cost	19.7	78.8
Capital costs				
Classroom construction	8,000	US$		
Partly subsidized (Community-based)				
Elements of recurrent cost				
Community level				
1 community teacher per	25	Children		
Public subsidy per community teacher	0.5	pcGDP	75	300
Top up per community teacher		Community		
Training of 1 community teacher	0.5	pcGDP	75	300
Consumables	0.6	pcGDP	90	360
Pedagogical kit	0.1	pcGDP	15	60
Adviser level				
1 adviser for	40	Community teachers		
Remuneration	3.5	pcGDP	525	2,100
Consumables	2	pcGDP	300	1,200
Training of advisers	0.3	pcGDP	45	180
General services				
Administrators (basic)	5	Administrators		
1 supervisor per	20	Advisers		
Remuneration (admin/supervisor)	5	pcGDP	750	3,000
Consumables	300	pcGDP	45,000	180,000
Recurrent spending per child enrolled	**0.077**	**pcGDP**	**12**	**46**
		Primary EFA unit cost	19.7	78.8
Capital costs				
Classroom construction	2,000	US$		

Source: Authors' calculations.

Note: EFA = *Education for All* Fast-Track Initiative; pcGDP = per capita gross domestic product.

provided for two different scenarios, one for a country with a GDP of US$150 and one for a country with a GDP of US$600.

Table 23.6 is similar to table 23.5, but for the 4–6 population. As noted, these children are ready for more social interaction and stimulation, which favors a center- or community-based program where children are gathered for five to six hours a day. This type of setting can be formal and look like existing preschools, but it can also be organized less formally, with the activities being implemented by the community, albeit with adequate support (financial and technical) from the state.

The unit costs presented in table 23.6 follow those used for teacher salaries, costs of teacher training, and provision of teaching and learning materials estimated for the *Education for All* costing.

For the fully subsidized preschool system, the first parameter is the average pupil-teacher ratio (set to 30 to1 in the example), but the numerical value of that parameter is obviously an important matter of choice. The second parameter to be set is the amount of teacher remuneration (expressed in per capita GDP units). The third parameter is the amount of the resources needed to cover all costs other than teacher remuneration (such as consumables, training and supervision of the teachers); these other costs are expressed as a proportion of the teacher salary cost (set to 40 percent in the example). From this element, the value of the unit cost, expressed again in per capita GDP units, is calculated (0.163 per capita GDP units in the hypothetical example). The cost of constructing a classroom is also used (US$8,000 in the example) to estimate the capital cost requirement.

In the partly subsidized (community-based) system, the structure of the unit cost estimate is similar to that described for the 0–3 population. The unit costs used in the example for training of the community teacher, consumables, and teaching and learning materials are equivalent to what was calculated for the fully subsidized option.

The Simulation Model: Putting It All Together

To determine what can and cannot be funded by the government, it is necessary to bring together data from tables 23.4, 23.5, and 23.6. Data from table 23.4 (share of public resources for education devoted to ECD activities, targeted coverage for the two age groups, and the strategy intended to implement the policy) and from tables 23.5 and 23.6 (recurrent public unit costs and public cost for construction of either the community center or the preschool classroom) are the crucial ingredients to help estimate the financial aspects of the policy at the country level. The costing model is presented in table 23.7.

The top part of the table helps determine the amount of public resources that could be allocated to ECD activities. Two sources for the funds are considered: (1) those that are likely to come from education and (2) those that are to be allocated from the health budget.

For education, the model follows the same structure as that used for the EFA Fast Track-Initiative costing exercise. It starts with the projection of the country's GDP and population. From there the evolution of the per capita GDP over a given period is calculated, and the amount of public revenues is calculated based on a projection of the fiscal pressure (the 2015 target depends on the per capita GDP of the country). Then the public resources for education are projected as a proportion of public domestic revenues that it is assumed will evolve progressively from what it was in 2000 to a target value of 20 percent in 2015. Finally, the amount of public resources that are dedicated to ECD from the education budget is derived by projecting the proportion of the public resources for the sector as a whole from what is observed in the base year (2000) to the target value identified in table 23.4 (the policy box), that is, 6 percent in the hypothetical example.

For the resources coming from the health budget, the target value is expressed as a proportion of GDP in 2015; this proportion is hypothesized to increase progressively from its initial value in 2000 to the targeted one in 2015 (0.1 percent in the hypothetical example). The amount of resources available derives directly from this figure (and from the GDP) to determine the hypothesized evolution of public resources for ECD coming from health. The last line of the first block consolidates the public resources available for ECD from both the health and education budgets.

The second block in the model estimates the recurrent cost of ECD activities in the country, given the objectives stated in the policy box (coverage and type of service delivery), as well as in the unit cost box. The estimation process starts with the population projection in the two age groups. (Data are from the United Nations–World Bank database.) From this population base, based on the objectives stated for coverage in 2015 in the two age groups as well as in the fully and partly subsidized systems, the projections (2000–2015) of the number of children in the two age groups and in the two systems can be made.

For the formal preschool system (ages 4–6), a further distinction needs be made to describe the respective roles of the privately and

Table 23.7. Costing Model for Government-Funded ECD Programs

Year of projection	2015	2000	2003	2006	2009	2012	2015
Public resources							
GDP (million LCU)	5.0%	20,343,400	23,550,028	27,262,102	31,559,290	36,533,824	42,292,468
Population (million)	2.5%	14.592	15.7	16.9	18.2	19.6	21.1
Per capita GDP (LCU)	16.0	1,394,147	1,498,667	1,611,021	1,731,800	1,861,632	2,001,199
Domestic revenue as % of GDP		10.6	11.7	12.8	13.9	14.9	16.0
Domestic revenue (million LCU)		2,164,800	2,758,422	3,485,398	4,373,018	5,453,863	6,766,795
Public recurrent resources for education as % domestic revenue	20.0	18.8	19.0	19.3	19.5	19.8	20.0
Public recurrent resources for education (million LCU)		406,500	524,712	671,519	853,223	1,077,440	1,353,359
Public recurrent resources for ECD as % public spending on education	6.0	2.4	3.1	3.8	4.5	5.3	6.0
Public resources from education for ECD (million LCU)		9,553	16,161	25,585	38,736	56,781	81,202
Public resources from health for ECD as % of GDP	0.10	0.0	0.02	0.04	0.06	0.08	0.10
Public resources from health for ECD (million LCU)		0.00	4,710	10,905	18,936	29,227	42,292
Total public resources for ECD (million LCU)		9,553	20,871	36,490	57,672	86,008	123,494
Recurrent spending for ECD							
[0–3] Population (thousands)	1.8%	2,193	2,270	2,354	2,450	2,521	2,579
[4–5] Population (thousands)		996	1,051	1,104	1,150	1,193	1,235
[0–3] % Coverage	20.0	0.0	4.0	8.0	12.0	16.0	20.0
[0–3] % Coverage in the partly subsidized system	75.0	75.0	75.0	75.0	75.0	75.0	75.0

(continued)

Table 23.7. Costing Model for Government-Funded ECD Programs (continued)

Year of projection	2015	2000	2003	2006	2009	2012	2015
[0–3] Coverage in the partly subsidized system (thousands)		0	68	141	221	303	387
[0–3] Coverage in the fully subsidized system (thousands)		0	23	47	74	101	129
[4–5] % Coverage	30.0	5.7	10.6	15.4	20.3	25.1	30.0
[4–5] Total enrollment (thousands)		57.0	111.2	170.4	233.3	300.0	370.5
[4–5] Enrollment in the formal preschool system (thousands)		57.0	67.8	78.7	89.5	100.3	111.2
[4–5] Enrollments in the private formal preschool system (thousands)	30.0%	26.0	28.6	31.2	33.7	36.3	38.9
[4–5] Enrollments in the public formal preschool system (thousands)	35.0%	31.0	39.2	47.5	55.7	64.0	72.2
[4–5] Enrollments in the community-based system (thousands)	70.0%	0.0	43.3	91.7	143.8	199.7	259.4
[0–3] Unit subsidy for partly subsidized community centers (pcGDP units)	0.051	0.040	0.049	0.047	0.045	0.044	0.042
[0–3] Unit cost for fully subsidized community centers (pcGDP units)	0.082	0.060	0.080	0.078	0.076	0.075	0.073
[4–5] Unit subsidy for community centers (pcGDP units)	0.077	0.060	0.063	0.067	0.070	0.074	0.077
[4–5] Unit cost for public formal preschools (pcGDP units)	0.163	0.220	0.209	0.197	0.186	0.175	0.163
Recurrent public spending for [0–3] children (million LCU)		0	7,706	16,610	26,983	38,572	51,457
[0–3] Community centers (million LCU)		0	4,982	10,680	17,254	24,529	32,545
[0–3] Formal centers (million LCU)		0	2,724	5,930	9,729	14,043	18,912

Recurrent public spending for [4–5] children (million LCU)	9,508	16,397	24,990	35,489	48,255	63,735
[4–5] Formal preschool system (million LCU)	9,508	12,274	15,100	17,957	20,810	23,615
[4–5] Community-based-system (million LCU)	0	4,123	9,889	17,531	27,445	40,120
Total recurrent public spending for ECD (million LCU)	9,508	24,103	41,600	62,472	86,827	115,192
Capital spending for ECD						
[0–3]Partly subsidized system: number of groups	0	851	1,766	2,756	3,782	4,836
[0–3] Fully subsidized system: number of groups	0	284	589	919	1,261	1,612
[4–5] Public formal preschool system: number of groups	1,033	1,308	1,583	1,858	2,133	2,408
[4–5] Community-based system: number of groups	0	1,734	3,669	5,753	7,986	10,374
Capital public spending for [0–3] children (million US$)	1.3	1.4	1.5	1.6	1.6	0.0
Capital spending on [0–3] community centers (million US$)	0.6	0.6	0.6	0.7	0.7	
Capital spending on [0–3] formal centers (million US$)	0.7	0.8	0.9	0.9	0.9	
Capital public spending for [4–5] children (million US$)	1.8	2.0	2.1	2.2	2.3	0.0
Capital spending on [4–5] community centers (million US$)	1.1	1.3	1.3	1.5	1.6	
Capital public spending on [4–5] formal public schools (million US$)	0.7	0.7	0.7	0.7	0.7	
Total capital public spending for ECD (million US$)	3.1	3.4	3.6	3.8	3.9	0.0

(continued)

Table 23.7. Costing Model for Government-Funded ECD Programs *(continued)*

Year of projection	2015	2000	2003	2006	2009	2012	2015
Recurrent financing gap (million LCU)		−44.7	3,232.1	5,109.9	4,800.0	818.9	−8,302.3
Exchange rate (LCU per US$)	6,745						
Recurrent financing gap (million US$ of the year 2000)		0.0	0.5	0.8	0.7	0.1	−1.2
Total financing gap (million US$ of the year 2000)		3.1	3.9	4.3	4.5	4.0	−1.2
% of recurrent spending domestically financed		100.5	86.6	87.7	92.3	99.1	107.2
% of total spending domestically financed		31.2	44.5	55.5	65.3	76.0	107.2

Source: Authors' calculations.

Note: LCU = local currency units; pcGDP = per capita gross domestic product.

publicly financed sector in delivering the services. The model takes into account four steps: (1) defining a coverage target for 2015 in terms of percentage of children to be enrolled in private programs, (2) identifying the progression between the existing coverage in 2000 and that estimated for 2015, (3) subtracting the number of children estimated to be enrolled in the private programs for that same period, and (4) calculating the progression of children enrolled in the public system by estimating the difference between the total enrolled in the public system and those in private programs. Then, the model takes into account the recurrent unit costs from the data in tables 23.5 and 23.6 to estimate the amount of recurrent spending in the two age groups separately for the partly and fully subsidized systems. The last line of this block provides the evolution of total recurrent public spending for ECD in the country between 2000 and 2015, based on the policy elements described in tables 23.4 through 23.6.

The next block focuses on capital spending. Only the capital costs at the local level are considered here. It starts with the identification of the number of "groups," that is, the ratio between the number of children covered in the two age groups and the two systems and the number of children per community leader or teacher. This ratio provides the evolution of the required number of offices for community leaders and the required number of classrooms. From this information, the estimate of the capital cost is simply the product of the public unit cost, or subsidy, of either a community center or a classroom (given in tables 23.5 and 23.6) and of the incremental number of such centers and classrooms to be built during year (y) to accommodate the incremental number of groups between (y) and ($y + 1$). Because the unit costs of construction in tables 23.5 and 23.6 are expressed in U.S. dollar terms, the total capital cost requirements are also expressed in those terms.

Finally, the last block provides estimates of the financing gaps. Because it is anticipated that public domestic resources are first to be used to cover recurrent expenditures, the recurrent financing gap for each year between 2001 and 2015 is calculated as the difference between the recurrent spending to achieve the stated objectives and the amount of domestic public resources that could be allocated to ECD activities. This recurrent financing gap is expressed in local currency units and calculated in U.S. dollars by using the exchange rate in 2000. The total financing gap is calculated as the sum of the recurrent financing gap and of the total capital spending. This block ends with an estimate of the proportion of both recurrent and total spending that is covered by domestic budgetary resources.

Summary and Conclusions

Obviously more work should be undertaken from an implementation perspective to identify the concrete design of appropriate quality community-based ECD programs. What is the practical description of the activities to be implemented? How can they be best organized? How is the system to be structured and what would be justified in terms of staffing and support to help the system deliver the expected outcomes? How is the training of personnel, in particular of community leaders, organized? How are the resources (consumables, financial resources, training, and support) to be made available at the local level, particularly in remote areas? Which monitoring and incentive mechanisms are to be implemented as part of the system to maximize effective outcomes? These questions need to be addressed when designing these programs, and important cultural and specific country contexts need to be accounted for.

In summary, it is difficult to suggest a normative figure for the percentage of the education and health budgets that would be reasonable to allocate to early childhood programs. The allocations will depend to some degree on policy makers' convictions about the importance of the early years and their beliefs that preschool is a good investment for the country; advocacy obviously plays a role. However, because preschool is an objective of the EFA Dakar forum, it seems that a commitment of 5 percent of the total recurrent education budget in 2015 can be considered a reachable target; below 5 percent would not be consistent with the EFA Dakar goals, and beyond 7 or 8 percent is unlikely, given the competition for resources between levels of schooling and the limitation of the resources available (domestic and from external aid).

However, any ECD program should be holistic, and ECD programs have a mandate well beyond preschool. For these reasons, funding is sought beyond the education sector. Because it is not easy to identify a particular budget to attach to activities, and activities can potentially be implemented using different mechanisms, it is better to simply identify an envelope for the financing of the ECD program (for its part that is not included in the education budget) and to attach it to the budget of the Ministry of Social Affairs, or Youth and Family, or a similar ministry, depending on national arrangements within the government. In terms of the amount that could be seen as reasonable, again, there is no normative figure. A benchmark of one-tenth of 1 percent of a country's GDP can be suggested, which would amount to about 5 percent of a health budget in a typical Sub-Saharan African country.

Because the two figures cautiously suggested here (a target of 5 percent of the education budget in 2015 and 0.1 percent of GDP at the same date) are subject to variation from country to country, it is probably safe to analyze the financial sustainability of ECD programs for different levels of resource mobilization. It is useful to stress the sensitivity of the amount of resources for ECD with small variations in the parameters suggested here. For example, in a typical Sub-Saharan African country, if ECD gets 4 percent of the education budget and 0.07 percent of GDP, then the public resources for the ECD program could amount to 0.21 percent of GDP, but this percentage would be increased by more than 50 percent to reach 0.33 of GDP if 6 percent of the education budget were devoted to preschool and 0.12 percent of GDP were allocated to the Ministry of Social Affairs for ECD activities.

To analyze the level of financial commitment required for ECD programs, an extension of the costing model to resource mobilization is likely to help at the national level. With this tool, national teams are able to calibrate the ECD programs that could be proposed to variations in the level of resource mobilization. If the team has determined the best operational arrangements for the delivery of ECD services, adjustments based on different levels of resource mobilization could be made, depending on the coverage to be achieved by 2015. If resources are not adequate, the national team can revisit the initial choices and adjust some of the characteristics or parameters of service delivery, without decreasing quality, to maintain a minimum level of coverage. It is critical to document these trade-offs so that the options can be explained to policy makers, helping them to understand what could be gained by marginally increasing the resources or could be lost in terms of coverage and quality of services if the amount of public resources mobilized for ECD were too low.

In summary, the argument has been made that investment in the early years has both short- and long-term outcomes that represent a savings to society—in terms of the efficiency of the education system, as well as social and economic benefits to the society as a whole. Nonetheless, choices have to be made, but they should be educated choices, with a clear understanding of the gains to be achieved by greater investment in early childhood programs and the threats to children's overall development if a government chooses not to invest in the early years.

Notes

1. Excerpted from *Early Childhood Care and Education in Sub-Saharan Africa: What Would It Take to Meet the Millennium Development Goals?* Adriana Jaramillo and Alain Mingat, World Bank, Africa Region, October 2003.

2. The *Education for All* Fast-Track Initiative (FTI) is a global partnership between donor and developing countries to ensure accelerated progress toward the Millennium Development Goal of universal primary education by 2015. All low-income countries that demonstrate serious commitment to achieve universal primary completion can receive support from FTI.

3. The term *community-based* is used in this chapter to refer to all forms of community structures—physical or human resources—to provide early childhood services. Funding for these programs may come from the community, from national and international nongovernmental organizations (NGOs), from private industry and individuals, as well as from public resources; it usually includes a combination of these sources.

4. Although ECD includes education, health, nutrition, and social protection, the reference here is with the education sector because the share of expenditures to cover these services is higher than for health.

5. For a review of the literature on the costs and benefits of ECD investments, see Haveman and Wolfe (1995), Myers (1995, 2000), Young (1996), van der Gaag and Tan (1998), and Evans, Myers, and Ilfeld (2000).

References

Bruns, B., A. Mingat, and R. Rakotomalala. 2003. *A Chance for Every Child: Achieving Universal Primary Education by 2015.* Washington, DC: World Bank.

Evans, J. L., with R. G. Myers, and E. M. Ilfeld. 2000. *Early Childhood Counts: A Programming Guide on Early Childhood Care for Development.* Washington, DC: World Bank.

Haveman, R., and B. Wolfe. 1995. "The Determinants of Children's Attainments: A Review of Methods and Findings." *Journal of Economic Literature* 33 (4): 1829–78.

Jaramillo, A., and K. Tietjen. 2001. "Early Childhood Development in Africa: Can We Do More for Less? A Look at the Impact and Implications of Preschool in Cape Verde and Guinea." Human Development Working Paper Series. World Bank, Africa Region, Washington, DC.

Lokshin, M., M. Glinskaya, and M. Garcia. 2000. "The Effect of Early Childhood Development Programs on Women's Labor Force Participation and Older Children's Schooling in Kenya." Policy Research Working Paper 2376. World Bank, Washington, DC.

Meyers, C. 2000. "The Case of Preprimary Education: The Cost Effectiveness of Shishu Kaksha Centers, Nepal." In *Early Childhood Counts: A Programming Guide on Early Childhood Care for Development*, ed. J. L. Evans, R.G. Myers, and E. Ilfeld. Washington, DC: World Bank.

Myers, R. 1995. *The Twelve Who Survive: Strengthening Programs of Early Childhood Development in the Third World*. Ypsilanti, MI: High/Scope Press.

———. 2000. *Summary: The EFA Global Thematic Review of Early Childhood Care and Development*. Mexico: Consultative Group on ECCD.

Soucat, A., W. Van Lerberghe, F. Diop, S. N. Nguyen, and R. Knippenberg. 2003. *Marginal Budgeting for Bottlenecks: A New Costing and Resource Allocation Practice to Buy Health Results*. Washington, DC: World Bank.

van der Gaag, J., and J. P. Tan. 1998. *The Benefits of Early Childhood Development Programs: An Economic Analysis*. Washington, DC: World Bank.

Young, M. E. 1996. *Early Child Development: Investing in the Future*. Directions in Development. Washington, DC: World Bank.

CHAPTER 24

A Tri-Part Approach to Promoting ECD Capacity in Africa: ECD Seminars, International Conferences, and ECDVU

Alan Pence with Abeba Habtom and
Francis R. W. Chalamada

The Early Childhood Development Virtual University (ECDVU) represents a unique approach to promoting leadership and building capacity in early childhood care for development internationally. Designed to achieve "traction" in moving forward country-identified agendas for child and family well-being, the ECDVU bridges theory and practice and Western and local knowledge in an effective learning community approach to development. The ECDVU is fully accredited through the School of Child and Youth Care, University of Victoria (Victoria, British Columbia, Canada). One-year certificate and diploma programs and a three-year master's degree program have been delivered. The pilot delivery of the master's program took place between August 2001 and September 2004. An external impact evaluation of the program, funded by the World Bank, concluded: "By any measure ECDVU has been singularly successful in meeting and exceeding all of its objectives" (Vargas-Barón 2005, 12).

This chapter will situate the ECDVU within a larger context of building capacity through a multipronged approach. We will briefly discuss the ECDVU's development as the third component of a tri-part set of capacity-building initiatives and then examine each of the three initiatives more closely. Collectively, these interrelated initiatives represent a demonstrably effective way to address not only early childhood development (ECD), but also other health, social, and educational technical capacity-building efforts in the Majority World.

A Tri-Part Set of Initiatives: Seminars, Conferences, and the ECDVU

In 1994, the United Nations Children's Fund (UNICEF) asked the University of Victoria to establish a series of ECD training seminars for mid-career professionals within UNICEF and its partner governments and organizations at a country level (C. Dalais, personal communication with A. Pence, 1994). The intent of the seminars was to help staff trained in other disciplines to better understand the intents and possibilities of ECD and to promote enhanced intersectoral cooperation in addressing those objectives. The ECD seminars (initially termed summer institutes) were held regionally, typically lasted 2–3 weeks, and brought together country-identified professionals with regionally and internationally recognized ECD specialists. Over time the seminars focused primarily on Africa. They represent the initial component of what would become a tri-part set of ECD capacity-building activities.

At the ECD seminar held in The Gambia in 1998, the World Bank requested development of an international conference on African ECD. Subsequently, the African International Conference on ECD was held in Kampala, Uganda, in September 1999 (M. Garcia, personal communication with A. Pence, December 1998). The conference, which built on fledgling ECD networks and the ECD seminars, was deemed a success. A second conference followed in Asmara, Eritrea, in 2002, and a third was held in Accra, Ghana, in May 2005. The African International Conference on ECD Series represents the second component in the set of capacity-building initiatives. The ECDVU is the third.

Participants in the ECD seminar series had identified a need for a graduate-level, applied ECD education program that would build on the seminars' success and would link participants from Sub-Saharan Africa (SSA) electronically and continuously so that ongoing intra- and intercountry synergies could be achieved. A draft proposal for such a program, the ECDVU, was submitted to the World Bank prior to the

1999 Kampala conference (Pence 1999). At that conference, the World Bank committed to using Norwegian Educational Trust Fund dollars to support the *development* of the ECDVU program, noting that *delivery* of the program would need to incorporate additional international partners. The ECDVU would advance country-identified ECD objectives and would allow participants to study parttime while continuing to work fulltime in their countries. Thus, within six years, 1994–2000, three interrelated activities emerged to support ECD leadership and capacity building in Africa.

Work to develop the ECDVU began in January 2000. In April of that year, an international advisory group consultation was held in Washington, DC.[1]

The advisory group discussed issues that included the historically weak role of universities in addressing ECD and, more specifically, ECD capacity promotion (this was deemed to be true not only in Africa, but internationally); challenges encountered by the Early Childhood Development Network in Africa (ECDNA) in efforts to "take off" in a sustainable fashion (this had also been discussed in a special session at the Kampala conference); and several Africa-specific ECD initiatives, including the (then) recently evaluated "More and Better" program developed by the Bernard van Leer Foundation. A discussion of problems encountered in that and other initiatives allowed the group to identify several lessons learned:

- A lack of organizational connection in-country limited program effectiveness.
- A need existed for a "critical mass" of participants (three or more) in-country.
- Learning must be connected to, and facilitative of, work objectives.
- Employers must support participants' activities.
- Local content and local knowledge must be recognized.
- Programs must be flexible for learners (Zuckernick 2000).

Consensus was reached on a number of points related to applying these lessons to mounting the ECDVU program:

- Rather than using a model of 15 countries with 2 participants each, go with fewer (9–10) countries and more (3–4) participants per country and promote a "learning pod" (team) approach within countries.
- Provide participants with a very high level of technical, personal, and professional support throughout the delivery.
- Relate coursework and expectations to country-identified objectives.

- Ensure a high level of African content and strong African leadership modeling.
- Use the Generative Curriculum Model (Pence and McCallum 1994), a generative, transformational learning approach (Zuckernick 2000).

Generative Curriculum Model

The Generative Curriculum Model (GCM) referred to during the meetings was familiar to several members of the advisory group. The GCM was developed through the First Nations Partnership Program (FNPP) at the University of Victoria in response to Aboriginal communities' requests for university-accredited and culturally relevant ECD training for their tribal members (Pence et al. 1993; Pence and McCallum 1994). The FNPP—a multicultural, coconstructed approach to ECD education that did not privilege Western knowledge—proved extremely effective in increasing education completion rates for Aboriginal students (76 percent completion of a two-year, in-community FNPP diploma program versus less than 40 percent completion countrywide; Statistics Canada 2001); reducing community "brain drain" (95 percent of the graduates remained in their communities); and promoting a range of child, youth, and family services. The program was one of only 20 worldwide to be highlighted in a United Nations Educational, Scientific, and Cultural Organization (UNESCO) indigenous knowledge publication (Ball and Pence 2002).

The GCM is predicated on a culturally sensitive constructivist approach to understanding children and programs for their care. The curriculum incorporates culturally and community-based perspectives, ensuring that local voices as well as Western sources are presented and considered.[2] The impact of this educational approach in participating First Nations communities in Canada was dramatic, not just in terms of extraordinarily high completion rates, but in terms of broader community development impacts (Ball and Pence 2000; 2006). Indeed, awareness of the GCM approach was one of the factors that influenced UNICEF's original request to the University of Victoria to develop ECD seminars for delivery in the Majority World.

The GCM approach can be seen as one manifestation of a broader, growing concern with top down, Western-centric development approaches to topics ranging from agricultural practices to economic development and child development (see chapter 7). While the GCM grew out of partnerships with Aboriginal communities in Canada, awareness of the potentially corrosive impacts or failed sustainability of Western-identified "best practices" was increasing globally. International development specialist Robert Chambers (1994, ix) noted: "...'we,' who call ourselves professionals, are much of the problem and to do better requires reversals of much that we regard as normal."

Increasingly, the need for local and regional involvements and voices was being seen as fundamental to achieving sustainable development in the Majority World. The ECDVU, with its philosophical origins in work with indigenous communities, was well positioned to address this need.

Promoting Capacity through Multiple Approaches

Next, we will examine more closely the tri-part set of capacity-building initiatives we have just introduced.

Seminar Series

As noted, the ECDVU represents one of three prongs of a broader ECD capacity-building agenda. The initial thrust, the ECD seminar series, proved particularly effective in identifying country-level leaders in ECD, highlighting worthwhile but little-known ECD initiatives in SSA, and forging the personal and professional bases for enhanced networking and information sharing across SSA.

Data from these seminars indicated that opportunities were extremely limited for sharing ideas and developments across SSA; even more limited were opportunities to "workshop" ideas over time in ways that would advance new developments across participating countries. Ongoing communication was difficult, and access to international development ECD specialists was limited. Participants found the seminars useful in shedding light on problematic issues and identifying potential ways forward.

The ECD seminar series proved effective as a capacity-building activity itself, and also as the foundation for creating other vehicles to promote capacity. When the World Bank expressed its interest in creating a "first" African International Conference on ECD, a rudimentary network was already in place as a result of earlier ECDNA networking activities and ECDNA cosponsorship of the seminar series. Consequently, a core group of approximately 40 individuals in 20–25 countries were easily accessible, had some familiarity with each other, were conversant with a generative approach to capacity building, and were able to extend networking into their countries. The theme for the first conference was "Showcasing Early Childhood Care and Development: Innovation and Application in Africa." From conception to "birth" the conference took nine months (January–September 2000)—an extraordinarily short period for an inaugural event that attracted more than 200 participants from approximately 20 countries. Such rapid development, with the range of countries and presentations showcased, would not have been possible without the groundwork laid by the ECD seminars.

Ideally, the seminar series would have continued on an annual basis, perhaps with an increasing focus on Francophone and Lusophone Africa, while the ECDVU team developed more intensive ongoing programs and others focused on planning a follow-up to the Kampala conference. The fact that the seminar series has not been picked up since 1999 does not reflect disfavor or lack of impact, but rather indicates limited capacity to undertake two new initiatives (ECDVU and the conference series) while still maintaining the earlier set of activities. Recent comments among African and international communities suggest that the time has come to use the recently increased capacity and leadership to reestablish this first of the three prongs in the ECD capacity-building agenda.

Conference Series

The ECD conferences address a different agenda than that of the seminars. Much larger in size (typically 200–300 participants versus 30) and shorter in duration (3–5 days versus 15–20), the conferences provide a useful opportunity to take a large-scale "snapshot" of ECD in Africa, to showcase certain African programs and people, to share one's work and ideas with colleagues from many other African countries (39 of 48 SSA countries participated in the May 2005 Accra conference), and to engage in broadly significant Sub-Saharan African advocacy. For example, the *Asmara Declaration* (2002) came forward from participants at that 2002 conference. The *Accra Communiqué* (2005) was endorsed by more than 25 ministers or ministerial representatives who attended the Accra conference, and subsequently helped to inform the Association for the Development of Education in Africa (ADEA) biennial, which took place in March 2006.

The ECD conference series has helped place children's care and well-being on the SSA political and professional agenda. The conferences have also brought together governments and professionals from across Africa with major international organizations. The Accra conference, for example, was cosponsored by the World Bank, UNICEF, UNESCO, ADEA, the World Health Organization (WHO), the Consultative Group on ECCD, and the ECDVU.

Table 24.1 provides an overview of the growth in size and complexity of the series of African International Conferences on ECD. However, before considering those indicators of growth, a key point should be

Table 24.1. First, Second, and Third African International Conferences on ECD, Compared by Size and Scope

Conference location	Date	Attendees	Presenters	African-based	Ministerial component
Kampala, Uganda	1999	200	35	75%	3 national ministers
Asmara, Eritrea	2002	200	60	80%	6 national ministers and 1 African international minister
Accra, Ghana	2005	300	80	85%	6 national ministers and 27 African international ministers or representatives

Source: Authors.

noted: Starting with planning for the first African International Conference on ECD, the series has been primarily focused on Africa and on reaching African participants. Many international conferences privilege Western speakers (for example, as keynote speakers) above regional and local presenters, which conveys a not-so-subtle message that "good and best" reside in the West. As part of capacity building, it is critical that Africa appreciate its own ingenuity, leadership, and existing capacity. The Accra conference featured more than 80 presenters; by design, more than 85 percent were from Africa, including all three keynote speakers. The Accra conference was a testament to the growth of ECD capacity in Africa over a short period.

ECDVU

Another testament to the growth of ECD capacity in Africa are the 27 participants (90 percent of the 30 who enrolled from 10 countries) who completed the full three-year ECDVU program in September 2004. The first ECDVU cohort was a remarkable group of ECD leaders from all parts of Anglophone Africa, and they are now positioned to identify policies, programs, publications, training opportunities, and other advances in support of child and family well-being not present in their countries when they commenced the program. Twenty-seven graduates may seem like a drop in the bucket of African ECD need, but the true measure of the 27 is the ripples they can create—the dozens, hundreds, and thousands that their work can, and does, reach.

While much of the ECDVU's postcolonial educational philosophy was derived from earlier experiences with indigenous communities and a key part of its structure had come from the ECD seminars, a new challenge focused on how to create a "virtual family" of committed learners and actors located on the other side of the world from the institutional base at the University of Victoria. It seemed that the only way to meet this challenge was through the World Wide Web. The proposal presented a compelling vision, but it was not certain it would work.

The ECDVU's first major activity was to undertake a technology feasibility study. That research yielded a cautious, "Yes, it should be feasible—most of the time." But there were caveats: For maximum connectivity it would be better if participants were located in, or could access, larger urban centers; the program should be purposefully redundant, duplicating the materials provided on the Web with discs and print materials; and the developers should create an unusual educational support position, a "cohort manager," whose job would be to provide ongoing support for and connection among learners, instructors, and the central office.

Other reviews were also undertaken, including guidance regarding which Web platform to use, criteria for selection of a server facility, and other technical and administrative issues. Coterminous with these reviews was the elaboration of a curriculum design based on generative curriculum principles of respect for multiple sources of knowledge and the importance of local context. The curriculum needed to mesh smoothly and appropriately across six months of Web delivery combined with a midpoint, two-week, face-to-face delivery. In all ways possible, the curriculum had to advance the program's three main objectives: leadership promotion, capacity building, and network enhancement. All aspects of the program were designed to address these central objectives, including assignments within and across courses, discussion sessions, use of local teams, personal support messages, and inclusion of local leaders at the two-week seminars. The ECDVU was fortunate to locate a curriculum design team with experience in developing university-level courses for Web and face-to-face delivery, and they were keen to take on an international program (Schachter et al. 2005).

While curriculum development work was moving forward, it was also necessary to create a system for identifying participants for the new program. When the World Bank announced at the Kampala conference in 1999 that they would support the development of the program, a flood of students approached the ECDVU director to request applications. It was clear that a system for student identification needed to be established within participating countries. The international advisory group assisted in identifying priority countries and also contributed to the development of criteria that could be used in-country to select participants. The approach that evolved linked back to the seminar series, using network participants from the seminars, in coordination with UNICEF and World Bank staff, to create an ECD country committee composed of key ECD groups and individuals from each country. The country committee's task was three-fold: first, the group would create an ECD goals and objectives statement spanning a 5–7 year period; second, they would advertise the ECDVU program, identify the criteria that would be used in selecting country nominees, and solicit applications; and third, the committee would nominate to the ECDVU administration up to four individuals, from different sectors and organizations, to take part in the program. Applicants were required to discuss their interest in applying with their employing organization and to seek some level of employer financial support—typically support for travel or accommodation, or both, for participation in the seminars. In order that personal financial situations would not be a factor in student applications, the program was tuition-free. All program delivery costs were covered by various core donors, including UNICEF, the World Bank at country levels, UNESCO, the Bernard van Leer Foundation, and the Canadian International Development Agency (CIDA). In addition, approximately 60 percent of the employers were able to contribute support to their employees.

Program delivery commenced in late August 2001. A great amount of data were collected as the initiative moved forward: country reports on children and women were a first-term country team assignment; various assignments supported or initiated other in-country activities; evaluations of courses, instructors, support services, and seminars were ongoing; broader assessments of overall program effectiveness were collected every six months; and evidence of capacity building was documented. Every six months the seminars rotated to a different part of Africa (South Africa, Tanzania, Ghana) and in each different region, ECD specialists joined the faculty (selected from around the world and in that region) in presentations and discussions. Site visits to key programs were made in conjunction with each seminar and a wide variety of academic and "network bonding" activities took place. The pattern of courses, seminars, and materials rotated through the six-month terms for the first two years of the program; the final (third) year focused on the students' identification, implementation, and write-up of a thesis or major project, in coordination with an individual committee. Each student's committee included an in-country academic, an in-country chairperson, a University of Victoria faculty representative, and a supervisor (the supervisor's work was shared among ECDVU staff with the director/professor). Defenses were taped, distributed, and signed off by committee members before the office submitted all necessary graduation documents.

A remarkable 90 percent of the participants (27 of 30) completed the full program within the pilot delivery period of 39 months. The World Bank evaluator noted that these results had been achieved at a "considerably lower cost" than for comparable master's degrees available in Canada or the United States (Vargas-Barón 2005, 43).

From its inception, the ECDVU was envisioned as an information creation and sharing resource. One way to achieve that objective is by publishing participants' projects and assignments on the Web. Thus, the theses and major projects, country reports, and key assignments produced by the 10-country cohort are posted on the ECDVU Web site, with participants' photos, biographies, and contact points. Other publications relating to the ECDVU's work include a special issue of the *International Journal of Educational Policy, Research, and Practice* (Pence and Marfo 2004) that includes overviews of all participants' major projects and theses; reports on various aspects of the ECDVU program in *Coordinators' Notebook* (Evans and Pence 2004), the *Journal of Education for International Development* (Schafer and Pence 2006), and *E-Learning* (Pence 2007); a book chapter, *Perspectives on the Future of Higher Education in the Digital Age* (Schachter et al. 2005); a UNESCO monograph, *ECD Policy Development and Implementation in Africa* (Pence 2004); in-country publications such as professional newsletters produced in Ghana and Uganda; and this first substantial volume on ECD in Africa, which contains contributions from numerous ECDVU participants, faculty, advisors, and committee members from across Africa and internationally.

As the impact evaluation noted, the ECDVU met all of its objectives. At the core of those objectives was the promotion of ECD capacity that could reach hundreds and thousands in participating countries. Two such large-scale stories of ECDVU-supported capacity building in Africa have taken place in Malawi and Eritrea.

Malawi—The training of four ECDVU participants has resulted in various successes in Malawi, including the subsequent training of 245 social welfare officers in ECD and about 1,800 caregivers as well as an increase in the number of ECD centers from 1,155 in 2000 to 5,899 in 2005. The ECDVU graduates are taking the lead in running the National ECD Network, strongly supported by government and development partners.

The ECDVU team has worked together to put ECD on the agenda of programs' implementation, including development and launch of the *National Policies on ECD and OVC* (orphans and vulnerable children); development of the *National Action Plan for OVC*, the *ECD Syllabus*, the *ECD Curriculum*, the *ECD Program Document*, the *Caregivers and Parents Guide in Child Care*, the *Training Manual on ECD*, and the *Operational Guidelines for ECD*; annual plans of action; and research reports on key household and community child care practices for 2003 and 2004.

In addition, child participation has become not just ceremonial but practical; issues are dealt with hands-together with the children. The ECDVU has supported Chancellor College to further develop ECD as a main topic, and Mzuzu University has started teaching ECD.

The ECDVU team has engaged in training and presented papers at community, national, and international levels. International examples include the second and third African International Conferences on ECD in 2002 and 2005 respectively, the Mauritius Biennial on Education and ECD in 2004, and the 2005 South African ECD Conference (Francis Chalamanda, ECDVU participant).

Eritrea—Eritrea is developing a Training-of-Trainers (TOT) strategy that aims to facilitate the implementation, monitoring, and evaluation of the Integrated Early Childhood Development program through the development of human resources for ECD—an integral part of which is the Parenting Enrichment strategy. The ECDVU program was crucial in advancing these objectives by imparting a philosophical approach as well as through specific feedback at key points:

- Identification of participants for ECD courses. The local communities identify potential participants, with decisions based on evidence of the applicant's commitment to children and to their community. A further consideration is the need to address the existing uneven development for such activities so that remote areas of the country are also covered.
- Identification of TOTs' existing skills in order to address professional preparation needs and, over time, to strengthen necessary skills.
- Preparation of manuals and other training resources and development of techniques in organizing, conducting, and implementing activity programs using a consultative approach learned in the ECDVU program.

- Familiarization with existing structures and strengthening such structures at Zoba (regional), sub-Zoba, and Adi (village) levels.
- Introduction of flexibility at all levels of ECD activity in choosing and using the context-appropriate topical theme (Abeba Habtom, ECDVU participant).

Next Steps

Having demonstrated the overall effectiveness and cost benefit of the ECDVU approach to leadership promotion, capacity building, and network enhancement, next steps focus on program transition to Anglophone African tertiary institutions. It is anticipated that one institution will be based in West Africa and one in East or Southeastern Africa. In addition to these two institutions becoming the western and eastern bases for ECDVU program delivery, it is planned that each will, over time, become a regional center supportive of ECD research and development. Proposals to fund this transition stage are in submission, and the World Bank approved funds to address certain aspects of these next steps through a one-year ECDVU certificate program delivery that commenced in late 2006.

The second priority in Africa is responding to long-standing requests from Francophone Africa for the development of a similar ECDVU program and, ultimately, an institutional base at a Francophone institution. Discussions, coordinated by the West African UNESCO office and supported by ADEA and the West African office of UNICEF, took place with interested Francophone countries at the Accra conference in May 2005. Several English-speaking participants from Francophone countries have been nominated for participation in the one-year ECDVU program.

For both Francophone and Anglophone African countries, it is desirable that the missing prong of the three-prong approach—two-week ECD seminars held annually in different parts of Sub-Saharan Africa—be reinstituted. The seminars were a valuable, initial-level networking tool. They allowed key issues to surface and innovative problem-solving approaches and initiatives to be shared. Donors, on-the-ground implementers, government officials, and international specialists came together in a supportive and interactive environment that laid the groundwork for other initiatives described in this chapter. Through these ECD seminars, SSA country-to-country consultations were promoted and recent thinking from outside Africa was also presented and considered. The seminars address a need filled neither by the conference series nor the intensive ECDVU program. They are a practical, affordable, effective complement to the other two activities, and they should be offered for Anglophone, Francophone, and Lusophone speakers.

Conclusion

In this chapter the storyline of the ECDVU focuses on ECD and Africa—but it could as easily take place in any development region of the world addressing a range of technical areas in need of leadership promotion, capacity building, and network enhancement. Aspects of education, health, nutrition, and social services, to name several sectors, have related development needs in particular niche areas. Through the purposeful, planned interaction of respected and committed local leaders with regional and international leaders, in an environment that is respectful of what *each* can bring to the discussion, locally suitable and sustainable ways forward can be found.

Tertiary education institutions should play a key role in promoting coordinated, thoughtful approaches to capacity formation, but they seldom do. Universities, as noted many years ago by Clark Kerr (past president of the University of California, Berkeley), are one of the social institutions that have changed the least over the centuries. Brick and mortar bastions, dominated by lecture halls and "chalk and talk" presentations, are as familiar in all parts of the world today as they were for the elite few in certain parts of 15th-century Europe. Universities have a role to play in promoting capacity in a development context, but the role is a very different than the one it has played to date. For universities to become the force they could be in promoting local capacity, they must come out of the "ivory towers" into the streets and communities that surround them; accept that there are many sources of knowledge and that all should be considered, without prejudice, in identifying useful solutions to community-identified problems; work with cross-cutting groups and promote teamwork and interaction across groups; strain to hear the voices less heard, consider them, empower them, and bring them into other discourses; bring technology into educational practice and use it to extend and amplify students' work; and, perhaps most importantly, be unafraid of "not knowing." If universities can do these things, they can play a useful role in capacity promotion in the Majority World.

Notes

1. See http://www.ecdvu.org for members of this advisory group, the African students' thesis and project committee members, and other key individuals, organizations, and donors associated with the ECDVU program.
2. See http://www.fnpp.org for references.

References

Accra Communiqué. 2005. Retrieved August 16, 2006, from http:// www.adeanet. org/downloadcenter/Focus/COMMUNIQUE%20-%20final.doc.

Asmara Declaration on ECD. 2002. Retrieved August 10, 2006, from http:// www.ecdgroup.com/asmara_declaration_on_ECD.asp.

Ball, J., and A. R. Pence. 2000. *Program Evaluation Report: Strengthening Community Capacity for Early Childhood Care and Development.* First Nations Partnerships Program, University of Victoria, Victoria, B.C.

———. 2002. "The Generative Curriculum Model." In *UNESCO-MOST Best Practices on Indigenous Knowledge (I.K.).* Paris: UNESCO.

———. 2006. *Supporting Indigenous Children's Development: Community-University Partnerships.* Vancouver, B.C.: UBC Press.

Chambers, R. 1994. *Challenging the Professions.* London: Intermediate Technology Publications.

Evans, J., and A. R. Pence. 2004. "The Early Childhood Development Virtual University." *Coordinators' Notebook* 28: 46–47.

Pence, A. R. 1999. Proposal to the World Bank for the Establishment of the Early Childhood Development Virtual University (ECDVU). Unpublished manuscript.

———. 2004. *ECD Policy Development and Implementation in Africa.* UNESCO Early Childhood and Family Policy Series 9. Paris: UNESCO.

———. 2007. "ECD and E-Learning in Africa: The Early Childhood Development Virtual University (ECDVU)." *E-Learning* 4 (1): 15–22.

Pence, A. R., V. Kuehne, M. Greenwood, and M. R. Opekokew. 1993. "Generative Curriculum: A Model of University and First Nations Cooperative, Post-Secondary Education." *International Journal of Educational Development* 13 (4): 339–49.

Pence, A. R., and K. Marfo, eds. 2004. "Capacity Building for Early Childhood Education in Africa" [Special issue]. *International Journal of Educational Policy, Research, and Practice* 5 (3).

Pence, A. R., and M. McCallum. 1994. "Developing Cross-Cultural Partnerships: Implications for Child Care Quality Research and Practice." In *Valuing*

Quality, ed. P. Moss and A. Pence, 108–22. London: Paul Chapman Publishing; New York: Teachers College Press.

Schachter, L., A. R. Pence, A. Zuckernick, and J. Roberts. 2005. "Distance Learning in Africa: From Brain Drain to Brain Gain." In *Perspectives on the Future of Higher Education in the Digital Age*, ed. M. Beaudoin, 165–86. Hauppage, NY: Nova Science Publishers.

Schafer, J., and A. R. Pence. 2006. "Exploring and Promoting the Value of Indigenous Knowledge in Early Childhood Development in Africa." *Journal of Education for International Development* 2 (3).

Statistics Canada. 2001. *Aboriginal Peoples Survey*. Ottawa: Government of Canada.

Vargas-Barón, E. 2005. *Impact Evaluation of the ECDVU*. Evaluation report for the World Bank. Washington, DC: World Bank.

Zuckernick, A. 2000. Minutes from the ECDVU international advisory group meeting, Washington, DC. April.

Index